The
Night
Sky

The Night Sky

RICHARD GROSSINGER

JEREMY P. TARCHER, INC.
Los Angeles
Distributed by St. Martin's Press
New York

Library of Congress Cataloging in Publication Data

Grossinger, Richard, 1944–
    The night sky/Richard Grossinger. (revised edition)
      p. cm.
    Originally published: San Francisco : Sierra Club Books,
© 1981.
    Bibliography.
    Includes index.
    ISBN 0-87477-489-6 (pbk.)
    1. Astronomy—Popular works.   I. Title.
    [QB44.2.G765 1988]   88-13974
    520—dc 19   CIP

Jeremy P. Tarcher, Inc.
9110 Sunset Blvd.
Los Angeles, CA 90069

Book design by Wolfgang Lederer

Manufactured in the United States of America
10 9 8 7 6 5 4 3 2

For Richard Crowne, Roy Whong,
Ginny Stangeland Johnson,
Abdisalam Y Mohammed, and those
other shadows who lie behind
this book; and for Robin and Miranda
in the year 2000.

Contents

Preface ix

Introduction (1988) xxi

1. The Night Sky 1

2. Scientific and Occult Astronomy 15

3. Ancient Astronomy 32

4. The History of Western Astronomy
   I. The Sun in the Center 53

5. The History of Western Astronomy
   II. The Planets 65

6. The History of Western Astronomy
   III. The Gravitational Field 77

7. The History of Western Astronomy
   IV. The Stars 87

8. The History of Western Astronomy
   V. The Elements 100

9. The History of Western Astronomy
   VI. The Space-Time Continuum . . . 110

10. The History of Western Astronomy
    VII. The Atom 122

11. The History of Western Astronomy
    VIII. The Creation 140

12. The History of Western Astronomy
    IX. Pulsars, Quasars, and Black Holes 152

13. Language, Mind, and Astrophysics . . . 166

14. The Planets
   I. The Solar System 181

15. The Planets
   II. Mercury and Venus 192

16. The Planets
   III. The Moon, the Earth, and Mars 205

17. The Planets
   IV. Jupiter and Its Moons 226

18. The Planets
   V. Saturn, Uranus, Neptune, Pluto,
   and Their Moons 242

19. Science Fiction
   I. The Origin of Celestial Worlds 271

20. Science Fiction
   II. Self and Cosmos 287

21. Science Fiction
   III. Jesus of Nazareth 303

22. Astrology 313

23. Star Myth 334

24. Flying Saucers and Extraterrestrial Life . . 362

25. The Pop Star Cult of the Fifties and Sixties 395

26. The Light Within 403

   Appendix: Giving Them A Name . . . 406

   Notes 419

   Bibliography 444

   Index 457

Above us, only sky.   JOHN LENNON, *Imagine*

Preface

THE NIGHT SKY is a book about the stars, the planets, and the creation—that is, about the attempt of our species to locate itself in the vast universe in which it has arisen. It is an account of the various myths, sciences, and other systems that have developed over the several million nights of our brief sojourn in this physical cosmos.

Each creature experiences itself as alive and perceives the abundant nature all around it. Existence has no implicit meaning and no explanation. Meaning comes into being only through living animals themselves and as part of the mystery of their life. It is as originless and boundaryless as the universe; in fact, it is coterminous with the universe. The night sky is an irrevocable statement of this condition. It gathers infinity into a radiant field and envelops the Earth. It is at once the most blatant clue to the origin of all this and the shroud which negates any possible resolution and leads every trail into wilderness. The night sky expresses the order and cohesiveness of the creation, but also its chaos and arbitrariness. The constellations were one of our species' first attempts to impose its own order and meaning onto the impinging randomness of nature. All astronomical systems repeat the desperation and peril of this initial act.

We are beings who require a context for each little thing we do but have no context for the whole big thing. This is the primary disturbance within human society and the force that drives us through structures and symbols in search of an impossible resolution. We are a process in coming to terms with the night sky and its implications. We may ignore it consciously, but this does not change the fact. When we stare into it, we feel the chilling brevity and smallness of life, but we also feel the something else that feels that. It is this second thing that makes all the rest possible and to which this book speaks.

The modern universe may be random and disordered, but it is also exquisitely interrelated and connected down to the minutest layer. Astral mythology and magic reflected this symbolically and sympathetically; later astrophysics has shown that all matter obeys the same laws—that the stars appear where they do for the reason that the wind blows, the grasses sprout, and cells divide. These laws are more than inviolable. They are the basis for a physical universe whose manifestation then falls into their only domain. In criticizing modern astrophysics for its moral and spiritual emptiness, we must not forget that it also gives us a magical sense of how humble and obscure animals arose, magnificently and unexpectedly, from the bare primal complexities of raw atoms to stand presently among the stars in a condition of consciousness and observation. This, in many ways, is more spiritual than the various dead theological versions of creation by an external deity or force.

This is an astronomy book not because the structure of stars and planets or the physics and geography of the heavens are its main subjects but because they stand both functionally and symbolically for its actual subject: the creation. Although everything we know and experience is the creation, the stars come closest to providing a context for all the rest. They are the eternal perceptible manifestation of unity and infinity in concordance. The venous patterns on a maple leaf, the thousands of insect larvae in a cocoon, the interstices of frost on glass or limestone in a cave, the webs of Spinoza, the flashes of Proust, the harmonies of Johann Bach, the dreams of Sun Chief all stand in correspondence to star-stuff, and all ostensibly originate from it in the fine rare pulp of the planets.

This book does not favor the night sky above these other replicas, but it does set its unity, amplitude, and originary qualities as yardsticks for the rest. In a black sea of discrete incandescent entities and luminous dust, we were born. Or this is how we come to comprehend it.

———

Earth and sky are inseparable. In ancient myth and cosmogony, their single body cleaved and differentiated. In modern science and astrophysics, there is no world outside of night; the starry field is a two-dimensional illusion. We now know that the tides, the winds, and the glaciers are star effects. Flowers, worms, and honeybees also reflect the night. All share its texture, light, and gravitational unity.

Deep within matter, the shape of the sky is repeated. There is a void sparsely filled with tiny nuclei and their orbital systems. These are stars, and the atomic microcosm is their night. Nuclear forces incorporate stellar gravitational fields while providing their substance in minute packets of which there are enough for a physical universe. Matter differentiates from and also builds upon itself in a network from the minute to the massive. No part of it is ever out of touch with the rest of it. Furthermore, infinity may have once been contained in a subatomic space from which it continues to propel outward across all dimensions. The night sky thus stretches from a microcosm to eternity. We see but one "night." We contain others, and still others pile up beyond our range.

Poetry, philosophy, government, and industry are all stellar phenomena. Our bodies and minds are star fabric material, and they occur in the phenomenological context of starfields. That we know the stars *is* the stars. Somewhere in that paradox and mystery is our destiny.

What makes this book larger in scope than most astronomy books is that it expresses the fundamental dichotomy of the creation (or universe) and the incarnation (or our existence in and of that universe). In any true astronomy, these are the same phenomenon and must be understood in terms of each other.

Science unwittingly misleads us. We can certainly explore the stars and the planets with instruments. We can know the physics of materials on Earth and can study elements, molecules, atoms, and subatomic particles with a high degree of refinement. We can understand the mechanism by which life propagates and the laws by which diverse living systems come into being. Embryology and astrophysics are subtle, complex, and progressive self-critical systems. So are psychology, anthropology, and linguistics.

We know a great deal about what is around us, what we are, how we interact, and how we perceive, cognize, and express the nature of things. But for all this, we cannot know and express the creationary event. We can only manifest it.

As important as astronomy and physics are in our knowledge of the creation, they must finally be satisfied with limited territories, any grasping outside of which distorts them. They are most distorted when they pretend to get to the bottom of things. The great physicists, like Newton and Einstein, laughed at the delusion that such was even possible. They were delighted to know anything at all.

It is not enough to look into the night with the confidence of scientific knowledge. We are wrapped in a fire-filled abyss. It is not an abstraction, a postulate, or a model. It is our experience. Just as our experience of being born is unalleviated by our knowledge of genetics and embryology, so our experience of the creation is direct and intimate in a way that astronomy cannot lessen.

To find the stars outside of stellar science, we must explore ancient myth, theogony, ethnoastronomy, astrogeny, interior astronomy, astromancy, and astrology. These systems are not scientific by contemporary standards, but we do not ask of them a description of the scientific universe. In cross-cultural anthropology we can use their structural and historic relationship to our own science to define hidden elements of it. And we can take them on their own terms as expressions of the creation by creatures within it.

We have images of galaxies, electrons, and atomic nuclei. Prior to them, we had other images, which led us to develop instruments by which we see these new and present ones. Non-Western and tribal peoples have had their own images: of spirit forces, gods and goddesses, divine energies, totem stars, astral realms, karma, stellar sentience, and star-incarnated shapes. Their explanations for how we got here are expressed in totemic and mythological codes and enacted and reexperienced in ceremonies, vision-quests, and meditation. The pre-Columbian American Indians did not know about quasars, atoms, or embryonic meiosis, but that does not mean that they did not experience the universe from within and come to some unique and accurate conception of its nature. Science may give us facts about the interactions of physical systems, facts crucial to an overall knowledge of the night sky, but ethnoastronomy and astrology give us facts about the riddles of creation and incarnation, facts which are not only inaccessible to science as it is currently practiced but which are contained in other forms within its fundamental structure because of our history and phylogeny.

So astronomy is born of the occult and requires it to make conscious its own language and instrumentation. We ourselves are born of unknown forces that we explore intuitively every day. The creation encompasses all of these modes, and the incarnation literally incarnates them, in our species and in the long evolutionary chain of plant and animal life.

What this book is about, since it cannot be about the creationary event, is the means we have of imaging the wholeness and complexity and mystery of what we are. It is a history, an anthropology, and an epistemology of stellar systems. The images we have of the formation of the universe determine the types of values we have, the societies we develop, and the moralities and aesthetics by which we live. How we think we came into being is who we think we are. And this was never in deeper crisis than in the present—when we know, it seems, too much, and knowledge itself has become fragmented and debased. We can criticize the ignorance of our ancestors, but we have covered ourselves in a new ignorance.

Clearly we know something that we call "the stars" and "the creation." But then there is something we do not know and cannot know. If we did, there would already be millions of books on it, or books on it would be totally unnecessary, and probably *we* would be unnecessary too. Because we don't know it and because we don't face it squarely and unblinkingly through the increasing layers of bigness that are imagistically provided out of our present knowing of something, there are no books on it. This is a primitive attempt at such a book—a book about our struggle to know something which is unknowable, using the stars as our measure and guide. That struggle shapes our lives and our society. But what is the thing that gets described instead of the creation, and by what distortion?

This book shifts from one system of creationary events to another. None of them can be wholly right, but none of them is wrong either, for all are part of the universe and reflect it from within. What makes a particular system or image more or less interesting is how it engages us in understanding our own coming to be in this pool of light, how it somehow parts time to give us a glimpse of the beginning which our being contains. From these single images and their interaction, we can regain the bigness and the unity which modern astronomy has stolen from us, and we can use the fruits of modern astronomy as crucial antidotes to its own poison. In fact, we *must* use them, for we have brought them into being, and if we do not swallow and transform them, they will surely swallow and transform us.

Throughout this narrative, I have tried to encompass and beat back the infinity and to work against the nihilism it proposes. The modern materialist universe has no place for us, and we would be fools to try to survive in it. We must assault it in its own terms, and not from any false idealistic ground. Eventually it will crumble anyway; but unless we are active in making a new universe, it will leave us only with ravaged fields. We must stare down the shafts of infinity; we must enter the violence and the emptiness, experience them in ourselves, and transform them into something livable. I have tried to prove, in some small way, that this is possible, that it is a human thing and not one of *their* things. Coming to terms with it is coming to terms with ourselves as much as with the seeming physical fact of the universe.

To this point, the astronomical and spiritual universes have both failed us. It does little good anymore to accept uncritically a vitalist universe in which spirit is always present in matter. The conviction of spirit must still be reconciled with the constancy and intricacy of the physical manifestation. The ambiguities of quantum theory and the resulting taos of astronomy merely pose a limited and idealized view of the dilemma. To claim a cosmic dance on false or apostate grounds is to remove us even further from the possibility of such a dance. In writing this book, I found the crisis of faith almost unbearable. It was certainly more than I had counted on. Not only was there no easy way in which to confront the spiritual/material dichotomy, but the very posing of such a dichotomy seemed to be an evasion of some more fundamental truth, some other unknown pattern hidden in the material.

At first, the imposition of a vital force behind the physical agency of creation seems to provide a spiritual alternative to a purely mechanical evolution. On closer inspection, however, vital forces come to look like fictitious mechanical devices, and they cannot be naively slipped into creation without betraying spiritualism too. Linguistic philosophers, conceptual artists, and grammatologists all provide models that locate the true complexity in ourselves. The models are not particularly starry or creationary, but this tells us that the universe lies closer to our disjunctures and paradoxes, especially in symbolic processes, than to our cybernetic replicas of remote galaxies. The formal elegance, however, betrays our emotional and psychic connection to the universe, and our need to make things conscious and visible. It is brilliant, but in the face of the great danger and crisis of incarnation, it comes to feel like pretense and dilettantish dabbling. Finally, it was very difficult to find a mode of astronomical analysis that satisfied even the conflicting positions in myself. Again and again I saw, across the surface fabric of my work, nothing but mind games and intellectual pieties, and it hardly mattered whether these were physical or spiritual in their bias. I had to transcend these without submerging the book in a lyrical muddiness.

Against the simple universe of the narrative of this text, with all its spiritual and physical variants, another universe breaches, shadowy and incomplete, and through it, another, fragmentary and illogical. These universes engage with the problem of language itself, and they must be allowed to distort the righteousness of the text. The occult sky and the physical sky must interfere with each other and create the rough edges of an unknown cosmology. Otherwise I must side with either the eternal archetypes of the astrologers and star magicians or the progressive scientism of the professional astronomers, or pretend to syncretize them in New Age jive.

In the end, I am probably guilty of exactly such a rapprochement. Astrology, science fiction, ethnoastronomy, astrophysics, linguistics, and New Age thought all merge in this book, for I hope to speak to the practitioners of each of these arts. But I also intend to propose an unknown direction, a direction unknown even to myself. Astrology and astronomy both cast falsely confident smiles over the great unknown soul of being, but they are modes that we can use en route to new systems of thought for which our age is the true midwife.

A good portion of this book is simply a history of Western astronomy from the time of Copernicus to the present, with an emphasis on overall philosophical and civilizational issues. Other chapters explore occult astronomy, the astral sky, star myth, ethnoastronomy, ancient astronomy, astrology, flying saucers, extraterrestrial life, and science fiction themes. There are also sections on viewing the night sky, the politics and sociology of stellar images, star dreams, the space program, the cognitive and linguistic issues of night sky systemization, and star themes in popular American culture.

In the way that Herman Melville "violated" the structure of the nineteenth-century novel to say everything there was to say about whales (while still writing a novel), I have redefined the format of the twentieth-century science/anthropology book to show the many contexts, both objective and subjective, in which stars occur in our culture—from the broad exterior heavens to the myriad internalized skies and asterisms. It is a sixteenth-century view of the universe reconceived in terms of twentieth-century structural anthropology, Freudian linguistics, and Oriental metaphysics. As the French historian Michel Foucault said in writing of the naturalist Aldrovandi and his contemporaries:

> When one has the story of an animal to tell, it is useless and impossible to choose between the role of a naturalist and that of an anthologist: in one and the same form of knowledge must be gathered all that has been *seen* and *heard,* all that has been related by nature or by men in the language of the world, of tradition, or of poets. To know a beast, or a plant, or anything from the earth is to collect the whole thick layer of signs that have been deposited in them or on them; it is to recover all the constellations of forms when they take on the characteristic of emblems.[1]

Aldrovandi's list of topics for a chapter on serpents in his natural history is the forerunner of my own table of contents on stars:

Equivocation (the different senses in which the word *serpent* can be used), synonyms and etymologies, differences, form and description, anatomy, character and habitats, temperament, sex and reproduction, voice, movements, places, food, physiognomy, antipathy, sympathy, ways to catch, death and wounds by the serpent, methods and signs of poisoning, remedies, epithets, designations, marvels and omens, monsters, mythology, gods to which he is consecrated, fables, allegories and mysteries, hieroglyphics, emblems and symbols, adages, coins, miracles, enigmas, devices, heraldic signs, deeds, dreams, reproductions and statues, uses as food, uses in medicine, diverse uses.[2]

Foucault concludes that "nature, itself, is a seamless fabric of words and marks, of stories and letters, of discourses and forms. . . . There can be no commentary unless beneath the text that one reads and explicates, runs the sovereignty of an original Text."[3]

As we have attempted to move deeper into the heavens, we have gone back through our own historical and linguistic conceptions of star terminology—so that the origin of time and space at the quasar disintegrates into the origin of star terminology and the human mystery in the Old Stone Age.

This is the second book in a series currently planned as three. Each book stands alone and contains no specific references to the others, but the series, as it is assembled, contains a second subject matter beneath the surface, which develops as the overall themes and meanings change. The first book, *Planet Medicine: From Stone-Age Shamanism to Post-Industrial Healing* (Doubleday Anchor, 1980), dealt with the history and anthropology of healing, including ancient medicine, non-Western therapeutics, and the origins of contemporary holistic health. Insofar as it was explicitly an exploration of medicine and the second book is a history of star-viewing and astronomical images, there is no connection. However, on the deeper level, *Planet Medicine* asks the following questions: What is mind? What is body? How are they joined? What is health? What is disease? How does a cure work? How do the definitions and meanings of health, disease, and cure change historically and from culture to culture?

Planet Medicine is based on the perception that ancient medical systems and healing methods from other cultures can never be recovered. They can only be invented anew—by anthropologists, who give us their partial and external versions of internal systems as they perceive them, and by radical healers, who rediscover ancient principles in the open context of their own work.

In *The Night Sky,* the opening questions are: What is matter? What is the universe? How does life come to be? And who are we?

These touch upon unasked questions in *Planet Medicine:* How do we have such histories, bodies, and minds? And what is the cosmic source of the life-energy that lies behind all vitalistic healing systems, Western, Oriental, and tribal? *Planet Medicine* must necessarily define the cure and life in human terms. *The Night Sky* redefines life in the universe at large within the limits that the universe places on human meaning and development.

It is a mistake, though, to think that *The Night Sky* provides an external context for *Planet Medicine* and is bigger and more cosmic. If the titles were switched, each book would reveal a new aspect of the conceit under which the other was written.

Both of these are pieces of writing, books. One is not a disease or a medicine, and the other is not itself the sky. Insofar as they belong to the same period of American literature and come from the same author, they share territories, themes, and meanings, and are interwoven with each other. Neither one can have a bigger territory.

To the unknown malaise that confronts us, both are medicines. The first is a medicine that discusses healing; the second is a medicine that discusses our imaging of the night sky and the stars. The actual disease is beyond both books, and each is written as an act of healing—self-healing and community healing. They ask the reader to be active, to reach to the same levels of paradox and disquiet in himself or herself, and to work with the text in making a curative act of vision.

Modern science has concluded that we are the minutest fleck of scum within an expanding atom, and that the "vastness" of the night sky is simply the innards of that atom strewn through hollow and warped space-time and composed in centers of gravity. We are dust motes upon eternity, specks of chemical texture in a puddle, held to a large molten stone which itself is a dot in the pool of debris. No wonder we are also the poor specimen in whom modern medicine diagnoses and discovers discrete diseases from mere random somatic interference. Even so-called genetic illness is external, for it comes from arbitrary disorder in the genes and not from within the organism's personal process. In such a universe, diseases must be as meteors, and the only cure for them is physical and mechanical manipulation. No one denies that all is internal to the cosmos, but it is now a barren internality of subsurfaces. The old medicines are discarded with the old systems of astronomy, and the New Age holistic sciences are vilified as fantasies and deceptions. In either case, the universe is dead, and its sprat are minute robots.

While *Planet Medicine* precedes *The Night Sky* in my own development of these themes, I actually began exploring astronomy far earlier in my life. It was a childhood interest, and I did more writing on stars, planets, flying saucers, and science fiction than on medicine right up to my research and writing for *Planet Medicine.*

The underlying medicinal theme of both books explains the order of their writing: unconsciously, I perceived the need for curative activity and radical personal change before continued exploration of cosmic issues. The culture also requires inner transformation, or all space exploration will be sterile and disappointing. The universe presented to us by NASA scientists and "image teams" and self-aggrandizing media astronomers is simply not satisfactory. There is nothing wrong with their data, but the universe they promote is a symptom of our cultural disease. Their superstar demands are no different from those of baseball players or politicians or Las Vegas performers; the only additional problem is that they mislead themselves into thinking that the neutrality of science protects them. But it does not. We are sold their unexamined social images, including macho and capitalist roles, along with outer space and the stars. We still await a creative public astronomy.

My own order was to confront the starry abstraction first within my own being: as a deeper breathing, an ability to move through conscious pain, and a dream within dreaming. Then it was necessary to test this medicinal insight against the vastness of the stars. In our dilemma, a commitment to healing must precede and then engulf the night sky. We must literally flood it with homeopathic remedies and *chi* flow, with color therapy and chanting. It is alone the power of the infinitesimal, the microdose, projected into infinity, that can cure the expanding universe, or heal us of its plague.

1981

Introduction

The Night Sky was originally published in 1981 by Sierra Club Books. This 1988 edition substantially updates and revises that version. The updating highlights three events: the post-1980 mission of Voyager 2 to the Saturnian and Uranian systems, the purported discovery (on a NASA data tape) of a "face" carved into a Martian mesa, and the present epidemic of UFO "abductions" and "cosmic conspiracy" theories.

I have also revised the text, not with the aim of changing the book's nature but in hope of bringing out its essential themes and making them clearer. Eight years' distance and perspective have allowed me to reconsider my own book as an outsider and to measure it against an echo of the original intention I still hear in myself. I found the old "Night Sky" visionary and powerful but lacking an ordering principle. I remember that when I wrote it, the job of getting all the material into one book was overwhelming, and I had neither the time nor the energy (within the deadline) to refine the statement. Also, because the book was written under the aegis of Sierra Club, I imaginarily addressed their audience without being aware I was doing so and thus produced a false subtext.

By my own present standards, I wrote too amorphously and allowed metaphysical questions to arise somewhat randomly. I am no more able to answer those questions now, but I have tried to hierarchicalize their asking. When I assembled *The Night Sky*, I knew I was posing unanswerable questions; in fact, I considered that to be the main goal of the book: to frame them in a way that invoked wonder and pushed people toward an understanding of the vastness of the mystery rather than to any unifying theory. I haven't changed on that point one iota; I think "the night sky" is insoluble, and I offer this book as a gift to our own mortality and finality. However, I have tried in this version to make the layers of insolubility subtler in their reflections through one another and to downplay the time-honored tautologies of existence.

The sheer passage of time has contributed the most to this reconsideration, but two events have also changed the ground on which *The Night Sky* rests, at least for its author:

By 1984 I had completed the trilogy of which *The Night Sky* is now the middle book. *Embryogenesis* is an account of the origination of our lives, our bodies and psyches, through a profound ontogenetic process that defines biology and being. Following *The Night Sky*, it addresses incarnation and mortality directly. It is an animal; *The Night Sky* is a constellation. It is the hunger for life and death; *The Night Sky* is the hunger for a beginning and an end. With *Embryogenesis* now supporting it, *The Night Sky* can more single-mindedly address our cosmological background.

It is also impossible not to reconsider the original "Night Sky" in terms of people's reactions to it. There were generally positive reviews in the New Age media. However, there were many mean-spirited reviews, especially in city newspapers. People who didn't like *The Night Sky* had little ambiguity about it. There were half a dozen "worst book I ever read" types of responses and others that were equally derisive and condescending. Most of these reviewers came from the science community; that the book was even given their attention was the result of a false expectation from Sierra Club Books being its publisher.

Politically liberal scientizers are not necessarily liberal in other ways; often, science is a religion, and its practitioners see it as mankind's only path out of the present morass. Those who seek other paths are viewed as ignorant and benighted (consider not so much the reaction to the news that President Reagan has used astrology as the self-assured tone behind it). The writers of the reviews simply didn't accept my premise that science is another mythology, so—as far as they could bear to read (and it usually wasn't very far)—this book came off as "uninformed" and meaningless. Since I did not offer any new theories or facts, it looked as though I had taken on the great institution of astrophysics only to sully it. "A book like this just shouldn't exist anymore" was the general message.

My themes haven't changed, so the book still may be opaque to that audience. However, I have changed the presentation and made it harder to *misunderstand* what I am doing and to renounce the book for the wrong reasons. *The Night Sky* is not an apologia for astrology or a celebration of the visionary heavens. It is as much an apologia for astrophysics and a celebration of the materialists' stars and planets. My premise is as unacceptable to rigid astrologers as it is to academically-bound scientists. And it is equally unacceptable to advocates of East-West syncretism. I have tried to redefine the entire territory on which each of these different inquiries is based and to allow them to be understood as part of the same open-ended search for meaning among the stars. I understand, of course, that astrology is incompatible with astrophysics, but I am not trying to reconcile them; I am trying to make a ground on which each of them has its own space. After all, both are human, both arise from speculation in stellar hermeneutics.

Insofar as many critics felt the original version of the book said, "Anything goes," I have searched for the basis of that misreading and tried to correct it. But *The Night Sky* must remain a book of ambiguities and contradictions. I am trying to tear everything inflated down to a common level, even myself. That does not excuse unclear writing, but it does explain why there is no thesis or easy summary to the book. The reviewers closest to my intention understood, if not the application, at least the aesthetics of that possibility.

If I were to try at this point to simplify *The Night Sky* to a single series of statements, it would go something like this:

The answers to the great riddles of who we are and what this all is cannot come from astrophysics and biology. Scientists cannot solve the cosmological problem either by mathematics or subatomic experimentation. Even their falling short is not an asymptotic approach to the solution; they fall short in another dimension entirely. The closest thing we will hear to an answer will be in the truths we experience in our own lives, and it will not be in words or ideas. It will be in obscure feelings and brief lucidities, joys that come and go in an instant, clarities at the heart of meditational practice, agonies of personal loss. These will not be metaphors for astronomical cosmology; these will be *the true cosmology for which any astronomy is the metaphor*. At the same time, we cannot ignore the actual night sky as an aspect of our existence, a source of feelings and ideas, and a riddle posed exactly against our lives. We cannot just go within because we *are not* only a "within." To the degree that we want an intellectual and artistic vision of the sky, and even a true scientific astronomy of it, we must be willing also to consider the entire history of astronomy and star-gazing among our species, including the occult and pre-scientific varieties, for when every path leads to paradox, the combined paradoxes of all paths reflect a deeper verity.

1988

1

The Night Sky

SPRING IMAGINE YOURSELF on a road leading
out of the village. It is a clear moonless night. The land is a
mixture of blindness and shadows with a few smudges of man-
made light. Against your skin the breeze awakens memories
brighter than daylight.

> *This is not the start of a mystery novel.*
> *But it is.*
> *The mystery is eternal and goes on generation after gen-*
> *eration unsolved. Hundreds of detectives lie in cemeteries*
> *on a planet in a system of planets. Newborn frogs appear*
> *on the margin of the pond, in the fresh weed. They are*
> *suspects too. And they are agents . . . spies.*
> *Who brought these creatures here to enact this episode?*
> *Do they know how moist and dark it feels inside?*

You stand alone and solitary, against the bigness of time, the
bigness of space. The sky is more than a visible plane. It is a
black translucent sea on whose edge you hang upside down—
filled with stars beyond number and beyond comprehension.
The Pleiades dance in a flecked cluster. The Dipper and the
horns of the Bull emerge; the Hyades sit above Taurus, bearing
the sigil of Aldebaran. The large reddish marker is Mars, and it
will wander from night to night in an ancient path. Bright Sirius
glows near the horizon in the treetops, casting a faint light on
the blossoms. Through the clearing, Regulus sits at the heart of
a Lion, dozens of fainter stars in his fur and on his paws. Cassiopeia rests in her cradle, tipping across another plane, overlooking this wildness from the dome. On the old Great Lakes,

1

the Indians saw an eagle, a snake, and three deer; in Brazilian jungle clearings, the same stars became a jaguar and a pig, as the Amazon rushed from one eternity to another. These fragments do not diminish the immensity or challenge the mystery. Our knowledge of the sky, in its complication and bigness of proposition, can never replace the actual bigness.

When we stand beneath the night sky, we stand beneath the history of the whole of creation. It is a miracle that so much of it is perceptible—a miracle we might appreciate more if it had not occurred and we did not have senses to discern it.

The stars alone, scattered in a black pool, speak both for and against the lifeless corpse. The young woman in the morgue, the old man in his bed, the warriors bloody on the hillside: these too in their stillness are the night sky.

When the dead leave us their bodies, where do they go? Do they vanish, and does their being dissipate? What, if anything, exists beyond the skull and the mask?

The stars do not answer the question, but they alone stand for a possible answer, for the hope that there even is a question. However remote and enigmatic they seem, random in their design, they are all we have now, all we've ever had.

To look at the sky is to look at your own death. This is as true for the Pawnee priest for whom the stars are spirits whose glyphs are emblazoned on buffalo hide as it is for the late American village-dweller for whom they are the leftover light of objects which continue to burn elsewhere or which burned out millennia ago.

But the sky is also the truth, and it has the power to draw us beyond our petty concerns and compulsions and temporary goals. We see what we are and what all this is, and we are stunned and exhilarated. It is, perhaps, a terrible truth, but the feelings respond to it, the heart opens.

Man under the night sky is man alone with his destiny. The stars inspire him to create the biggest things of which he is capable: gods, odes, number systems, and the temples and observatories that house them. It is not a matter of the absolute bigness of these things, for nothing man does is physically big before the stars. It is a matter of the internal bigness he feels, which his experience of the night reaches to. The stars expose something deep and true. Scientists and lovers know this each in their own ways. The unconscious shock of a flaming infinity without enables a tangent space within to break free.

This is different from and yet suggests the objective truth that we contain galactic-like clusters set in darkened distances through whose collective electricity we feel anything at all. It is different from and also suggests the astrological intimation that our destiny is written in and by the stars.

It is closer to the perception of Immanuel Kant that the creation has a dual form. "Two things fill the mind with ever new and increasing admiration and awe," he wrote, ". . . the starry heavens above and the moral law within."

SUMMER   HERE ON THE DESERT, the hot air escapes and the sand turns into heaps and shadows. Daylight is gone and we stand on the beachhead of the universe. A few stars appear, and then a billion of them—far more than we expected. The simple group of Pleiades explodes into hundreds of densely clustered stars. Arid zones are filled with unfamiliar clusters and wisps of Galactic haze. Even without the Moon, they light the desert—forming shadows of creation itself.

The Galaxy is so thick its far robes sweep about the mountains. Sage dew sweetens the air. All about, meteors race through the stars, then return to darkness.

The monuments of Hohokam peoples stand against the eternity they thought once to measure. They are now ruins, but the Sun and Moon and some of the planets still return—in the numerical order of the heavens—to the windows and grindstones the pre-Papago star-priests cut into their observatories. How many other temples and measuring devices sit on the deserts entangled in the second-growth shrubs of other planets, having outlived their makers, continuing to measure the local cycles against the backdrop of all of time? The universe passes from muteness to knowledge into hieroglyphic again and again, even as stars are born and die.

Now the desert sky is as full of stars as the densest field of white blossoms. It is an overwhelming perspective dashed down upon mortality. See them as sound, see them as light, see them as harmony, see them as discordance: it doesn't matter, for one sees something that is more than any of those things and more than all of them. They are light, but they are primary spectral white light, as no other thing is. They are sound, but their silence is deafening. Heard on a radio telescope, they are eerie and alien, like the intelligence of the dolphin and whale whose sounds bypass us. We are left out, but, in another sense, the thing we are left out of is the thing we *are* and cannot know.

We both fear and desire an infinite universe. Now we know that beyond every galactic center, every climax forest of stars, lies another. Trillions of miles from the center of a stellar empire, the simple inhabitants see it as a star. But what empire: ours, theirs, or another? And do they know that the star is an empire, or is it simply part of a giant bird of an unknown species or some other creature alien to us and to the emperor's people but not to them? In the outlands beyond these imaginary observers, there are those who cannot even see the empire, or another empire lies out in a different direction, another star. All the people on planets around other stars in this Galaxy, to say nothing of people in other galaxies, come into being, live and die, and cease being without knowing of us and without our knowing of them. This is the question in terms of which our own life/death is posed. And if there is no other universe, we must move anyway into another universe, for our minds cannot withstand or comprehend eternal sameness either. The egg is so rich that maybe the white stuff does pour out forever, stars and snows and thoughts and campfires of pygmies in Africas beyond Africas and through the systems of Antares, of Sirius, one eternity bright and fiery upon the heels of another. Continuous. Simultaneous.

The night sky is a photograph of eternity. The thousands of lights, standing for billions of billions of lights, that we look out upon at the moment they stand there for us, they are the creation. We cannot expand it; we can only add to its richness. Each single breath of ours, filling our mind, is matched by a counterbreath within the absolute of space and time. What joy is there, but what sorrow too, what infinite sorrow.

We read in science fiction books that Antares was once the center of a great empire of star cities. Could this be true?

Undoubtedly it is not. Already it lies in our own past and we move on to new imaginary planets and beings. We weep for the cities of Antares as we do for the Minoans and Picts; we weep for our own loss, that we were there, and now we are here. We weep for how deep in our own body we feel what it is we know. Not what we want. Nor what we desire. It's what we know. What we know we know. To set it square, right; to come out of this undiminished.

We appreciate that it is mainly still a mystery because there is not enough here to explain all of this or our place in it. We are born into daylight, but we are also born into darkness; and the darkness of the night sky confirms and reflects our suspicions of the darkness of our origins.

It is even imaginable that this entire universe is something like one atom in a "ladybug" in another universe, which is an atom in a meteor in another universe, and so on. Likewise, deep within the subatomic particles of this universe, which number in the trillions of trillions, there may be countless other universes.

We are like the figures in a deck of cards shuffled for an instant in the tinder of light. We see by a lantern that is already being extinguished, which we breathe into being by vision itself that passes from our lungs into our chests up the thin passageways into cranium, nose, and eyes.

We have moved north to the Bay of Fundy, in the last stand of coniferous forests before the Earth vanishes from history into that other timelessness of glaciers, beyond the habitations of men.

We float in the sky, but in something more than the sky. The solid Earth does seem almost like a rustling in infinity, and the trees stir in the wind, unconnected to the stars but as a further state of cosmic night. Darkness lies in those collective leaves— the same darkness filled with light-bearers that bridges the gap above us.

Lightning bugs swim in the altered air. Their lives are short, a few weeks; but all lives, the great books tell us, are of the same length. In the quick successions of images that flash in their sensoria, they see everything, they know all there is to know.

They are not alienated from their creation, though we stand outside their zone and watch them as if a tragedy, disappearing and reappearing in broken pulsation.

Where do we float? Whence came we to this clime?

By our consciousness, that other night sky—cupped as a lightning bug its light—we suffer the riddle imposed in thought. We are the gods whom those in darkness have set against the darkness. They may bear the candelabra through halls of pure nectar, but we cannot see them or know them or be so assured. They perhaps cannot see us. They are vanishing into oblivion. They perhaps never existed.

They are our fathers.

Our only fathers.

The agony they pose for us is not to stumble blankly back. When we signal them from this bare turf under the complete cosmological sky, their answer is the obvious one: terror is a luxury too; behind our panic is a witch who will not take us no matter how we submit to her. But then we are all afraid of the same thing—that we will not be afraid in time.

There is no other life, not only for us to live but to refuse to live. Better to plunge in that dark pool with its bright rays, to risk being pulled up out of it like a rat on the end of a cyanide pole.

It is all held together on a thread, great suns as well as lightning bugs, each one, where they are, across our system as galaxies across the bands of telescopic haze, haze caused only by our limited senses and the limits too of thought. The Milky Way twists around behind us, and out across the sky, the center of our Galaxy seen across the plane of its own tail. It is so far away, and yet it penetrates us. The Galaxy is umbilical. It touches us gently on the forehead, between the eyes; it touches us as our belly button, because we are made of it, as it ascends, curls, and vanishes into infinity, its main branch an ancient river revealed each night by night itself, as if that were meant to teach us something, as if being instructive were the first order of being present.

The fierce edge of creation cuts the hierarchical arrangement of existences. Yes, there are messages, sent between incommensurate locales, but they are no different from the rest. The things happening are the messages—lightning bugs, memory, stars—their staccato and rhythmic order is all that meaning can be.

That which exists through itself is meaning, the magus said.

We come here once, and it all happens, from the birth of cosmos to the rebirth in fire, in water, in the ellixis alleghensis of light. It is a primary transformation that joins us to Sun, as two chunks of embryonic scum in the same contaminated pool.

Look back at us in the Martian night sky. Through the oceans and conifer forests of the north, the blue-green of old Earth shows, a singular glow among astral birthstones: plankton aura, mist in solar wind—bioluminescent. All creatures are whelped in it, joined to their material line by murky matter, strewn as sour milk in a black sea. Strands cling to their prior strands like worms in a heap: the red fox limping through the morning, the giant crow picking at the woodchuck corpse, the clams breathing in their caves of muffled gravity, the minnows in flurries of light flesh. The Moon's body rolls in the Bay without touching it.

This is all the initiation we will have. We are no different from firebugs; at times of being brought into creation, we lie in an eternity untouched. As carriers of the light, this far from homeland, we stand in darkness.

Orion is the single most sentient-looking object in the sky, with its two rows of three stars set angularly toward each other within a triangle of three bright stars. Rigel, Bellatrix, and Betelgeuse form the torso. At the edge of the glittering Sword is a swab of haze indicating an enormous luminous cloud, the Great Nebula in Orion. The Belt is made of three almost evenly-spaced stars of equivalent brightness. The upper one, Mintaka, is brilliant white; the middle one, Alnilam, is of flatter hue and named for a string of pearls; the bottom star, Alnitak, the girdle, is yellow and purplish, and actually a triple star.

In India the Belt was an arrow. In Greenland these same stars were seal-hunters lost in the ocean. The Australian aborigines believed that the stars of the Belt were young men, cavorting with the young women of the Pleiades.

It is the set of the Belt in the sky, with the Sword falling beneath it, all within the seeming bounds of Rigel and company, that gives Orion its singularity. It is not a matter of complex aesthetics. Orion is raw creation in the semblance of a hieroglyph. Its name most likely comes from the Akkadian Uru-anna, who was not a hunter but "Light of Heaven," a chief of unknown lineage and sorcery. Only in Roman times did Orion become a warrior or a figure engaged in the hunt. For the Egyptians, it was Horus, in a boat surrounded by stars, and bright Sirius beneath was a Cow, also traveling in a boat. In the *Egyptian Book of the Dead* it is named: "I see the motion of the holy constellation Sahu."

In Hindu myth, Orion was part of the superconstellation Praja-pati; he was a stag called Mriga, who chased his daughter Rohini, a red deer we know as Aldebaran. Mintaka, Alnilam, and Alnitak are arrows stuck in him by the hunter we call Sirius.

In China, Orion was a White Tiger.

In Ireland, he was an Armed King.

Flammarion, strangely, called it "California of the sky." Whether he meant that it was like the coastal border of the West on the great Eastern sea we do not know. [1]

The seventeenth-century writer William Derham, in his *Astro-Theology,* described the pale light in Orion as the one spot in the night sky where the empyreal heavens shone through. The luminosity did not belong to Orion itself, but came through an invisible crack in the higher astronomical spheres. [2]

The ginseng hunters of Asia seek an almost transparent, gnarled wild root, shaped like a man with head and limbs, a root which squeals when pulled from the ground and which has a universal curative power lost in the cultivated varieties. This rare medicinal plant they know by the local names for the constellation Orion. [3]

In matters of this star-group, one is struck by a simultaneous obscurity and intelligibility. Orion most forcibly expresses the mystery that all stars do, which is the mystery of creation itself. It strikes to the heart and goes through us like a knife. The mystery of our flesh.

In a sky where wonder is everywhere, Orion is the closest thing to a feasible object, a clue. But, of course, it is no such thing astrophysically. It is a random set of events associated by the accidental plane of our Solar System in the Galaxy. It is a radio disturbance of jewels. It is a bag of glowing gas hung on a Sword. And yet, is anything up there, in here, random or accidental?

If there were a message from a higher intelligence—not even to us—Orion is it. From a higher intelligence to another higher intelligence. From before history until beyond our history. Ours is the privilege only. Because it is utterly lucid. More lucid than we are. But we can see it. We are inside it. We alone create the glyph.

On cold winter nights, when the winds blow to 100 degrees below zero and mice are born in the pipe straw, Orion is a heat, a priorness, a omneity that balances it. When summer settles in these parts, Orion is gone.

Lyra is the answer. A silence in three essential notes. Without reprieve.

AUTUMN DEATH ALONE, they say, gives life its meaning. And it must be true, for each of us exists briefly inside an eternity of nonexistence about which we can know nothing because knowing ends too. There are hundreds of explanations and reprieves, but they belong to life, not death. Perhaps our karma follows us, perhaps some aspect of the mind (not memory), perhaps the spirit remembers this in a way which explains why *it* is the spirit—though not to us, not while we are alive. Perhaps life is eternal, and death a mirage, so we live this same life over a billion billion times, each time experiencing different parts of it, like this one, until consciousness is entire and there are no boundaries.

All this may do us some good someday, but we are tiny, fragile, hungry, and afraid of the unknown, afraid of not living. We resist the smaller changes; how could we not resist the change of everything we hope and know? The animals teach us that life does not die easily, even if it dies willingly. Or perhaps we do not live

easily either, and death is the only resolution. We complicate
our lives until they are hopeless. Then we say, "at least we will
not live forever, so there is no need to straighten all this out."
Death allows us our waste, our cruelty, our agony of disappointment in who we are, for it will eventually swallow them, and
then all the people who are alive at this time, and then all the
people and races on this planet, and then all the graveyards and
even the planet itself. So why do we care? Why do we even try
to set it right? As bad a mess as we have made of things (or so
some claim), we have also created an order of things, a way of
being, and even an honor, in a transitory country in an unknown
place. Within life, we have made nations and languages and laws;
and though none of these will survive, we have made them as
well as they can be made here. We have somehow served that
renegade within night who arranged for our brief flash of consciousness, and we have left him with something else, as final as
death, for his pains.

Our complication resembles the complication of the stars in
the original formation, however that is theorized. New layers
keep getting laid down on what's already very complicated. All
these things were complicated from the beginning—and then
they begin to accumulate our memories and references and
glosses of early attempts to solve them onto later attempts, as
our life moves on also. By the middle years, we realize that we
cannot resolve everything, we can only complicate it. There are
some people we will never see again, though we do not know
who they are; there are some languages we will not speak, some
places we will not ever visit: we always assume there will be
another chance, for everything. Our memory interferes with the
present, and the present interferes with itself. We think we can
make more time for ourselves to get these things cleared up,
but the attempt to make more time, and the time in which we
do it, makes less time, and complicates them still more. So it
requires infinite time. This is the way it was in the primal nebula,
which might have expressed itself by now, except that it made
galaxies of light and expanded them through a prior void. They
might have resolved light and time, only they brought new light
and time, new properties of matter and shape into being. And
then stars and worlds arose, and on them the chemicals carried

even more complicated meanings into being, meanings which could no more recover the beginning and explain it than they could attain eternity or than the beginning could regain its priority and omneity. So we are born into life in the middle of things that are in the middle of things, in the middle of ourselves, in a continuum of memory and desire.

We cannot get out of this. And the sky, even if it were a sky of frogs and lily pads, spreads itself out as the widest ramification of conditions. Clearly, this is it.

The idea that the Sun was created for man is ridiculous, but so is the idea that it just sits there randomly in exactly the right place to give us heat and light. Twentieth-century cosmology has given the Sun and us inherence in the same cloud. It has passed the real question on to the time before the cloud, and the cloud before that. So we sit in our solar paradise, allowed to be by an accident of stellar evolution we also do not believe.

"What is life like?" the lawman asks the rustler in *The Missouri Breaks*.

"It's like nothing else I've ever seen."

"Against his will he dieth that hath not learned to die. Learn to die and thou shalt learn to live, for there shall none learn to live that hath not learned to die." So says *The Book of the Craft of Dying* in the English translation of the *Tibetan Book of the Dead*.

It is the unlived in us that cries out to the Creator for its chance to come into the world, even as the unborn, in our imagination of them, must cry to be born. Or else why would they risk so much for so little when in the end they must be worse than unborn, they will be dead?

"One sticks a finger into the sand to see what country one is in," said Søren Kierkegaard. "I stick my finger into existence and feel nothing. How came I here? Why was I not consulted?"

We come into being in a way we cannot account for. Memory does not follow us back to the first words, and then before them to the precipice. Language is more complicated than that, right from the beginning. By the time we know anything, it too goes back to the beginning. We forget not knowing.

Life is shaped from within as Einstein shaped the universe we now inhabit, a flux of energies creating their own boundaries outside of which nothing can exist, not even war. Come to any point on the wall and it will very articulately throw you back to a space inside that wall, whether in the language of your own breathing, the precise equations of physics, or the dialects of some ancient people. Push English to the limits of conscious-ness, and Old English will gradually replace it, or French, or German; push it far enough back to the melting of the glaciers and the last solstices of the Ice Age, and it could even be Tibetan or Apache, Cro Magnon. But it will keep on talking about the formation of all these things, and its own formation, from within itself within earlier languages within protean speech.

We cannot go beyond thought, though we precede thought in every way.

When we die, all this will change. The blue vellum of the sky, the green parchment, the trees and fields will be peeled away. The night of stars and galaxies, though it is as undiminished and hollow as death, will be peeled away also.

Death does not allow an easy way out. We may think: "This is the nature of things. I did not ask to be born, and yet I am here. I do not ask to die, but that is the destiny of all living things." We can offer ourselves to death by our reason, but we contain far too much energy to make peace with death. All those eggs within eggs and languages within languages are no preten-sion. The memories and memoryless tissue formed within us are a thirsty lattice. When we lean over the drinking fountain and put our lips and gums and tongue into the water and cannot drink fast enough and want to drink forever, filling ourselves, whose thirst do we think we are? Whose thirst do we feel through the cells also longing to be filled? We may crumble in the grace of old age or yield to some other death agony, but *they* are not quenched. Something does not die—this hungry thing which embraces the animal. Something lives forever or not at all.

Shore up the fort as we may, at odd times we must know it— deep in daytime naps or beyond passion—there is an ocean dashing on the rocks below; it goes on until it meets the night. We are a hurricane of light and nerves and space. Water rushes through us, more than the whole ocean, more than the oceanic mass of planets, so ripe that meaning itself rings and aches. There are terrible storms in the universe, light years long, light years thick. There are equally violent storms inside the universe, long in consciousness, thick in consciousness. We are those. Such storms cannot be snuffed out by the end of life as simply as an ant seems to be crushed and is forgotten. Those in the storm must swallow it in and take it to eternity, with them if they go on, and to eternity anyway if life is the end.

After all, none of these kingdoms could exist without us, not as they do now. Death likewise.

It is only our purpose that is at odds with mortality. All this has another purpose too.

WINTER "THE SKY over a modern city is occulted by smoke & industrial throwaway, its proper atmosphere," writes the poet Robert Kelly. [4] But the cities are also celestial replicas, as any night view from an airplane reveals. The streets of New York look like the nervous system of a great creature still being born or the dense center of a galaxy. Man and woman have constructed something nerve by nerve and star by star from within, and its synthetic biology engulfs them.

For a child growing up in the city, the land of the stars is the Planetarium. In a room surrounded by silhouettes of the local skyline at dusk, a computer resembling an alien vehicle flashes the full heavens onto the ceiling to a haunting timeless music. Suddenly the buildings are gone and the disk is full of antique stars, as when the land was wilderness and Indians lived by the river.

Outside the star room is a night sky museum, with hunks of meteoric rock; scales for taking one's weight on the Sun and the Moon and the other planets; and epic kodachromes of the deep galaxies showing the vastness of space—the exploding nebulae with their reds and blues and aboriginal white light in shapes and figurements as exotic and primal as the fish and sea-plants in the nearby aquarium. It is dizzying to leave such a building and return to the city streets. Once, all human events occurred within the brightness of the night sky. That was the original cinema we attended each day as the Sun set.

"Countrymen are unlikely to forget," writes Kelly, "how after a quarrel with the wife and a quick getaway, they came out to see the Pleiades flirting in & out of sight at the top of a cold sky. Or 'Orion blazing.' "[5]

The man fights, then bursts out into a bigger world of himself, a world of fires, a world of origins.

In D. H. Lawrence's *The Rainbow,* Tom Brangwen falls in love with a Polish woman whose remote beauty he cannot penetrate, even in passion:

> Such intimacy of embrace, and such utter foreignness of contact! It was unbearable. He could not bear to be near her, and know the utter foreignness between them, know how entirely they were strangers to each other. He went out into the wind. Big holes were blown into the sky, the moonlight blew about. Sometimes a high moon, liquid-brilliant, scudded across a hollow space and took cover under electric, brown-iridescent cloud-edges. Then there was a blot of cloud, and shadow. Then somewhere in the night a radiance again, like a vapour. And all the sky was teeming and tearing along, a vast disorder of flying shapes and darkness and ragged fumes of light and a great brown circling halo, then the terror of a moon running liquid-brilliant into the open for a moment, hurting the eyes before she plunged under cover of cloud again. [6]

All the woman's strangeness and distance is set off against the strangeness and distance of the night. But the night is also familiar and reachable in a burst of solitude. The greater strangeness lies within us, Lawrence is saying. The distance of the sky is flat and illusory compared to the foreignness in our own souls and between two of us. It is in ourselves that we feel the vastness and passion of creation for which the night sky is the externalized image.

2

Scientific and Occult Astronomy

Acording to modern scientific cosmology, the universe ostensibly manifested itself in an all-engulfing explosion, an explosion we still sense in the background radiation of space. The "Big Bang," as it is called, occurred on such a grandiose scale that we are bare cosmic seconds into the pop. In our own time, fifteen billion years later, its nearly spent blast can be heard as a murmur.

The idea of space or location or even time in such an event is meaningless. It was everywhere and everything. Material, thrown in all directions, created space. There was no space otherwise for this explosion to expand into. But if it created space, then out of what? We have no answer. "Nothing" does not explain it because, for us, it is a hole. But there was nothing for there to be a hole in.

Where did this explosion get its matter and energy from? The frightening answer is either that we do not know or that it is debris from the last creation.

What was the last creation like?

As long as it obeyed the ultimate laws of substance, it could have been anything. It could have contained planets, babies, painted pots, chipmunks, lichen, electricity, and gravity, just like this one. Or it could have contained different things.

If we ask: was there life on Earth in those times?, we must answer: what Earth?, what time? A different explosion would have led to a different creation, another space, a time before time itself, a unique outlay of planets, galaxies, and stars, if even there were such things.

15

If somehow we were to enter this last creation, we would not be able to tell where we were in it, what "where" meant, or how it fell in any hypothetical sequences of universes coming before or after. There could have been billions of such universes, or more, each within their own parameters of space and formation in cosmic time, endlessly created and destroyed, forever unto eternity.

The destruction implied by this is in no way partial. The obliteration of planets or whole galaxies does not rival it. In the "Big Bang" at the end and beginning of time, all things are destroyed. Suns and planets of course are destroyed; people are destroyed; their artifacts are destroyed; the memory that there ever were people is destroyed; continuity ceases; philosophy ends; every clue even to the implication of our existence is wiped out. All are ground into atoms and subatomic particles and stored in a single inclusive mass as if they had never existed. They are scrubbed clean. And then they burst into the milky fleece of new stars and worlds. Creation starts over again: reference points, matter, meaning, life. Then it ends.

The Big Bang Theory is currently popular, for it apparently solves many puzzles: Why are the galaxies rushing away from each other? How came to be the loosely distributed stars of the night sky? Of what origin is the background of radio noise in the universe? How does time begin and end? Perhaps it is not so surprising that the papacy gave its approval to the Big Bang Theory because it seemed also to be a confirmation of a single divine origin of the universe.

As long as there is an expanding universe to explain, alternatives to the Big Bang are few. In fact, there is only one basic alternative, the Steady State Theory, in which the matter of the universe is seen as continually created, either uniformly or in certain hot spots, with old matter continuing to move into space or beginning to dissipate and collapse. This theory does not require a cataclysm, and it allows the present universe to be as old as time itself, to retain its basic archaeological integrity. This that we see *is* the creation, instead of just one in a series of "creations."

Where does the matter come from in Steady State? What was the initial creation?

According to one of its propounders, Fred Hoyle: "It does not come from anywhere. Material simply appears—it is created. At one time the various atoms composing the material do not exist, and at a later time they do."[1]

If we were to suggest that this is difficult to accept, he might well point out that Big Bang doesn't solve the problem of original matter either; it just gives the impression that it does. Either we have new matter emerging from an explosion, or we have it dribbling into space at a few remote points—not very many, but then not very many are needed in a big universe. To answer any further question, we must go back, which is impossible, to before the creation.

Hoyle suggests that if a film were made from any point in the universe, galaxies would be seen emerging from the background material. Though galaxies would also be "blowing" away into the hindmost zones of space, the film would not show much change because new galaxies would replace these. "How long would our film go on?" Hoyle asks himself. "It would go on forever" is his answer.[2]

Steady State Theory makes the universe homogenous in time as well as in space. If the galaxies are moving away from one another, new ones *must* be formed to take their places; otherwise the universe would eventually thin out. Once a galaxy reaches a place where its light can no longer overcome the speed of its recession from us, then we cannot know its existence. It will have been lost to the expansion of space. But new galaxies are being formed, which could not happen without the spontaneous creation of matter in space.

Of course, all of these explanations come to the ultimate problem: how did the universe begin? does the universe have a beginning? an end?

Either way we are in trouble. If it does not have an end (or a beginning), then truly we dwell in an incomprehensible eternity. If it does have an end, if it did begin once upon a time, then what lies beyond it? Nothing? Gods?

The temporal origin of the universe is much more difficult to comprehend than the spatial dimension (though these are, finally, the same). Time is a theological, mythological, or epistemological question. No matter how many beginnings and ends

scientists define, there will always be the question: and what
before that? Before the universe, what? Why did it come into
existence? Did it happen right away? Was there a delay? What
stalled it? How did it move from nonbeing into being?

Of course, the other form of this same question is: Where
were we before we were here? Where shall we be after we have
finished our allotment? What delayed us from coming into being
at the beginning of things?

Science will never answer these questions satisfactorily, for it
will always give secondary causes in place of first ones, or its so-
called first causes will suggest even prior causes. It takes a "spiritual astronomer" like Da Free John to comprehend the utter
insolubility of the astrophysical riddle:

> Physicists are currently . . . confronting the unavoidable con-
> clusion that everything that preceded the "Big Bang" can no
> longer be discovered and known. In other words, scientists
> cannot in this case find the ultimate material cause they are
> seeking, because any facts or information that existed prior
> to the explosion that created the material universe have
> been totally obliterated or transformed beyond recognition
> by that explosion. . . .
>
> If we trace the one-dimensional chain of material events
> (or apparent effects of causes) back far enough, even if we
> could discover what existed before the "Big Bang," there
> still may be no End to apparent effects and causes. But if we
> accept the factuality and implications of the "Big Bang"
> itself, it does seem that, at least with the ordinary, mental
> equipment of Man, we will never be able to go beyond a
> certain point, and so our prideful presumption of attaining
> complete knowledge about (and thus superiority over) the
> universe in which we are appearing will, we must admit,
> inevitably be frustrated. Today's scientists may be busy dis-
> covering all kinds of things, but they are, by virtue of this
> consideration, beginning to realize that they are all some-
> thing like plumbers now.[3]

He concludes elsewhere that, as long as "conventional physicists are stuck in material conceptions of the stars and ideas such
as the "Big Bang" as the origin of physical events . . . they do not
conceive of the subtler and Transcendental dimensions in which

those processes are taking place."[4] This is the essential dilemma of purely materialistic astronomy.

The Big Bang seals us into a dead universe that is also dying. We too are extinguished without a ghost or a trace. We huddle around the random embers of a sun-star, nursing the faint currents of heat: the hot springs, the electron baths, the summer grains and flowers, the glows in our bodies, and the fossil fuels of their antecedents in the DNA blueprint. Not only does nothing else remain: nothing else ever existed. But this is the present endpoint of only one line of inquiry into the heavens: external, objective, and, in the modern sense, progressive. The other is internal, magical or telepathic, and inherently teleological. At one pole of the universe, the Big Bang is everything. At the other pole, it is only a perceptible shell, a vivid externalization, and we are the spawns of a profoundly internal spiritual force. The Sun may heat the physical universe, and barely so at that. There is an archetypal Sol which lights the spiritual universe and will continue to forever, or until there is no longer a need for this manifestation.

It would be a mistake to call one universe intuitive and the other empirical: both are intuitive and both are empirical, though in different ways and in relation to different ostensible objects. Both are equally subject to psychological and cultural biases. We can best understand the history of astronomy as a dialectic of the lineages arising from these poles. Occult and scientific astronomy inspire each other, they become one another, they mistake the other for themselves. In modern times, they work not toward a rapprochement but toward a deeper and more final polarity: on one side, the Big Bang; on the other, the astral universe in which all things endure forever.

The prototypical internal astronomer is the Egyptian priest in his pyramid. As he meditates on star images and decans (the thirty-six gods of the 10-degree divisions of the zodiac), the meanings of the sky come to him in his mind and spirit. The internal astronomer believes he can tell the difference between the images of his own brain and the messages of the stars. His methods are rigorous and certified, having been passed down for generations from the dawn of time. He knows the stars because he trains himself to be on their channels of intelligence, because he is the mirror of their life. His own knowledge is a version only of their cosmic and eternal wisdom.

Internal astronomy is our idea—not theirs. The priests do not think their stars are internal. Those are the real stars, the bright supernaturals in the sky and in magic texts, communicating clairvoyantly as well as visibly. Their messages fall into the bodies of plants, animals, and other entities. Magicians are actually internal astrologers who operate from this astral and planetary residue. Early man drank potions and went on vision-quests to get into the mind of the heavens. He stood outside in the night, night after night, and prayed for admittance and truth. What he learned he considered sky-intelligence. It is this visionary lore, this system of correspondences from a journey, imaginary or not, that sets the basis for internal astronomy with its star charts and sigils.

In one Taoist system of "interior astrology," as the translator renders it in English, the stargazer finds the stars by pressing the tips of his fingers just at the corners of his eyes and wiggling them until "the stars" appear. This is not some other arbitrary sky; for purposes of divination, it is the same sky, and the sage Shih K'uang tells Duke P'ing that he should use it "if the sky is cloudy and the stars are invisible." He goes on to remark that Alcor can still be found as a Helper Star, though no longer next to the Big Dipper.[5]

Duke P'ing is ecstatic at learning this method. "I will have [it] engraved on jade tablets and stored in my treasure chest," he says, "so that I can look at it often."[6]

"If a man's heart is true," Shih K'uang goes on to say, "he can see celestial lights and take their visibility into his heart through his eyes, or he can generate spirit lights and take them in through his breath and nerves. It is the same."[7]

To the external astronomer, this is not the sky at all, and it is not the stars. He observes the actual night sky in order to understand its patterns and cycles—the passage of different star-groups across the dome in the course of a night and the seasonal and millennial changes. Later in history, in the West, he comes to explore, by analysis of the electromagnetic band, the composition of the stars and the shape of the universe as a whole.

It is the same activity carried on with new instruments from a cumulative bibliography. The external astronomer is concerned to know what the sky *is* in some absolute sense, just the way a biochemist might want to know what the ocean is. To him, the celestial sphere is imaginary, the constellations are imaginative projections, and the night sky is actually a field of infinite radius upon which the celestial objects appear to be placed. There is not one field but many individual fields, depending on the location of the viewer. The stars are far apart and moving at hundreds of miles per hour, but distance absorbs their variability and motion, casting this temporary "stable" sky.

The internal astronomer is less concerned with the stars as they are in abstract nature and more with what they are in *his* nature. His nature is fused with the whole of the universe; he looks always into one through the other. From the point of view of the external astronomer, the internal astronomer is condemned never to know the actual stars, only the aspects of his own consciousness (and unconsciousness) assigned to the heavens by tradition, mythology, and lore.

Internal astronomy may come first in the history of mankind, but it is a totally hypothetical priority: our awareness of our own existence precedes our awareness of the sky. Internal astronomy is never entirely divorced from external astronomy. It could not be. Man knows the stars only from seeing them. Though the internal sky may have been intuited visionarily at some apocryphal moment before he looked upward, it was not then the sky but a field of unknown composition and shape extending infinitely within, filled with sparks and talismans. A series of insights joined this at once to the night sky, and a ritual methodology sealed the marriage for as long as we are together on this world. The darkness without and the phenomenological field within became the night sky, so now we can barely imagine what preceded a prehistoric system millions of years old. By the time we hear of astronomy, in our voyage backward before it disappears into the mute darkness of our own ancestry, it already includes uncountable varieties of astrology, astromancy, and astral magic.

Divination, magic, and the calendar share an origin in this larger system. The association of Sirius with the inundation of the Nile at the summer solstice may be a "scientific observation," but the larger system of which it is part is experienced internally. One school of contemporary ethnoastronomy argues that the origin of writing systems—Egyptian hieroglyphics, Chinese ideograms, and Canaanite-Phoenician syllabic alphabets—long a mystery, must lie in this same ancient astro-philosophy. Specifically, Hugh Moran and David Kelley propose that the twenty-two letters of the Hebrew alphabet and the twenty-eight letters of the Arabic alphabet "are based on the signs of the lunar zodiac, which long antedates the twelve signs of the ecliptic or solar zodiac." The age of this system is demonstrated by global correspondences which suggest a pre-Indo-European, even an Ice Age, origin. It includes Chinese and Hindu lunar mansions, Jain symbols for the lunar constellations, Aztec day gods and day names, Mayan glyphs and day names, Burmese constellations, and Cambodian lunar animals. Of course, the Greek and Roman alphabets, and our own Romance ones, follow from the Semitic.[8] It is as though the Moon herself, in our magical and mythical devotion to her and her numbers and symbols, gave us the system of recording from which all history radiated. No wonder she has an astrological association with memory, the unconscious, and the duplication of codes. Earth and sky have been coeval since the dawntime, and every ancient tribe and civilization viewed their marriage as an active account of cosmology smelted in radiant metals.

The traditional Western name for the spiritual sky is the astrum. This astral realm is not organized according to normal linear geometry. Things small in real space (like the planet Pluto) may be astrally equivalent to Saturn, or even the Sun. Physical remoteness of the stars does not change their astral nearness. Those bodies we see distributed in "outer space" are simply three-dimensional footprints of bodies of many dimensions.

Strictly speaking, in order to "see" astral space, one must enter an astral body. In that form a person can travel and visit other worlds while his physical body remains on Earth. The astral realm is a manifestation of the ultimate night sky, so knowledge of correspondences gained on these transphysical journeys is applicable to the visual sky. The astral and the astrological are definitely related: the planets move visibly in the zodiac, but the meaning of this movement is perceptible only in astral form. That is not to say that astrology derives from astral projection. It may well precede it, coming not from that method of "seeing" but from its own long tradition of celestial and terrestrial observation and intuition.

In the astrum, stars and planets show things most inherent to them. They appear with their original colors; they hum their natural sounds.[9] At the same time that they reach upward into a divine and supernal realm, they are imbedded in a physicalizing hierarchy that requires the Earth at its other pole. Sky and stars and gods came into being in the lotus burst of creation. As the petals of this lotus continue to unfold and create the outermost and the profound, its fine roots grow downward through the rich humus of the Void, a fertility associated in hermetic tradition with the number Zero, the Fool of the tarot, and the egg of the Gnosis. When Zero opens, it contains All.

The flower of the heavens reaches down over us and covers us; the elemental life of the world surges up within it as different octaves of occult vibration. The Earth is the sphere of magical operation. It is removed from the center of creation, where magic is natural and influence direct, but it has a direct rhythmic and sympathetic connection to this realm through the astrum. Inasmuch as the physical world was brought into being invocatorily and magically from the Source, it can reach the Source by invocation and magic. The lunar alphabet and calendric number systems are the most important tools.

The trees, the animals, the flowers, the fish all originally had counterparts in the sky, stars or constellations that reflected their essential being, that arose from the same archetypes. To look into the night sky was to look at the different flowers in the fields, to see the fish of the deep. It was also to see the character of mankind, for the different types of human beings, the idiosyncratic nations and occupations, the various clans and totems, were all written in the sky. A particular tree or herb or stone may be associated with a planet or star, such as juniper with Saturn or the lemon-yellow gem apatite with Mercury.[10] The Star of Bethlehem coincided with the advent of Christianity. Some modern astrologers have claimed that the comet Kohoutek deposed numerous heads of state, including Richard Nixon.

The hermetic texts contain the cumulative attempt of Western mystics to discern the hidden correspondences between man and the cosmos—from their own experiences and those transmitted from the non-Western world. The importance of these symbols and correspondences is not that they have been fixed by occult authority, nor that they are ancient. Their significance lies in the fact that they are our only history of the spiritual universe to this point, that they have been found satisfactory on an unconscious psychological level over millennia, and that they represent a collective cultural experience over many aeons and lifetimes: they are our single thread going back to the beginning.

An hermetic description of the Creation appears in *The Divine Pymander,*[11] an Hellenic mediaeval work attributed to a much older Hermes. This contains the background theology for internal astronomy and an explanation for the merging of astrum and night sky: The spoken Word of God touches the creative Mind, and a speech-driven impulse hurtles through an infinite Below. It becomes entangled in the whirlpool of incipient Nature and is spun around and around in circles and circles within circles. There it loses its simple relationship to the origination and is "turned from an indefinite beginning to an interminable end."[12] Seven paths, or vibrations, connect back to the Creator, for there is a Seven within Him that He has imparted to the Creation. He smiles with love upon this maelstrom; then He sees reflected back an "insatiate beauty," the form of Man rippling in the shadow, carried through light and water. So taken is He with this appearance that He "willed to dwell within it" and "begat the irrational form."[13] Nature looks back through this beautiful image of God and longs to embrace the Man. Man also sees himself for the first time in his reflection in the body of Nature and in her desire for him; he is enamored and reaches down through the shells and embraces himself in her. The shells break, and Man and Nature are locked eternally in an embrace. Neither can escape the other.

There is still no sky, only the movement of forces—Mind, shadows and water, the turbulence of disturbed fields. The sky comes into being after and in correspondence with the "beasts, quadrupeds, and reptiles, and aquatics, and winged, and every fruitful seed, and grass and green herb, having the seed of reproduction in themselves."[14] The seed seals the circles and the Seven into the world. The whirlpool becomes the microcosm.

From the beginning, there is another "Sky," the cosmic background against which Creation emerges. As long as there is no starry night, nothing separates time from the eternal. Finally, a thin translucent layer turns the Earth inside the Creation and gives the illusion of geography, space, and time. Later astronomers will see that the illusion is infinite and goes on galaxy upon galaxy, but the infinity is not what removes the Earth from the Creation; it is a secondary effect. What removes the Earth is the mirage of geography and sky, the perceptual trick, or, in Qabalistic lore, the whirling sword which God placed to keep man and woman from returning to Eden, a sword which could now only be the speed of light, as it relates both to the physics of particles and the physiology of the eye. The original Sky is woven through the Earth and reachable in intermediate form as the astrum.

The optic image and the hermetic one fall simultaneously upon man in his intuition that he is inside something that has formed around him not once but many times, and not in one way but in many ways, and so that he cannot tell the difference between the source inside him and the source outside him. The whole geography of future worlds from which we might come before birth and later worlds to which we might go after death hangs in the balance of this unresolved episode in a whirlpool, with the sole significant clue being the number Seven. We talk of spirit and matter, or the divine realm beyond the stars, even the physical realm of galaxies and quasars, and all these things follow from the way in which we believe that the world was imbued with life and meaning in the first place.

After the formation of the night sky, the Seven Circles worked their way up to the top of our sphere. The divine aspects in them took on stellar forms, and the constellations were made. Then the circumference was wrapped around, forming a visible plane in which these original creationary forces shone. The night sky is thus the last vestige of matter where matter becomes more and more permeated with spirit as it moves toward spirit.

Some mediaeval and Renaissance occultists believed that the material part dominated and the stars showered the Earth with poisons and destructive influences which man could ward off by amulets and signets. Others saw those same influences as free stellar energy, useful to create medicines, perform magic, and even to escape astrological destiny.

In Hebrew Qabalistic tradition, the creation emanates from God's intelligence as a series of primes generating other numbers, the sheaths of subsequent landscapes emerging as dreams within dreams until they manifest far beyond His images and He can no longer touch or alter them. They are subject only to the rule of the original numbers and the derivations from them.[18]

Taoist astronomers believed likewise that the true heavens lay behind the transient visible sky, or within it, as candles in a glass lantern: "Outside the sky the Luminous Ho throws up waves of jade."[15]

We can picture these purple-black waves, like an ocean, washing up against the universe.

By the cosmology of the twentieth-century Russian mystic G. I. Gurdjieff, the visible universe of stars and planets is merely one aspect of a vast multidimensional creation. A ray of light-sound carries information from higher worlds into lower ones; at every level where it meets a critical octave it must change and its vibrations are translated into matter and form. The night sky reveals one such crisis of manifestation. The liquid biosphere of our world is another.

> The *Protocosmos* is the Absolute in the ray of creation, or world 1. The second cosmos is the *Ayocosmos*, the holy cosmos. The *Macrocosmos* is our starry world or the Milky Way. The *Deuterocosmos* is the sun, the solar system. The *Mesocosmos* is 'all planets,' or the earth as the representation of the planetary world. The *Tritocosmos* is man. The *Microcosmos* is the 'atom.'[16]

Gurdjieff proposed a full universe of "seven dimensions, from zero-dimension to the sixth dimension.... Beyond this period there is either nothing or the same period may repeat itself on another scale."[17]

As a three-dimensional body the earth is something quite different for itself from what it is for us. Our view of it is incomplete; we see it as a section of a section of a section of its complete being. The 'earthly globe' is an imaginary body. It is the section of a section of a section of the six-dimensional earth. But this six-dimensional earth can also be three-dimensional for itself, only we do not know and can have no conception of the form in which the earth sees itself.[18]

Creatures on the earth can manufacture souls out of gross physical matter, but they must first learn how to transmute physical nourishment, breath, and thought into finer substance. Those beings which do not develop souls from this stellar debris and which are unable to transcend three dimensions at death become light itself. They are damned to return unrequited to the stars and, with their flawed energy, light the cosmos for eternity.

Everything living sets free at its death a certain amount of the energy that has 'animated' it; this energy, or the 'souls' of everything living—planets, animals, people—is attracted to the moon as though by a huge electromagnet.... In the economy of the universe nothing is lost, and a certain energy having finished its work on one plane goes to another.[19]

From this perspective, physical astronomy describes only one sector of the universe. As its tools of inquiry improve, its replica becomes more and more complex and refined, but it is complexification and refinement of only certain dimensions of a much vaster manifestation transcending ordinary definitions of time and space. We are encouraged by occult astronomers to look anew through the night sky of physics at a density of cells, souls, and vibrations traced by the riddle of light representing the archetypal data of creation.

In fact, a number of contemporary spiritual writers have translated the concepts of science back into a hermetic astronomy. Rodney Collin, a Gurdjieffian astronomer, gives us a simultaneously spiritual and physical definition of the universal constant:

If light can diffuse and endure undiminished for half-a-billion years, it can surely do so for ever. This means that all light, from a candle or from a super-sun, sooner or later fills the entire universe. Light is *undiminishable, eternal and omni-present*. In every religion that existed these qualities have been recognized as divine. So that we are forced to the conclusion that light—actual sensible light—is indeed the direct vehicle of divinity: it is the consciousness of God.[20]

So we can look at the sky as a screen of hydrogen fires, or we can look at the same light as the divine component of creation transmitted eternally. The Sun is the local embodiment of this material, and the Earth is constructed of solar material. When we imagine the primordial seas with their millennial rains and steam, the upheaval of the molten core, the emergence of bare rock, and the clinging life mantle, we can intuit an inside to this process so that the astral is transmitted through the elemental. Then the Sun becomes something more than an incandescent cloud of molten seas and gaseous corona. Beyond its granularity and molecularity is another characteristic. Collin says:

> Go out and stare at the sun in the sky. Why are you blinded? Why are you unable to define or describe what you see? Why is the impression incomparable with anything else you know? It is because you are looking through a hole in our three-dimensional scenery, *out into the six-dimensional world.*
>
> The matter of the Sun, or electronic matter, is beyond form and beyond time. It is even beyond the recurrence of form and the repetition of time. . . .[21]

The Jesuit anthropologist Pierre Teilhard de Chardin has a modern evolutionary version: The mass of the Sun contained a psychic interior which it inherited from the origin of the cosmos and the beginning of time itself. The Earth is an interstellar germ, endowed with a sidereal aspect by the Sun. This aspect emerges through the combination of complex molecules. Cells differentiate from a native hydrosphere, then the organs of larger animals from cells, and still more complex layers of animal life upon these. None of this could have happened, argues Teilhard, if it were not already present at the beginning. Life is an expression of inner substance attempting to return to an original spiritual state. As plants and trees reach up to the sky for light, transforming that light by photosynthesis into the food of creatures from the food of stars, they are reenacting a pure divine form, they are reaching for the Sun. Their "without" projects the patterns of nature; their "within" is archetypal. In one aspect of their being, they penetrate the six-dimensional cosmos; in another aspect, they differentiate, spread, branch, think, and make philosophy, art, and science—to imitate, by intelligence, the pre-intelligent source. [22]

Teilhard calls it "a doubly related involution, the coiling up of the molecule upon itself and the coiling up of the planet upon itself. The initial quantum of consciousness contained in our terrestrial world is not formed merely of an aggregate of particles caught fortuitously in the same net. It represents a correlated mass of infinitesimal centres structurally bound together by the conditions of their origin and development." [23]

These coilings take place simultaneously across the entire planet as a series of waves. First there is chemical activity, then simple cell growth and bacteria teeming across the surface, then animals, then a wave of thought which sweeps the planet first as telecommunications and later as an actual noosphere. At this stage, the Earth merges again with the spiritual cosmos.[24]

The astral and astronomical universes obviously share nothing today, and it is difficult to make a case for a relationship. I had not thought this problem through when, in January of 1972, I stumbled onto it in an interview with the astronomer Carl Sagan.[25] He expressed contempt for the occult arts and indicated that it was far simpler to dream up a planet than actually to go there and see what it was. This seemed an ethnocentric and technocratic point of view, so I challenged it, saying that there was a relationship between the planets in the astrum and the planets in the sky. He laughed and asked me to prove it. My quick response was that the Mars being photographed then by Mariner cameras was only known at all insofar as it had existed in the whole history of our trying to visualize and understand it, and that that history was inextricably interwoven with the photographs even before they were taken. Sagan objected that this was to say the unconscious mind could have some knowledge of astronomy apart from what the conscious mind tells it. He argued that some sort of scientific tests would have to be carried out before data could be considered valid. Otherwise it was just wishful thinking. As we talked longer and longer, it became clear that this was an important issue to him. His sense of personal maturity came from not believing in occult things and from having grasped and taken the one opportunity there was in this age to visit other planets. He had translated a boyhood fantasy into a real adult life, and these other things seemed to him like the indulgences of adults who could not grow up and were probably not good scientists anyway.

"In my mind," he said, "there's a big difference between something I want to be true and therefore pretend inside my head is really true and something that's really true. . . . Suppose you lived your whole life in a very subdued and puritanical and uptight way because that was what you had to do to get to heaven, and then you die and that's it. Well, I think you would have been had."

"You wouldn't know it," I said.

"Nevertheless, it makes a difference to me. The fact that you would have foregone all sorts of satisfactions and pleasures for a supposed infinite reward and then that infinite reward was never delivered."[26]

One would hardly want to deny us the treasures that the space program has brought back from the nearby planets, and in any case Sagan's point of view is the conventional materialistic one and does not engage the astral problem except to dismiss it, which is certainly a legitimate stance. There is, however, another aspect of our experience, and we lose it if we are this quick to do away with the spiritual sky. The stars may be made out of hot gas and atoms, but that is not what they *are*. In fact, we do not know what they are.

The modern astral tradition does not deny scientific information; it feeds off it. As the planets change from animals and luminous bodies to worlds, these worlds have new kinds of astral fields and auras. We live in our internalizations of our images, which themselves change the nature of things. We unknowingly forge new talismans in the lineage of those Egyptian priests who said their charms held the spirits of individual stars. The NASA photographs are among these now; they are syncretized in contemporary astrology and divination, even as bits of European machinery and junk are incorporated as trinkets within sacred

Crow Indian medicine bundles without undermining the bundles' sacred power.

Of course, there is only one real universe. There are the two vying impostors of our modern times: the spiritual and the material. Though the law of creation demands that these be absolutely merged at every moment, they have hardened now as two separate systems of belief which divide the world. The difference between capitalism and socialism palls besides this.

To look at the heavens and realize that one is staring into a vast mirror of correspondence and sympathy is very different from looking out into the expanding body of the fireball. We cannot do away with the radio sky or the sky of the Big Bang and its galaxies and cosmic rays and hungry suns. But we can impose those two skies on each other and realize that they are opposite terms in an identity that for us is not resolved—that they are both inevitable, and it is up to us to square them in ourselves. The astral and astrological sky is what we contact as we go back into our own history, our infancy as a species, but also into our moment of identification with the cosmos, which is still inside us in some way. The physical expanding sky is what we contact as we go outward into contemporary physics and astronomy and the dismissal of all unproven synchronisms and correspondences. Both are there in our heritage and both are necessary. They deny each other, but then we deny each other. They also require each other, and so do we. Without astrology, there never could have been astrophysics. Not only does astrology give birth to astronomy in the minds of Kepler and Newton; it does so again in the minds of us all.

But the modern dilemma is reflected decisively in astronomy, no longer in pure astral magic or astrology. This is the legacy behind Sagan's unexamined bias. Our dilemma may one day return to a spiritual sky, but only through the present secular heavens. Until then, the sky of astrophysics must be part of the astral and astrological skies as well, and we will struggle all our lives toward a reconciliation.

If we look into both skies at once, we stare down a strange and chilling tunnel into the thing we are. And the deeper we look into the contradiction, the paradoxes on either half of the contradiction—zodiac symbols and fleeing quasars—the more we can see and the more we realize what it took to get us here.

3

Ancient Astronomy

PRIMITIVE MAN and modern Western man share the intuition that we come from the heavens. To primitive man we are the incarnation of fiery spirits in the sky. To modern man we are the formation of life in space debris. Either way, the night sky is the dark ethereal chasm through which we look back toward the beginning.

Early man was ten times the devotee of the heavens that even our best scientists are. To him they were necessity, not a job or a conundrum he could escape from. He observed their lights and motions and changes. He experienced the warmth-giving Sun and the brilliant sparkle of the night sky, and he came to the conclusion most suggested by the appearances and his experience of his own insides—that he was looking into the radiant world of the gods, the place from which either he himself came or the instruction for his creation came. Instead of pushing the stars away by his intellect, he took them into his bloody taste of the universe. Our skyfield is flat and disconnected, essentially arbitrary. His was alive and vibrating; it pressed down on him with messages, beyond wisdom.

The sky is our universal clock. With one hand, the Sun measures the hours of the day, and the stars measure the hours of the night. With their other hands, they measure the seasons of the year. The Earth's wobble gives a third hand to this clock, and it measures the epochs of history by the displacement of constellations. The changing heavens are a great calculator wheel lodged between our transient world and the cosmos at large.

The Earth *is* the sky again, and vice versa. The sky houses the Earth and provides numbers for its movement through space and time. As violent and portentous as the sky can be, it is the only trustworthy guardian of the Earth. It is the one assurance that we can never fall entirely out of this incarnation. If we were transported, kidnapped, to another world, another dimension, another system, the first reference point would be the sky. If the sky were partially lost, partially twisted, we might find our way back to the Earth or have some understanding of what had happened to us. If the sky were totally unfamiliar, we would be lost forever. The closest we come to this without starship travel is in the migrations from one hemisphere of our world to another. As seafarers enter unknown waters, stars close to the horizon behind them disappear, while, in front of them, new stars appear. Only on the approximate celestial equator do some horizon stars and star-groups remain in this altered company. It must have been a great shock to ancient navigators to find the sky as well as the sea changing, but it was an event in keeping with the mythic scope of the journeys. The sky was another vast "ocean" filled with luminous beacons and hieroglyphics.

The aboriginal inhabitants of Micronesia, Polynesia, New Zealand, and Australia journeyed there by canoe from Southern Asia by stages through Indonesia, the Philippines, and Melanesia. No doubt a certain amount of blind adventuring and chance landfall occurred during this millennial process, but the systematic migration of clans of men, women, and children took place by celestial navigation according to a system of star compasses the fragments of which still survive.

In Hawaii, certain stars are called "guiding stars" because they rise over certain islands as seen from given locations—for instance, on a specific route, Arcturus rises over the Hawaiian Islands themselves, and Cygnus rises over Tahiti. For longer voyages, sequences of stars, i.e., star-paths, are necessary. One passes from zone to zone, with navigation realigned according to successive fixed points at sea.[1] In 1774, Andia y Varela described Polynesian navigation:

> When the night is a clear one they steer by the stars; and this is the easiest navigation for them, because, these being many in number, not only do they note them by the bearings on which the several islands with which they are in touch lie, but also the harbors in them, so that they make

straight for the entrance by following the rhumb of the particular star that rises or sets over it.[2]

In Tikopia, the 70 miles northeast across the sea to Anuta was traveled by successively pointing the bow of the canoe toward nine stars. A star is followed only when it is low in the sky, after which its successor is picked up. The necessary stars come up over the horizon all through the night, with the earlier guides having set. Only the last star or two remain when the Sun breaks through the map.[3]

For the Carolines, a sidereal compass survives, with the rising and corresponding setting points of nineteen stars, including single stars from Scorpius, Crux, Cassiopeia, the Big and Little Dippers, Aquilla, Corvus, plus Vega, Aldebaran, the Pleiades, and so on. Polaris stands at the North; the upright Cross can be used to interpolate a southernmost point; and Altair and Orion's Belt mark the equator of the chart and the true equator, respectively. What makes this compass so useful is that it contains an unlimited number of possible relationships between stars that appear at different heights above the horizon and that rise and set at different times.[4]

Eldon Best gives the Maori sequence for the voyage to New Zealand as passed down in oral tradition: "Atutahi (Canopus), Tautoru (Orion's Belt), Puanga (Rigel), Karewa, Takurua (Sirius), Tawera (Venus as the Morning Star), Meremere (Venus as the Evening Star), Matariki (the Pleiades), Tama-rereti (the Tail of the Scorpion), and Te Ikaroa (the Galaxy)."[5]

This was the sea-road once taken through the sky to the homeland from the ancestral land of Irihia. The blazing lights over the Pacific were the present manifestation of a phenomenon that lay behind the Maoris' whole history and made them, in a sense, space voyagers, ancient mytho-astronauts. The heavens were made up of circular domes, or cupolas, set one in another, the various skies raised by pillars and set in enveloping tiers. The roundness of the heavens was created by the intersection of these tiers with the Earth. To travel across the sea was to travel from heaven to heaven.[6] Maori myth has it that the ancestors forced their way through the hanging sky. The Samoans in fact called the Europeans *papalangi* (heaven-bursters).[7]

The mariners of prehistoric times were astronauts insofar as their passage broke through cosmological systems and placed them in new ones as remote to their experience as we imagine other habitable planets to be. They did not know the sky as an extension of pure space. But they traveled through the sky as they understood it to exist.

The intertwining of number systems, stellar observation, and sacred architecture is a hallmark of ancient astronomy. The Meso-American temples are so complicated that dozens of stars and planets, as well as the Sun and the Moon, are built into their architecture. The vast plaza of Teotihuacan is as much the night sky as the Earth. This is a cosmological necessity. If men were not free to construct and visit representations of stellar relationships, then they could not study their own destiny. They would be cosmologically illiterate. Teotihuacan was apparently constructed so that the Pleiades passed visibly from its Eastern to its Western cross; this is the same star cluster that rises with the Sun on its first annual passage across the zenith in that locale. The Zapotec site of Monte Alban appears to have its baseline set according to the path of Capella for exactly the same reason.[8]

The Caracol is a prehistoric tower in Yucatán later used by the Mayans and named in historical times for its resemblance to a snail shell. Inexplicably asymmetric, it speaks architectural nonsense but stellar wisdom. Many of its windows and structural angles mark positions of Venus, including the extreme northern and southern points reached every eight years. Another window allows a direct line of sight to the equinox sunset; while another series of windows and staircase openings lines up with the star Achernar. What is misshapen on the ground is caused by a building "in" of the sky. The Caracol contains other viewing lines for Castor, Pollux, Canopus rising, and Formalhaut setting, events which could seem almost compelled by the zigzags of the structure, as if the stars had no choice but to obey the ancestor-architects generations after their death.[9]

To the North are American Indian mounds, many of them, if not all, set in the ground in the exact pattern that stars form in the sky. Some of the large conical mounds represent individual stars of great importance. Other effigy mounds trace out the constellations by the paths of their protrusions. These are both

better and worse than telescopes; they do not reveal the actual
bodies of the stars, but they bring the experienced and imagined
essence of those stars down to Earth where man can experience them.

The Great Serpent Mound in Ohio could well be the Little
Dipper; nearby bird and bear effigies suggest the Big Dipper
and Canopus. Mounds and posthole circles in central Ohio,
southern Illinois, and the East St. Louis area seem to mark extreme northern moonrises, and also sunrise at the solstices and
equinoxes. Some of these mounds were still used in historic
times by the Plains Indians of central Kansas. The Big Horn
Medicine Wheel is set like a proper observatory 9,600 feet up
in the clear mountain air of Wyoming. It is a series of rock cairns
and postholes 90 feet in diameter. Lines drawn through the central cairn to the outer spokes mark summer solstice sunrise and
sunset and also the rising of Aldebaran, Rigel, and Sirius just
prior to the Sun in summer, i.e., their heliacal rising before the
dawn drowns them. From the heliacal period of Aldebaran, at
summer solstice, to the period of Rigel is twenty-eight days; it
is another twenty-eight days to the period of the beacon Sirius.
Twenty-eight is also the approximate number of days in the
Moon phase and of ribs in the buffalo; the Big Horn Wheel has
twenty-eight spokes.[10]

One of the East St. Louis sites is a star observatory at the
center of a pentagram. Mounds are situated at the various angles
and on lines bisecting each other passing from angle to angle.
In these hillocks are buried the officials and players of an American Indian game like hockey and lacrosse, played in historical
times by the Creek. It is a kind of prehistoric Indian Coopers-
town, and also a museum in which the pattern of the burial
ground is determined by the stars. The athletic stars are buried
with the celestial stars, whose brightness they perhaps reflected
with their scintillating plays. It was not as tame a sport as either
lacrosse or football. Archers with slings were poised on the field
to shoot down the ball-carriers.[11]

Stonehenge is the work of priests, but the precision of its
architecture leads one to consider it a primitive computer, a "machine" that remembers positions in the sky to allow exact cali-

bration, at the solstices and equinoxes, of moonrise and sunrise, moonset and sunset. In fact, these positions are stones on the heel of which or through the minute openings between which the Sun or Moon appears at appropriate times. The larger temple, including the so-called Aubrey Holes for sticks to be set in, served as a general computer for the prediction of eclipses.[12] If this was 3,500 years ago, as is generally believed, some 20,000 years earlier the ostensible ancestors of these people in France and Spain kept track of the phases of the Moon with tiny notches on antlers, bones, tusks, and pebbles.[13] As Alexander Marshack indicates in his studies of these objects, they correspond so exactly to lunar cycles in their mathematical series that they could hardly, within reason, be anything else—especially, we might add, given the lunar obsessions of later, historically-known peoples or the rich and complex development of lunar symbolism by the time we receive it in written text. The earliest lunar (and solar) imagery is so exquisite in its interpenetrating themes and counterpoints that it is more like the remains of a dying civilization on another planet than the inheritance of the dawn of our race. No doubt this is part of the temptation of various mythographers and other exotic historians to assign this imagery to visitors from other worlds, other times, other galaxies.

The particular crudeness of the scribbles Marshack discovered, such that they had been overlooked by all prior archaeologists, is far outweighed by their mathematicity. The people of the late Stone Age may have had rough tools to record with, but they understood cyclicity and its relationship to stellar events. The sky was the biggest and most obvious text to study, however it got there. It was blazing reality. It contained the basis of time and number in space, concepts so large that they seemed to contain the universe. Ancient man studied this luminous text nightly for generations and learned the whole system, made of it a noetics and a poetics without having to know what the stars were made of; they were made, in a sense, of the numbers they generated, numbers which were also generated by flowers, seasons, rivers, and man's mental and biological rhythms, hence sacred numbers, giving rise to the divine beings who also appeared in dreams and visions. It is not happenstance at all that

when the gods of the sky appear in historical times in the early
civilizations, they are involved with mathematics, or that early
astronomy *is* astrology. And as far as Stonehenge itself is concerned, the twenty thousand years between those ancient counting boards of the Moon and the temple observatories of both
the Old World and the New are enough to engulf all of history
since many times. They are certainly enough to allow a linear
phase-count to be transformed into three-dimensional reflecting
pools of stone.

The mathematics of prehistoric peoples survive in the astronomical systems of ancient Middle Eastern civilization. Time-
tables in clay tablets date from the fourth millennium B.C. in
Mesopotamia. A Chaldean ephemeris from 568 B.C. shows the
precision of this calendric measurement:

> On the eighteenth of the month, Dilbat (Venus) was 2°
> 55' above the King (Regulus in Leo).
> Night of the eighth, evening, Sin (Moon) stood 6° 15'
> under the Scales of the North.
> The tenth, Mercury at evening behind the Great Twins
> enters.

Other observations were collected by the astronomer Labashi
in a "book" translated as "Appearances of the Planets, Behind
You It Will Return" and dating from 577 B.C.:

> Appearance of the Goddess Dilbat, 8 years behind you
> she will return, 4 days you subtract, you observe.
> Mercury 6 regular years behind you returns.[14]

Mercury does not have a cycle of six years, but Venus is accurate: there are eight years minus four days before it returns
to its exact place in the night sky. The figures for Mars (47 years
minus 12 days) and Saturn (59 years) are relatively accurate.

> Year VIII, Simanu 10, the goddess Dilbat in the evening
> into the head of the Lion entered, Simanu 27 at morning,
> in the place of the Crab she made her appearance.[15]

This is an entry from a tablet of 523 B.C., and it has a music to it,
even in English. Venus is wearing a luminous gown; she comes
forth one place after sunset, another place sixteen days later
before sunrise, as the Mesolithic forerunners of the Maori noted

also from their boats.

Without any instruments for measuring time or viewing space, the Babylonians calculated with remarkable exactness the positions of the Sun, Moon, and planets. The fourth-century B.C. astronomer Kidinnu corrected earlier turning points of the seasons to bring them in line with the precession of the equinoxes, a phenomenon itself undiagnosed at the time. He developed an arithmetical progression for the deviance of the position of the Sun from one full Moon to another. He calculated the period for the Moon's movement along its path closer to and further from the ecliptic, where eclipses were more likely, and he measured synodic periods for conjunctions of the Sun and Moon. All of this he did with an accuracy only fractionally off modern calculations—and better, in most cases, than the accuracy of astronomers through the nineteenth century, who, of course, because of gaps in transmission, had to repeat these experiments.[16]

The astronomy of Kidinnu came to the Greeks through the Persians, who knew him as Cidenas. It was brilliant mathematics, but it was mathematics to serve the gods, carried out by a priest. The Greeks were different insofar as they were the first people in the continuity of Western science to wonder what those things up there were made of. It was not enough to predict and derive their positions by number. Those positions themselves hid motive of some kind, impulse sacred or earthy. Somewhere within the flat tablet of deities sat a spacious world of bodies. If they were bodies, they had to be made of something. The Greeks never resolved this dichotomy, but they always worked towards its resolution, a process we inherit from them. They never gave up the notion that the planets and the stars were gods, but, in not giving it up, they never clung to it as passionately as the astronomer-priests of the Near East. Almost unconsciously, they committed a gradual act of sacrilege. They considered, at the same time, that the planets were gods who were cosmogonically bound in sacred paths, and also that they were bodies which must be substantial and must use the sacred circles of geometry to carry out their motion.

Hesiod's version of creation was predominantly mythological and shared as much with the Sumerian as with the later Greek

versions. In the two centuries following Hesiod and leading to
the Ionian astronomers of the sixth century B.C., an elemental
philosophy gradually supplanted the theogony. The meaning of
divine Eros was transformed, and the burden of Creation was
taken on by the humors and elements. No one told the gods
that they had been displaced, and no one told the Greeks. But
with the old Eros went the Chinese box version of matter generated from matter, day from night, sky and stars from Mater
Gaea. Elements now separated the dark and light, the cold and
hot, the wet and dry, extending the properties of raw nature into
matter. In the aeons since, we have only temporarily lost sight
of these elements. They are surprisingly modern and inextricably woven into the later molecules and atoms.

The pre-Socratic philosophers had the first visions of how the
universe might work mechanically. At least they are the ones we
place at the beginning of our own techno-historical sequence.

One of the earliest Ionians, Thales of Miletos, floated the
Earth like wood on water. Aristotle later complained that Thales
did not solve the logical problem of what the water rests upon.
Thales also predicted eclipses from the Babylonian tables and
deduced from the lunar phases that the Moon is lit by the Sun
and travels concurrently with it. He reasoned that eclipses of
the Moon are caused by the terrestrial shadow cutting off the
Sun's light, and that eclipses of the Sun occur as the Moon, from
the perspective of the observer, cuts across the Sun's light.[17]
Like so many early ideas, Thales's propositions were discovered
anew rather than inherited from ancient times, though, on some
deeper level, each historical occasion (even those which are totally lost to us, of which there are far more) adds to the context
of discovery and rediscovery. The texts we inherit, especially in
fragmentary condition like those of the Ionians, stand for millions of others as the one extant clue to a profoundly unconscious and collective process.

For instance, of another sixth-century B.C. philosopher, Anaximander, only a one-sentence fragment remains, but we know
of him from his later classical and Christian critics. St. Hippolytus writes in his *Refutation of Heresies:*

He [Anaximander] held that the earth is a body suspended
in the sky, not resting on anything else but keeping its

position because it is the same distance away from all; that it is in the shape of a cylinder like a stone column with a curved top surface; and that it has two faces, the one of them being the surface on which we walk, the other opposite to it.

He further held that each of the heavenly bodies is a wheel of fire surrounded by air, which separates it from the fire at the extremities. The air has little breathing holes somewhat like the holes in a flute, and through them the orbs are seen.[18]

According to St. Augustine in the fourth century A.D., Anaximander "believed that worlds are infinite in number, and that they contain everything that would grow upon them by nature. He held further than those worlds are subject to perpetual cycles of alternating dissolution and regeneration, each of them lasting for a longer or shorter time, according to the nature of the case."[19] Augustine regretted that Anaximander, like Thales, did not attribute this activity to a divine intelligence.

In the sixth century A.D., Aetius of Constantinople wrote: "Anaximander held that the stars are hoops of fire, compressed by air, and that they breathe out flames from little openings in the air."[20]

Another Ionian, Heraclitus, explained the stars as bright exhalations that ignite in the concavities of pure space. The Sun is hotter and brighter only because it is close to us. The Moon is a similar exhalation, but, since it is nearer the Earth, it is darkened by the Earth's impurities. Heraclitus proposed that bright exhalations in the hollow orb of the Sun are turned into flame, but that when the dark and moist exhalations take priority, the Sun is extinguished and night ensues. He is most remembered for his conception of a fiery principle within matter such that the world is a continuous flux and one never steps into the same river twice. The whole cosmos is such a river. Not only do we not challenge this, we still approach it.[21]

Another school of the sixth century B.C. followed the work of Pythagoras into a different aspect of the cosmos. Perceiving that it was the different lengths of strings in musical instruments that gave them their notes, the Pythagoreans discovered the harmonies as a regular progression of simple numerical ratios (the octave, the fourth, the fifth). The moving planets must equally form a musical harmony, they thought. Pythagoras himself assigned the intervals: from the Earth to the Moon was a tone; from the Moon to Mercury was a semitone; from Mercury to Venus was also a semitone; from Venus to the Sun was a minor third; from the Sun to Mars was a tone; from Mars to Jupiter was a semitone; from Jupiter to Saturn was a semitone; and then from Saturn to the sphere of the fixed stars was a minor third.[22]

The Greeks believed that something qualitative lay behind the cosmic manifestation, so they interpreted matter as form rather than quantity. The fifth-century B.C. natural philosopher Democritus proposed a theory of atoms that continued to interest Werner Heisenberg in his search for a unified field theory of physics. All of creation, said Democritus, is made up of an infinite number of tiny particles. These move around in the Void. Of different shapes, they become twisted, snarled, and entangled with each other as they bump and brush. Their contacts generate all substances in the world. For instance, the fire of the Sun and the stars comes apparently from those round particles which generate heat and light as they interlock. The atoms also create the human senses. It is the elemental atomic aspect of man's knowing that recognizes the elemental atomic aspect of things in nature.[23]

Democritus laid the basis for understanding the symmetry of the universe, said Heisenberg, though the Greek philosopher mistakenly assumed that the protean principle was a particle. But our elementary particles go back to Democritus and to Plato's *Timaeus*. "They are," according to Heisenberg, "the original models, the ideas of matter. . . . These primitive models determine all subsequent developments. They are representative of the central order. And though accident does play an important part in the subsequent emergence and development of a profusion of structures, it may well be that accident, too, is somehow related to the central order."[24]

In the last century before Christ, atomic theory in the context of an infinite universe attained a startling clarity in the work of the Roman poet-philosopher Lucretius. As the Platonic and Aristotelian branches of the great Greek river passed into the Christian Middle Ages, Lucretius wrote at the end of a small Latin tributary:

In all dimensions alike, on this side or that, upward or downward through the universe, there is no end. . . . The nature of space makes it crystal clear. Empty space extends without limit in every direction and seeds innumerable in number are rushing on countless courses through an un-fathomable universe under the impulse of perpetual motion. . . . Our world has been made by nature through the spontaneous and casual collision and the multifarious, accidental, random and purposeless congregation and co-alescence of atoms. . . . There exist elsewhere other congeries of matter similar to this one which the ether clasps in ardent embrace.[25]

The atoms are in continuous movement and process; otherwise all matter would be lying in heaps. Instead:

Each thing is born and emerges into the sunlit world only from a place where there exists the right material, the right kind of atoms. . . .
Atoms of matter bouncing up from below are supplied out of the infinite. There is therefore a limitless abyss of space such that even the dazzling flashes of lightning cannot traverse it in their course.[26]

Objects and species may vanish or perish but the indestructible seeds remain. "Nature does not allow anything to perish till it has encountered a force that shatters it with a blow or creeps into its chinks and unknits it." These seeds, however, must have become inactive, for the Earth now seems unable to produce even animacules, let alone new beasts and tribes of men.[27]

From the fragments of the fifth-century B.C. philosopher Anaxagoras, we can see the early understanding of the relationship between the physical universe and the complexity of the mind:

Neither in speculation nor in actuality can we ever know the number of things that are separated out.[28]

In everything there is a portion of everything else, except of mind, and in some things there is mind also.[29]

By the time we reach the fourth century B.C. and the work of

Plato, the mainstream of the West had turned from elementalism and atomistic psychology to an archetypal and numerological idealism. Plato hypothesized that the World-Soul transmits a harmonious order from which the individual properties of the visible world arise. The atomic templates are: cubes (earth), octahedra (air), pyramids (fire), and icosahedra (water); the Cosmos itself is a dodecahedron. These are not things in themselves but qualities which mix together like Democritus's atoms in the composition of substances. They are unchanging, ungenerated, and indestructible; they are also imperceptible and in perpetual motion.[30]

Plato was not a notable astronomer. His night sky was a giant clock created by the Demiurge in order to bring Time into being. The Sun and Moon and five planets were harmonic units of this time. The Sun was created to "fill the whole heaven with his shining and so that all living things might possess number,"[31] learning it from the zodiac, the phases of the Moon, and day and night. The overtaking of the Earth by Venus, and of Venus and the Earth by Mercury, was a peculiar subtlety of the divine clock. All of these events had esoteric and profound causes that were hidden from common people because they would cause panic if they were known.

> This was the plan [wrote Plato] of the eternal god when he gave to the gods about to come into existence a smooth and unbroken surface, equidistant in every direction from the center, and made it a physical body, whole and complete, whose components were also complete physical bodies. And he put the soul in the center and diffused it through the whole and enclosed the body in it. . . .
> And when he had compounded the whole, he divided it up into as many souls as there are stars, and allotted each soul to a star. And mounting them on their stars, as if on chariots, he showed them the nature of the universe and told them the laws of their destiny.[32]

Plato's circles and souls are ultimately psychological and epistemological, but if they are taken as natural and scientific, they trap mathematical astronomy in an impossible search for their coordinates. It is from this that the systems of Eudoxus and

Ptolemy arose in the following generations and passed into the Middle Ages.

We find Plato interesting again in the contemporary context created by Jungian psychology and quantum physics. Prior to the twentieth-century reinterpretations, Platonism threw a cover upon the heavens.

It was Aristotle who surrounded an immobile Earth with nine concentric spheres, each transparent and showing through to the next: the Moon, Mercury, Venus, the Sun, Mars, Jupiter, Saturn, the fixed stars, and the Prime Mover. The Prime Mover of Aristotle is the Deity of Aquinas and Augustine. As one moves out through the planets to the stars, toward God on His throne, spirituality increases. The elemental chaos of the Earth extends only up to the sublunary sphere and the Moon itself and includes clouds, rain, snow, meteor storms, and comets. The stars are pure and perfect. The planets are less pure, but they are set eternally like gems in their mild powerful circles—circles that led mathematicians to go on imagining complicated contraptions of wheels on which these perfect forms could be manipulated into the paths in which they occurred in the actual sky with both retrograde and forward motion.[33]

The late fourth-century B.C. Aristotelian universe breaks with the Ionians and the Atomists in being finite, with the Earth at the center. No wonder Anaximander and Democritus were disowned. Heavy bodies now move toward the center of the Earth only because the Earth and the universe have the same center.

Though Platonic and Aristotelian astronomy trapped European thought in an artificial cosmos for almost two millennia, there was another Greek tradition whose fruits were ignored and all but forgotten. A scientific renaissance flourished in Alexandria, notably in the third century B.C. This Egyptian city was the crossroads and marketplace for the flourishing Hellenic culture that followed the conquests of Alexander the Great. At that time, Greek culture spread to and incorporated Egypt, Persia, and western Asia; the Hellenic world-view was actually a pan-Eurasian synthesis, gathering the wisdom of both classical civilization and the so-called barbarians of Europe and Asia. The science of Alexandria was a cumulative achievement of the many traditions that coalesced there. The Greeks inherited what was left of the Sumerians, the Egyptians, the Persians, and the other empires from past golden ages, but, even as they extended Hellenic civilization to the northeastern and southern Mediterranean, it was transformed by local cultures.

In pure technology, Alexandrian culture was a marvel for its own time: among other things, it had the chain pump, the water-lifting screw, the threshing drag in the fields, the sternpost rudder, a copying machine for sculptors, and a lighthouse at the port of Alexandria whose fire could be seen for thirty-five miles. Holy water was dispensed in the temples by a slot machine.[34] Some persons claim that if the Hellenic scientists had prevailed, we would now be traveling to the stars, perhaps even to other galaxies, for two thousand years of almost total ignorance intervene between the academies of Alexandria and the post-Copernican revolution in Europe. This is no doubt a misreading of history. Although certain surface features suggest the possibility of a shortcut, other more profound elements obviously required the long years we now call mediaeval. It is still an interesting fantasy that has us exploring the Solar System at the time of religious schisms and the Crusades.

The library of parchment scrolls at Alexandria was the major depository of the knowledge of the world to that point. Centuries later, in A.D. 415, religious fanatics burned and destroyed the library, and we retain only tantalizing fragments. The desecration of the Alexandrian library is notorious as an act of blind sacrilege against the planet; it robbed us of Heraclitus and most of Greek physics. But how many other crucial documents and species have we lost without even knowing of them? Civilization is as much a process of returning to unconsciousness as it is one of bringing to light. Our modern astronomies tell us this. And the poet Robert Kelly seems to be reminding us of both the dark gods who rule history and the frustratingly provocative quality of the extant fragments when he laments: "The only trouble with the person who set the torch to the library at Alexandria is that he didn't do a good enough job."[35]

We can review the achievements of the late Greek world as a prelude to the very different science of the Middle Ages. Even at the time of Aristotle, Heracleides put the Sun at the center of the paths of Mercury and Venus—the innermost planets, which circle the Sun faster than the Earth—though he still had the Sun and its satellites circling the Earth. Aristarchus of Samos, born the year of Heracleides' death, 310 B.C., and the last of the Pythagorean astronomers, declared unequivocally that the Sun was the center of a system of planets, including the Earth. His one surviving work is a treatise entitled *On the Sizes and Distances of the Sun and Moon,* a scientific work both in perspective and methodology.[36]

During the third century B.C., Euclid derived the basic formulas of geometry, and Archimedes discovered the mechanical laws by which machines would be constructed for more than a thousand years; he also taught the Aristarchan heliocentric cosmos. Using geometry, Eratosthenes, director of the library at Alexandria, computed the Earth's circumference to within less than one percent error by measuring the angles between the Sun's rays and the vertical at Alexandria and comparing these with figures taken at Syene after measuring the distance from Syene to Alexandria. The experiment came from the insight that the noon Sun on the longest day of summer shone on the bottom of a deep well at Syene but never in Alexandria.[37] This is not one of our modern mass-produced experiments with monkeys or computers. A moment of sunlight at the bottom of a well is a clarity and a mystery both. Such insight is repeated only as the overall aeonic conditions change. For instance, the astronaut Michael Collins recalls seeing the succession of night and day from space. Day is simply night with the closest star smashing light through the atmospheric window, but not all of it getting through, giving the illusion of sky.[38]

In the second century B.C., Hipparchus, a Greek scientist in Asia Minor, upon discovering a new star, took to counting the stars in the sky, measuring their positions, and comparing these to the measurements of the Babylonians. This immediately revealed that the zodiac had become displaced. His instruments were so good that he determined the length of a year within six minutes and the distance from the Earth to the Moon as 33 Earth diameters (30 is the more accurate figure). By noting that the Sun and Moon were both sometimes larger and sometimes smaller, he concluded that their distance from the Earth changed. In all, he measured the positions of more than a thousand stars, and he put them into six categories of brightness. This task was not continued until Tycho Brahe began again almost two millennia later.[39]

When Ptolemy built his master system of Greek astronomy in the second century A.D., it was based essentially on the observations of Hipparchus. In every other way, the Ptolemaic System was a restoration of the Platonic and Aristotelian cosmos that Hipparchus's findings should have fatally fragmented.

The third-century B.C. mathematician Apollonius of Perga had used Euclidean geometry on curves like parabolas, ellipses, and hyperbolas, and he had shown how the irregular motion of Mars could have a regular motion at its basis. In the *Almagest,* Ptolemy placed the Earth at the center of the universe and derived the motions of all the planets and the Sun and Moon as combinations of circles with their collective orbit centered on the Earth—or almost on the Earth. In the Ptolemaic model, they actually moved eccentrically, with the center of their orbits being a point in the Void slightly apart from the Earth. Ptolemy used Apollonius's idea, but he added an extra overlapping circle to equalize monthly irregularities in the distance covered by Mars. "Uniform motion in a circle corresponds to divine nature," he said. "To reduce all apparent irregularities to such motion may well be called a feat."[40]

Ptolemy retained the moral basis of the homocentric system by replacing the Earth-centered spheres with complex eccentric circles and epicycles. This also preserved Aristotle's physics, since Aristotle had claimed that circular motion was natural and primary. Circular motion was prior to any rectilinear variation on it, so it must be the basis of the heavens.

Planets now moved in series of circles, cycles, and epicycles, abandoning one circular path for another not according to any discernible law but as the equations of the terrestrial astronomers required to "save the appearances," the sacred and divine appearances. To many, fact itself had become a sacrilege.

Geometry as a mode of reality was a particular obsession of the Occident. The Chinese had their own sacred astro-geometry, but they did not believe in circular occult motion and crystalline spheres. Taoism implied nonrepresentational algebraic motion. No further impulse was imposed archetypally. Motions arose from intrinsic characteristics in the chaos of the elements and in the powers of opposite interacting forces, yin and yang.

Ultimately, the Western theory of reality was to bear fruit, in physics and technology, but not before cosmology was recreated out of simple quantifications so that any number, however short of an integer, and whatever shape, however irregular, had a reality within the conditions that generated it. This could not happen until the sacred circles were broken and their natural circularity was separated from their theological circularity.

It is one of the paradoxes of historical process that this happened in Europe rather than China, in a tradition that had to wrench the vectors out of fixed archetypes rather than in a philosophy already committed to creative chaos. A different science developed in the Orient, for the East internalized sacred number and developed from it the mantras and interior alchemies and methods of yoga and meditation that led to a representation of cosmology not as the night sky and the universe of gravity, quantity, and atoms, but as an attention fixed within the universe of human physiology and transmental process. In the East, they discovered gravity and atomicity as laws of consciousness rather than laws of space and substance. They went into the meditational inside of cellular structure with reality fixed at their own being; the West went into the outside of cellular structure and external shape until reality was reflected in the starry heavens of astronomy. The machine age was the counterpart of those heavens on Earth. Apparently, the externalization of sacred number, however rigid and unpromising a path it seems in retrospect, was a more likely forerunner of physics and technology than the externalized algebra of yin and yang. But all this is not resolved. Meditation now enters the West and transforms astrophysics, and astronomy is practiced in China. If the outward stars do not compel the inward stars to change in the Orient itself, then they do in the West, where meditation is practiced in the context of physics. If humanity is willing, these two paths join in the future and lead to the new science promised back in Hellenic times to both the East and the West. A so-called Dark Ages stands in the way now, even as it did then.

The dimensions and distances of outer space which we now

take for granted were not even remote possibilities to the ancient Greeks. It is those distances, and the sizes they portend,
revealed by the optical telescope and the radio telescope, that
separate our universe from theirs. The Greeks could not have
known the scope of nature because they had nothing with which
to discern creation at such vast distances and in such irregular
pockets. The hierarchy of matter, from large raw suns to infinitesimal creatures in droplets of water, eluded them, but they
perceived an elemental set of relationships and intimated their
mathematical basis.

It is for us now to try to imagine the Greek sky as real, not
by being childlike and pretending that we know nothing about
space (which implicitly demeans their views), but by considering
again that space could still be anything. Those who lived and
died under such a sky are no more benighted than we who shall
live and die under an equally abstract version. The richness of
apperception supersedes a sterile kind of knowing. Most people
today project a flat unvarying eternity upon the sky, and even
astronomers approach the sky as an arena of contest in the com-
petitive brilliance of their theories rather than as a real thing. It
is the absolute cosmic priority of the night sky and our existence
simultaneous with it that stirs us to knowledge and truth. We
are indeed privileged to have the instruments we do, and they
are a gift of time itself and of the collective human race which
has led to us. But there will be yet better instruments, and they
in themselves will not automatically enrich the sky. In fact, they
may deplete it by calling to our attention so many more bits of
data and events that we are thrown out of the remaining oneness
and singularity into astronomical jargon and clichés.

Mediaeval cosmology was more than the theocracy of the
Babylonians restored. Democritus and Archimedes had spoken,
and their voice would not be quelled. The scientifically progressive Arabs surrounded the West geographically and
economically. Throughout the mediaeval period, an Enlightenment hung in the wings, which is why it was so magical and so
joyously proclaimed when when it seemed to come late, after the
millennium. But that is also the reason why there is no absolute
Middle Ages and no clearcut Renaissance. Some of Europe slept
in Christian cosmology and feudalism. Some of Europe kept loyal

to Greek and Arab science and the hermetic laboratory that yielded astrology and alchemy. Some of Europe had remained pagan from ancient times; its loyalty was to the old Atlantic and its Mesolithic industries. Even though the Christian theocracy dominated cosmology, engines and machines were intuited and built, new currencies were minted, and local inquiry into planets, animals, caves, anatomy, and navigation established a more substantial basis for a scientific revolution than a few Ionian philosophers. The remains of Greek natural science were the spark, but by the sixteenth century there was something to ignite; and when the explosion was finished, we knew about the stars, the circulation of blood, and the animals inside a droplet of pond water.

The Ptolemaic cosmology of the *Almagest* was the basis of the mediaeval universe, but flat Earth models were also popular within the confines of Church doctrine. Kosmas's *Christian Topography* of the sixth century is typical. The originator was a merchant turned scientist-philosopher who had traveled in the Atlantic as well as the Mediterranean, the Persian Gulf, and the Red Sea. He declared that the Earth, on account of its heavy nonspiritual nature, must lie at the bottom of the universe, not the center. The cosmos itself was designed, he thought, like the Tabernacle of Moses, with Heaven raised on four perpendicular pillars joined to the edges of the Great Ocean and shaped like a semi-cylinder. The firmament was a veil separating the divine world from the dwelling place of man. The Sun, Moon, and stars were carried below the firmament by angels who had this duty until the end of time.[41]

It was no doubt incredible to watch angel-borne sparks nightly beneath the sanctum of God in the nonindustrial air of the Middle Ages. But the translation of that vision into theology and cosmography had a deadening effect. It denied the Greek heritage, and it bound the European world into a cloister. How could navigators sail very far on a flat ocean that spilled over at the arches of heaven? Kosmas Indicopleustes might have have known better, for he actually reached Equatorial waters. But the image so dominated that Columbus's men actually feared the "black horizon" that they would tumble into as they continued to sail beyond recorded lands to the edge of the map. Even Ice Age European seafarers understood the "infinity" of the global ocean, but the new clerical and scholastic order was paranoid and intentionally confining. It was a time when people saw angels in the sky and the shadow of Satan across the night.

Plato and Aristotle marked no golden age. They stood before dark times scientifically, and a whole other civilization had to pass before the West returned to the point it had attained at the height of the Greek enlightenment.

Dante, for instance, six centuries after Kosmas, is still in the Ptolemaic universe. His passage through the spheres of the planets is a journey into more and more radiant zones of light, which represent not just increased brightness but the unveiling of the spiritual component of light. The *Paradiso* is a fourteenth-century voyage into the Solar System. With Beatrice—Eros—imparting divine motion, Dante visits the various planets: Mercury, Venus, the Moon, the Sun, and so on. Each one is inhabited, not by beings on a terrain but by souls in stages of transmigration. As one ascends through the stars, or into the celestial fabric, the light of God which "impenetrates" the cosmos becomes direct and blinding. Even the stars wash out beside it. This spark contains the pure flame of God's love.[42]

There are also elements of Christian topography in the *Paradiso*. One sails across the ocean to the conical pit at the center of the Earth. Hell is a geometrically defined position, a bottom to the universe, sucking all that is antispiritual into its core. Mount Purgatory arises out of the sea directly beneath Jerusalem. Climbing this mountain, one ascends into the celestial spheres, the planets.

This cosmology leads one way into a totally tabernacular universe; but on another path, the hermetic magicians were transforming the Ptolemaic spheres into zones of the astral world, and the stars impregnated plants, animals, stones, and all of nature with pagan influences. The Renaissance astronomers came into this muddle and spent their lifetimes addressing it. They transformed the night sky, and they changed the West with it. Ancient astronomy ends in a single tradition leading across a few short centuries to men walking on the Moon. We should also note that, except for this single brilliant thread, it is still a dark sea surrounding us and we are in an aeon of war and ignorance.

4

The History of
Western Astronomy
I: The Sun
in the Center

THE TRANSITION from ancient astronomy to modern astronomy is generally seen to occur through five main starwatchers: Nicolas Koppernigk (or Copernicus), Tycho Brahe, Johannes Kepler, Galileo Galilei, and Isaac Newton. Copernicus, the first, was born in 1473. Newton, the last, died in 1727. So the period we are talking about begins with the sixteenth century and ends at the beginning of the eighteenth century. It is specifically European, but it is pan-European. Copernicus was a Pole of Slavic ancestry. Kepler was a German Protestant. Brahe was a Dane born in a region which is now Sweden. Galileo was Italian. Newton was English. The work of each of these astronomers contradicted the work of one or more of the others, but what they stand for as a lineage is the transition from the Ptolemaic sky of heavenly bodies composed of numinous crystal moving around the Earth in perfect circles and driven by vital force, to the pre-modern sky of ordinary planets moving around the Sun in ellipses established by gravity and centrifugal force. Copernicus was born too early to consider the ellipse, but there is little doubt he would have rejected it, as did Brahe and Galileo, because it violated perfect circular movement. Kepler considered gravity too mystical a force to assign to physical motion. However, from the combined work of these astronomers, a single new system is carried into the eighteenth century.

It is also important to note what these theoreticians did not do. They did not abandon the idea of God behind the heavens. They did not perceive the real distance of the stars or their arrangement in galaxies, though they understood that they were a great deal further away from Earth than the last planet, Saturn. They did not abandon the view of the heavens as an harmonious arrangement of perfect movements inspired by invisible occult sources and orchestrated by a Prime Mover (though Galileo came right to the threshold of the modern secular sky). These men sought to know how an esoteric agency had set physical matter into eternal motion and elemental exchange. The mathematician in their center, the German Baron von Leibnitz, was a bare shade from Pythagoras on this issue. The latter saw God wrapped in geometric forms; the former saw Him interacting with His Universe by calculus.

It is quite easy to credit each of these astronomers with the wrong discovery by judging their activities mainly in modern terms. The heliocentric revolution of Copernicus is apocryphal. Copernicus did not put the Sun in the center; it had been done before him by Aristarchus, among others, a fact that was general knowledge in educated circles. Copernicus was not the only "astronomer" to attribute motion to the Earth. Nicholas of Cusa, for reasons having little to do with physical astronomy, had concluded a century earlier that the Earth was in motion and that this was unknown to us only because we had nothing fixed to perceive it against. Cusa also said that since the universe has no boundaries, neither the Earth nor any other place can be the center. That Cusa arrived at these insights for theological reasons means only that his system was not in the modern lineage, but the heliocentric model of Copernicus was.

Copernicus was less theological, and this, above all, sets him at the head of the lineage of modern astronomy. He put heliocentricity and a moving Earth into a form that led them to be taken seriously by both the Church authorities, who banned his work after his death, and the astronomers, who followed him.

Copernicus was not a stargazer; he was a mathematician and church cleric. He sought to put the heavens in order, and to do so he created a better bookkeeping system for the stars. There is little doubt that he realized how flawed his own system was. He had set out to simplify Ptolemy, but he ended up with more, not fewer, epicycles and artificial devices. Ptolemy's system required thirty-nine spheres and one for the fixed stars. Copernicus used at least forty-eight epicycles. The *simplification* of the Ptolemaic system is one achievement erroneously attributed to Copernicus.

Copernicus made only twenty-seven observations on his own: twenty-seven measurements of the stars, most of them inaccurate. All the rest of his system was based on Greek and Arab texts which he never checked even for the inevitable errors of translation and transcription.

In addition, he had neither the equipment nor the deep curiosity about the sky to make more observations and base his system on his own sightings. From the outset, he chose to work with secondary materials: the Ptolemaic system, the catalogues of Aristarchus and Heracleides, and the star observations of ancient times. Those twenty-seven observations of Copernicus stand out because they represent twenty-seven discrete moments at which this man looked into the actual sixteenth-century sky and tried to see it for what it was, tried to measure it. Otherwise, he assumed the heavens as a fixed imprint and worked in tables.

Ptolemy had created imaginary points in space—the equants—from which uniform motion would seem to exist. However, if uniform velocity were actually imposed, the planets must give up their circles. He must have known he was making a fiction, but, like so many other scientists, he no doubt assumed the fiction was better than the chaos that preceded it and would give some future astronomer a basis on which to make corrections.

This turned out to be Copernicus. He adjusted the Ptolemaic schema of circles and equants by using a central Sun and a moving Earth. To his dogmatic mind, the violation of uniform motion was blasphemy greater than the heresy of a moving Earth. The equants and epicycles he took as nothing more than a calculating device for appearances. He intended his own device as a better one, but he never abandoned the doctrine that the planets moved "with uniform velocity in perfect circles."[1]

Yet, Copernicus did something slightly more than adjust an illusory heavens. He made it possible for large numbers of people, especially educated people, to see the apparent motion of all the stars as stillness against a moving Earth. He did not initiate heliocentricity, but he wrote it in such a painstaking pedantic manner that it left a special imprint on the European mind not only in his own time but for centuries to come.

Since the Earth cannot be the center of the orbits of the other planets, and since they obviously move both toward and away from the Earth, the Earth must have "another motion in addition to the diurnal rotation." Beside rotation, the Earth "wanders with several motions and is indeed a Planet," a view which, Copernicus points out, was ascribed to Philolaus, the Pythagorean philosopher. The heavens, on the other hand, "if we assume them to be infinite, and bounded internally only by their concavity, so that everything, however great, is contained in them," could hardly move about the Earth. It would be like a vast eternity circling about a point. "Why then hesitate to grant Earth that power of motion natural to its shape, rather than supposing a gliding round of the whole Universe, whose limits are unknown and unknowable?"[2]

Because Copernicus was a mathematician and argued from a stubbornly pragmatic point of view, his argument had a particular credibility. Yet, the Copernican vision had no great widespread public appeal at the time, and the thousand copies of *De Revolutionibus orbium coelestium*, published in 1543, never sold out. Reprints came approximately every one hundred years. The system was communicated to the world quite secondarily through other books, such as Thomas Digges's proclamation of the infinite Copernican universe in his *Perfit Description of the Caelestiall Orbes,* which had seven quick printings. The differences between Copernicus's original ideas and Digges's recapitulations became blurred with popularization. Copernicus had retained the cohesive orb of fixed stars, but Digges scattered the stars helter-skelter through the realms of infinite space. He intuited the major cosmic import of local heliocentricity: it was not Sun-centeredness as such; it was what the dislodging of the Earth did to everything else. On a mere mathematical adjustment in an illusory system rested man's whole place in the cosmos—but wasn't it always so, then as now?

The pious canon would have been shocked by his appearance in the poetry of John Donne. The Copernican system had become the work of Lucifer, raising the Earth into the heavens and building a modern Tower of Babel to challenge God. Decades after Copernicus's death, the Church elders heard of this famous heretic and wanted him burned at the stake. That they were too late astonished them. How had he eluded them?

But Copernicus had other problems. By historical accounts, he was a troubled man, given to petty squabbles. A bizarre chain of entanglements led to his adversaries' overseeing the publication of his work and butchering the text for their own purposes. A preface was written in his name claiming that the system described in the book must be a fiction because the path proposed for Venus was an impossibility. Copernicus did not deny this. He was certainly aware, if from nothing else than the discrepancies in the positions of Mars, that he had failed to correct the Ptolemaic heavens. Yet, he refused to allow that his system was a fiction in the same sense as Ptolemy's, even though he also failed to do the work that would allow him to take it seriously as a real proposal of physical dynamics. He was trapped between his system's possible heresy and a host of errors on the one side, conditions which tended to ameliorate each other, and its dramatic correctness on the other. He had done away with the disturbing retrograde motions of the planets by showing that they were simply appearances arising from the Earth's simultaneous revolution about the Sun. Also, by implication, he had declared the fixity of the stars. Since they were no longer "responsible" for movement around the Earth, they began to drift out toward their actual distance from us.

But it is ironical that Copernicus never got as fresh a look at the sky as he gave to others. He did not have cosmic imagination. *De Revolutionibus orbium coelestium* is exactly what its title states: a book on the revolutions of the celestial orbs. It is not a statement of how the planets actually move; it is not an attempt to understand their nature; it is not even an attempt to give the Sun its real size and central position in this sytem. It is a correction of tables and a way to view the mathematical properties of the figures traced by the planets' successive positions.

In attempting to preserve order, Copernicus contributed to dislodging it. It is peculiarly fitting that a conservative church cleric should have created such a giant wave that so little befitted him, for it shows how specific and concrete are the pins that hold the background to the foreground in our world. We hardly know what they are. While others screamed for various sorts of revolution and change (and there were wars and famous heresies in his time), Copernicus accidentally dislodged one of the bolts in the mediaeval world. He displaced the stars; he introduced the tiniest element of eccentricity, the merest wobble, and it eventually picked up other wobbles and became an earthquake, a skyquake.

Almost at the moment that Copernicus turned to the Sun, the hermetic and Gnostic tradition in the West turned with him. In fact, it had always been there, and the association with the Sun of Hermes himself, planetarily as Mercury and theosophically as the source of light and the metal gold, was an ancient and significant one. Like Cusa, and without realizing it, Copernicus had laid the basis for a new hermetic interpretation of the universe too:

> In the middle of all sits Sun enthroned. In this most beautiful temple could we place this luminary in any better position from which he can illuminate the whole at once? He is rightly called the Lamp, the Mind, the Ruler of the Universe; Hermes Trismegistus names him the Visible God, Sophocles' Electra calls him the All-seeing. So the Sun sits as upon a royal throne ruling his children the planets which circle round him.[3]

If we were not told this was Copernicus, we might have guessed one of the hermetic or neo-Platonic philosophers.

Heliocentricity and the discovery of the New World by European mariners went together in the transformation of cosmography. Just as Copernicus did not discover the moving Earth, so Columbus did not discover America. Cyrus Gordon makes a case for Phoenician trade expeditions to Brazil as early as 800 B.C.[4] Carl Sauer suggests that there was Irish settlement in North America by A.D. 900, following the Norse invasions of the North Atlantic in 850.[5] In 1000, the millennial year, the Vikings sent a polar bear from North America to the Sultan of Egypt.[6] Rune carvings in stone have been found from Newfoundland and Vermont clear to the Mississippi.

By A.D. 1200, the Vikings were established in the Western Hemisphere and Basque fishermen were bringing back their catch off Nova Scotia to market in Spain. The Norse finally abandoned Greenland and the West in 1400.[7] So when we come to 1492, that famous date, we must ask: what is it a date for? Surely not the discovery of the New World. The Indians were there for at least twenty-five thousand years before. Surely not the European contact with the West. The "discovery" of America was as problematic as the Copernican "revolution"; both define breakthroughs in mediaeval self-deception and public ignorance.

1492 is the date for fusing two contradictory European images of the world. One Europe was grounded in the old Mediterranean culture with lingering hopes of restoring the Roman Empire (or at least the Roman cosmology), perhaps through the Church, and thus starting a new golden age. It was aware of the riches of Asia but ignorant and afraid of the Atlantic—the direction (West) of primitivity and darkness. It was a Europe concerned with international finances, trade fairs and markets, and rearranging national boundaries for political purposes. It was the Europe of Verdun, and it became the Europe of King Philip of Spain, De Soto and his ravages of Southeastern Indian civilization, Cortez, and Napoleon (even that late, with his desperate sale of Louisiana, the one strategic land he held).

The other Europe was specifically grounded in the old Atlantic; it never entered into Christian orthodoxy or mediaeval philosophy. It was forever pragmatic, pagan, and tribal. It was represented most purely by the descendants of the Druids, the fishermen of Biscay and Bristol,[8] the Cretans and Basques, and those otherwise educated "Christians" who searched for Hermes, incorporated him alchemically into Church liturgy, and saw Egypt as the base of an ancient and powerful magic.[9] In this other Europe, the Irish priest-voyages were known, and there were secret maps and routes, old "scientific" documents. It was the Europe not of Plato and Aristotle but the Arabic and Persian encyclopedias—the Europe of John Dee, John Smith, Hesiod,

Homer, and the Norse *Sagas*. It became a Renaissance Europe relatively unconcerned with either Christian orthodoxy or the Reformation, and it rejected the scholastic uses of ancient humanist philosophy. [10]

But neither Europe held America as such. The first one was afraid and ignorant of it; the second was involved in astral magic and navigation without a complete cosmography. Columbus took the Atlantic from its natives on both sides, Algonquian and Basque, and gave it to Spain and Rome, to Cortez and Pizarro. He brought together the round world and the flat world, the pagan world and the Christian world; he merged the secret trade maps and unknown kingdoms with public grants and acknowledged sources. By so doing, he lost the Homeric sea and its wondrous peoples, even as we have lost the angelic heavens. He set sail into the old Atlantic and found lands in it in such a way that they stayed found, not as mere rediscovery of the Indies. He made it impossible for Europe to ignore what it already knew.

The year 1500 was a turning point. Columbus and Copernicus were both stubborn enough to change the world-view and make it stick, but rigid enough to believe in the old cosmology to their dying days.

Born a few years after the death of Copernicus, Giordano Bruno, the Italian astral philosopher, was probably the first to integrate the heliocentric proposition with traditional hermetic magic. A contemporary of Kepler and Galileo, he alone was executed by the Church for his heresy.

The view of the heavens that Bruno proposed in the sixteenth century was so idiosyncratic and so nonmodern that it has been regularly misinterpreted as a brave forerunner of an astronomy that was to develop only centuries later. Bruno died for magic not science, though the distinction between them is ours, not his. He grasped intuitively at things which look like twentieth-century discoveries when we read them in excerpts of his writing, especially when these are chosen to exemplify an early martyr of the Enlightenment. No doubt Bruno died in the name of truth, but it was a different truth: the truth of the Sun City and the Egyptian awakening, the vision of machines run off astral power, stellar energy drawn by signets and sympathetic magic. Bruno would have honored electricity if he had lived that long, but he would not have accepted its utter secularization. The poet Diane di Prima recently heralded Bruno's vision:

> The City of the Sun comes soon, cannot be far
> yes, you are right—what's a millennium
> or two to us, brother? The gods can wait
> they are strong, they rise—the golden tower
> flashing the lights of planets, the speaking statues
> that guard its four gates, the holy wind
> that carries the spirit of heaven down thru the stars[11]

Bruno saw that the stars and galaxies must be infinite and eternal, that such systems must contain sensible and intelligible beings. He did not use the word *galaxy,* but he spoke of systems of stars with their own customs and beliefs and their own right to centrality quite apart from the position of the Earth. He was a "modern" for decentralizing the universe and getting not only the Earth but this whole region of constellations out of its special position at the center of creation.

> Sky, universe, all-embracing ether [said Bruno], and im-measurable space alive with movement—all these are of one nature. In space there are countless constellations, suns, and planets; we see only the suns because they give light; the planets remain invisible, for they are small and dark. There are also numberless earths circling around their suns, no worse and no less inhabited than this globe of ours.[12]

What Bruno found attractive in Copernicus was both the central Sun and the moving Earth. He also felt that the Copernican vision was a kind of Promethean seizing of our true heritage among the stars. The spheres which the Ptolemaic-Aristotelian tradition had imposed barred man from the sky and kept the magical principle elevated away from human access, in the angelic realm where only the Church could mediate. But the Egyptian universe, or at least the universe of Hermes with its Egyptian affinities, allowed human beings to travel in astral spheres on their own, gave formulas for drawing directly on stellar energies, and populated the heavens with alien intelligences. To de-Christianize the sky was not to blaspheme God; it was, to Bruno, acknowledgement that God could create more than just a Christian universe. It was, in fact (and here is the blasphemy for which he died in 1600), to imagine a universe in which God made things that could not be known by scholastic and Thomist law but could be derived by magicians and hermetics using their own principles of divination. Said Bruno:

> Open wide the door for us, so that we may look out into the immeasurable starry universe; show us that other worlds like ours occupy the ethereal realms. . . .[13]

Ptolemy had attached the stars to envelopes, but Bruno then said: "It is not to be believed that there is any firmament, or foundation to which are fixed these great animals which form the constitution of the universe, the infinite material of infinite divine potency."[14] The Earth moves in order to increase its attributes and because it is first and foremost alive and has a soul which it must express by movement.

Infinity is what makes Bruno most astronomical. He had an early vision of the great bestiary into which telescopes would later explode. He saw the *anima mundi* spawning stars, spilling sidereal energy into the microcosm as elements, imprints, signatures. So the true art of the heavens was not astronomy but astromancy, talisman-crafting. Intimacy likewise is what makes Bruno least modern. He did not mean outer space in the current nihilistic sense; he did not mean infinity dwarfing man. All of creation was available to humankind by magic and divination. The Earth was not relegated to a remote corner, for there are no remote corners, only hearths and creationary fires.

He regarded the failure of man to stargaze creatively as his failure to ascend, with Copernicus, into spheres of luminous energy:

> Some men [he wrote], resembling the dim-eyed mole, who, the moment he feels upon him the open air of heaven, rushes to dig himself back again into the ground, desire to remain in their native darkness; others are like those birds of night which, because of the weakness of their eyes, retreat into their shadowy haunts as soon as they see in the brightening east those bars of crimson which are the sun's ambassadors. All those creatures who may not gaze upon

the lights of heaven but are destined to dwell in the infernal circles of Pluto's dark prison-house, when they hear the dread summons of Alecton's furious horn, spread wide their wings and veer away in rapid flight toward their abodes. But those who were born to see the sun, being full of thanksgiving when they come to the end of loathsome night, dispose themselves to receive in the very centre of their eyes' crystal globe the long-expected rays of the glorious sun, and, with unaccustomed gladness in their hearts, they lift up hands and voices to adore the east. . . .[15]

This theme echoes in the poetry of the twentieth-century hermetic Robert Kelly—once again the call to the Sun-star:

& if we do not get up and destroy all the congressmen
turn them into naked men and let the sun shine on them
set them down in a desert & let them find their way out,
north, by whatever sexual power is left in them, if we do
    not
seize the president and take him out in daytime and show
    him
the fire & energy of one at least immediate star, white
    star,
hammer that down in his skull till he can hear only that
rhythm & goes and enters the dance or makes his own,

we will walk forever down the hallways into mirrors and
stagger and look to our left hand for support & the sun
will have set inside us. . . .[16]

But Bruno died at the hand of mediaeval senators; and three hundred and fifty years later, Wilhelm Reich was to die in federal prison in Connecticut for the medicines he derived from stellar "orgone" through machines that curiously resembled Bruno's blueprints for tapping cosmic energy and by a process still unacknowledged by science. Reich saw the galaxies as meeting-points of two sexually charged streams of particles discharging new star material, and he considered the use of such energy, as it rained down through our planet's atmosphere, our birthright. It was, he said, the only cure for cancer, fascism, mass neurosis, and desertification of the Earth.

The terms of the heresy may have changed, but astral paganism still challenges a clerical establishment. Bruno refused to recant before the Church, Reich refused to appear before the Food and Drug Administration. If it is not the stars men die for, it is certainly the radical effect of stellar visions on society. Bruno's last words echo across the centuries:

"I await your sentence with less fear than you pass it. The time will come when all will see what I see." [17]

And we might wonder if that time is still in the future.

5

The History of Western Astronomy II: The Planets

I F THERE IS one astronomer whose work marks the watershed between the ancient occult system and the modern scientific one, it is Johannes Kepler. Kepler was that rare combination of cynic and mystic. He was an astrologer. In fact, he attributed his own perspicacity in solving the problem of Mars's orbit to the arrangement of the planets at his birth. More clearly than any historical figure since Pythagoras, he heard and transcribed the music of the spheres. He wrote some of the most beautiful and enduring testimony to the mediaeval cosmos. Yet, he alone of his contemporaries was pragmatic and resourceful enough to break with the perfect circular orbits and the inherent divine motion and discover the actual laws of the movement of the planets.

It is difficult to know whether to credit Kepler with discovering the harmony of the spheres as occult music or as the mathematical properties of their orbits, because to him they were the same phenomenon:

> The sun in the middle of the moving stars, himself at rest and yet the source of motion, carries the image of God the Father and Creator. . . . He distributes his motive force through a medium which contains the moving bodies even as the Father creates through the Holy Ghost.[1]

And elsewhere:

Why waste words? Geometry existed before the Creation, is co-eternal with the mind of God, *is God himself* . . . ; geometry provided God with a model for the Creation and was implanted into man, together with God's own likeness—and not merely conveyed to his mind through the eyes.[2]

In his epic work on the history of Western astronomy, *The Sleepwalkers,* Arthur Koestler places Kepler at the heart of the book, in the center of the series of chapters entitled "The Watershed." Koestler's portrayal of Kepler is profound and thorough, a far more accurate and insightful case of applying psychology to an historical figure than the more heralded work of Erik Erikson on Martin Luther. Koestler understands that Kepler was unlike anyone else of his time. His insights were far more radical and sustained than those of Copernicus. The laws he discovered had barely been prefigured, if at all.

What Koestler captures is the combination of the mystic and the scientist: a man who believed in astrology enough to write criticisms of the corrupt astrology of his time; a devotee of astral magic who had nothing but contempt for superstition and who gave up years of his life to defend his mother against a charge of witchcraft, preparing the defense with the same care he had exercised on the positions of Mars; a scientist who abandoned previous theories because of minute flaws, in an era when most people were competing to save the appearances only; a cranky husband and father and friend who blamed much of his troubles on astrological influences, yet wrote brilliant psychological self-analyses in the characterological language of the zodiac; a compulsively careful mathematician and theoretician before any other astronomer understood the usefulness of painstaking exactness.

Kepler's mind remained clear throughout innumerable exiles and banishments occasioned by prejudice, superstition, and war. He lacked access to the best data of his time, but, unlike Copernicus, he could not accept a partial system. He could not finally perpetrate a cosmos sustained by a circumstantial combination of actual mechanism and traditional belief. Vital forces lay at the source of the heavens, but their translation into physical motion was absolutely physical and thus describable without recourse to authority or orthodox cosmology. If the symmetry of the skies could not be maintained by circles and natural uniform motion, then the Creator must have set some deeper and more perfect riddle within.

The moral basis for Creation was a central issue through all of Kepler's work. When he discovered, later, that the distant stars were immobile in relation to the Earth and that this might be a result of their great distance, he argued that this disturbing infinity could not affect the moral consequences of man's life. Otherwise the crocodile and the elephant, for being larger than man, would be more in affinity with the Creator. This is reminiscent of Herman Melville's later insight that whale and insect are each obedient to a single volition, i.e., a single nerve impulse.[3]

Kepler accepted Copernicus's model with the Sun in the center, and from there he tried to work out the mathematical secret contained in the orbits of the other planets. Initially he meant to establish a ratio between the sizes of the principal epicycles of each planet. This led nowhere. He placed an unseen planet between Mars and Jupiter, then a second one between Mars and Venus, thus violating the numerological laws based on the seven bodies of the night sky (six planets and a moon). He tried trigonometric ratios between orbits; he applied different astrological principles, then various forms of geometry. But he was plying an impossible riddle. The orbits were not circles, and the placement of the planets was not the key to a Pythagorean harmony.

At this stage, Kepler did not distinguish between the attempt to arrive at a mathematical solution to the problem as a description of physical reality and the attempt to arrive at a numerological solution to the celestial music. The two skies were the same sky to Kepler. The wonder is that he was able to observe the "hermetic" sky closely enough to discover mathematical principles that had no basis in traditional occultism.

He constructed his first hermetic Solar System in *Mysterium Cosmographicum* (1597). The full title states the basis of the work: *A Forerunner to Cosmographical Treatises, containing the Cosmic*

Mystery of the admirable proportions between the Heavenly Orbits and the true and Proper Reasons for their Numbers, Magnitudes and Periodic Motions. Kepler's solution was to place the orbits of the planets within the five perfect solids, which separated them from each other:

> The earth is the sphere, the measure of all; round it describe a dodecahedron; the sphere including this will be Mars. Round Mars describe a tetrahedron; the sphere including this will be Jupiter. Describe a cube round Jupiter; the sphere including this will be Saturn. Now inscribe in the earth an icosahedron, the sphere inscribed in it will be Venus; inscribe an octahedron in Venus; the circle inscribed in it will be Mercury.[4]

Kepler recalls the moment of discovery as rapturous. So convinced was he that the same God who created only five symmetrical solids could not help but place them between the six planetary orbits, he expected a perfect fit. When he got only an approximate fit, he assumed that the data was inaccurate and he corrected it (i.e., changed it) to fit his hypothesis. Having evaded other magical universes, he created one of his own.

Years later he was to make a small but significant shift in his concept of the movement of the planets as conceived in *Mysterium Cosmographicum*. From assuming that the planets were driven by souls, he switched to the image of a force emanating from the Sun. The difference between a soul and a force was a small one, but he had made a subtle adjustment and was now approaching the actual terms of the arcanum. Copernicus had set the corporeal center in the Sun itself. If the Sun was in the center, perhaps a force radiating from the Sun held the planets in their orbits and gave those orbits their shapes and frequencies.

Kepler understood almost at once that his geometrical universe was another myth. There was still a real solution, a purely physical solution that would not violate sacred law because sacred law was inviolable. Whatever shape God had made the universe, it was there in the heavens to be perceived and known. So Kepler rejected his own theory.

Mysterium Cosmographicum was written when Kepler was twenty-four years old. His major scientific work, *Astronomia Nova (A New Astronomy Based on Causation or A Physics of the*

Sky derived from Investigations of the Motions of the Star Mars Founded on Observations of the Noble Tycho Brahe) was written when he was in his forties. The title tells the story. Kepler had finally gained access to the astronomical observatory and star tables of Tycho Brahe.

A wealthy court astronomer, Tycho had been adopted by his childless uncle who bestowed a rich estate. Tycho's interest was observational astronomy, and he had the best equipment in the world assembled on his grounds, which he renamed Uraniburg. According to Arthur Koestler, Tycho mapped the accurate positions of 777 stars, though he added 223 approximate places and guesses to make a table of an even 1,000. Despite that numerological tendency, he declared that the 1572 nova in the vicinity of Cassiopeia was a fixed star and not a tailless comet or a symbol of God's wrath.

Tycho shared precision and fastidiousness with Kepler but little else. He worked mostly for ego and fame, to make astronomy a noble calling and to glamorize his otherwise idle existence. Kepler was *compelled* to solve celestial mysteries, and he lived at their cutting edge all his life. Tycho was superstitious and lacked any insight into either physics or hermeticism; Kepler was both mystical and empirically brilliant.

Kepler was also a man in a trance. He felt that he alone could solve the stellar puzzle. The solution would not come just from abstract mathematics and geometry; the failure of *Mysterium Cosmographicum* proved that. Kepler knew that accurate figures and good instruments would change the traditional data and, with it, the basis of the mystery. Tycho wanted his work to contribute to a great heavenly synthesis, but he lacked the imagination, so he "hired" Kepler to complete his own system. He was the nobleman, Kepler the commoner. Hence, it was to be Tycho's theory. Deep down he might have understood that Kepler had the better mind, but he lived in a courtly world, centuries from such an admission.

Kepler sought only the freedom to work on his problem and to have unhindered access to the records. Their collaboration was interrupted on numerous occasions by temper outbursts and Kepler's bolting; but, in the end, Tycho gave in, and what he did not give to Kepler, Kepler either stole from him or whisked away after his death before the survivors could get their hands on it. For years afterward, the noble family of Tycho Brahe tried to hinder Kepler's publications or to attach their name rather than his to them because the observations themselves, the entries of the night sky, were considered family jewels. It was upon these jewels that Kepler based his new astronomy.

Very early in the relationship of these two astronomers, Kepler wrote:

> Tycho possesses the best observations, and thus so-to-speak the material for the building of the new edifice; he also has collaborators and everything he could wish for. He only lacks the architect who would put all this to use according to his own design. For although he has a happy disposition and real architectural skill, he is nevertheless obstructed in his progress by the multitude of the phenomena and by the fact that the truth is deeply hidden in them. Now old age is creeping upon him, enfeebling his spirit and his forces.[5]

This is the story of mankind—the multitude of the phenomena, the lack of a cohesive theory, and a brief period alive among these phenomena to solve them. It was as true of Einstein as of Tycho or Kepler.

Just as the Moon was to be the key planet for Newton because of its location in the Earth's gravitational field, and just as Mercury was to be the key planet for Einstein because of its passage close to the disk of the Sun, so Mars was Kepler's planet because of the eccentricity of its orbit, the most elliptical of the six inner planets (Venus and Neptune, by contrast, travel around the Sun in almost perfect circles).

Kepler waged a personal "war" against Mars—Mars who had made a career out of mocking astronomers, who brazenly kept his secret, who defied mathematical resolution even when the other planets obeyed. So long as Mars was a planet and not a chimera, Kepler had to deal with it. He suspected that it held the key. For all its inscrutability, Mars must follow the law; and when its riddle was solved, then the other planets could be understood on Mars's terms.

Mars's positions told Kepler that it moved in toward the Sun and then back away from it. But if the orbit was circular, its center could not be the Sun. The Sun's influence could only be uniform, so if Mars traveled about it in something other than a circle, then another force, originating in the planet, pulled it off course. A circle still lay at the bottom of things, but a circle distorted by some other shape.

Most accounts tell us that Kepler brilliantly deduced that the orbits of the planets were ellipses. Koestler actually follows the logic of the *New Astronomy* and shows how Kepler arrived at his ellipse painstakingly and only after many years. First, he tried different circular orbits. He came quite close to a "solution" in the old approximate terms. But now he had Tycho's appearances to save also, and no matter what orbit he came up with, it was contradicted by some corroborated position of the planet.

Of course, Mars's positions are determined by its own movement and the Earth's movement. Kepler needed both, so he took to computing the Earth's position as if he were an astronomer on Mars, and he found that the Earth did not revolve evenly around the Sun either. It seemed to move at velocities inversely proportional to its distance from the Sun, as if controlled by a solar force. In the course of working with this problem, Kepler articulated his second law, which gave him a basis for determining the position of a planet at a given time in its orbit: a line connecting the planet to the Sun will sweep out equal areas in equal times, no matter what the distance. When it is closer to the Sun, it will move faster at a rate that will increase the width of the area swept out to exactly the degree that its length is diminished.

Now Kepler could handle the deviation from uniform speed, but he still did not know the shape. For more than a year, he worked with ovals—or "eggs," as he called them. He made continuous errors of simple mathematics and transcription which magically canceled out, leaving him where he would have been anyway. Some deep unconscious guide watched over his quest. A chance perception of an odd number in two different contexts gave him a formula for the shape prescribed by the planet's variance in its orbit in accordance with its distance from the Sun. The semidiameter of the Martian orbit, where it varied most from a circle, was 1.00429 of the radius of the circle. At the same time, Kepler was exploring the angle formed by Mars simultaneously with the Sun and with the center of the Martian orbit as seen from Mars. If the distance from Mars to the center of its orbit was divided by the distance from Mars to the Sun, it gave a figure that was also the secant of this angle. In Kepler's own words: "I stumbled entirely by chance on the secant of the angle 5° 18', which is the measure of the greatest optical equation. When I realized that this secant equals 1.00429, I felt as if I had been awakened from a sleep."[6] (Hence the title of Koestler's book.)

Kepler had hit upon the formula for the ellipse without knowing it. He saw only that he had a curve with a bulge. After a geometric error led him through an excruciating battle with this shape, he tried an ellipse as a hypothetical stand-in, only to realize that the ellipse and his formula for the law of the planets' positions were one and the same. This is Kepler's First Law of planetary motion: the planets move in ellipses around the Sun. The Third Law, stated in *Harmonice Mundi* (a work in which he also tried to develop a notation for the heavenly music), is that "the squares of the periods of revolution are proportional to the cubes of the mean distances from the Sun."[7]

Kepler did not understand gravity, inertia, or centrifugal force, but his laws contained everything needed to derive them. To him they were mystical and numerological relationships, so he went no further in uncloaking the sky. He had meant to show that the clockwork of the cosmos is inhabited by a soul which manifests itself in motions carried out synchronously between objects across distances without mechanical connections. This he demonstrated. It was Newton who made the connections, and even for him they were of a spiritual nature. Yet, we today, who consider them physical, have no clearer sense of their actual nature.

Galileo lived during almost the same years as Kepler, but he was an astronomer in a different spirit, and he had almost no contact with him. Galileo was more like Tycho, vain and arrogant, concerned with reputation. Tycho may have wondered if astronomy was an important enough calling for a nobleman;

Galileo had no such pretensions: he was an intellectual snob. The role of master astronomer and pioneer of the heavens was a lofty enough podium. He prided himself on knowing things in the cosmos before anyone else did, and he enjoyed pulling rabbits out of the night sky.

Galileo's contributions to a modern view of the sky are on two levels, the first of which was pure exploration through the best telescopes of his time. Through his eye, he walked on the Moon. He passed over deep craters, he saw mountain peaks covered in bright sunlight while their lower slopes were in shadow, and from the shadows he calculated their heights. He discovered the initial four moons of Jupiter and the appendages of Saturn; and turning his spyglass into the depths of outer space, he saw something that was truly awesome, which Tycho and Kepler had simply intuited: everywhere "other stars, in myriads, which have never been seen before, and which surpass the old, previously known stars in number more than ten times."[8] Each of the constellations is thus a far denser and more complicated object than had previously been considered. The Belt and Sword of Orion alone had eight additional stars. The Praesepe cloud in Cancer, known as the Beehive Cluster, resolved into component stars. This was the beginning of a barren infinity. But at first glance it was magnificent and beautiful.

Galileo's book *Messenger from the Stars* introduced the notion of the infinite sky to the world at large in 1610. Since Galileo, the sky has been a dynamic opening into eternity rather than a flat projection of the code from the higher spheres. Now we more or less assume that the stars we see are the ones closest to us, the ones that happen to be in this part of the universe. Quasars, for us, appear to mark the end of the universe, but we do not have the divine sphere to place outside it that people still had in Galileo's time. If we should discover that quasars are part of our tiny corner of the universe and the creation goes on exponentially into other realms of matter, we might experience again a fraction of the shock that people received from Galileo's sky messenger. "The infinite is unthinkable," said Kepler.[9]

"The eternal silence of the infinite spaces terrifies me," wrote Blaise Pascal.[10]

We do not even bother to acknowledge it very much anymore.

We have reached the point where it is worse than infinite spaces: it is the infinite without meaning. Milton would write of "a dark / Illimitable ocean, without bound, / Without dimension."[11]

It was as though we hung, in a moment of history awakening from one dream, between dreams. Galileo snapped the trance; he spoke what we already must have known. Look, he said, the heavens are not a vast clairvoyance or a diamond of our destiny; they are a fiery corruptible thing like the Earth. Even the brilliant Sun is pocked with decay when seen through the glass.

> What greater folly can be imagined [he wrote] than to call gems, silver and gold noble, and earth and dirt base? For do not these persons consider that, if there were as great a scarcity of earth as there is of jewels and precious metals, there would be no king who would not gladly give a heap of diamonds and rubies and many ingots of gold to purchase only so much earth as would suffice to plant a jessamine in a little pot or to set a tangerine in it, that he might see it sprout, grow up, and bring forth such goodly leaves, fragrant flowers, and delicate fruit?[12]

It is this very jewel that we were to search for later among the planets as soon as we fully understood they were worlds like ours—not angels, not sigils. But those first astronomers experienced the last waves, at least in the West, of the sweet astral heavens with their celestial music, and they plotted the night sky with harmony in their brains: the bounty of astral white marking the past; modern scientific instruments pointing toward an equally unknown future.

Galileo's other contribution to a modern view of the sky was astrophysical in a totally different way. He showed that bodies fell to the earth at the same speed, not in proportion to their weight. It took Newton to generalize this finding into universal gravitation, and Einstein to generalize that to relativity and include time in the formula for space. Galileo's law was meant for terrestrial application only.

Galileo seemed to require a circus atmosphere for his discoveries, and he laid claim with flourishes: the Goddess of Love imitates the shapes of the Moon; the highest planet has a triple body; the face of the Sun is marred and corrupt. So the world learned that

Venus went through phases, Saturn had a multiple form, and the Sun had spots. These discoveries upset the mediaeval sky, for the planets and Sun and Moon moving through the constellations were the key to celestial harmony. Now there were things beyond our prior knowing which enlarged the universe through a welter of random, inexplicable shapes. Perhaps the fact that it was his *tour de force* made the new vastness and variety of the sky less fearful for Galileo.

Kepler had merely applied mathematics to the visible. Galileo reported secrets hidden by God Himself. When he insisted that these wonders be made into dogma, the Church authorities balked. What right had this unspiritual mechanic to demand the absolute truth of things which were still hypothetical and whose meaning could not be absorbed so quickly!

Galileo's difficulty with the Church came not from the things he discovered or the new boundaries of the universe he proposed. These were accepted by religious people, enthusiastically by some, begrudgingly by others. It was Galileo's arrogance that trapped him. He came to see his own discoveries as more important than the whole Catholic Church with its millennial tradition, and he proclaimed that the Church could no longer have a say in matters of the sky. This gratuitously angered the elders in Rome.

Like a practical joker, Galileo enjoyed shoving the telescope into the hands of disbelievers and Church officials, making them look at Jupiter's four captive planets and the crescent of Venus. "There," he would deride. "Challenge that if you can!"

It was not the heavens that disturbed people; it was Galileo's attitude. He was the prophet of doom for a whole world-view, but he did not handle his position with humility or sobriety. He did not even seem to know what it meant. He careened through town slapping people on the back, saying, "See, I told you!"— offending and frightening even Kepler. The skies were serious business. One could not announce that Pan was dead and then cheer or laugh. These were terrible visions. How terrible, time would tell. The authorities, in their aged wisdom, somehow knew.

The Church theologians cornered Galileo finally on the matter of the Earth's movement. They did not dispute that the

Copernican model was an excellent calculating device and an hypothesis that might yet be proven true. They denied that it was proven beyond doubt. Galileo had to accept this and back down.

But it was the last time. The priests would not again have a chance to hold the secular scientist before his works and say, in essence, "Look at the consequences, look at what you have done to the world."

6

The History of Western Astronomy III: The Gravitational Field

THE SEVENTEENTH CENTURY stood on the verge of a new universe much in the way we might again today. The pieces were in place, but no unified theory connected them. Copernicus's universe was not Kepler's universe, and neither of them were Galileo's Solar System or realm of falling bodies. Something was required to sew these into a single fabric, to reveal the shape that was emerging through collective humanity. In the early part of the century, Francis Bacon and René Descartes had set what seemed to be the poles of scientific inquiry. Bacon advocated exploration of actual physical systems and their components without recourse to metaphysics or abstractions and with an aim toward the ultimate technological improvement of society. Descartes had created an abstract and mathematical system: his universe was a thin fluid composed of minute dust particles which rotated in vortices and whirlpools around the Sun and distant stars.

Newton did not need to decide between Bacon and Descartes, even as he did not need to decide between Kepler and Galileo. He subsumed them, and in so doing, he subsumed their

contentions, which were real and are still real. The universe did
not need to be *either* an abstract mathematical invention or a
collection of limitless discrete causes and effects. These described the same reality. Newton combined the astronomical
laws of planetary motion formulated by Kepler with the laws of
falling bodies and projectiles developed by Galileo. He supplied
the mechanism behind Kepler's elliptical orbits, which was also
the basis of heliocentricity.

Newton accomplished what Kepler and Galileo could not do,
despite their contemporaneity: he brought them together by
showing that there is no distinction between outer space and the
Earth and that all bodies obey a universal Law of Gravitation.
So Earth and Sky were re-wed not in the hermetic axiom but by
the realization that they are not separate domains.

It is hard, at times, to distinguish the laws of Newton and the
twentieth-century Newtonian universe from the work of Isaac
Newton the man. The laws mean a different thing against a
backdrop of mechanical theories of life than they did in the
spiritual universe still bright on seventeenth-century nights. In
their own time, Newton's laws were the solution of a divine
geometry. In the centuries following, they became the foundation
for a materialist reality.

The fact that any high school student knows Newton's laws
now hardly diminishes their original grandeur. It was not facts
and formulas that created this turning point in the history of
science; it was Newton's sudden realization of the meaning
behind the night sky—the physical agency of its composition and
motion. To see this for the first time—at the edge of history, a new
thing—was incredible. Now his laws are mass-produced; they are
the mechanical bottom line on which industrial civilization runs.

The link between Kepler and Galileo was the Moon, which
could be considered at once as a planet in orbit about the Earth
and as a projectile which was fired from the Earth but which,
for some unknown reason, did not return to it. This unknown
reason was the Moon's tangential velocity, which created enough
centrifugal force (as we have come to call it) to counteract the
pull of the Earth. Conversely, what counteracts the Moon being
pulled into the Earth (or the planets being pulled into the Sun)
must be a force strong enough to hold satellites in place. The

attraction necessary is staggering. A body the size of the Earth must be halted, as it tears at breakneck speed toward the outermost point of its ellipse, gradually slowed, turned inward, and drawn back until velocity and centrifugal force again carry it to apogee. Kepler had certainly proved that such a thing happens, and by a law which causes it to sweep up equal areas of space in equal times. But how? He thought that it could only be an invisible astral force emanating from the Sun.[1] He did not understand that this was the same force affecting all bodies in any space. It could be applied to balls thrown in the air, or rolled down a hill: these were "planets" too.

The law of universal gravitation proposed by Newton states that every particle—every particle of matter anywhere in the universe—attracts every other particle with a force varying inversely as the square of their distances and directly as the product of their masses. This held for stars and planets, and it held also for insects whirring their gossamer wings in the fields, and for pebbles washed up on the beach. Furthermore, it held all of these together in the same universal field. This was, in fact, the universe.

Newton laid the mathematical basis for gravity and the laws of motion and interaction, but he had no idea what gravity was. An invisible force transmitted millions of miles from its source with incredible power was so mystical a notion that it had only been idly considered or considered and rejected by scientists and mathematicians before him. The difference was that, for Newton, gravity was not an abstract concept in the tradition of Kepler or Descartes; he defined it only by its effect. "Whether natural or supernatural," he said (for it made no difference), it is that which has "placed the sun in the center of the six primary planets, placed Saturn in the center of his five secondary planets and Jupiter in the center of his four secondary planets, and the earth in the center of the moon's orb."[2]

The power of gravity was awesome. "It must proceed from a cause that penetrates to the very centers of the sun and planets, without suffering the least diminution of its force; that operates not according to the quantity of the surfaces of the particles upon which it acts (as mechanical causes used to do), but according to the quantity of the solid matter which they contain,

and propagates its virtue on all sides to immense distances, decreasing always as the inverse square of the distances." The Sun's
gravitation is made out of the particles of which "the body of
the sun is composed," and although it weakens as distance from
the Sun increases, it continues "as far as the orbit of Saturn, as
appears from the quiescence of the aphelion of the planets; nay,
and even to the remotest aphelion of the comets."[3]

The conviction that some great metaphysical truth lay behind
gravitation did not cease for Newton's lifetime or in the decades
that followed, and has ceased now only insofar as gravitation has
been joined to relativity in a larger mystery. Newton believed
that he had discovered how God was in contact with all parts of
His Creation at once. Through this force, everything responded
to the same will. In fact, God's will was a necessary component
of gravity, to keep the entire universe from being pulled together and crushed.

Each point of matter, Newton realized, seeks unity at the
center of a great sphere, which is the center of matter itself.
This replaces Ptolemaic geocentricity as a statement of divine
astronomy: "every particle of space is *always,* and every indivisible moment of duration is *everywhere,*" hence God is always
and everywhere. "He is omnipresent not *virtually* only but also
substantially; for virtue cannot subsist without substance."[4]

Newton at once turned the universe into both a mammoth
field of influence which satisfied all idealist conceptions, spiritual
or philosophical, and a simple machine which no performance
of material effects exceeded or contradicted. He moved away
from abstraction, either physical or spiritual. Words such as *time,
space, place,* and *motion* were to be understood only in mathematical terms as actual measured relationships and quantities.
These were constants, with their own nature, not requiring additional explanation. Absolute space occurred in a Euclidean
geometry, and absolute time flowed equably from the past
through the present to the future. Bodies occupied actual place,
and absolute motion translated them from one place to another.

What follows are laws of motion: Every body, terrestrial or
celestial, continues in a state of rest, or of uniform motion in a
straight line, unless it is compelled to change that state by forces
coming to bear upon it; if that happens, the change will be pre-

cisely proportional to the force and in the line of direction in which that force is itself operating; thus, two bodies always act mutually upon each other in such a way that every action has an equal and opposite reaction. Since Newton was talking about the masses of bodies, it was important to distinguish between weight and mass. Mass was a quantity of matter deriving from density and bulk taken together. Motion, as a numerical entity, required mass (an amount of matter) and velocity, multiplied by each other. Mass multiplied by accelerative force originated motion in a specific course and at a specific speed. Newton foresaw what was almost impossible to believe: that without the mass of the Earth, people would float away.

Another effect of Newton's laws was to dispel any lingering notion that geometry was somehow different from mathematics, with a special archetypal claim on nature. Kepler believed in the perfect solids; Newton did not. This is the fundamental difference between them, minor in its subtlety at the time and major in its implications for future times. Take away the special case of geometry, and mathematics replaces spiritual essence as the key to the universe. One need no longer look for spirit, only for number. In his preface to *Mathematical Principles of Natural Philosophy* (1687), Newton wrote:

> Therefore geometry is founded in mechanical practice, and is nothing but that part of universal mechanics which accurately proposes and demonstrates the art of measuring. . . . Rational mechanics will be the science of motions resulting from any forces whatsoever, and of the forces required to produce any motions, accurately proposed and demonstrated.[5]

If Newton could not have expressed gravity in mathematical terms and applied it to the actual mechanics of astronomical and terrestrial objects, it would have been dismissed as another mystical stopgap. Perhaps his interpretation of his own proposal was metaphysical, but those who followed him cast out the theological parts even as he had dismissed the geometric mysticism of Kepler and Kepler had discarded the circles of Copernicus. Newton's gravity became the foundation of a new system, and his sources were forgotten, his intention overlooked. The astronomers and physicists who followed him built a tidal and mechanical universe from the laws he gave them.

It took time, but Western science slowly began to see the web into which the secularization of Newton's theories had woven them, and the suspicion began to dawn that they would not get out of it for a long time; they might never get out of it. Before Newton, the night sky was a divine parchment, a demonic sigil, a display of cosmic philosophy. After Newton, it became a laboratory in elementary physics, a demonstration of simple large-scale interactions of gravitational fields, and a remnant of a primitive original system of matter. The night sky shows the universe as it is eternally under multiple influences, and, in a certain sense, as it *was* before the formation of galaxies and stars. The black heavens embracing the whirling compacted blobs of matter bare the fundamental symmetries of nature. In a hot universe, we have only the particles and their original structure. In a cold universe, as here on this planet, a jungle of camouflage grows up around this original atomic and pre-atomic scenery. Not only does it grow up around it; it incorporates it in itself and hides it in a diversity which is home to us but entirely foreign to the original atoms. This is where we enter, and it is the only way we could enter—latecomers to the mystery. At least this is how science chooses to explain us, its one inexplicable embarrassment. Beginning with Newton, we work our way out of the jungle into a clear sight of nature. It is inhospitable, but its saving grace is a gargantuan lucidity. We face the curious problem that, as we work toward protean nature, we work against our own nature.

The night sky not only demonstrates mathematical laws to the latter-day astronomers; it *is* those mathematical laws, written simply in things that are larger than we are and much bolder and less duplicit. Stephen Weinberg sums this up very succinctly in *The First Three Minutes* when he says: "That which we do now by mathematics was done in the very early universe by heat—physical phenomena directly exhibited the essential simplicity of nature. But no one was there to see it."[6]

We might also consider Bertrand Russell's warning: "Physics is mathematical not because we know so much about the physical world, but because we know so little: it is only its mathematical properties that we can discover."[7]

Newton left behind a thornier riddle than we have generally recognized, and one that expresses our own crisis of meaning and identity as accurately as the one which Newton addressed did for his own time. We have looked at Newton's night sky for three hundred years, following the rationality of a universal mechanics and measuring each new thing as we have uncovered it. And we have continued to find a machine which generates an abstraction which generates a machinery. Centuries after Newton reconciled Bacon and Descartes, the problem of mind and matter is a contention again. It was a Christian riddle; now it is a zen riddle.

It is incredible to realize that the only thing that stands between our mathematics and the night sky is ourselves. Otherwise, numbers and creation would embrace each other and the universe would be sealed. We are the only disturbance.

Newton did not foresee this. "Why there is one body in our system qualified to give light and heat to all the rest, I know no reason," he wrote to Richard Bentley, a theologian who sought to square gravitation with Christianity, "but because the author of the system thought it convenient."[8] This was not Church politics; Newton believed it. He made no attempt to construct a purely "Newtonian" universe. He wrote Bentley on another occasion:

> It is inconceivable that inanimate brute matter should, without the meditation of something else, which is not material, operate upon, and affect other matter without mutual contact. . . . That gravity should be innate, inherent and essential to matter, so that one body may act upon another at a distance through a *vacuum,* without the mediation of anything else, by and through which their action and force may be conveyed from one to another, is to me so great an absurdity, that I believe no man . . . can ever fall into it.[9]

For the next three hundred years, science has defined gravity exactly as innate, inherent, and essential, or, to the degree that it has not done that, it has redefined gravity as curvature of space and time according to Einstein's theory of relativity and has passed the onus of agency ("material or immaterial," wrote Newton in the same letter[10]) on to an equally innate, inherent, and essential characteristic of things. The face of night was shattered, and when it settled again—the enigmatic smile of glittering motes and dusky luminescent trails—it showed a new aspect of its sphinx.

Newton did not do this to us, or did he? The current cosmos is not his, even by extension, but his seeing was so clear, for all of us, that it made it inevitable. A century after this spiritual man's life, William Blake's Newton is already an enemy—an enslaver of mankind, a smotherer of light and vision. By then the telescope had replaced the imagination as the instrument for delving into nature, and the simple coefficient it put against the night sky came to define our primary relationship to the stars. No longer did we even *see* the sky; instead, Newtonians told us, we have optic nerve registrations.

In *Jerusalem,* Blake sets "Bacon & Newton, sheath'd in dismal steel," terrors binding mankind. The "Loom of Locke" is "Wash'd by the Water-wheels of Newton: black the cloth / In heavy wreathes fold over every Nation: cruel Works / Of many Wheels I view, wheel without wheel, with cogs tyrannic / Moving by compulsion each other, not as those in Eden, which, / Wheel within Wheel, in freedom revolve in harmony & peace."[11]

But Blake, as those who follow him, can no longer attack science from a purely theosophical position. Science has become part of knowledge itself, part of religion. All men and women are its advocates, even those who deny it. The Rosicrucian enlightenment of the seventeenth century even tried to invent a mathematical nonscholastic magic (as per Bruno). Their paradise was wiped out in Bohemia by the Thirty Years' War, and the Eden they dreamed of never came, even with the later machinery of the pagans. Conversely, the present malaise of industrialism is in part Western man's loss of his own sources and his concommitant failure to credit astral intelligence with its role in civilization.

There are no more saints on either side. Blake's "strong wing'd Eagles" in "The Four Zoas" are clearly, despite Blake's attack on Newton, post-Newtonian, and, in so being, they radiate Kepler and Descartes:

> . . . thro' darkness deep
> They bear the woven draperies; on golden hooks they
> hang abroad

The universal curtains & spread out from Sun to Sun
The vehicles of light; they separate the furious particles
Into mild currents as the water mingles with the wine.[12]

In Shelley's poetry, the Earth is a planet as much as a zone of creation; light may be divine, but it is also defined by Newton's experiments with a prism. Shelley writes of the "intense atom" of life, which "glows/ A moment, then is quenched...." He tells us:

The sun comes forth, and many reptiles spawn;
He sets, and each ephemeral insect then
Is gathered into death without a dawn,
And the immortal stars awake again.
....
Life, like a dome of many-coloured glass,
Stains the white radiance of Eternity....[13]

This is the real heritage of Newton, not the mechanical universe. It is a great irony that the Einsteinian universe is held as the model of cosmic creativity and surprise against the universe of Newton. It was Einstein who doubted God most deeply and whom God failed, first in seeming to play dice with particles, and later at Hiroshima. It was Newton who believed in the spirit and who was the truer mystic.

Newton's laws were developed specifically in the context of the Solar System and the Earth and were directly applied to the motions of planets and moons about each other and the Sun and to the interactive aspects of terrestrial substances. When Halley's comet arrived as predicted in the mid-eighteenth century, showing a periodicity of 76 years, it was considered a confirmation of Newtonian physics, and, in particular, of the role of the Sun in determining the positions of all the orbs in its immediate field. Halley's comet showed how big this field might be.

Newton's method of formulation, a theory of fluxions whereby changes of quantities were taken as infinitely small variations, was rough and required constant refinement when applied to actual phenomena, as the path of the Moon or the mutually influenced orbits of Jupiter and Saturn, which, like those of all planets, were incredibly complex and displaced from a pure solar-directed ellipse.

In his 1848 essay "Eureka," Edgar Allan Poe summarized Newton's relationship to celestial mechanics:

> He was forced to content himself with showing how thoroughly the motions of an imaginary Universe, composed of attracting and attracted atoms obedient to the law he announced, coincide with those of the actually existing Universe so far as it comes under our observation. [14]

Pierre Simon Laplace, the mid-eighteenth-century French astronomer, was the first post-Newtonian to complete a system of the heavens as a great machine. He pointed out that the difficulties confronted in squaring heavenly events with Newtonian theory actually ended up proving it, because the necessary refinements could only come from Newton too.

Laplace published his immutable cosmic machine in 1799 in five volumes entitled *Mécanique Céleste*. He even imagined the genesis of its motion: the Sun once must have had a gaseous outer atmosphere of greater circumference than the whole Solar System. As this burning sheath rotated, it contracted, increasing in speed and casting off material. These were the planets: soot from the Sun. Further rotation knotted them into sold matter; and as the knots condensed, bits of them were tossed off and formed the moons. of the planets. The resulting Solar System was a clock— eternal, unvarying. [15]

Laplace (and later, Immanuel Kant) reasoned backward, as Newton had not. Since all the planetary orbits occupy roughly the same plane, then this must once have been a flat, rotating disc of material, with the tidal force of gravitation molding the planets in their orbits out of coalescing matter. In "Eureka," Poe extended Laplace's theory outward to Neptune, the most recent planet discovered at that time, and suggested that the outer portions of the disc were originally broken into fragments, and that this explained the oddities of the new planet, its moon, and its phantom ring.

The self-regulating machine was so shocking that Napoleon Bonaparte said: "Monsieur Laplace, they tell me you have written this large book on the system of the Universe and have never even mentioned its Creator."

"Sire," Laplace replied, "I had no need for any such hypothesis." [16]

7

The History of Western Astronomy IV: The Stars

WHILE NEWTON was developing a new "astrophysics," other astronomers were exploring the Solar System and the Milky Way. As lenses improved, Europe plunged through the dome of fixed stars into a sea of suns whose limits were not apparent. Persian and Greek deities crumbled and fell. The map of the West had been obliterated.

John Flamsteed, an English contemporary of Newton, marked the positions of three thousand stars. Another Englishman, Edmund Halley, catalogued hundreds of southern stars from an observatory in St. Helena. He checked discrepancies in their positions from the days of Ptolemy, and this revealed that the sky was not fixed and stable; the stars had moved.

Halley is best known for his discovery that comets have elliptical orbits like planets; and the return of the 1682 comet in 1758, thirteen years after his death as he had predicted, was perhaps the first new application of astromancy since the Babylonians, and was impressive enough to give that comet his name thereafter.

Meanwhile, on the European continent, the Sun King, Louis XIV, had assembled the great scientists of many nations at the French Academy of Science. A Dutch astronomer, Christian Huygens, used Galileo's mathematics of the pendulum to control the rhythm of a gear and make an accurate clock and a jewel-box planetarium of the Solar System. As a pure astronomer, he discovered that Jupiter had a bulge at its equator, Mars had polar caps that changed size, and Saturn's protuberance was actually a ring. He also discovered the first moon of Saturn.

Like Newton, he studied the nature of light, and he came to an opposite but complementary conclusion. Newton had decided that light was made of corpuscles passing through empty space. Huygens, accepting Descartes' ether as the substance of the void, decided that light "does not move; it merely strives toward movement" like a wave.[1] No material changed place, but motion was propagated through the ether as the waves through the sea. Newton's corpuscles better fit the mechanical universe of the time, but Huygens's vibrations and oscillations awaited the rays and radioactivity of a future science.

The Italian astronomer Giovanni Cassini, working outdoors with 150-foot air telescopes and lenses suspended from towers, participated with Huygens in deriving a rotation period for Mars close to that of the Earth. Huygens theorized that bulging Jupiter must be soft material rotating very fast. Cassini confirmed a Jovian day of ten hours. He also found a division between the rings of Saturn, discovered four more Saturnian moons, and mapped the hemispheres of Jupiter.

Cassini, like William Herschel in the following century, attempted to name new bodies after enlightened monarchs rather than mythological beings in order to distinguish the age in which these bodies were discovered from the superstitious aeon in which the planets and constellations were named. Mythological names, however, always replaced historical ones, especially within the Solar System. Simon Marius's method of naming the Galilean satellites of Jupiter after the lovers of the god was followed in the naming of Saturn's moons after beings of the Saturnian age. In this one way, the astral sky triumphed, for in astrological and magical work, names carry the archetypal meanings and influences of the worlds.

Meanwhile, the true distances in the universe were becoming evident to these astronomers, and light was the key to the riddle. Most scientists then thought that light was timeless and instantaneous everywhere. Galileo himself had been uncertain, so he devised an experiment with a lantern-bearing assistant. The results were inconclusive, and Galileo had decided that, in any

case, the speed of light was too great to measure with his appara-
tus. Olaus Roemer, a Danish astronomer working at the French
Academy, arranged a novel experiment. After measuring the
period of revolution of the satellite Io around Jupiter at 42 hours,
27 minutes, and 33 seconds, Roemer persistently timed the reappearance of Io from Jovian eclipse between August and November
1676. If light had a finite speed, the reappearance of the moon
might be retarded as the Earth moved away from Jupiter. A
difference of seconds would have proven the point, but light was
even slower than that: there were a full ten minutes of lag at
Jovian apogee, decreasing as the Earth reapproached Jupiter over
the next six months. Now Roemer had a figure for the distance
that light travels in a second: 186,000 miles. He derived it from
the rate of retardation of Io's reappearance caused primarily by
the Earth's movement in its orbit.[2] It was to become the unit by
which all cosmic distances were measured. Huygens later figured
that it would take a bullet from a cannon twenty-five years to
reach the Sun. Looking at the Sun through a tiny hole in a plate, he
concluded that it was 27,664 times as bright as Sirius by the laws
of dioptrics. If Sirius were the same brightness as the Sun in its
own vicinity, then it would take the same bullet almost 700,000
years to get there.

"What a wonderful and amazing scheme have we here of the
magnificent vastness of the universe!" he wrote in *Cosmotheoros,*
translated into English as *The Celestial Worlds Discovered or
Conjectures Concerning the Inhabitants, Plants and Products of
the Worlds in the Planets.* "So many suns, so many earths, and
every one of them stocked with so many herbs, trees and animals,
and adorned with so many seas and mountains!"

It was around the middle of the eighteenth century that astronomers began to explore the shape and size of the Milky Way. The
discovery of its nature is usually credited to Thomas Wright, who
wondered why this sector was denser than the rest of the sky. Was
it because we were looking along a single plane in which more
stars were visible? Fantastic as it seemed, perhaps we were looking into the core of a system of which we were also part. Furthermore, the system might be lens-shaped, so that we would see
fewer stars out toward the rim, and almost through it like glass
where there are no stars.

> Imagine [he wrote] how infinitely greater the number of
> stars would be in those remote parts, arising thus from their
> continual crowding behind one another, as all other objects
> do towards the horizon point of their perspective, which
> ends but with infinity: thus, all their rays at last so near
> uniting, must meeting in the eye appear, as almost in con-
> tact, and from a perfect zone of light; this I take to be the
> real case, and the true nature of our *Milky Way,* and
> all irregularity we observe in it at the Earth, I judge
> to be entirely owing to our Sun's position in this great
> firmament. . . .[4]

Wright was also a man after the heart of Kepler and Newton:

> We cannot long observe the beauteous parts of the visible
> creation, not only of this world on which we live, but also
> the myriads of bright bodies round us, with any attention,
> without being convinced, that a power supreme, and of a
> nature unknown to us, presides in, and governs it.[5]

Immanuel Kant, a contemporary of Wright, intuited that the
stellar galaxy was the clue to a larger system of cosmic evolution.
Since Nature repeated fundamental shapes, if there was one
Milky Way, there might be more. Perhaps there had been a primal
nebula at the beginning of the universe, a cloud containing molecules in random movement amassing by attraction. Gravity
caused the the stars to fuse, leaving space among them. Kant
proposed this theory in his *Universal Natural History and Theory of the Heavens*, and, in a sense, he "waited" 175 years until
1925 to have it confirmed by Edwin Hubble.

Kant complimented Wright:

> He regarded the fixed stars not as a mere swarm scat-
> tered without order and without design, but found a sys-
> tematic constitution in the whole universe and a universal
> relation of these stars to the ground-plan of the regions of
> space which they occupy.
> . . . The eye which is situated in this plane when it looks
> out to the field of stars, will perceive on the spherical con-
> cavity of the firmament the densest accumulation of stars
> in the direction of . . . a plane under the form of a zone
> illuminated by varied light.[6]

Once this system is established, we see that there must be more Solar Systems, more Milky Ways, all from the same primal nebula. . . . The worlds and systems acknowledge the same kind of origin . . . ; attraction is unlimited and universal . . . ; in the presence of the infinite, the great and small are small alike. . . .[7]

Millions of years may have passed before nature reached this present perfection; millions more may pass before it extends itself into new spheres and evolves new forms. "This infinity in the future succession of time," wrote Kant, "by which eternity is unexhausted, will entirely animate the whole range of space to which God is present. . . ."[8]

Kant's faith in divine law was unshakable, but he did admit, as more have admitted after him, that "there is here no end but an abyss of real immensity, in the presence of which all the capability of human conception sinks exhausted, although it is supported by the aid of the science of number."[9]

And already Pierre Simon Laplace was on hand, creating stability without God.

The most famous astronomer of the late eighteenth and early nineteenth centuries was Frederick William Herschel. He began his adult life as a music teacher in Germany, and ultimately settled in England. After constructing the best telescopes of his time, he set to making a catalogue of celestial objects. Naturally, he noted thousands of stars, but he also discovered the multiple stars—that many sparkles contained two, three, or more discrete sources. He estimated the periods of revolution of double stars and put into the public imagination the idea of worlds with two sunrises, twin shadows, and variations of night and day within day and night. He realized that double stars were not merely twins that lay in the same line of sight. They orbited about each other and were physically part of the same system. So Newton's law of gravitation stretched deep into the sidereal realm. Not only could planets stand in mutual attraction to planets and to suns and moons, but suns could be impressed by other suns. Herschel then discovered the movement of the Sun itself trailing the Solar System behind it toward an area of the sky marked by Lambda of the constellation Hercules. His inability to calculate solar move-

ment accurately was the result of an incorrect hypothesis; he
assumed that a star's apparent brightness was determined only by
its distance.

He discovered the first dark nebula, calling to his sister
Caroline to come and see the hole in the Milk. He named it
"The Coalsack." He also found other nebulous clouds that did
not seem to be made of stars. "What a field of novelty is here
opened to our conceptions!" he wrote. "A shining fluid . . . of
a nature totally unknown to us . . . of a brightness sufficient to
reach us from the remote regions of a star of the 8th, 9th, 10th,
11th, or 12th magnitude, and of an extent so considerable as to
take up 3, 4, 5, or 6 minutes in diameter! Can we compare it to
the coruscations of the electrical fluid in the aurora borealis? Or
to the more magnificent cone of zodiacal light as we see it in
spring or autumn?" [10]

Perhaps, thought Herschel, he was staring into the primitive
yolk out of which stars themselves were born.

He resolved the Milky Way from whitish haze into small stars
which he counted; and from just those that were visible, he
dead-reckoned its shape as a grindstone with a diameter of six
thousand light-years. That the Milky Way, the via lactea as he
called it by the Latin, was a system of stars to which the Sun itself
belonged became clear to Herschel as he went up and down its
branches and swept across and through it, mapping its major and
minor arms. He also became aware that this "stupendous sidereal
system we inhabit"[11] with its millions of stars is itself detached
from other nebulous clouds of stars.

(You can try this experiment yourself. Look down from Cassiopeia toward Pisces, go between the bright star of Aries, Hamal,
and the bright star of Pegasus, Alpheratz. The eye is stopped by a
smudge or blur in the sky—the great Andromeda Galaxy, two
million light-years away.

You are not just looking at another world or a big star. You are
looking at a hole in our own Galaxy of billions of stars at an object
which is the combined light of billions of other stars.

It is our absolutely straight-on view of an island universe. That
we can see so far with comprehension is incredible. If only a
fraction of the stars in that galaxy have planets, and only a
fraction of those have life, we are still looking at the single beacon

of millions of inhabited worlds, hundreds of thousands of species and civilizations, virtually as remote from one another as they are from us, and which see us as a single obscure object out a hole in their galaxy—and not even us, just the hazy oval of which we and all the rest of the Milky Way are part.)

Herschel also studied nearby worlds. He explored the belts of Saturn, the polar caps of Mars, and he found satellites around Saturn. Most notably, though, in 1781 he discovered the Georgium Sidus, which we now know as Uranus. "On Tuesday the 13th of March between 10 and 11 in the evening, when I was examining the small stars in the neighborhood of H Geminorum, I perceived one that appeared visibly larger than the rest; being struck with its uncommon magnitude, I compared it to H Geminorum and the small star in the quartile between Auriga and Gemini, and, finding it so much larger than either of them, suspected it to be a comet."[12]

Later study showed no tail and a circular orbit. So this was a planet. He named it Georgium Sidus because it was "a star which (with respect to us) first began to shine under his [George III's] auspicious reign. . . ."[13]

Sir Joseph Banks, in presenting Herschel with the Copley Medal of the Royal Society later that year, extolled: "Who can say but what your new star, which exceeds Saturn in its distance from the sun, may exceed him as much in magnificence of attendance? Who can say what new rings, new satellites, or what other nameless and numberless phenomena remain behind, waiting to reward future industry?"[14]

In 1787, Herschel discovered two moons around Uranus, which were subsequently named Oberon and Titania after fairy and magical beings from Shakespeare. Of Oberon, Herschel wrote: "I saw this satellite faithfully attend its primary planet, and at the same time keep on, in its own course, by describing a considerable arch of its proper orbit."[15] He made remarkably close estimates of the moons' periods of revolution, and he found that their orbital motion around Uranus was retrograde, counter that of the Earth, the other planets, and the other moons known at the time. This was a tremendous blow to the Laplacian hypothesis which required a uni-rotational ring.

Herschel also participated in the discovery of the asteroids during the eighteenth century, and, in fact, he gave them that name. He was not notably involved in meteor work, but in 1798, the year after the discovery of the retrograde moons, two German students compared their observation of the same meteor from sites far apart and concluded that meteors were not "meteorological" at all, but must originate far out in space, beyond even the Moon's orbit.

Herschel was a pure astronomer, not a system-maker. He adored the black tablet in which he said he saw "myriads of worlds springing up like grass in the night."[16]

Interestingly, he tried always to schedule his necessary visits to the royal court on Moon-lit nights. Royal support required that he attend, but he had only one lifetime of dark nights in which to see all the stars. Since he constructed telescopes for a living, he was often forced to work months upon months at a time in the daylight hours grinding reflectors for himself and others. The light-gathering mirrors in telescopes at that time were made not of aluminum-coated glass but of speculum metal. The glass eyepieces, in which the magnification occurred, were confined to a certain size by technology, but more light could be gathered by bigger reflectors. These required constant repolishing to maintain their sheen. After painstakingly constructing a mirror of four feet, Herschel focused it on Saturn the first night and instantly discovered two unknown moons.

When he had to be away, he had his sister work with the telescope "every starry night on wet or hoarfrost-covered grass, without a human being within call."[17] She discovered eight comets.

His son, John Herschel, had a twenty-foot reflector built near Capetown, South Africa, and from there he catalogued over 2,100 double stars and almost 1,700 nebulae. By counting stars in different fields of view and then putting the fields together, he estimated that there were 70,000 stars in his telescopic sky. Behind the visible night, another sky was expanding exponentially. This would happen again when archaeologists uncovered semihuman bones in deep strata of that other ancient coffin, the Earth. There was another world of human creatures before this one, and there were other stars beyond the night. The universe was getting older and older, and man himself was becoming an unknown thing.

Stars were now everywhere unfixed, in various densities, double and triple, with no end in sight. Even the numerological basis for the Solar System was undone by a new planet. Herschel was born into a sky that would have been impossible for Kepler or Newton and, without realizing it, he made it impossible for anyone born after him to see that same sky. God was vanishing; there was no reason why, among millions of stars, He should not begin to seem further rather than closer, and less rather than more engaged in the Creation.

An 1803 astronomy book brings us up-to-date:

> The Galaxy or milky way must not be neglected; it is one of the most remarkable appearances in the heavens; it is a broad circle of a whitish hue, in some places it is double, but for the most part consists of a single path surrounding the whole celestial concave. The great *Galileo* discovered by the telescope, that the portion of the heavens which this circle passes through was every where filled with an infinite multitude of exceeding small stars, too small to be discovered by the naked eye, but by the combination of their light, diffusing a shining whiteness through the heavens. Mr. *Brydone* says, that when he was at the top of Mount Aetna, the milky way had the most beautiful effect, appearing like a pure flame that shot across the heavens. . . .
>
> The number of the stars almost infinitely exceeds what we have yet been speaking of. An ordinary telescope will discover, in several parts of the heavens, ten times as many stars as are visible to the naked eye. *Hooke* in his Micrographia says, that with a telescope of twelve feet he discovered seventy-eight stars among the Pleiades, and with a more perfect telescope, many more. *Galileo* reckoned eighty in the space between the belt and the sword of Orion, and above five hundred more in another part of the same constellation. Antonia Maria de Rheita counted in the same constellation above ten thousand stars. Future improvements in the telescopes may enable us to discover numberless stars, that are now invisible; and many more may be which are too remote to be seen through telescopes, even when they have received their ultimate improvement. . . .

Who can say, how far the universe extends, or where are the limits of it? where the Creator stayed "his rapid wheels"; or where he "fixed the golden compasses"?

With the discovery of a seventh planet, rings, moons, and the nature of meteors, and then with Laplace's perturbation theory of the origin of the Solar System, the eighteenth century had come to a new understanding of the moving hands of the cosmic clock. One "local" problem was the gap between Mars and Jupiter. In 1722, Johann Titius had developed a mathematical progression for the distances of the planets from the Sun. That same year, Johann Bode, in his *Introduction to the Study of the Starry Sky,* restated the progression with the specific recommendation that there was another planet at 2.8 times the Earth's distance from the Sun (or seven times Mercury's distance and four times Venus's distance). When Uranus fit the progression so closely, the search for the "missing" planet was intensified, but it was not until New Year's Day, 1801, that Giuseppi Piazzi, an Italian astronomer, found an 8th-magnitude star in Taurus that changed position over the next two nights. On January 14, it ceased its retrograde motion and began moving forward. Assuming it to be a planet, he named it Ceres. Then he lost it when Taurus passed into sunlight, and he became sick and was unable to continue the tracking. It was not found again until December, when Karl Friedrich Gauss, using an orbit computed from only three figures, relocated it. Thereafter, astronomers flocked to see this second new planet. Ceres fit Bode's progression almost perfectly, but it was so tiny that it showed no planetary disc. While astronomers were puzzling over this, H. Wilhelm Olbers, in April of 1802, found a second object in a proximate orbit, and this was named Pallas. Juno was found in 1804, and Vesta in 1807. By 1852, there were twenty known planetoids; and by 1870, there were 110. Once their existence was known, they were found all the way down to the twelfth magnitude, including some that passed out beyond Saturn and others that passed within the orbit of Venus. Hermes, Eros, and Icarus have all approached the Earth itself in recent times.

In 1846, John Adams, the British astronomer, and Urbain Leverrier of France simultaneously predicted the discovery of an eighth planet, using Newton's laws and computing its positions by the hypothesized perturbations that an unknown planet had caused in the positions of Uranus. Neptune was actually first observed, at least with awareness of what it was, by Johann Galle, a German astronomer using Leverrier's predicted position of September 23, 1846. After finding an 8th-magnitude star that was not in a new star chart he was using, Galle continued to observe it and found that it was moving in a retrograde direction in close proximity to Leverrier's estimates of size and speed as well as location. He then wrote to Leverrier that "the planet whose position you have pointed out *actually exists.*"[19]

On September 10 of that year, Sir John Herschel looked through his telescope at this new world and said: "We see it as Columbus saw America from the shores of Spain. Its movements have been felt trembling along the far-reaching line of our analysis with a certainty hardly inferior to ocular demonstration."[20]

Later that same year, William Lassel, using a new mirror telescope, discovered Triton, the large moon of Neptune, which is brighter from Earth than any of Uranus's moons. But in 1851 Lassel also found Ariel and Umbriel (as they were later named) circling Uranus.

It is interesting to note that, even though a planet is discovered at a certain historical period, it is often known before that as a star. The ancients saw Uranus, but it was too faint and slow-moving to excite interest in its planetary nature. The American astronomer Sears Walker searched Lalande's eighteenth-century catalogue for unknown stars on the nights and in the positions where Neptune would have been visible, and he used these likely sightings in constructing his improved elliptical orbit in 1847. When Neptune was found to be way off its expected position from Bode's progression (30.05 times the distance of the Earth from the Sun instead of 38.4), the "law" lost any credence. It actually belonged more to Kepler's universe of geometric solids and Pythagorean harmonies, and its main historical role had been in encouraging the search for a missing planet.

The prediction of Neptune by two independently searching astronomers in the same year was not without controversy. Leverrier was the more famous and also the more egotistical of the two, and Adams's prior discovery went unreported for many months because the British Astronomer Royal, George Airy, did not believe in the existence of trans-Uranian planets and did not take his results seriously. When Adams's prediction was announced later, Leverrier and his French supporters vigorously fought against sharing the historical credit. In fact, Leverrier wanted the new planet given his own name and self-servingly suggested the name Herschel for Uranus.

This relatively insignificant competition masks another far more interesting controversy that has been forgotten but not resolved. The credit for discovering a planet generally goes to the person whose formulas predicted its position, often instead of the person who actually finds it. Galle found Leverrier's planet for him. But Galle's "star" also corresponded to Adams's prediction for the same night, even though, remarkably enough, Adams and Leverrier had different orbits for their planets, neither of which corresponded even remotely to Neptune's actual orbit, nor to each other, except at the periods when they all intersected. That the three ellipses should have come so close to perfect intersection (the hypothetical ones of Adams and Leverrier and the real one of Neptune the planet) on the night that Galle chose to look is a stroke of luck almost too fantastic to believe.

Both sets of calculations were based on Bode's inaccurate estimates of Neptune's size and distance from the Sun. They were also based on the extremely subtle calculations of not only Uranus's perturbations of the unknown body but also that body's perturbations of Uranus, and on an accurate Newtonian orbit for Uranus, with all of the other gravitational influences on it in the Solar System. This is a "solution" difficult to arrive at for many of the outer planets today, and it was impossible then. In fact, the hypothetical planet that lies between Mercury and the Sun, Vulcan, was "observed" many times throughout the nineteenth century because so many astronomers were looking for a body to resolve the anomalies in the motion of the perihelion of Mercury.

Given these difficulties, the officials of the time chose to credit Leverrier with the discovery of Neptune because it was found through using his formula, *even though* his hypothetical planet and Neptune crossed at only a few points. Having done this, the officials were compelled later to give Adams equal cred-it, since his planet crossed both Leverrier's and Neptune at the discovery point. The dilemma becomes far more provocative later, after it is clear that neither the existence of Neptune nor the later discovery of Pluto resolve the anomalies in Uranus's orbit. The Neptune situation is summarized well by the historian William Graves Hoyt, quoting from the American astronomer Henry Norris Russell: "Leverrier and Adams . . . had assumed too great a distance for their unknown planet from Bode's law, but their calculations also 'made the orbit considerably eccentric (although it is really very nearly circular),' " and this "spurious eccentricity brought the predicted orbit toward the sun in the region where the planet actually lay at the time, and went far to undo the error of the two original assumptions." [21] Apparently Neptune was ready to be found.

There was also another issue that troubled nineteenth-century astronomers. It was first known to be stated by Halley in 1720, but was later credited to Wilhelm Olbers, who put it forward as a paradox in 1823. As Halley realized it, the universe must not be infinite, for, if it were, the collective light of all the stars to infinity would fill the night sky to the brightness of the disc of the Sun. Galileo had concluded that light exhausted its "instaneity" over shorter distances, but this was no longer an acceptable solution. Olbers solved the problem for himself by attributing the blackness of the sky to the existence of dust and particles in space which would need only to dampen a small fraction of the eternal starlight to create the dark night. Even a substance much more transparent than water would absorb enough light over the great distances of space to eliminate sight of the furthest stars. To this degree, the nineteenth century still believed that there was sand to put its head into, and that the teeth of eternity must be blunted somewhere beyond the vil-lages of Earth.

8

The History of
Western Astronomy
V: The Elements

OWARD THE latter part of the nineteenth century, telescopic
equipment improved, and, with the invention of the photographic silver bromide plate, modern astronomy of the heavens
began as the painstaking recording of all regions of the heavens
on replica film. The plates were so sensitive that they could pick
up objects that the human eye would never see, even through
a lens. Already the cameo of William Herschel with his sister
Caroline standing in the night with hoarfrost on their telescope
was quaint.

Furthermore, the world inside, or below, opened out as star-
rily as the night through the microscope. Both lifeless chemicals
and fertile pond water showed stars and animacules as deeply as
resolving power would go. No more than the telescope showed
the face of God, or a Golden Compass in the Void, did the
microscope show the vital force that guided all substance or the
crystal sparks of primordial ether. It was the same instrument,
only it enlarged things in a different plane. Atom and star were
eventually to prove that. And man found himself in a strange
new hierarchy with suns and nebulae above him to infinity and
animals inside animals inside animals, and atoms inside everything, including himself. A lens made the night sky also the
atom, and the atom filled the night sky with light.

Since the time of Galileo, Western man has "known" that

those things out there are neither spirits nor gems, but stones, pebbles and dirt. Some of them are frozen; most of them are molten. The display itself is created by the gargantuan sizes of the objects, the distances between them, and the primary forces that govern their arrangement. If we could look inside a flower or a bug or our own flesh and blood on an equally long focal plane, we would see a similar display. The microscope gives us such vision. We see that we contain replicas of the night sky; in fact, all matter, animate or not, is filled with skies.

As the poet Theodore Enslin taught: When we crack open the walnut, we find, not the kernel, but simply another husk. In order to find the kernel, we must change the nature of our perception and move into other dimensions.

It was a contemporary of Isaac Newton, the Dutch naturalist Anton van Leeuwenhoek, who discovered that a miniature cosmos had apparently existed unseen since the origin of the Earth.

Leeuwenhoek was brought a ganglion from the leg of a woman, in which, it was reported, worms had generated spontaneously. Under the microscope, he recognized insect larvae, maggots from eggs deposited by flies, but the anatomist who had brought the ganglion was not satisfied. Leeuwenhoek removed the larvae to a piece of beef; they became pupae and hatched into flies; then a pair of these were mated and the female laid 115 eggs like the original ones. Joseph Addison wrote:

> Every part of Matter is peopled; every green Leaf swarms with Inhabitants. There is scarce a single Humour in the Body of a Man, or of any other Animal, in which our Glasses do not discover Myriads of living Creatures. The Surface of Animals is also covered with other Animals, which are in the same manner the Basis of other Animals that live upon it; nay, we find in the most solid Bodies, as in Marble itself, innumerable Cells and Cavities that are crouded with such imperceptible inhabitants, as are too little for the naked eye to discover.[1]

The world of microscopic things had a revolutionary impact on nineteenth-century stargazing and set the stage for astrophysics. In 1805, John Dalton, an English chemist, advanced an atomic theory of the elements reminiscent of Ionian philosophy. He proposed that basic substances are made up of atoms, which are indestructible and indivisible and from which all structure is assembled. Chemical combinations occur based on the unions of these atoms according to simple mathematical properties. Yet, the atoms maintain their essential identity through all physical and chemical changes.

In 1869, the Russian chemist Dmitri Mendeleev discovered that the chemical properties of the elements are periodic functions of their atomic weights, i.e., of the number of protons in their nuclei. When he arranged the then-known elements in a series, he found that there were familial resemblances among elements at regular numerical intervals. For instance, carbon, silicon, and tin lie in a series for which the member between silicon and tin was then apparently missing. This was later found to be germanium. Fluorine, chlorine, bromine, and iodine constitute another family. Then there is a group of lithium, sodium, and potassium; another of nitrogen, phosphorus, arsenic, and antimony; and so on. Nature contains a hidden periodic function which is basic to form and order in the world. All the other elements are based on the simplest one, hydrogen with its single proton, which is also—we were to find out—the fuel of the stars.

Mendeleev's periodic table, and the reality that lay behind it, gave a new basis for understanding the history and evolution of matter. Mathematical relationships determined the seemingly limitless display of forms in nature, from plants and animals to stars and galaxies. It was hauntingly Pythagorean, as Heisenberg would remind us.

Despite the breakthrough, there was no reason initially to assume that man would ever be able to "touch" the stars. With the advent of spectroscopy, though, the elemental chart suddenly became a cosmic laboratory using light as its "chemical." The technology arrived in the second decade of the nineteenth century when an optician in Munich, Joseph von Fraunhofer, noticed that the spectrum of the Sun, when passed through a slit and then through a glass prism, developed hundreds of dark lines over it, each one a shadow of the original slit. In sunlight and in the spectra of the Moon and stars, these lines were always found at the same wavelength. Fantastic as it seemed, these minute scratches revealed the inner structure of materials light-years away, from the absorption of specific wavelengths as they passed from burning stars through their cooler atmospheres.

In 1859, another German, Gustav Robert Kirchhoff, discovered that each element, when vaporized, generates a specific spectrum. No two elemental spectra are the same. Not many stars had analyzable spectra at first, but the nebulae did, and they showed such familiar elements as oxygen and nitrogen, which meant that even at the great distances of interstellar space, the same chemistry was sustained (the expectation, left over from the days of an ethereal cosmos, was that entirely unknown elements abounded in the heavens). The sodium, magnesium, calcium, chromium, and iron found on the Earth turned out to be composed of the atoms also detected in stars. In fact, the first "exotic" element was found in the Sun (so named helium), but it too turned up on the Earth.

Until spectroscopic analysis all the different kinds of nebulae and starry hazes were indistinguishable from one another. The ambiguity of this period of history persists when some people still call galaxies nebulae. William Huggins was the first to demonstrate, in 1864, that not all of the nebulae are star clusters; some are simply clouds of luminous gas. Today we know that the colored Great Nebula of Orion is a large gaseous cloud surrounding a number of stars. Other nebulae, the Pleiades for instance, are actual star groups.

Analysis of the stars showed that, if anything, they were less complex than the Earth, for they were so hot that only simple atoms survived in them (a few red stars show compounds of carbon, oxygen, and iron, but nothing more intricate). With a universal chemistry as their yardstick, astronomers could begin to interpret sequences of star types and derive the familial relationship between the stars and planets.

We might also note that it was not until the 1930s that it was possible to analyze the composition of the planets from spectral light filtered through their atmospheres. To this day, with the exception of the Viking soil analyses on Mars, our spectral analysis is confined to the planetary atmospheres; these reveal great amounts of methane, ammonia, and hydrogen on the larger worlds of our Solar System, making them akin to small suns.

Until such experiments, it was possible to imagine these planets as habitable by beings like those on Earth.

Charles Darwin, working primarily with animals and their fossils, provided a theory of evolution that was to incorporate universal chemistry into a scientific history of the cosmos. Darwin showed that living creatures varied in their basic forms from generation to generation, and that such random variations eventually spawned utterly new species, species selected by nature according to their fitness. Hence, extinct life forms known only from fossils might have been the prehistoric links between various contemporary species of plants and animals.

Darwin was not talking about the origins of suns and planets; he did not foresee the extraterrestrial implications of his theory. But, from the simple fact that he was able to define a mechanism for life without referring to vital energy, he made creatures into stellar phenomena—not right away but as the consequences of random variation and natural selection became clear to scientists. If the planets had their origin in the Sun, if suns had their basis in galactic hydrogen, and if the elements on suns and planets spread in happenstance combinations, then creatures might emerge even as fire and rain, from natural forces and without the intercession of a creative consciousness or a prior life energy.

There was no need to separate the animate Earth from the inanimate universe and look for a special cause for life. The Periodic Chart alone gives the basis for making people out of stars (no new matter or energy is needed, the spectroscope proved). Life is a modification of the same hydrogen that burns in the stars. The Law of Natural Selection peoples the planets of other stars with the kinds of beings that would be favored by their environments.

Newton's gravitation lay behind Darwin's natural selection. The mechanical universe has only one thermodynamic source, and it cannot make special allowances for life or mind. Once geneticists tied elemental chemistry to biological speciation, they realized how life itself could have developed mechanically from random chemical interactions. It was starstuff, with the Earth as its loom.

George Ellery Hale, one of the first New World astronomers,

credits Darwin's *The Origin of Species* with giving him a relevant model for the stars. "It taught me," he wrote, "to regard the sun as a typical star, a link in a long evolutional chain, and thus helped me to avoid becoming exclusively a specialist in solar research."[2]

Later, Hale summarizes the philosophical impact of the new cosmogony:

> We are now in a position to regard the study of evolution as that of a single great problem, beginning with the origin of the stars in the nebulae and culminating in those difficult and complex sciences that endeavor to account, not merely for the phenomena of life, but for the laws which control a society composed of human beings. Any such consideration of all natural phenomena as elements of a single problem must begin with a study of the Sun, the only star lying near enough the Earth. . . .[3]

Baron Hermann von Helmholtz and Lord William Kelvin independently developed theories of stellar life cycles. With their explanations came the shock that the Sun was mortal; it was consuming itself, being compressed into its center from the pull of its own gravitational attraction. The energy for its light and heat came from radiation released. As long as there was material to draw on, the star would remain lit, but it would eventually extinguish itself. This would happen to all the suns in the universe.

The life cycle of stars could be seen strewn throughout the heavens: embryos, newborns, children, adults, "conjugal pairs," elders, and fossils of extinct forms. Astronomers viewed interstellar clouds of gas, young white giants, red dying stars consuming the last of their energy, eccentric white dwarfs, and an abundance of common yellows.

A few decades later, they developed a system of classifying stars according to heat. The hottest and brightest were the young blue-white stars at 20,000 degrees C. Then came alabaster-white Sirius, only half as hot. Pale-yellow Polaris was hotter than our own yellow Sol (10,000 degrees C.). Pumpkin-colored Arcturus typified the next category, followed by poppy-red Antares, half the heat of Arcturus at 2,000 degrees C. Old Antares was a red giant, so bloated it would engulf the orbit of Mars as our sun.

The perishable Sun is a koan of our cosmology. Intuited in the nineteenth century, it was another death blow to the mediaeval cosmos. Adding the speed of light to the distances of stars, astronomers began to understand that they were looking at corpses, perhaps dead over millions of years.

Or dying. For ancient explosions were still visible in galactic spirals, one in Andromeda, another in the Hunting Dogs. This meant that devastating amounts of material, whole systems in fact, could be destroyed. All civilization suddenly hung at the mercy of godless fire. The nineteenth century could perhaps handle the orderly birth and death of stars and even the creation of new stars from nebulous material. It was not quite ready for supernovas—explosions beyond comprehension, consuming philosophy.

Over time, Darwinian thought salvaged the crumbling universe and invested it with a new kind of order. It wasn't elegant by either Ionian or Copernican standards, but it was strict and formal in its own terms. It was bleak and nihilistic, but it heralded the beginnings of European industrialism and was the ideal handmaiden of the factory. What it gave up in spirit and divinity it gained back in functionalism and scientific hegemony. After all, the Rosicrucian "machines" never produced a volt of electricity, and we still await Bruno's astral city. But Darwin had redefined energy, and the machines of his successors ran factories.

In the modern version of the Darwinian logos, species of living things come into being in complex interdependent relationships with their environments. Under the constantly changing conditions of planets, new organisms appear. Natural selection does not provide them; it is merely the circumstances whereby certain variations that occur accidentally are preserved. Order and harmony may seem to emerge later, in our own time, but anarchy and anomaly brought these present species and their accoutrements into being. Mutation and accident are the only "laws," and atomic and molecular morphology are their single foundation. Inanimate chemicals become cells, as it were, by imitating them first. Cells become organs and organisms, slight roughnesses become guts and spinal columns, fins become wings and limbs, primitive sensing cells become brains. Organisms always use ancient structures for new functions because there is no exogenous source. Without gills to work on, the universe could not invent lungs. Even the abilities to assimilate food and produce offspring—the distinguishing features of living organisms—come about in non-living compounds from the chance interactions of compounds. Thus, it is possible to appreciate why scientists today do not expect to find humanoids elsewhere in the universe. We are the fluke outcome of trillions of random events in the terrestrial environment.

Nothing appears *ex nihilo*. Matter simply exhibits its properties in a cumulative chain or a series of cumulative chains; some of the lineages diverge and differentiate further; others die out. This random dispersal replaced The Great Chain of Being which once hung down from the astral sphere and whose links were archetypes which could not be crossed by transitions of species.

A generation after Darwin, Sigmund Freud would show that the beliefs and customs of mankind were a consequence of the same law. His theory of consciousness posited a mode of "natural selection" for thoughts, images, and emotions. Even our ideas and motives now have a "gravitational" basis. Twentieth-century social science incorporates all human activity in this structural and statistical universe. Taken from the sky by Newton, gravity now rules the cosmos, with man's soul as its hostage.

In short, the universe has become a sophisticated version of Laplace's celestial mechanics. Hydrogen gas swirls into spirals, and planets congeal under the force of gravity; structures and compounds are elaborated by the atomic nuclei. The properties of carbon, hydrogen, and oxygen lead to complex chains of molecules; proteins and amino acids form. Creatures crawl out of the muck and sea salt. Those life forms that are best suited to their environments, which are also changing, survive to give birth to lineages, which are themselves altered by the changing universe. After a few billion years, at least one very complex life form on one planet uses its intelligence to tame fire, invent language, and domesticate plants; or, more accurately, these things are unconsciously developed, and individual creatures, like us, are born in their midst. But not even this complex creature has a spirit; it is simply a clever arrangement of chemicals. Mostly it is unconscious, but a minute portion of its being passes into consciousness against extremely strong forces of suppression. Such life forms develop societies, and some of these survive and amalgamate, mostly by harnessing greater amounts of environmental energy. Ultimately, they even develop theories of celestial mechanics and understand that the matter in their bodies came from the stars and that they themselves are nothing special, just debris in its chance assortment. It is a perfect circle. Astronomers exist by grace of the same celestial mechanics as suns.

Something in us may cry out against this common ancestry even for kings and queens and philosophers who were sired by the sires of earthworms and frogs. It may be an outrage, but there is little reason for hope and great expectations anymore. Our clearest statement of something else is our need to make a statement at all. The something in us that cries out may be just the illusion of a spirit in a puppet who thinks he is alive, or it may be the spirit of the infinite, whatever that is, and if it even has a spirit, and if we have a right to be that spirit through the glass darkly. Our outrage is either exactly who we are, or it is our most pompous and painful delusion. Soon none of this will be here anyway—none of it, none of it at all. What a surprise! What a comeuppance and surprise! D. H. Lawrence, among countless others, has answered the challenge:

> The purpose, what was the purpose? Electricity had no soul, light and heat had no soul. Was she herself an impersonal force, or conjunction of forces, like one of these? She looked still at the unicellular shadow that lay within the field of light, under her microscope. It was alive. She saw it move—she saw the bright mist of ciliary activity, she saw the gleam of its nucleus, as it slid across the plane of light. What then was its will? If it was a conjunction of forces, what held these forces unified, and for what purpose were they unified?
>
> For what purpose were the incalculable physical and chemical activities nodalized in this shadowy, moving speck under her microscope? What was the will which nodalized them and created the one thing she saw? What was its intention? To be itself? Was its purpose just mechanical and limited to itself?
>
> It intended to be itself. But what self? Suddenly in her mind the world gleamed strangely, with an intense light,

like the nucleus of the creature under the microscope. Suddenly she had passed away into an intensely-gleaming light of knowledge. She could not understand what it all was. She only knew that it was not limited mechanical energy, nor mere purpose of self-preservation and self-assertion. It was a consummation, a being infinite. Self was a oneness with the infinite. To be oneself was a supreme, gleaming triumph of infinity. [4]

In that sense, creatures form the opposite pole to molecular rigidity and galactic vastness. Without them there would be only an unknown turmoil traveling blind and senseless in a void. With them there is a wondrous sky filled with sparks that they either have no name for or they call gods or hydrogen fires. Without creatures, a rough simple universe roars, an unabated cataclysm. With them there are senses to reflect the inside of this cataclysm, words to describe it, and images to build temples which contain representations of the paths of heavenly bodies, and radio telescopes which record the background noise of outer space.

When men drill through the Arctic snowcap and ice into the ocean beneath, and go in diving suits and swim in that cold sky, they find living mites in the freshwater ice-crystals that have burst into the ocean edge. These creatures spend their entire existence in these fragile crystals. For them the night sky is simply their being; they look out through the cellularity of their bodies at the infinite.

9

The History of
Western Astronomy
VI: The Space-Time
Continuum

THE COSMOLOGY of the universe in the first decade of the twentieth century was leftover Newtonian mechanics, which were assumed to be able to handle all new phenomena. Newtonian physics had proved satisfactory enough in explaining dynamics within the Solar System and among stars and fields of stars. But there were shadows over the Newtonian model, one of them cast by Faraday and Maxwell.

In the 1840s, Michael Faraday, working experimentally with a magnet, discovered lines of force continuing into space from the poles. These seemed to support Leibnitz's image of space as the relationship of objects to one another, in direct contradiction to Newton's empty space. Moving a magnet near a coil of copper, Faraday excited an electrical current: the mechanical energy of the magnet had been transformed into electrical energy. The experimental work of Faraday and, later, of James Clerk Maxwell with electric and magnetic energies led to the concept of a force field. Outer space was newly conceived as a field with waves of electricity and magnetism as well as light. In 1861, Maxwell suggested that light itself might be a form of electromagnetic energy.

It was difficult for these experimenters to accept that fields were real phenomena. Previous models had proposed stress operating mechanically in a medium of space-filling ether. The ether had never been discovered, but it was ostensibly a real thing. What electromagnetism changed was the definition of "real." We know now that electrical fields are created by the mutual interactions of bodies with electron charges, and magnetic fields are electrical in origin. We also know that all the light and radio noise from space are essentially electromagnetic radiation. But these discoveries separate our century from the last by a gulf wider than that separating Newton from the Greeks.

In 1899, the German physicist Max Planck discovered that the unsteadiness that appears in thermal phenomena (and atoms) is not a consequence of imprecise equipment or interference; it is a basic and independent feature of nature. Planck's quantum of action allowed scientists to make a model for why two colliding atoms return to their "normal" states after collision when two colliding planetary systems obviously would not. The atom changes its energy by discrete quanta only, so it recoils to its underlying "harmonic." In addition, the radiation from atoms generates wavelike interference patterns but particlelike photoelectric effects. And there is no way to describe either the position of the electron between any two observations or both its position and its momentum.

> The predictability which held for molar aggregates (stones and other inert objects) is not possible with ultimate particles. It might be objected that the uncertainty is *introduced* by the act of observing them (epistemological). But it has been found that the particles carry or possess the uncertainty anyway (ontological). There is only a probability that they are in a given place. The electron is now referred to as a "probability fog."[1]

The mechanical model is accurate only when the internal dynamics of the atom and the relationships of atoms are not taken into account.

It is misleading to think that space is different for being a field rather than a concrete thing. There are no "things" anymore in the old sense. Bodies are not solid concrete substances. They arise only as singularities within fields, electromagnetic and gravitational, and the fields of their own nuclear forces. Matter is nonporous only to our crude faculty of sight. If we could look at it more closely, we would see something resembling the Solar System or the galaxies. The twentieth-century occult astronomer Rodney Collin describes the Solar System itself as a fiery train or body in about the proportion of a human figure standing erect and racing toward Vega at 12.5 miles per second—that is, if seen by a being with a moment of perception eighty years long:

> The planetary paths, drawn out into manifold spirals of various tensions and diameters, have now become a series of iridescent sheaths veiling the long white-hot thread of the sun, each shimmer with its own characteristic colour and sheen, the whole meshed throughout by a gossamer-fine web woven from the eccentric paths of innumerable asteroids and comets, glowing with some sense of living warmth and ringing with an incredibly subtle and harmonious music. [2]

We have entered a world in which Newton's laws do not hold in the way that he originally proposed them. Potential has surpassed actual force, so finite equations must be replaced by differential equations describing fields in which this potential acts along a gradient, giving rise to the illusion of force.

There was another rupture in the Newtonian universe, one that Newton himself had foreseen: if the universe were finite and matter were equally distributed in it, and if gravity were the only force determining the relationships of astronomical bodies, then everything would be drawn by collective gravity to a single point. Only if the universe were infinite could this fate be avoided. Gravity would be saved, but there would be the conundrum of an infinite universe. A universe that goes on forever is not only big; it stands against identity and reason.

In 1842, at the University of Prague, Christian Doppler had constructed an experiment that was to yield the protean image of twentieth-century astronomy: the red shift. Using the changing pitch of a moving object as a clue to whether it is approaching or receding, Doppler created an analogous model for light. If the distance between the Earth and a star were increasing, the spectral lines would shift toward red wavelengths; and if the distance were decreasing, they would shift toward the blue. A Dutch meteorologist, Christoph Hendrik Didericus Buys Ballot, tested the Doppler effect in 1845 by using trumpet players on an open car of a railroad train pulled along through the fields by a locomotive. This strange cacophony heralded our present expanding radio universe.

The colors of the star spectra were not altered, but, as was shown by William Huggins in 1868, the dark lines were shifted one way or another from their normal positions. The degree of shift, if interpreted as the same effect found in the moving orchestra on the train, was a consistent and unerasable clue to stellar velocities. For instance, Capella, with a .01 percent shift, is moving away from us at that percentage of the speed of light.

Early in the twentieth century, astronomers discovered certain stars that changed in brilliance for inherent reasons. They were not double or triple stars. They were simply variables. The Americans Harlow Shapley and Henrietta Swan Leavitt were able to derive a period-luminosity curve for these stars, called Cepheids after the test one, Delta Cephei. In other words, astronomers could calculate the absolute luminosity of stars by their periods, and if they knew the absolute luminosity, then they could calculate distance on the basis of apparent brightness. Suddenly the size of the Milky Way more than doubled, so that, in 1915, Arthur Eddington estimated it at 15,000 light-years, a mere fraction of its presently-estimated diameter but a staggering figure at the time. By 1923, Edwin Hubble had succeeded in finding Cepheids in the spiral arms of the Andromeda Galaxy. He measured its distance from Earth as 900,000 light-years. We now accept the figure 2.1 million light-years.

Meanwhile, there was still the Doppler Effect to deal with. The red shifts of stars boded something. Vesto Slipher, working at Lowell Observatory, had shown in 1914 that the spiral galaxies were moving isotropically outwards (away from us and away from each other). This was not taken seriously until the late 1920s, when Edwin Hubble began to work on the velocity-distance relations between our Galaxy and others. An expanding universe did solve one problem: Olber's paradox. Shapley had concluded that space must be extremely transparent, too transparent to resolve the paradox, or else other problems regarding the brightness of distant globular clusters would arise. At the time, he said, "Either the extent of the star-populated space is finite or the heavens would be a blazing glory of light."[3] But not only was the universe infinite, it was expanding! Astronomy was desperately in need of a successor to Newton.

It took only one man, Albert Einstein, to resolve these difficulties. From 1917 through the middle of the century, he invented the twentieth-century night sky. By adding gravitation to electromagnetism, Einstein made latter real and so placed us in a space-time continuum.

The Newtonian universe, Einstein initially agreed, should have a maximum density of stars in the center; it should be "a finite island in the infinite ocean."[4] But it clearly is not. There was also no place theoretically for both Newtonian matter and the Faraday-Maxwell field; the field is what survived.

Einstein established that gravitation is a field, like electromagnetism. Mass itself is relative, depending on velocity: the faster a thing moves, the more massive it becomes. Time depends on mass. If the force of gravity is great enough, time runs slower. These were bitter pills: almost by the year, the universe was becoming less secure, but at least there was now a way out of the celestial machine.

Gravitation, Einstein realized, is independent of things which influence all other observed phenomena. While electromagnetic fields affect only charged bodies, gravity operates on all bodies everywhere in the same way without regard for heat, chemical makeup, or electromagnetic charge. It is the universality of gravity that makes it impenetrable. We cannot dissect it. It simply is.

Using Bernhard Riemann's 1854 formula, adapted by Riemann from Karl Friedrich Gauss, Einstein extrapolated a universe in which time was added as a fourth dimension and matter was homogeneously distributed (all viewpoints in it were isotropic). Gauss's theorem had allowed the hypothetical two-dimensional inhabitants of a universal plane to find the curvature of their world in a third dimension. Riemann used algebra to generalize this theorem so that it could be applied to a space of any number of dimensions, i.e., to measure the curvature of the space.[5]

Einstein developed a curved space for his universe, and he

placed three terms—*space, time,* and *gravitation*—in an interdependent series. Gravitation was "explained" as an effect of
the curvature of time and space; that curvature gave a limit to
the universe with nothing left outside. It was not an exterior
curvature, but an inherent one. Around the high gravitational
field of a star, the curvature of space might be greater than in
interstellar space.

If we assume, for instance, that matter creates the space (or
illusion of space) that it occupies, then the universe is intrinsically
everywhere; and if it is growing bigger, the space into which it is
growing is literally the extension and complexification of its own
fabric.

Einstein tried to do away with the problem of inside space
and outside space when he mapped space itself as a kind of
hyperspace such that all which is outside is also back inside. Not
only can we not get outside this space, we cannot even touch the
outside from the inside. It is a space that continues to emerge
from its own properties only. It has as an outside barrier the
speed of light, which is threaded through its inside, and the
bending of space-time, which is probably an illusion. This universe can have no inside or outside, and its original point is
everywhere; hence the microwave background in space.

Because this universe was static, Einstein accounted for its
failure to close in upon itself by a repulsion at large distances.
This force between remote objects he called a cosmological constant. The expanding universe of galaxies required an expanding
space ultimately, but Einstein's universe was adaptable because
of its infinite curvature. The expansion could create space-time.
Finally, Einstein gave his universe a negative curvature, with
open and infinite space, like a western saddle with a radius of
curvature of five billion light-years.

The nineteenth-century German physicist Hermann von
Helmholtz foresaw this universe as a bright silvery Christmas
tree globe whose distorted mirror transposes the whole of the
space around it into a sphere. The further away a thing is, the
tinier it looks and the closer it is to the center of the sphere. If
we come up close to it, we can dominate it, but we lose our
shape.

Relativity theory is *not* a metaphysical device or an image; it is a physical theory designed to explain observed facts and to bring seemingly contradictory rules into one law. There are no more special "laws" such as conservation of mass and energy or the principle of least action; these are all included in the equation of relativity. There are no more special fields; there is one universal field in which matter itself is a mere confluence. Like Newton, Einstein rested his theory on facts. He predicted the curvature of light close to the Sun, and his confidence was borne out during the solar eclipse of 1919. Relativity theory also explained why Mercury does not behave according to prediction at perihelion and why the dwarf companion of Sirius (discovered in 1844 from Sirius's wavy path) has such a large red shift.

Einstein's gravitational space was discovered mathematically, and the images we have of it are after the fact. We cannot imagine four-dimensional space simply by analogy with three-dimensional space to two-dimensional being. Another dimension would add a whole new quality to space itself. Things in three dimensions are radically different from things in two dimensions. The fourth dimension is revealed mathematically by tracks of material particles and rays of light. We can predict its coordinates, but we cannot experience its nature. Insofar as this four-dimensional world is "real," space and time as we know them are mere conventions. Events can happen either forward in time or backwards. In observing particles, we do not really know. Positive charge may simply be negative charge moving backwards in time. What we call force may be interaction. Two-dimensional beings might see the third dimension as something like time and attracting force, or it might add something totally different to their world. It has even been suggested that gravity is the fourth dimension and that this is why it pushes everywhere on everything equally from a source which is inherent but invisible. It shapes our entire universe and we feel it from within, but we cannot see it. How else would a fourth dimension act?

In the Einsteinian system, apparent time is also real time, and all time is relative to movement and space. Previously, it had been thought that the time showed by moving clocks was a local fiction. It is. But there is also no other "true" time.

Einstein demonstrated the primary relationship between inertia and energy: the electromagnetic energy stored by the

electron increases its inertia and thus its mass. From this com-
mutability of mass and energy, made famous in the formula that
combines them with the squared constant of the speed of light
($E = mc^2$), substances and force become versions of the same
thing.

In general, Einstein combined phenomena of gravity, mass,
and energy in a four-dimensional space-time manifold. He
understood the nature and relationship of light and heat and
matter implicitly, and he was able to relate these to Planck's
quantum. He intuited that radiation itself comes in quanta, and
that they are also the source of pure light. The photon, which
has the chemical energy of one electron volt per atom, is the
intrinsic capacity of sunshine to engage in photosynthesis.

But Einstein balked at the uncertainty factor in quantum theory because he believed there was a real external nature quite
apart from probabilistic functions. He demanded an objective
night sky and a natural landscape of creation. Because of his
involvement with the torso of space, he was able to paint the
deepest night sky of the century. Time and space exist only as
an inextricable pair, and the night sky is the visible form of them.
The richness of this relativistic drawing stands out like the starry
heavens themselves—utterly motionless, yet moving at the
speed of light. We are post-Einsteinian by birth.

It is possible to understand these issues more deeply by review-
ing the transition from the universe of Newton's era—in which
matter was concrete and substantial and plants and animals were
eternal forms on the Great Chain of Being—through the field of
Maxwell and Faraday and the random biochemical assemblages of
Newton, to the preconscious, relativistic universe of Planck,
Freud, and Einstein. One work in particular radiates the turbulence of cosmological revaluation beneath the placid naturalistic
surface of nineteenth-century land- and sea-scapes.

Moby Dick could have been written as it was only during the
profound global transition of the mid-nineteenth century. Herman Melville's whale was a creature of early nineteenth-century
biology—at least to the degree that its sheer size and power as
a creature gave it the cosmological weight to carry the novel. It
was also a forerunner of the alien intelligent whales of twentieth-

century cosmology and a remnant of the sea monsters of eighteenth-century teratology. The nineteenth-century whale was one of the indisputable rulers of the animal kingdom at a time when both science and the humanities were committed to life—to the exotic creatures of the jungle and the ocean depths and to the tribes of precivilized humans found in the aboriginal worlds of the Americas, Australia, the South Pacific, and Africa.

We have broken our agreement with the animal kingdom. We had already broken it by the time of Melville and Darwin, yet their works were filled with exotic beasts and tribes. This was the golden age of zoological and anthropological expansion, but it was also the death knell. Our search for original form has moved beyond the purely biological into realms of force fields and speeding star-systems. The genetic, where the whale reigned, is now inextricably buried in the morphological. Simultaneous investigations of primary elements and the physical makeup of heavenly bodies have married living and nonliving entities to the same chemistry, compromising not only the whale but the lion, the African shaman, and the Roman priest. As chemistry becomes universal, the whale merges with a new class of objects. In a cosmic framework, it is just another animal, neither chemically nor anatomically unique. Melville foreshadowed this in his drama, and he intuited it in other ways: for instance, in his discussions of the taxonomy, history, and mythology of the whale, which "interfere" with the narrative field of the nineteenth-century novel in the same way that Faraday and Maxwell interfered with the Newtonian field of simple "narrative" forces, or in the way that Janos Bolyai and Nikolai Lobachevski transformed the Euclidean universe into a universe of discontinuous fields and transformations. Melville could write of the "confluent measureless force of the whole whale . . . concentrated to a point" in its tail.[6] This is the new universe of fields and singularities. Or, elsewhere in *Moby Dick:* "Silence reigned over the before tumultuous but now deserted deck. An intense copper calm, like a universal yellow lotus, was more and more unfolding its noiseless measureless leaves upon the sea." [7]

It is not necessarily what Melville declares; it is the subtlety of how he sees things:

The air around suddenly vibrated and tingled, as it were, like the air over intensely heated plates of iron. Beneath this atmospheric waving and curling, and partially beneath a thin layer of water, also, the whales were swimming. [8]

The ladders and hierarchies of the nineteenth-century taxonomist, who presided over the whale's unofficial coronation, stand as trivial before the overall taxonomy of electrons, cells, polarities, and intelligence. But it is a mistake to think that the whale has lost its crown only because the stars are larger and presumably house larger oceanic beasts elsewhere, just as it is a mistake to assume that its size entitled it to the crown originally. The scope of the heavens had been known before. It is because the stars are essentially similar to whales that whales are no longer needed to mark the outer limits of morphology and mythology. Stars and animals arise in a single elemental pool. Stars rival living systems in their complexities albeit of a different order. Or perhaps it is that the intricacy of life arises in the intricacy of stars without an intermediary.

There is also the psychological issue: by "reducing" creatures to star debris, science has devalued sentience and intellect. Ethologists have consigned the so-called motivations of animals to genetically compelled patterns of activity. So the stars are no more "inanimate" and unwilled than we.

By itself, this is a dead-end, but an even more profound revision awaited us at the turn of the century. Philosophy not only had its roots in biology but was merely a veneer. Even astronomy was a superficial gloss on a dense and unconscious process of mind.

In 1899, Sigmund Freud published his classic *Interpretation of Dreams*. As far outward as we look, Freud said (by implication), we do not see our actual condition, which is also infinite but in another dimension:

One is inclined [he wrote] to regard the dream-thoughts that have been brought to light as the complete material, whereas if the work of interpretation is carried further it may reveal still more thoughts concealed behind the dream. . . . It is in fact never possible to be sure that a dream has been completely interpreted. Even if the solution seems satisfactory and without gaps, the possibility always remains that the dream may have yet another meaning. [9]

So it is, entering the twentieth century, not only for dreams but for stars, and in fact for everything. As man attempts to make the universe simultaneously conscious and complete, it will evade him in an absolutely new way that will make the original paradox seem minor. Like King Sisyphus, he has pushed his huge stone to the top of a hill in Hades only to have it roll down again. The universe cannot be made conscious and complete, Freud declared, but he did not deny that the attempt would still have to be made. From then on, we would have to be aware of the layering and infoldedness of our location in the cosmos. No longer could the exploration be complete in its own exteriorized terms:

> It is essential to abandon the overvaluation of the property of being conscious before it becomes possible to form any correct view of the origin of what is mental. . . . The unconscious is the larger sphere, which includes within it the small sphere of the conscious. Everything conscious has an unconscious preliminary stage; where what is unconscious may remain at that stage and nevertheless claim to be regarded as having the full value of a psychical process. The unconscious is the true psychical reality; *in its innermost nature it is as much unknown to us as the reality of the external world, and it is as incompletely presented by the data of consciousness as is the external world by the communications of our sense organs.* [10]

From his analysis of dreams and the unconscious mind, Freud taught his generation that this was a species in trouble. Barely three decades later, the radio telescope showed that this was a universe in trouble—renegade and violent in its conception, unable to keep order in its parts, and careening toward disaster.

As more and more data about the stars and the universe were discovered, the fabric began to crumble in on itself. It became clear that what is underneath it all is a thing that is neither sensible nor knowable. Newton's laws had turned the creation into a laboratory, but there was no place in it for man except in his guise as objective scientist. Now he will look in three places, distinctly, for the thread which connects him to what he is. He will search to the ends of the night sky for his origins; he will look inside matter for the principle of his formation; and he will explore his own mind through mathematics, philosophy, psychology, and linguistics. The night of stars is also the night of cells and atoms and is the unconscious fabric of myth, dream, and language itself.

Melville diagnosed the coming schizophrenia: "Better might one be pushed off into the material spaces beyond the uttermost orbit of our sun, than once feel himself fairly afloat in himself!"[11]

It was not the bigness of the sky that threatened man, but his own shadows and eccentricity against it.

We begin to see that it is the stargazers, not the stars, that determine cosmogony. The stars are required, but as a face of infinite, not the infinite itself. A Zen law is operating here: the further we stare via instrumentation into what is meant to be complete and knowable, the more the basis of our being and the knowable will change. That is the role of star- and cell-gazers; their truths determine our relationship to meaning. We cannot help learning at the same time that the bottom is bottomless and that the realm of concrete appearances will never resolve its own paradoxes. There is no question that we have some ingenious solutions to problems of matter, stars, and origins, but it is no longer enough to keep adding more knowledge; the factor of incompleteness is not going to change. We turn almost reflexively back to social issues, saying, "What have the stars to do with us?"

Everything and nothing.

We can replace our insolubility only with contradictory solutions that have nothing in common except the distant and obscure link that we perceive and forge by our being: depth psychology, linguistic philosophy, quantum physics, stellar art forms— whatever we choose. We are unconscious and *it* is unconscious, so that is where it will happen, for scientists as well as improvisational dancers. One makes models, the other moves: both are "stars."

Any astronomer from here on in wrestles not only with the stars but with his or her own nightmares, relationships with other men and women, and survival as a creature on the Earth, and all these things find their way into the theories, no matter how diligently he or she works to keep them out.

10

The History of
Western Astronomy
VII: The Atom

THE TWENTIETH-CENTURY NIGHT SKY is an offspring of
the field that arose first in the work of Faraday and Maxwell.
Gravity preceded electromagnetism, but then both were integrated in the larger cosmic field of Einstein and the later intra-
atomic field. The "atom," in effect, both replaced and became
coterminous with the "star" in determining the shape and meaning of the night sky. For the last century scientists have sought our
cosmology more by cyclotrons than radio telescopes. We have
moved slowly and gradually through the starfield, but any discussion of the atom carries us at laser speed from Freud and Planck,
to Los Alamos and Hiroshima, to strings and quarks.

There is no simple image for the atom, or its properties and
components, so we must peer through confusions of language and
syntax to understand its enigma. In truth, we have come to
something that is at once a terrifying, limitless energy dwarfing
even the hydrogen bomb, and an abyss that goes on forever,
emptying by veils until it is less than nothing.

It was only yesterday, at the dawn of the twentieth century, that
Ernest Rutherford bombarded atoms with alpha particles and,
from the way in which the particles were deflected, derived an
image of atomic structure. Atoms turned out to be anything but
tiny marbles. They contained as much void, in scale, as intergalactic space. Small planetlike charges whirled about a sunlike center

122

which held them by electric force. Later it was discovered that the nucleus was only one hundred thousandth the size of the whole atom.

Inquiry into this new primary unit confirmed the existence of two subnuclear particles, first the proton (so-named) and then the neutron. While the proton had a positive charge, the neutron had no charge. Each had a mass two thousand times that of the electrons that circled the nucleus, and they were so close to the system's center that they themselves sped continually through the nucleus at 40,000 miles a second. This demonstrates clearly the limitations of our senses and our ability to grasp the relationship between matter and energy. Something moving this fast is not "matter," even if it is.

Research showed that all chemical behavior arises from the electrical characteristics of these atoms. Hence, the looseness of electrons through a metal allow electrical current to move through it. Meanwhile, the atoms, in their struggle to recoup the lost electrons, crowd close together, making the metals also hard and durable.

Light was now understood as a very smooth mask for the chaos of electrons annihilating each other, which itself was only one possible way of looking at the complex interaction of opposite charges. The particles of light born in the Sun carry their electrical (electron) energy to the Earth, where they are converted into living materials by structures built out of previously arriving atoms from the Sun and the local nebular cloud. The Earth continues to incorporate an infinitesimal part of the unraveling Sun.

Heisenberg discovered that there was extra energy within the atom—not very much, but enough to make particles of light and gamma rays that lasted for a fraction of a millisecond. The energy was fictional in that it never existed in a concrete locatable sense, but it was real in that the world stood on it. The light may have been borrowed, but the loan had been repaid in time since the dawn of the universe. Its absolute limits were set in a term discovered by Planck and called Planck's Constant. Along with Einstein's measure of the conversion of mass into energy, this inexplicable process laid the groundwork for the very existence of nature.

These "virtual" particles were light itself. Drawn between electrical charges, they carried the message of the electrical force because they *were* the electrical force. Electricity was a chain of transmission, not action at a distance.

If an electron and its anti-electron actually exist, then they have already annihilated each other and left a particle of light. So, although no antimatter is discernible, somehow it is as responsible as matter for bringing particles into being. Scientists and science fiction writers have since imagined whole universes of antimatter necessarily separated from this one.

By the 1930s and 1940s, force-carrying particles were hypothesized on the basis of the same borrowed energy. These were later found in cosmic rays. Named mesons, they came from the violent destruction of protons, prior to which they held the atomic nucleus together. Particles and forces were becoming more and more the same thing.

In the new universe of subatomic matter, particles collide continuously at high speeds. They are split into other particles, but these are not different or smaller or less; they are new particles of the same kind. There is no further partibility. Matter can be divided, subdivided, torn apart, but it never falls into more primary pieces, because the energy of its dismantling goes to create new particles. The mucilage of light and the particle field holds together substance.

It is the light quanta that give rise to the name quantum theory in the context of Planck's Constant, which gives a range to uncertainty relationships. Light quanta are neither a wave nor a particle, neither a singularity nor a radiance spread over space, and yet they are both. Matter has become like our experience of ourselves—it has a topology with qualities of dimensionality, orientability, and indivisibility. But it has no real locatability in time and space. Particles are not waves in three-dimensional space and time, but they are, in three dimensions, waves of probability. "Isolated material particles are abstractions," wrote Niels Bohr, "their properties being definable and observable only through their interaction with other systems."[1]

Nineteenth-century observers of the Sun assumed that gravity alone bound it, and that as the Sun burned off its matter, it would shrink. This might be true if the Sun were a normal sea of chemical fire. But Einstein's theory of the convertibility of mass and energy and the discovery of a strong binding nuclear force (fulfilling Newton's prophecy that there must be *another* power-ful attraction in nature holding bodies together) transformed our model of the Sun. Hydrogen is not "fire"; it burns on an atomic level under the influence of the strong nuclear force. A hydrogen Sun consumes and radiates, making new material to consume, creating particles out of energy. It is not immortal, but it is far longer-lived than the nineteenth-century star.

But what is the strong nuclear force? We can no more answer the question than we can answer the same question of gravity. We know that the strong nuclear force works in the heart of the atom, in the nucleus, and that it holds the protons and neutrons together. It is a million times stronger than the electromagnetic force which holds the electrons to the same nucleus. All parti-cles, not just those in the nucleus, have strong nuclear interac-tions, except the photon, neutrino, electron, and muon. The latter three are called leptons as a class, to distinguish them from the other particles called hadrons, which include the meson and baryon. The leptons interact by the weak nuclear force—a to-tally other characteristic of fields of matter, which neutralizes electric charges in about half the nuclear matter of the stars, thereby allowing atoms heavier than hydrogen to be created without annihilation first by the electric force. In a sense, the weak force creates the neutral basis of matter by changing pro-tons into neutrons. It is a minor deed carried out in a very small place, but that small place is everywhere and everything, and without it we would not have much of a universe. It is the weak force inside the atom which causes changes in the atomic nucle-us, protecting complex elements as they build up in the stars.

The tiny neutral particles called neutrinos are by-products of the weak force. Until 1980, they were thought to have no mass, but recently an infinitesimal mass was discovered, which be-comes significant when we consider the number of neutrinos in the universe. Still, they travel right through the core of the Earth without interaction. They react only to gravity (and barely, be-cause of their high velocity) and to the weak force. Since the weak force is truly weak, they act hardly at all. Predicted by

Wolfgang Pauli in 1930, neutrinos were not found until 1956 in a nuclear reactor. They are far too flimsy to build much with, but without their tiny adjustments, the universe would have been too electric to complexify and differentiate.

The weak force came to be understood as a kind of meta-electrical entity. If the electrical force became stormy, the weak force would ripple through it. In the death of a star, neutrino pressure via the weak force would generate swarms of elements and ultimately send out ripples, waves which work to break up the stellar body. In a very large universe, such brief disruptions spew a lot of complex matter.

Compared to all this nuclear activity and even to the electromagnetic force, gravity is extremely weak, but its power is its universality and action over a distance. It resembles not a force at all but the cosmological constant, the spider whose web is light and time. Gravity is minimal with small objects; yet, as matter becomes denser, gravity overrides everything else and sculpts stars, galaxies, planets, and moons out of raw material, ignoring the subnuclear forces that give it matter to amass.

In the 1960s, scientists came to prefer an alternative interpretation to protons and neutrons as the basic indivisible particles of matter. Yes, on one level, the weak force seemingly transformed a proton into a neutron. But on another level, it really altered something within the proton, a sub-subatomic entity that was named a "quark" by Murray Gell-Mann, an Israeli physicist working at the California Institute of Technology (for the James Joyce line: "Three quarks for Muster Mark"[2]). Protons and neutrons were now said to be composed of two kinds of quarks each. The proton had two up quarks and one down, the neutron two downs and one up. This was the basis of what they were. Now the weak force had a specific task assigned to it: it changed an up into a down quark.

Despite a subsequent worldwide search, including the bombarding of hadrons with extremely high energies, quarks have not yet been found; it is possible that they cannot be found, that proton and neutron are impenetrable. Moreover, there is a question of whether they really exist or are just a way of portraying the structure of subatomic interactions.

Where does this leave us? In molecules there are atoms, in the atom there is a nucleus, in the nucleus a proton, in the proton a quark. But is the quark the final denomination? Is the fact that quarks cannot be liberated from protons an indication that there is no more? Scientists have since hypothesized pre-quarks, called preons, that give the quarks their peculiar characteristics, but this can quickly become an endless path down another causeway. The eternal subdivision of matter, like the eternal universe, is a moral and cosmological issue.

The concept of quarks arose from a need to define an underlying symmetry in the world of particles. With three types of quark and anti-quark, baryon and meson patterns could be described as quark interactions. The quarks become actual points of singularity without structure but generating all structure. They could not really be totally structureless or nothing would form, but they must go beyond the limits of our ability to detect structure.

The first patterning characteristic of protons was discovered in the 1960s before the idea of quarks; it was called strangeness by Gell-Mann. Strangeness was a real thing, not a metaphor and not "another thing" that was also strange. (*Strange* shares a Greek root with the words *exterior* and *external*.) Strange particles existed longer than others, but their strangeness eventually ended. Neutralized by the weak force, the particles became ordinary. There were nonstrange particles, strange particles, doubly strange particles, and even triply strange particles. These went on to have one, two, or three extra lives before emerging without strangeness. During the process, they shed particles. Eventually, scientists added a sideways quark (determining strangeness) to up and down ones to create a triadic structure for quarks. It may sound like puzzles and mazes, but it is meant to be real. Somewhere inside us, particles are shifting and shuffling quarks, keeping not only us but our atoms "alive."

In the mid-sixties, a new force was introduced to the quark realm: color. The quarks were not themselves colored (they could not be, as they are prior to light), but they behaved in relationship to each other in a way that resembled color in the building up of white light. The quark-dynamic binding force could be conceived of as chromodynamic, with six metaphorical colors: red with its anti-color turquoise, green with its anti-color mauve, and blue with its anti-color yellow.

Color force was no mild thing; in fact, if quark theory was used as the simplifying base for nuclear theory, then color force was actually the prime source of the strong nuclear force.

Particles themselves had no color: they were white; but they carried color, and color was what held them together. Any of the quarks could take on any color, and any of the anti-quarks could take on any anti-color. The color relations were conceived as stringlike, operating at close distances and indissoluble, held together by forces called gluons. The gluons would flow between the proton's quarks, and the colors would consequently change. As one got closer and closer to a quark, the color force, because of its stringlike quality, would not increase; instead it would grow weaker, because quarks too close would have no tautness. If the string were snapped, however, one would simply have new identical particles forming at each end. This is why we could not isolate and free the single quarks. They were there in the symmetry, but any disturbance continued to generate the symmetry anew.

To upness, downness, and strangeness, another flavor of quark was added in 1974, the charmed quark. It was a fourth kind of quark, whose property was to increase the formation rate of proton-category particles from combinations of other quarks. Charm was subtle, and it was named in keeping with its behavior. Even though we could not actually point to what its elimination would mean. It somehow complicated the basic underlying symmetry of matter, adding new possible kinds of particles to the substratum of the universe.

Charmed quarks combined with strange quarks in weak force interactions. They were heavier and had more energy than ordinary quarks. In fact, charm and strangeness were linked and interdependent.

In the Big Bang, when the universe was tight and the nuclear and weak force dominated the actual deep sky of the heavens, when interstellar and intra-atomic were the same field, charm and strangeness were no doubt in abundance. Charm is a most ancient characteristic of the universe. It is pre-Cambrian on a cosmic scale. Strangeness is more Palaeozoic. Both forces retreated into the microscopic realm as the universe spread out. Then *we* formed to see the long-range dispersed sky and the foreshortened microscopic sky. Charm and strangeness were sequestered within, for they could not go outside into the thinness of space. We and they depend on each other, for they require beings such as us somehow to emerge from the Flux to name them in symmetry and number pairs, and we then require them to have been in existence virtually forever for beings such as we are to arise and describe them instead of some other sterile or vagabond universe.

There was no center to the explosion that created the universe. Everything detonated at once. Everywhere was the center. Everything was blown from everything else, spreading the conflagration into space. But the original substance was so dense that it took billions of years for it to thin out into our present array of black night with patches of creationary sludge. The sky, by this proposition, is a splatter—not a splatter *against* something, as white paint on a dark wall, but a splatter *into* waves of gravitation and time-space created by the electro-atomic composition of the stuff itself. It spread radiatively, vibratorily. And now it hangs there, ingots still burning, hot stars. Some of the original mulch is still stuck together in nebulae and galaxies, but even those are rushing apart.

The dynamics of the night sky are not that different from those of the Winnebago Indian creation myth in which the sky was "shat" by Coyote against the deep black, with the Milky Way the main stream of cosmic defecation. The old Greek image of milk squirted from Hera's breast, giving rise to the Via Lactea of ancient Rome and the Middle Ages, has some of the sense of splatter and streaming too. A deluge filling all space and time simultaneously is not a possibility in either Greek or Siouan mythology, but the explosion and the vibration are. The poet Gary Snyder takes an Asian image into a cosmic fertility vision:

> Our portion of fire
>   at this end of the milky way
> (the Tun-huang fragments say, Eternal Light)
> Two million years from M 31
>   the galaxy in Andromeda—

My eyes sting with these relics.
Fingers mark time.
   semen is everywhere
Two million seeds in a spurt.[3]

The unintentional lewdness of the "Big Bang" is appropriate to our identification with star violence and star ecstasy. The pulsing, gushing qualities of living tissue connect it to a primordial pollen. Our flood of consciousness in awakening is also the cosmic dawn. Even the famous peeing in the grass under the full night of white-hot ash brings on a oneness astronomers do not always experience in their eavesdropping upon the immortal act. The sheer coursing and warmth of fluid with its *chi* ember upon the ground and its whisper of molecules returns the sense of all fire as water. Flying squirrel, penguin, gibbon, rattlesnake—each softly fashioned upon the spine of yin and yang—contain the symmetry of the original universe.

Isotropy is established by the structure of the explosion: everything is rushing away from everything else; thus, all galaxies are fleeing from each other, as seen from any place in the universe. There was a moment in physics when it was thought that we were back at the center of things: they were all rushing away from us. They are. But we have no special privilege.

The Big Bang theory was formulated in the late 1930s and early 1940s after Hubble's interpretation of the red shift. The theory might have remained obscure, as at the beginning, but it has grown on us, and in recent years it has taken over astronomy. We had no real alternative. The sky was not static; it showed recession in telescopes and radio waves. The initial implication was that some innate force was thrusting creation into new zones, but no such force has been found. The universe is expanding because everything was tossed outward by an ancient explosion of unknown origin. It is as soulless and unredemptive as that. We just happened to get mixed up in the middle of it—perhaps at the beginning, surely when we discovered it. Now it seems that all those ancient bison at Lascaux and Egyptian pyramids and Mayan astrological temples and Ming vases are part of the terrible affair too. So are the Australian Aboriginal dreamtime beasts and the Bushmen hunters pursuing giraffes and zebras. There was a shoot-out on Times Square. Principals un-known. Motives likewise. And here we all are.

The Big Bang minimizes the problem of whether the universe was infinite or not at the beginning or is infinite now. If it was infinite at the beginning, the explosion was infinite too. If it was not, but still gave the galaxies escape velocity, then they are moving infinitely into a space-time that is determined by their properties, or, more accurately, by the properties of their sub-atomic particles.

The universe has no net electric charge. It does not annihilate itself electrically. The numbers of electrons and protons in the whole thing must be exactly equal, not 99.999 percent equal but exactly equal. This is a condition for us to have a universe at all, or for matter to form without being destroyed in the embryo. It is necessary that powerful electricity be balanced and at bay for the relatively weak charges of gravity to take over the mold-ing process and to shape a "big," or at least a chunky, universe, with atoms containing complex composite nuclei. Electrical charge is such that whenever it is changed locally, it creates its opposite charge in perfect and continuous balance. It is the pow-erful underlying yin-yang which allows an overlying amorphous geography.

If the explosion was not sufficient to propel the galaxies out-ward forever, the universe will eventually contract, condense, and bounce back out again. In such a view, there is no distinction between our past and our future. We can look forward, cosmic-ally, to exactly the thing that gave birth to us. Suddenly, the nearby galaxies will begin to blueshift, while the more ancient light of remote galaxies will continue to redshift—or, actually, we will see its red shift longer because it will take time for news of the change out there to get to us by light. Millions of years will pass, and the contracting universe will not affect us any more than the expanding universe does now. All of the hydrogen and much of the helium that provides the fuel for the stars was created in the Big Bang. There is no other way to create hydro-gen that we know of. Without the Big Bang, its origin is a com-plete mystery, and the posited explosion merely gives the mys-tery an agency. Millions of years from now, most of the interstellar gas will have been consumed in the stars, and few, if any, new stars will be being born. When the universe has reached a hundredth of the size it is now, we will have the night sky that Olbers saw in a conundrum or a nightmare once, as bright as the day sky. Eventually, molecules will break down into atoms, atoms into electrons and other nuclei. It will take thousands of years for big changes, but as the cosmos becomes a plasma millions of degrees hot, it will begin to change in a matter of days, rising by millions of degrees per hour. Not only will all matter disappear, but the more complex particles will vanish with it—the work of star and atoms—and stars and atoms will merge (the telescope will show the same thing the microscope does); the microwave background will collapse once again into a single howling roar. This will last for either an eternity or a brief fraction of a second, depending on how one views the obliteration of time. And then the Big Bang will occur again.

Wrote the poet Edward Dorn:

> every change of placement
> the shift of every leaf
> is a function
> of the universe which
> moves outward from its composed center
> 40 bilynyrs. Then returns. . . .
> our given pulse
> hits inside this
> everymoment we live
> to hear this
> COSMOS[4]

It is a pulse touching inside every mountain Ainu chanting, every juggler holding three or four stones in motion about him, every pair of lovers seeking their rhythm, every fern and starfish, every dervish dancing. It all happened one starry night, and we do not know if it is our faraway vision of spirit or simply, inside us, the complication of matter hung on the loom to the end of the universe. Gravity carries it to the wheels against iron in the clatter of the train along its tracks. It is our heartbeat. It is an avalanche. It is also delicate beyond measure, which is why we feel heartache as well and can neither relieve nor locate it. We must drift in a multiplicity. And then:

> the moment
> approaching when all of it
> will be stilled in a shimmy[5]

The ripple in the pond is also the explosion creating the universe. It begins and ends and hangs for an eternal second—the same one inside us when the insight comes and when we feel ourselves a unity.

The universe begins at an incredible temperature of millions of millions of degrees. Such a universe cannot be described, even hypothetically, for it is a universe only of quantum mechanical relationships. Gravitational fields would have been so powerful that particles themselves would be created by such fields, but that presupposes that the concept of particle has any meaning at such a temperature. No message about anything could get even as far as one wavelength, so size, shape, and location would be meaningless. There would be only one of each of them, and that one would be everything and everywhere. It is in perhaps this first ten-thousandth of a second that something primordial comes into being—the quarks. They buzzed around. This was their universe, their home. The strong and weak nuclear forces had as much range as gravity and electromagnetism. The Big Bang, with its quark-charmed strange universe, is the moment of determinative structure, and the millions of millions of years and other temporal units since then are nothing more than the particles fulfilling their potentialities as heat and pressure diminish.

To form the present universe from this bath of superheated matter, the first few minutes of cooling were crucial, if we can accept the eternity of minutes in the timeless flow before there was a Sun or an orbit in which to find units of time. The temperature first cooled enough for there to be protons and neutrons in the complexity of atomic nuclei. Hydrogen stands at the upper end of the pre-atomic series at a moment when it is doubtful whether atoms will be formed at all. Once the crisis is passed, cosmological and stellar nucleosyntheses begin to manufacture denser nuclei.

The early universe of the first few minutes was made primarily of photons, electrons, neutrinos, and anti-neutrinos. It was made of light and radiation, the same light and radiation that continues to flow from stellar centers. About a millionth of it became nuclear matter at first, and all of that was hydrogen and helium, about 75 percent hydrogen. After a matter of years, perhaps hundreds or thousands, a cool gas began forming, the gas of the galaxies and suns. Electrons joined with the nuclei to form atoms. Gaseous matter drifted in among the radiation, gravitation wheeled it off into galaxies, and galaxies spawned local space and systems of stars and planets.

A possible contradiction of the Big Bang theory is posed by the question: why were the thermal components not blown to bits far beyond the point where they could condense into galaxies? Theoretical physics requires that the universe have been in a state of statistical thermal equilibrium at a point before the formation of galaxies and stars. All subsequent prediction about earlier or later states comes from an assumption of an intermediate uniform state. In that sense, the Big Bang theory, like so many other modern suppositions since the application of natural selection to genetics and Emile Durkheim's discovery that suicide occurs in predictable percentages, is a statistical theory.[6] The Big Bang is not a concrete thing. We know it as the resolution of the distribution of things in time and space and their mathematics. It is a demographic conclusion about the universe. The 3° Kelvin microwave background of space, recognized first in 1965, is considered to be an echo of the explosion that occurred ten billion years before. It is a prediction of what would be found if a fabric, namely everything, had expanded a thousand times, with equivalently homogeneous cooling, from a time when it was 3000° K., at which time matter and radiation were in thermal equilibrium. The universal background of radiation is the universality of the explosion and the evenness of the dissipation from an opaque superheated space. In such a pure universe of heat and number, matter develops only as a contamination. That is a favorite word of contemporary cosmologists, and its irony must be intentional. It is lucky that this contamination is ultimately capable of feeling relative heat, looking into the fabric to see the portals of time, and developing "numbers" that must, in some way, be crude replicas of the aboriginal sky.

Once matter forms and coalesces into clumps and islands, the rate of expansion is handed over to gravitation. We return, almost nostalgically, to the Newtonian universe. If we go backward in time from here, we require Planck again and quantum mechanics—that is, we must go forward a few centuries in physics. If we proceed directly from here according to Newton, we go through Laplace to James Jeans, who determined mathematically the smallest mass that was capable of condensing gravitationally, thus leading to a theory of star formation. From Jeans's mass, we go forward to Heisenberg and Einstein, toward spacetime, uncertainty theory, and the microwave background. Once we get this universe cooled off enough, we can return to our daily Newtonian lives. All of these images and ideas flow in a circle, giving rise to each other.

Big Bang theory is unrelenting and unredemptive. We are trapped in it by the fact that our minds, like the primal nebula, are too dense to let go of it, in the same way that they cannot let go of materialism, progress, consumption of materials, and even an idea of themselves as something that requires explanation. We hold to these images as we hold to war. And as our reason tries to pull us away from war and destruction, something else compels us to return or risk having it thought of by someone else, and to our own disadvantage. We are drawn equally to pornographic events and torture. If it is possible, we must do it; our minds decree so, and we are never the first. Almost as we think it, someone else is there before us. So men are torn apart on wheels and thrown alive to hungry dogs.

But it was also a cosmologist of the night sky, G. I. Gurdjieff, who said that if soldiers in an army could see their true cosmic position *for just an instant,* they would all throw down their weapons and go home. That is, if they could see themselves against the stars, and the Earth in the universe, and their own being born, being incarnated in that universe.[7]

We have reaped the materialistic wheel that we naively sowed, and we have learned something from it. That learning is now alone what can change us. We could also get stuck here, and it is a barren place. If our destiny remains such, we cannot help destroying ourselves, for, as the humanist philosophers divined, there is no longer any reason to live.

In Big Bang theory, our identity is given only by such a cataclysmic event that it could be at best a scar, the earmark of a primal trauma that is borne by the individuality of everything. Thus, the echo of primeval fears in the jungles of ancient man was also the echo of our own matter forming at the bottom of our unconscious bodies and their simultaneous nightmare.

Steady State theory is still quite violent, but it does not require the single big devastation, and it even allows for creative fountains in multiple dimensions of matter, and for a stability and a grace. It is interesting and perhaps terrifying that all the new evidence is in favor of the Big Bang. But is the terror a cosmic one or a cultural one? And do we fear space more than our own nihilism and its residue throughout our civilization?

Touching and powerful, and also sad, is the ending of a popular modern cosmology by Steven Weinberg: *The First Three Minutes.* As Weinberg reviews the implications of Big Bang theory, there is rebellion from the readers in my library copy, with insults in the margins and at the ends of paragraphs. People seem to feel that if the author had had some imagination, in terms of uncertainty theory and black holes, he could have created a "happy ending" in the same way that *Star Trek* episodes discover a psychic universe within the dregs of this physical one. Whenever the warmongers and the materialists are about to have their way in the *Star Trek* universe, another aspect of creation emerges, usually personified by highly evolved telepathic and even bodiless beings who have found immortality and a collective nirvana. We have been brainwashed by these endings. They are our inheritance as much as Big Bang, but for a scientist committed to seeing the present era through, there is no other outcome than the one Weinberg resigns himself to:

> However all these problems may be resolved, and whichever cosmological model proves correct, there is not much of comfort in any of this. It is almost irresistible for humans to believe that we have some special relation to the universe, that human life is not just a more-or-less farcical outcome of a chain of accidents reaching back to the first three minutes, but that we were somehow built in from the beginning. As I write this I happen to be in an airplane at

30,000 feet, flying over Wyoming en route home from San Francisco to Boston. Below, the earth looks very soft and comfortable—fluffy clouds here and there, snow turning pink as the sun sets, roads stretching across the country from one town to another. It is very hard to realize that this all is just a tiny part of an overwhelmingly hostile universe. It is even harder to realize that this present universe has evolved from an unspeakably unfamiliar early condition, and faces a future extinction of endless cold or intolerable heat. The more the universe seems comprehensible, the more it also seems pointless.[8]

Since quarks and atoms bear so little relation to who we are now, except for the fact that we have dreamed them up from sparse evidence and use their mathematics, it appears almost as though we have originated from something alien, something that has no moral value. The cosmology of ancient and tribal peoples did not have this problem, because they began from moral value and moved outward. The myth hero of the Jicarilla Apache of New Mexico speaks:

This earth is my body. The sky is my body. The seasons are my body. The water is my body too. . . . The world is just as big as my body. The world is as large as my word. And the world is as large as my prayers. The seasons are only as great as my body, my words, and my prayer. It is the same with the waters; my body, my words, my prayers are greater than the waters. Whoever believes me, whoever listens to what I say, will have long life. . . . Don't think I am just in the east, south, west, or north. The earth is my body. I am there. I am all over. Don't think I stay only under the earth or up in the sky, or only in the seasons, or on the other side of the waters. These are all my body. It is the truth that the underworld, the sky, the waters, are all my body.[9]

In Qabalistic cosmology, the creation emanates from God in such a way that everything is contained in everything else. A single thought from the Divine Mind becomes many thoughts, and the many thoughts become boundless creation. It is another isotropy. Where anyone stands, he stands in the center of all worlds. The stars may be the detritus of an explosion, but that is the illusion of one layer; they are also the candles from which angels light worlds. They are the image through which we see such candles.

For some Oriental philosophers, our incarnation itself creates the world illusion. In Buddhist lore, this manifestation and our desire for it are the same thing and serve as a creative emanation of each other. From these perspectives, the Big Bang is a great paradox and a test for man.

Weinberg concludes his book:

> But if there is no solace in the fruits of our research, there is at least some consolation in the research itself. Men and women are not content to comfort themselves with tales of gods and giants, or to confine their thoughts to the daily affairs of life; they also build telescopes and satellites and accelerators, and sit at their desks for endless hours working out the meaning of the data they gather. The effort to understand the universe is one of the very few things that lifts human life a little above the level of farce, and gives it some of the grace of tragedy.[10]

Farce and tragedy are the two great muses who dance upon our century, and always together. Samuel Beckett provides us the same axiom. *Murphy* opens: "The sun shone, having no alternative, on the nothing new."[11] And at the end of *Waiting for Godot,* Vladimir says:

> All I know is that the hours are long, under these conditions, and constrain us to beguile them with proceedings which—how shall I say—which may at first sight seem reasonable, until they become a habit. You may say it is to prevent our reason from foundering. No doubt. But has it not long been straying in the night without end of the abyssal depths? That's what I sometimes wonder.[12]

This premonition falls like a shadow over all of human history from here on in—because we know so much about everything and because our despair cannot even contain in it the hope of a future golden age. The formal seriousness with which Weinberg states it almost belies the real seriousness of the problem. It is not a new problem at all; it is not a new paradox. Hindu sages thousands of years ago would have predicted exactly such an outcome for big State-funded stargazing programs in the West.

Estragon replies to Vladimir: "We are all born mad. Some remain so."[13]

11

The History of Western Astronomy VIII: The Creation

THE BIG BANG THEORY tells us about a creationary explosion from which matter came into being and continued to expand and dissipate—a fireball racing outward in all directions at incredible speeds. At first it wasn't even matter; it was pure radiation, energy, in which matter formed as a contamination in the way that ice will suffocate a pond in a severe winter. Summer ended for the original farmlands and vineyards of light, and in almost all areas of the cosmos they withered and died. But their seeds became the loom of a new cosmos. The first monstrous protogalaxies were torn apart, and billions upon billions of stars were formed in second-generation galaxies.

As the primeval nebula swirled tumbling through space, its fabric tore apart, radiated, and condensed anew. Tatters collected around cores, and from the cores gravitation reached out; whirlpools of starry tincture swept up the matter from space around them until they were all that was left, fiery beacons in a cold winter desert, only the thinnest of radioactive veils to settle over the rest of time and space. That veil is all the thinner now.

Big Bang tells us that the pure and original universe is fire, fire of a nature to make the fires of the suns themselves seem cold, fire in which matter cannot form. The stars are then the ice in this cooling pond, and the nebulae a flowing white field of cosmological hydrogen. They are cauls. Cauls hot enough to form suns. But these too are dissipating. Unless there is some unknown spring supplying fresh water to the cosmos.

The forces of matter are universal: gravity and its handmaidens work in the universe at large as they do in the minutest sphere. A galactic dust storm, giving birth to star systems, is obedient to the same ancient law as the fog off the ocean or the north wind carrying dust. Matter goes where it is compelled and where there is least resistance, be it silt, water, or hydrogen fire. The various spiral and ring shapes suggest the underlying turbulence, composition, and attractions.

Within the original hydrogen whirlpools, smaller eddies formed. Rotating clouds of hydrogen dust contracted into dense massive objects, hundreds of times denser than water in their cores and with millions of degrees of temperature. Of course, these are our flimsy millions, formed on the cold side of light. No doubt the savants of the original golden universe would consider the star centers the last almost burned-out embers of a moderate heat, almost too faint to measure. The planets are the ashes of those stars—the bits left when solar gravity claimed all the rest.

The primordial nebula was at least 99.999 percent pure hydrogen and helium. The galaxies formed in a brief time about a million years after the Big Bang, when matter was dense enough to overcome dispersive radiation. The other elements were built in the nuclear furnaces of the stars, where intra-atomic rearrangements took place and new atoms were formed. Although they no doubt take their character from the unknown particles that lie within them, they contain *the* original structures for us. Our entire world is built upon the properties arising from the numerical relationships inside these atoms. The shininess of metal, the bright flare of phosphorus, the cool miscibility of oxygen, the deep mimelike life-chains of our grandfather carbon atom are all the result of intra-atomic shuffling, like the shifting of beads in a moiré pattern. The elemental properties show up in flower shapes, animal behavior, and human thought. The "meaning" of the elements that stand within them is beyond us; it is of such a pure algebra that we can read it only as numbers set against other numbers, things we have come to call "color" and "charm" and "strangeness" because of their seeming resemblance in their mathematical behavior to secondary qualities and images of our own lavish microcosm. Since these characteristics come into being in the first thousandth of a second of the Explosion, when nothing can mean anything, scientists have compensated for the void by giving them garish and familiar images.

The interstellar gas would have remained hydrogen and helium if it were not for the supernova explosions that enriched it with the heavier elements for planets of water, stones, and flesh. In the primordial cloud, matter is young and simple. In the stars, it becomes complex *on an atomic level*. On the planets, atoms form molecules; characteristics that were utterly concealed on the stars startle the universe.

The transmutation of hydrogen into helium gives off the photons of the night sky. Without the stars to breathe hydrogen, there would be no planets, no stone, no water, and no life.

From helium, carbon and oxygen arise, followed by sulphur, silicon, etc. There are ninety-two such naturally produced elements (including hydrogen), but iron, the twenty-sixth, is about as complicated material as the stars' interiors generate before they are exhausted and fall to the weak nuclear force. Elements heavier than iron, such as gold, lead, and so on, could only have been formed in even greater explosions.

The deaths of stars are not simple; both gravity and the nuclear force must collect their due. Some massive stars become supernovae, burning their own ash, collapsing from gravity, imploding, and then erupting again suddenly and violently. During their last explosive gasp, heavy nuclei can capture additional neutrons and form elements more complex than iron. The debris splattered with heavier atoms is then broadcast to the universe in cosmic rays.

In the constant decay and regeneration of stellar material, there are many different types of cataclysmic events, each contributing its own grades of matter to the milk of the nebulae and galaxies from which new suns and stars are born. We inherit the molecules of our bodies and the iron and tin of the Earth's crust from a crumbling dynasty of original and secondary stars. The death of kings provides the primal stuff of a new world-age. We inherit our silver and gold and our radium and uranium from second-generation stars. Our Sun is a third-generation star, made of the slag of dead suns. All except its hydrogen and helium was synthesized in stars far away. The Sun came out of a stellar nursery somewhere in the Milky Way before arriving at its present locale in the System. Its sister suns, formed with it in the nebula, lie unknown to us in other parts of the Milky Way.

It was in the ancient rocks of the original Earth that the atoms of carbon, nitrogen, oxygen, sodium, potassium, silver, and gold gained their freedom from fire; they oozed upward, filling the oceans with water, the air with gases, and providing the variety of substances for accretion into the terrestrial scenery. The blue of our sky is a nitrogen hue.

Radioactive elements such as thorium and uranium were included in the original rocks, and they continue to provide a source of internal geological heat. Such heavy elements are unstable because the strong nuclear force in them is only about a hundred times stronger than the electric force. So electric repulsion between protons tends to decay their nuclei. When the nuclei split, the fragments rebound, releasing energy and eliminating some of the overburdening mass.

The Earth's size is a precise balance between the gravity holding it and the collective electric force in the atoms of all its materials, from its rare and noble gases to its shifting bedrock and molten nickel-iron core. When we think about energy these days—fossil fuels, nuclear energy, hot springs, volcanoes, tides, wind—clean energy or dirty energy—renewable energy or nonrenewable energy—we should realize that a bank of stellar energy is built into the planet. It is not some after-the-fact thing we invented, like automobiles or oil wells; the planet is held together by networks of atomic and molecular energy, a minute by-product of which we tap.

Once atoms build molecules and molecules enter into chemical compounds, the situation becomes very unstarlike, with solids, liquids, and volatile gases. Planets are cooled, molded jungles, woven of elements gathering thickness and texture over billions of years.

As atoms, molecules, and compounds join in overlapping lattices, fuse and differentiate layer after layer, a complex and delicate geography forms, totally different from anything in the stars and galaxies or suggested by the fireball. Matter is remarkable long before it spawns life or intelligence: it is a surprise and a delight in a universe of such violent and bastard ancestry.

On Earth the elements are in constant interaction on both the molecular and chemical levels. Water rushes onto the beaches and sweeps the residue of stones into its solvent; sea creatures are left on the sand to decompose and be ground into stones. Most notably, two gases, hydrogen and oxygen, under the proper conditions, can form a liquid, a liquid which remains at much higher temperatures than its constituents, and one with unique properties. Without it there would be no human life. It provides oceans, puffy clouds, glacial icebergs, rain, and the moist sweetness of our flesh.

If we look back over creation, it seems an unlikely thing. The planets are built of the materials of the stars, and the stars are simply the hot ash of the original explosion. What causes anything to happen, except for secondary explosions and gross distribution of matter, is the intrinsic capability of atomic substance to form texture and structure. Cooled off and organized on small spheroids, matter arranges itself in intricate patterns and generates materials that are inconceivable in terms of the separate stars or the vastness of space. These materials are everything we know and understand.

There is no evading the fact that we are made of star-stuff. We contain its atoms, its electrical fields, its particles and nuclear forces, its decay. It is our destiny, and we are its destiny. Anything we are, it must be too; but anything it is, we must share. No wonder Joseph Stalin and Mao Zedong worried about what science would find inside the atom. The future possibility for a social order lies in what men and women really are. And that lies in the nature of matter. For Mao, quantum theory was a confirmation of a revolutionary and communist social order, and he supported Heisenberg's atom. He even came out in favor of quarks and pre-quarks because he felt the dialectic should descend through matter to the minutest degree.

It is strange to think that the subatomic particles, in their brief mute lives, might spell out the destiny of the peasants of China in a world as far from them as the quasars are from us. But the issue is a real one, and Marxists have kept as close an eye on the products of cyclotrons as they have on the protean matrilineal and partrilineal configurations of primitive societies, searching for the inevitability of an evolving universe. After all, we come along a single and particular path, and our evolutionary line contains only one set of molecular and genetic potentials at any one point. On the path from star-stuff to consciousness, we incorporate everything we pick up along the way, every cell and every lizard, and any one of them is capable of a revolution or an act of vision in the darkness of a night.

The raw creation seems alien to us. We seem strangers to ourselves. The inner sky is not any more placid and domesticated than the outer one; our cells remain tiny stars, i.e., aspects of the same extension of space through the properties of matter. We are this, finally and forever. We are other things too, in our thoughts and philosophies, but these other things must also be true to protons, neutrons, electrons, and their components, or to the real things to which we have given such names. We look upon the sky in its vast openness, its cavernous depth, but the sky is simply a field of opacity.

And it is everywhere. It is the embryo, layer of cells by layer of cells, each of which is a sky to the infant bursting from the cocoon imposed by some previous cell, some previous sky. It is paramecia pouring into the lens like stars. It is the elemental rock of the planet, each individual gem of which cracks open to show another gem. All of this rock was resplendent galactic fire to the hypothetical inhabitants of another world at a far earlier time. It is inside the bud and the fruit of the flower. And it is also inside the mind of man, inside him so many times that he no longer knows whether he is coming or going but seems somehow to walk straight down the hallway of an invisible house in an unknown city.

It is no idle conceit that our Earth is a mirror of the heavens and we are made of the stars. Magical law says: "Every man and every woman is a star."[1] Science says this in its own way. We are so, first, in the Big Bang; second, as we are made of materials either directly from the body of the Sun or from the same hot cloud that the Sun came from; and third, as the Earth is showered with atomic materials from throughout the universe. Our hair and eyes and flesh and freckles contain atoms from remote stars, atoms that have been in suns, in Antares, Betelgeuse, Sirius, and Vega. But, once again, these are our names, not theirs.

Life seeps out of unruly electrical and molecular fields, but it tames them. In fact, it has tamed them layer by layer over billions of years, so the flowers and the flesh hardly show their fiery atomic makeup. Where in a kiss are the molecules? They have "disappeared" entirely into the structure; yet they have built for aeons for such a moment. Where is the hydrogen in a gull? Yet without hydrogen the gull would not nest. The sheer rigor of assembling and attuning these fields over time, assimilating matter through them and reproducing them hierarchically through themselves alone, gives a semblance of decency and philosophy to this realm. How else could the violent nuclear universe hold the delicate embryo, the soft robin's egg, in its ogre arms?

In one of the oldest Greek myths recorded by Hesiod, the sea was born of the earth asexually. She was a clone. She lay for the embrace of the sky, to whom she bore an offspring: "the thing which encloses everything, Okeanos." Eros followed, "flooding the mind and all gods and men into further nature."[2] Night was born from Chaos, and then—in loving union with its sister, the Underworld (Erebus)—spawned the Bright Sky, the Aether, and Day. The Earth bore also the starry Heaven and the high Hills to cover herself.

Chinese cosmology describes a somewhat different quality of the universe: Before the division of empty space into the clear and the turbid, a Vast Prime (*hung yuan*) alone existed. The All-Highest Lord Lao opened the heavens. A raw germinal stuff poured forth, immediately separating into yin and yang, the receptive and active poles of nature. All subsequent form germinated from their polarity. As in Steady State Theory, the Void is no longer a void; it is a loom of potentiality, a warp on which matter forms.[3]

The original stuff of creation was fleecy white like the Milky Way. The name for cosmos, *hun-t'un,* shares a root with *wonton.* As it drops down into the microcosm, it is a tasty dough indeed. It grows less by expansion and more by polarity, fission, and inversion. The sculpting of a universe from without is imaginary only. Nothing touches it on the outside. It contains, like the embryo, the principle of its own shape, and continues to emerge from itself by divisions more and more complexly.[4] In fact, embryogony and cosmogony may disclose the same topogenesis.

If we watch an embryo form, we have an illusion of there being an outside edge to it because we are outside it. But the principle is intrinsic. Hemispheres develop, and material passes from region to region. Some regions grow thicker and envelop others. Some material keeps reduplicating; other material "disappears." At certain unpredictable points, the embryo turns inside out, in whole or in part, and then continues to grow and differentiate. Limbs and orifices emerge as though drawn magically out of the interior substance. The creation of the sky was a similar process of turning something inside out again and again while differentiating its parts. The Chinese and the Greek versions intuit this in different ways. Creation is the simultaneous extraversion and internalization of matter. We are summoned up through the abyss, summoned by the same voice that summoned all the creatures. The birth which places each person here and repeats, for each one of them, the creation itself, is no simple matter. It is a subtle bond between cell and sky which seals us into the system. In the sixteenth century, Paracelsus wrote of a quality by which fire was joined to air, a chain which, somehow, without materiality or visibility, held nature together and bound its parts:

> As the chicken is sustained in its egg by its albumen without touching the shell, so chaos sustains the globe and prevents it from tottering. This chaos is invisible, though it appears of a light green tint. It is an intangible albumen, having the power and property of sustaining, so that the earth shall not fall from its position. . . . And as every morsel of flesh lies in its own liquid, or the generating seed in the sperm, so the stars lie in this albumen, and move therein like a bird in flight. . . .[5]

A Bushongo Bantu version from the Congo River has the entity Bumba surrounded by water and alone in the darkness:

> One day Bumba was in terrible pain. He retched and strained and vomited up the sun. After that, light spread over everything. The heat of the sun dried up the water until the black edges of the world began to show. Black

sandbanks and reefs could be seen. But there were no living things.

Bumba vomited up the moon and then the stars, and after that the night had its own light also.

Still Bumba was in pain. He strained again and nine living creatures came forth: the leopard named Koy Bumba, and Pongo Bumba the crested eagle, the crocodile, Ganda Bumba, and one little fish named Yo; next, old Kono Bumba, the tortoise, and Tsetse, the lightning, swift, deadly, beautiful like the leopard, then the white heron, Nyanyi Bumba, also one beetle, and the goat named Budi.[6]

In an Eskimo version of creation, the first man decides to burst out of the pod in which he is hanging from a beach-pea. He is astonished at himself, his arms and legs, the open pod on the vine, then this dark object with wings looking at him. It was a Raven who pushed up its beak like a mask and became a man. Then it asked the first man what he was and where he came from. When the man answered, the Raven exclaimed: "Ah! I made that vine, but did not know that anything like you would ever come from it."[7]

Zuni cosmology has the Maker and Container of All, Awonawilona, standing alone: "There was nothing else whatsoever throughout the great space of the ages save everywhere black darkness in it, and everywhere void desolation. In the beginning of the new-made, Awonawilona conceived within himself and thought outward in space, whereby mists of increase, steams potent of growth, were evolved and uplifted." He created himself in person and then caused the Sun "to exist and appear. With his appearance came the brightening of the spaces with light." Mist-clouds formed in the brightness and provided water for the "world-holding sea." Then, taking flesh-substance from his person, he "formed the seed-stuff of twain worlds, impregnating therewith the great waters." After shaping the raw lands, he spread them out with his palm downward "and into all the wrinkles and crevices thereof he set the semblance of shining yellow corn-grains; in the dark of the early world-dawn they gleamed like sparks of fire, and moved as his hand was moved over the bowl, shining up from and also moving in the depths of the water therein." So was the night sky formed and space and time wound together on the wheel. [8]

The Mayan creation myth begins by making the Void as empty as possible: "all was in suspense, all calm, in silence; all motionless, still. . . . There was nothing brought together, nothing which could make a noise, nor anything which might move, or tremble. . . . Tepei and Gucumatz came together in the darkness, in the night." They were "great sages and great thinkers," but they had been "hidden under green and blue feathers," a startling paraphernalia for pre-existence. "They talked then, discussing and deliberating; they agreed, they united their words and their thoughts. . . . While they meditated, it became clear to them that when dawn would break, man must appear." [9]

In the Aranda creation myth from central Australia, the ancestor Karora "was lying asleep in everlasting night. . . . Over him the soil was red with flowers and overgrown with many grasses."

Flowers before flowers? Grasses of the Cosmic Mind from which the prairie grasses flowed?

"And Karora was thinking, and wishes and desires flashed through his mind. Bandicoots began to come out from his navel and from his armpits. They burst through the sod above, and sprang into life." [10]

Creation occurs in primordial Tahiti when Ta'aroa breaks through his egg which "revolved in space in continuous darkness." He stands upon the great broken shell and shouts: "Who is above there? Who is below there?" There is no answer. "Who is in front there? Who is in back there?" He hears only his own voice echoing. Then the first thing he does is to take his broken shell and raise it into a dome for the sky. [11]

The Japanese embryogenesis resembles the Chinese one:

> Of old, Heaven and Earth were not yet separated, and the *In* and *Yo* [feminine and masculine principles] not yet divided. They formed a chaotic mass like an egg which was of obscurely defined limits and contained germs.
>
> The purer and clearer part was thinly drawn out, and formed Heaven, while the heavier and grosser element settled down and became Earth. [12]

Some eighteenth-century scientists believed in a primeval germ which contained in miniature an image of all of the creation that would follow, so that each succeeding generation was contained in the prior one. The skin would peel off the bud, and a new creature, identical to its ancestor (or subtly different), would arise. When all the material within the germ was expended (the microcosmic germs within germs), that line would come to an end. Ultimately all lines would come to an end.

It was only later that scientists imagined a field which could recreate itself almost forever so long as the blueprint contained in that field was not destroyed and there was nourishment to sustain it. It would take billions of years to form such a blueprint, and its survival was always a delicate matter; but once in existence, it could go on using existing mass and energy indefinitely.

"We are the end of the leeching that produced us," writes Edward Dorn. "A spoonful left at the bottom, very refined, pure stuff, the final dry powder, the dust that lives."[13]

Using the raw materials available on this planetoid in an ingenious fashion, our species has taken the smallest step back into eternity. It is also a big one, as Neil Armstrong intuited when he placed his hind limb, descendant of the phalanges of a frog and the spiny arms of a starfish, on the Moon. In overcoming an immense gravitational wall that held him in for thousands of generations, man has made a statement that would have seemed impossible, impossible forever, for a world of dragonflies and gulls. He has entered another space, however clumsily, however briefly. But this is not the way back into eternity, not the way he came. If he stares into space that way, he sees only a prison. The further he looks, in millions of light-years, the further he is from the center. Already the numbers are incomprehensible. The only way we make sense of them is to feed them into computers in greater and greater lump sums, making new exponential classes.

Our destiny in the sky is behind us and not before us. We and the stars float in the same cradle and are made of the same matter. In myth, we face each other in a concurrence beyond space and time. We are an indispensable part of their riddle, their own destiny. The consequences of walking on the Moon and sending satellites to photograph the outer planets of the Solar System are unknown at this point. But whether or not we adapt to outer space and pass to other planets, or even to another star, we share with the most remote galaxies we know, and those beyond them, a simultaneity on the inside of an unfolding virus. This is why Bumba's crocodile crawls out onto another planet in another galaxy too. This is why Karora's bandicoots flower with the birth gases of the remotest stars. This is why thought in the Mayan temples is akin, somehow, to something like thought in creatures who will never hear of us and whom we will never see. The real science fiction is the shared creation, which will never be known, and yet the intuition of it makes us who we are and gives rise to our images of fantastic beings derived from the same deep unconscious dark within us that atoms sprang from, and from them the earth and sky and protoplasm and genes of all those worlds and microcosms. Bumba's white heron is a white unknown bird flying toward the center of our galaxy, or away from it. His single bug appeared simultaneously throughout the universe, minute and unseen. This is true because there is no other truth to replace it, and any truth which replaces it will be of the same order. Because we cannot know, we must be; and in the unconscious origin of all things, knowing and being are finally the same. This is our oneness with both the Creation and the Void. And the night sky is the clearest statement, despite all that has happened to us in the subsequent turmoil of embryogenesis and local time, of who we are.

12

The History of Western Astronomy IX: Pulsars, Quasars, and Black Holes

THE 200-INCH MOUNT PALOMAR mirror was proposed in 1928, but it was not attempted for years. The glass was originally poured out of quartz by General Electric at half a million dollars' expense. It cracked, and Pyrex was used instead of quartz. Corning Glass did the pouring in New York State, and then the expensive disc was sent to Pasadena, where it was ground and polished and the mounting was built. Twenty years after it was proposed, this great eye stared into the galactic sky, and instantly man stood billions of light-years further out in space. Almost immediately, though, the radio sky, along with the X-ray, the infrared, and the ultraviolet skies, began to converge with the remote visual sky and overlap it.

The old sky was constructed of information from visible light sources. The modern astronomical universe was also made from light. But the postmodern astrophysical universe is primarily an interpretation of radio signals and other invisible wavelengths plus data from experiments in subatomic physics and relativistic equations.

When radio telescopes are aimed into the infinity of space, they record previously unknown structures and events; even if these events also give off light, their radio emission usually far exceeds their visible component. Locally in the Solar system, radio telescopes have picked up disturbed regions in the outer layers of the Sun and the immense radio noise of Jupiter, especially as broadcast in bursts during the passage of its moon Io. Used to scan our Galaxy, these devices have picked up the remnants of exploded stars, new embryonic stars, pulsing stars, and stars with flares, none of which have a visible display resembling the radio one, except for optical pulsars like the one in the Crab Nebula. If the radio "light" could be made visible, these stars would increase in brightness and dominate the sky.

Radio emissions have also been useful in "seeing" through the clutter of dust in mapping the structural features of the Galaxy itself, notably its spiral arms. Turning beyond the Galaxy, radio astronomers have discovered not only quasars but portions of other galaxies either exploding or colliding. And then all about our egg is the microwave background containing the echo of the fireball that shaped our present cosmology.

The relationship between music and the night sky is an ancient one. The stars, in their silence in the vacuum of space, are also an eternal cone of sound—sound first postulated in the Pythagorean number systems and orchestrated by Kepler in the music of the spheres. This same sound recurs in the system of Gurdjieff: the deep octaves carry something prior to matter through the dimensions of creation into this present realm of star-suns. The music of the spheres is a figure for the harmonic and orderly universe as late as the dawn of twentieth-century astronomy. The music of Bach and Mozart and Haydn is starry in the Kepler-Newton tradition, and even Chinese classical music suggests a highly ordered ethereal realm. But then radio astronomers began hearing discordant noises from the bellies of dying galaxies and stars. The modern cosmos of quasars and pulsars is also the primeval cosmos in its birth and death throes. It is the music of the primitive Earth: African drums, Balinese Ketchak, Australian Aborigine emu chanting, and the mantras of the Two-Horned Priests of the Hopi.

Pulsars were discovered in November 1967 by a British graduate student, Jocelyn Bell. Because of their extremely regular bursts of radiation, they were first thought to be intelligent signals from civilizations in space. Every possible source for such a pulse was checked: local static, equipment malfunctions, pigeons' nests in the telescope. It was not suspected until the very last that they were stars.

Since it was already accepted that stars contract and die, astronomers considered that a very large star, with enough density to convert its material into neutrons, could, instead of becoming a white dwarf, collapse into a superdense object. Such a neutron star would throb, giving off radio noise and x-rays.

The American astronomer Thomas Gold developed a hypothesis in which a rotating star could collapse into a neutron star. An old star, spinning more than a hundred times a second, would gradually slow down as it threw off its remains. The pulse would come from the whirling envelope of plasmas, an envelope held to the star by a magnetic field and strengthened ten billion times by the compacting of materials and the conserving of magnetic force lines.

The original pulsar showed up, in the words of its discoverer, as "this particular bit of scruff" in the constellation Vulpecula (The Little Fox), a modern figure which the seventeenth-century Polish astronomer Johannes Hevelius wedged in between the Arrow and the Swan at a point where the Milky Way splits into two branches. "I wished," said Hevelius, "to place a fox and a goose in the space of the sky well fitted to it; because such an animal is very cunning, voracious and fierce. Aquila and Vultur are of the same nature, rapacious and greedy." [1]

The most swiftly-rotating and powerful pulsar is the one in the Crab Nebula; in fact, it may have exuded the immense cloud of filaments making up the nebula itself. A strong young pulsar lies in the The Sails (Vela) of the constellation Argo.

Gold offered a model in which pulsars could serve as an explanation for the abundant "cosmic rays." Composed almost entirely of atomic nuclei and traveling the universe at speeds approaching light, these particles penetrate the Earth with so much force they have been recorded even deep in mines. But how did they become so accelerated? Gold suspected pulsars almost immediately, and he tried to get his proof from a statistical ploy: he compared extrapolations of cosmic ray density with pulsar density in the Galaxy and found these two figures precisely balanced each other.

Neutron stars and pulsars are models, based on the concept of a stellar body that does not have enough mass to form a black hole after exploding as a supernova. Its insides are dense and shrinking, while its husk keeps on burning, emitting particles. (Nigel Calder, the science writer, has compared using supernovae to create pulsars with using bombs to make glass goblets.)

In 1968 in Ann Arbor, I attended, by happenstance, one of Gold's first lectures on his theory of pulsars. A radio-astronomer friend invited me to what was advertised as an historic talk, the presentation of a radical new thesis concerning the origin of cosmic rays. In the spirit of syncretism, I suggested some other locals who would enjoy pulsars—or the idea of them anyway—the astrologers of Ann Arbor. My friend shrugged contemptuous assent when I asked if they could come along too.

Dr. Gold really hit the blackboard with chalk and put up some big numbers, lots of zeroes. We didn't see any stars, but, in fact, he said: all the energy in the universe, sufficient they were, his pulsars, his equations, to account for. And more!

"Wow!" said the astrologers, as those zeroes went up across the board.

There was the usual cocktail party afterward, and Dr. Gold stood there, throughly German and convinced, rigid in honor of his discovery. When I reached him on the receiving line, he was visibly disgruntled.

"What is an anthropologist doing at a lecture on astrophysics?" My explanations about ethnoastronomy only confused him further. And I wondered, "What's going to happen when he gets to them on line?"

Needless to say, he did not see the humor, let alone the irony, in it. But energy is energy, and those same astrologers, over the next ten years, rented the computers at the University of Michigan to chart the astrology of high-energy radio sources and, in a sense, invent radio astrology.

After all, just because we can see and hear the universe doesn't mean we should abandon our most profound pre-Egyptian legacy, that the sky is first and only and always messages from the gods.

The discovery of the first quasar preceded the discovery of the first pulsar by seven years. It was first noted as a very strong radio source that could not be identified with any star or galaxy. The area of the emission was ultimately pinpointed in an experiment with lunar occultation. A ninety-minute exposure of the suspicious area of the sky was taken with a five-meter reflector at the Mount Palomar observatory. What showed up was 3C 48, a bluish star accompanied by an elongated speck of material pointing back at roughly the 2:00 region of a clock. In the Cambridge catalogue it had been photographed thousands of times since 1886, and, though its brightness had changed radically over that time, this variation had not drawn attention. Faint stars are common enough in the unmagnified sky. In the telescopically enlarged sky, there are far too many for all of them to be monitored and explained.

Right from its rediscovery, 3C 48 caused problems. None of the normal spectral lines for a star appeared. And then there was the mysterious flashing. Even galaxies, made up of hundreds of billions of different light sources, do not vary radically in brightness. Seyfert galaxies sometimes resemble stars because their centers are so much brighter than their arms and they have a slight variability, but they are not nearly so bright as quasars. When more of these strange objects were identified, they were determined not to be stars in the conventional sense. They did not rotate with the Galaxy, so they must lie outside it; they had enormous red shifts, indicating also that they were moving rapidly away from us.

There are no such possible objects.

Experiments with the signal from 3C 273 showed that the radio noise from the quasar has two components, one from the star itself, stronger and fairly typical of other radio sources, and the other from the wisp beyond it, which was atypical. The wisp was actually moving directly away from the star; it was a jet. This has become the characteristic quasar image: an irregular star accompanied by a streamer.

The earliest spectra taken of quasars were fuzzy and inconclusive. Later ones showed their unusually high red shift. Their first rough estimated distance from us was between one and two billion light-years and rapidly increasing. Later examination of quasar spectrum lines upgraded this to between three and ten billion light-years; 3C 286, for instance, was receding at 55 percent of the speed of light. This means that we are seeing these objects as they were close to the beginning of the universe. They mark the portals of cosmology, like Titans and Cyclopses, vast personages left over from before the present universe.

We should be forewarned when the letter Q appears. In languages that come from Latin, Q is the harbinger of a fundamental mystery. Quarks and quasars may have other excuses, but Q knows better. If it was not chosen consciously, then unconscious fantasies govern its selection.

Whether apocryphally or not, the *Q* is said to come from the apple, from whose shape it was fashioned—the apple, called quert in many of the old languages, which Adam and Eve ate to get to the bottom of things at the beginning of mythical space-time. Look at our inheritance of *Q*'s from Latin:

Quis: Who? Quid: What? Quantum: How Great? Quinam: Which? Quando: When? Quam: How? Quanam: By What Way? Quia: Why? Quoties: How Often? Quot: How Many? Quotus: Which in Number? Quorsum: To What Place? Qualis: What Kind Of? Qua: Where? Quin: Why Not?

When we say quasar, i.e., quasi-stellar object, we are invoking the root: Where if? What supposing that?

Quasar theorists have imagined collisions at the fringes of space between antimatter galaxies and galaxies of normal matter. They have talked of black holes squeezing material out of the universe which then shoots back in at the distance of quasars. They have mentioned leaks from a universe further in the future than ours, slipping back over the time barrier. They have proposed collisions of huge groups of giant stars or multiple super-novae. Perhaps quasars are the residue of black holes or vast amounts of matter condensing into a black hole. Perhaps they are even aberrant chunks of matter flying out of the explosion at the beginning of the universe. Or remnants of a past universe never included in the Big Bang because they escaped too far into space and created their own dimensions.

The two main aboriginal sources of omens are the sky and dreams, for both of them are substantially rootless. That one comes from within and the other from without is a meaningless distinction as long as the degree to which we ourselves are inside or outside phenomena is unknown.

Dreams are "skies" in other senses. Entering them, we pass into discrete worlds, completed and inhabited.

When the night sky appears in dreams, the infinite universe is projected through the imagination of infinite space in the collective unconscious density of the cells. Dreaming settles deeply into our own tissue as stargazing presses out into the tissue of the universe, and both enactments merge into a vision.

Sometimes the dream sky is blacker than night; a heavy darkness permeates even the air. We find that the lake shore is just as black as the forest we have emerged from. The stray stars in the sky seem innocent enough, but at any moment a brilliant and intelligent set of constellations will burn their way through the ignorance and beam down on us. We must be ready, or escape. Flying saucers are looking for us; they will become so big, as they approach, they will be unbearable. They will take us into the arcane system of planets and suns. But are we ready? *No, we are not.* Not ready as Moses was for the burning bush. We must close our eyes to the darkness, stumble, and awake. And the question remains: Was this the astral universe in which our presence was so lucid and terrifying? Was it another universe whose name and place we do not know? Is that sky a blowup of our cellular tissue, fashioned by symbolism into night? Or is it some alien and primordial sky retained as a memory in the DNA of our species?

Star dreams are rare, and usually mythic. A notable one is the poet Robert Duncan's dream of 24 April 1963:

All the stars of the cosmos had come forth from the remotest regions into the visible. At first I was struck by the brilliance of Orion, but as I looked the field was crowded with stars, dense cells of images and then almost animal constellations of the night sky. It was as if we saw the whole over-populated species of Man and in that congregation of the living and dead, the visible and invisible members of the whole, we began to make patterns of man, animal entities whose cells were living souls.

"We see these skies here," the Poetess said, "because we are very close to the destruction of the world."[2]

The poet has left ordinary space and time. He is in a place where more than the naked-eye constellations are visible. This could be because he is seeing the Earth's skies from all of history, hence the same stars in their many appearances from the precession of the equinoxes, or because he is seeing through night and through the limits of the speed of light into centers of creation extinguished from our sensory field.

These "animal entities whose cells were living souls" must, on one level, be the constellations of the sky, whose cells are suns and planets. If we move from the Earth, and then from this Solar System, to other locations in the universe, the Sun becomes a member of our most familiar sky-beings: Cassiopeia, Ursa Major the Great Bear, Aquila the Eagle, Cetus the Whale. These forms, encoded as animals and mythological beings, are so large that they include us at the same time that we lie outside of them. If we journey far enough, they break apart only gradually, and in the process they give birth to other figures in other skies. The feeling is that mythological entities must go on, long after these things are obliterated from the chronological Earth, and long after all our seeming obsessions have broken us or been broken in the catacombs of this world's interior.

Far from the night sky itself the stars return, as organs of the body, god aspects, totem masks, ikons, archetypes, cells, gaps in thought and language, and visitants to dream skies. This is the true texture of starriness—blood and bark as well as cold fire and remote constellations. Where we stand, the stars can be mute figures who approach us with powers of divination and signs, or they can be cosmological furnaces.

Then there is my own dream of November 1975. I am filming the water pouring into Peacham Pond (Vermont). Suddenly the image through the movie camera lens becomes wild fat bugs which burst into orange, yellow, and red splotches; these become venous and luminous. They seem to be dancing to a music, but I cannot hear it. Now I see an aged forest. A river of stars flows through it. There are giant trees, bared on black humus; they hang over the edge of something, damp and rooty and quilled.

A loudspeaker mentions a war report from far away, perhaps the Holy Land. Unexpectedly there are jets in the sky, jets of varying shape and density. They approach not by engines but as our world is drawn to them. They are the work of artisans far beyond us: single jets with flares and double dumbbells. One group of seven or eight approach, growing bristly and grainy, and I understand that this is called the Pleiades fleet. As close as their bodies seem to be, they are stretched and fuzzy in the way that enormous enlargements of faint star clusters are.

Yet they are not stars. They are jets, silver gray jets with emblems on their sides in the overcast sky. Their emblems are constellations. This image replaces and then is replaced by the earlier one; something seems to hold the two together.

The figures are irregular and amorphous to raw sight. I sense that they are regular underneath in a way I cannot understand.

I am in a deeper universe. The jets fly in clear formation out of their extradimensional airport. Their flares leap out of density and bend back through space itself. I see now that some of them are perfect circles with single leaks and others are twisted rings.

They do not bomb our land, but this says nothing about their intention or ultimate plan. They do not have to attack, for their positions are perfect and they are being drawn into history.

I think that I have filmed them at last, the arrival of the armada. Then I see that I have opened the camera by mistake in my haste to work it. Perhaps I have exposed the film. The cartridge is a pyramid, perfectly sealed, and I cannot open it to reverse the film and shoot the other side. My immediate response is to try to change things by closing the camera and shooting, pretending there is film in it. During this interlude the sky has changed. There are enormous clouds, cirrus and altocirrus, but delicately crafted and wild and sinewy in a way I have never seen before. The color of the sky is a gem blue that is almost iridescent. Far away are other clouds that stand in long bands, whipped into spirals and sucked into cones that stand above the whole planet like mountains. In their foreground are intricately etched ivory figures that look like the work of a Mesolithic craft guild. They start as miniature statuettes and then expand; they retain their shapes and become white sea mammals, hunters with harpoons, and even fur-dressed ancient Europeans, members of the same Maglemosian communes that carved the figures.

The cones are smooth and eternal, without a single shred or fray. The air does not leave a ripple in them.

I realize that I have seen into the mythological world of quasars and that it is different from the tapestry of visible stars. Something about the quasars, I realize, was presaged through all of history, and their irregular shapes, like cancers of ancient worn objects, their suggested radioactivity and violence, are not modern but a prophecy of ourselves from creations before us. Their inscrutability merges with that of the Sphinxes and the pyramids and the gigantic Easter Island heads that sit in the Pacific as if looking at something beyond us, if not at us. And still they look at us.

Black holes are curious mixtures of the observable physical effects in the realm of the stars and the consequences of applying topology to topography; they are theoretical objects, mathematical predictions of what might happen if matter were squeezed to the point where its intrinsic structure collapsed to infinite density. As the gravitational field became stronger and stronger, the mass of an object, no matter how big it was originally (i.e., it could have been as big as the whole universe) would be reduced to a speck. Since the effects of relativity increase with density, the curvature of space would fold in upon itself, with infinite red shift. The object would be so dense that several billion tons or more could fit inside a pinhead. The black hole would continue to consolidate the mass of its ingredients, but the actual matter would be crushed. Hence, some suns upon burning out may go on collapsing indefinitely. Their waves of light, bent and elongated by gravity, would become infinite, so that no visual information could escape. In fact, a black hole leaves behind only its gravity. Starlight would fall back even as water from a geyser returns to the ground. In relation to this object, we would be nowhere at all.

This hypothesis comes directly from Einsteinian mathematics and was originally proposed by Karl Schwarzschild, a German astronomer, in 1915. It was meant to be a theory only, juggling supernuclear densities and large gravitational fields.

Einstein and Nathan Rosen had proposed, in 1935, that points of infinitesimally small size such as atomic particles might be viewed as singularities within which density could become infinite. A total singularity would raise immense difficulties, so they proposed instead that the gravity-influenced curvature of space could become so warped that it would bend into a whole other plane of space-time before actually entering the singularity.

What happens to matter supposedly crushed to zero volume in a black hole? It must leave the universe. But it cannot leave the universe. So it must appear elsewhere *in* the universe. The laws of nature require it. It cannot be obliterated. It can only be changed into some other thing. California Institute of Technology astronomer Kip Thorne gave us an unexpectedly memorable image when he said that it might come bubbling up, like spring water in the mountains, in another region of this universe or in some other universe. Even so, that "other" universe must still be part of the creation.[3]

Einstein and Rosen had been talking about the quantum effects of particles in the subatomic realm. They were not dealing with massive crushed stars. By the psychedelic sixties, the idea of a bridge between different regions of time-space had become a head trip for astrophysicists, science fiction writers, and metaphysicians of popular science. They have since invented such a range of exotic images that we reapproach black holes as high adventure, like caves at the bottom of whirlpools, kingdoms on the other side of the sky. As their light is sucked back, travelers disappear; they pass through wormholes into other universes. Only the storyteller can follow them.

William H. Press of the California Institute of Technology proposed that if through some asymmetry or deformation the event horizon of a singularity broke open, then the laws governing nature and its phenomena would break down completely. Anything could come out of a black hole on the other side of the universe—even, said Press, inventory ranging "from television sets to busts of Abraham Lincoln."[4] (Clearly, that bust of Abraham Lincoln ended up deep in outer space, dazzling Kirk and his crew on the *Star Trek* TV series.)

But this is a very optimistic reading of our lot. Black holes are also truly black, and they have darkened our philosophy more than brightened it. Having invoked a destructive capacity that goes beyond anything imaginable, we have begun to hope that it is possible to transcend destruction in ourselves. This suggests that, at least unconsciously, we have begun to know we have a far greater chance of acting out our destructive potential and blasting through it than of retreating and slinking away from it. Black hole journeys suggest such transformative apocalypses. Once we have trashed this universe—if we trash it absolutely to the bone—we will be blown into another universe. It would be foolhardy to trust this, though, and expect that, as at the end of *Dr. Strangelove*, the chorus accompanying the atomic bombs will be singing: "We'll meet again, don't know where, don't know when." But that macabre blend of fatalism and spunk dogs us all of our days.

Black holes need not be created by collapsing stars; according to the British astronomer Stephen Hawking, minute ones could have been dispersed in abundance in the Big Bang. The meteorite that hit Siberia in 1908, often explained as a comet exploding in the atmosphere, could have been a black hole that continued right through the planet. The entire Solar System could be following the Sun around a black hole, or several very tiny black holes could be orbiting the Sun at great distances like planets. These would have to be of the "mini-black hole" variety, for anything with more mass would have an appreciable gravitational effect on the bodies in the Solar System.

It has been suggested that the universe itself is a black hole, exploded from a singularity. Or perhaps the material for the universe has rushed in from black holes in other universes. (Quasars, correspondingly, are possible faucets, or white holes, at the ends of passages linking different orders of space-time.)

Some astronomers have suggested that one kind of black hole with an ergosphere could be captured and used for energy. Waste materials could be discarded into it, and the energy released by the addition of mass could be harnessed in its acceleration out of the hole. One of the possible technologies of the future is based on a dynamic network using the recoil from captured "mini-black holes." Charles Misner, Kip Thorne, and John Wheeler, described, perhaps fancifully, a black hole contained within a sphere upon which a great city was built, with gravity from the hole supporting the city.

Human creation must somehow reflect the deep cosmic sky. The artist is a "radio telescope" on a cellular level. He cannot see or hear star birth and star death and the passage of materials across dimensions, but he is the creature in whose senses these patterns are recorded and ordered, and he is the inner mesh of the stellar material of which distant atoms and suns are also made. Cubist designs show one aspect of atomicity; impressionistic landscapes show another. Abstract expressionism has stellar coordinates; Joan Miró's creatures are not science fiction, they are aspects of our own incarnation as we peel back toward unconsciousness and molecularity and toward the origin of thought. Dancers drop their weight suddenly and fall, then scoot across the floor. An arm extends one way, a leg another. One dancer carries another asymmetrically. Why? Is it simply decorative aesthetics, or do both the dancers and the audience reach out to the limits of gravity and anatomy? Where these meet, what exists?

As a jazz band plays, atoms and electrons seem to fly from their primordial sequences of notes. Centers emerge; then they disappear. Saxophone and keyboard grind out sound; we hear the violent atonal birth of stars. We hear the archetypal tune trying to break into the present chaos of matter. The drums carry bursts of protons into energy, and the bass imposes the weight of gravitational fields across the night black. Wrote the poet James Bogan, in his rhapsody for musician McCoy Tyner:

> Neptune's moon
> red Aldebaran
> far Hercules
> drawn now
> into our range
> the sufferings of our Sister
> Galaxy Andromeda
> felt by spiraling correspondence.[5]

Scientists do not invent the probabilistic location of electrons or put tons of materials in a thimble because they find these things in the universe. Contemporary physicists and astronomers are not unlike the Ptolemaics who struggled to find enough epicycles to save the appearances without abandoning the circle, except in this case it is the whole of Western logic they are trying to save, and at a time when the future of industrial society rests on the application of that logic. When Ptolemy "saved the appearances" of the sky in his day, he was trying to save the world of meaning that had developed under that sky. Subatomic particles, black holes, antimatter, pulsars, quasars, and the expanding universe are likewise mythical representations of physical things.

Then there is my dream of November 3, 1982: I am visiting an old folks' home, but it is more like a huge institution of learning, a college. Many of my uncles from childhood are there, but they have become blind or partially blind. It is daytime, but the night sky is visible through the blue. I see strange streaks of stars like cirrus clouds. Then one of the old uncles—a lawyer from Brooklyn—takes out a book he can apparently read without seeing. He says we must trace our present position in time and space. He turns the pages and allows me to view the stars as they are actually configured in three dimensions. There is a huge Mongol warrior's head, and successive photographs show that, as we transit it and look down upon it (year after year and century by century), more of the exquisite detail of the face, made up of literally trillions of stars, is revealed. The astrogeography is so complex, with so many layers, it would take thousands of lifetimes to examine it all, but our exploration is condensed into the dream. We turn the pages and view its holographic entirety. I think it is crucially significant that the stars have sculpted such a perfect figure in space. Then my uncle turns the pages of the book back to our present zone with its cirrus streaks and asks for my interpretation. It seems obvious that the Earth not only looks directly upon but is entering a disturbed zone. I tell them we will leave behind only monuments to ourselves (like tombstones and bones). And then I realize our thoughts remain too, even after cremation—that this complex sector of space requires we remain in the star-cluster Mongol warrior's head, still conscious, until our destiny is resolved.

13

Language, Mind, and Astrophysics

W<small>E EXIST</small> in a confusing time in which ambitious things are proposed and scientists and philosophers make grand syncretisms of things in mind and nature. We pretend that we are up against the borders of reality itself, but these might be different borders, within thought and within language, that merely seem like the borders of the whole. When geometry had problems with curved space, we extended into non-Euclidean geometry. Now we are learning, as Kepler did, that no geometry resolves all the issues. Nor any mathematics.

Our age will not proclaim the great synthesis of all forms of knowledge; it will barely survive its own paradoxes at best. Unavoidably, we must find parallels for the stars and matter in abstract mathematics, topology, Oriental religion, dreams, and parapsychology, for these are terrestrial things, and as we approach the night sky, we also approach the boundaries of thought and language, where celestial and terrestrial converge like non-Euclidean parallel lines. Let us not think, though, that by proclaiming a "tao of physics," we can unmask the underlying unity. We cannot evade the riddle by pretending to solve it, or by pretending that it solves itself collectively and unconsciously across the Indo-European and East-West gulfs.

We have come to see (like Sir James Jeans) that the universe looks more like a great idea than a great machine, that our description of it resembles thoughts more than unintelligent matter. We no longer mean the thought of a specific deity or an angelic energy within creation, as Kepler and Newton did; we mean that something like intelligence is present in the universe as a whole, or perhaps that we sense the progenitor of our own intelligence in space and matter at large—that thoughts, like the ones we have, shaped the universe. But how and why did it come to this arrangement? Were we present at the beginning or created solely through the extenuating properties of matter? "The atoms and molecules that make up the pages of this book are also, within their own level, aware," Seth said through his medium Jane Roberts.[1] Consciousness precedes matter and creates it. No wonder yogis legendarily materialize food out of the "air" to feed hungry people—but not often, it is said, because of the cosmic consequences.

The universe is externalized only in relationship to the mind. And the mind is internalized only through its experience of the external forms of nature. Our breathing and perception change the universe, but phenomena burst in upon them continually and change them as well. It is no wonder that meditation and science come to describe similar events. Focus of breath and discovery of quasars are equivalent not because the systems are isomorphic but because the one universe generates the same crisis of perception.

The famous question "Who?" is semantically simple. But try chanting it with normal rhythmic breath from deep in your belly where it originates, resonating it through the chamber of the chest. Each intonation will alter and deepen it until a being you barely know is asking the real question that needs no answer. It may even be "Ha." Cosmic laughter rings out through your body, seemingly forever.

It is at the center of the heart-mind that we ask any big question, and big questions include: Who am I?; What is this?; How did it all originate?; Why does it go on. What professional astronomers (and other academic cosmologists of the modern sensibility) fail to take into account is that the distortion and impedance of the body-mind are reflected not once (as superficial distractions) but hundreds, perhaps thousands, of times through their mode of objectifying and articulating. The quality of their question will be only as good as the absolute quality of their being. The degree of light seen in the world will be precisely the flow of enlightened consciousness through their minds (the impression of darkness likewise the flow of unredeemed consciousness). And the answers, of course, will be only as good as the questions. So, cosmologies that originate from fossil-fuel/junk-food/working-day addictions cannot improve on their base. The intrinsic purity of the scientific process wrings them remarkably clean and dresses them up pretty well for show under the circumstances. But the distraction and rigidity behind them is evident in their compulsive hype. They chatter and sell themselves, and, when they can get away with it, they bully the ignorant. No cosmology can escape this initial ring of cause and effect, for there is no universe outside the mind-body distortion.

Both modern physics and Eastern philosophy acknowledge in different ways that we look at the night sky and inside ourselves at the non-origin. There is no justification or rationale for our condition. We exist in the sky as we exist in breath. Ideas originate in the stars, and we may use them to explain being. At the same time, mental static flows through us as we generate an ego and a personality. We may picture other galaxies and planets around other suns, or make a model for the beginning of the universe; these are like the realms of Oriental iconography. We internalize gods as we internalize electrons and neutron stars. We have a model for salvation and a model for creation. They are secondary images. Buddhism and astronomy are also pure imageless sciences.

The balanced forces that make up the universe *are* the universe at any given moment, whether we know them or not. The Sun and planets and galaxies and so-called gravitation and electromagnetism exist and carry out their nature. We carry out our nature in imagining them. Breath separates mind from its attachment to images and forms; then both enter the eternal nullity and singularity. An externality grows larger and more complex as we stare into it; internality changes by our passage through it. There is nothing else.

Our pessimism is our projection onto the night sky and the gods when we see that they are not connected to our goals and do not take us into account. In our desire to create gods who share our values and destiny, we have created enemies who have turned back against us. There is a new sensibleness is letting the universe-that-is touch us like waves in our own silence, through our cells and through radio telescopes. We can try to see deeper with more refined instruments, and in doing this we refine ourselves. We also see into the universe directly. We impose form on nothingness, but nothingness alone generates form. We fear the destruction of ourselves and everything finally, but even our awareness of being is an aberration in the placid void. We try to perceive the concrete reality of matter, but all we experience is the continuous alteration of energy. Clarity eludes us at both the stars and the origin of being, but clarity also rushes upon us as a sudden wind that cuts like ice to the root of existence.

The Western fantasy is to relieve this boredom with rocket ships, to enter and explore an infinity of appearances. Even a rocket ship, with or without men and women inside, and minds inside them, has a consequence, direct and unadorned, in being the thing it is. We are lucky in this; the object is always turned back to within an altered field of perception. Otherwise we would be stuck trying to force our way into a universe that might not even exist. The certainty of the stars and matter, the appearance of a resemblance between Buddhism and astronomy, the seeming thread of reasonableness in this book are all bluffs.

The infinite energy that is exposed as being outside in the universe is also inside and beneath our personalities. We recognize the cosmos by a projection of the psyche. Not only are we atomic beings, but the sum total of all atomic fields everywhere is a larger collective unconsciousness from which we draw limitlessly into our personalities. The illusion is that we must be subject to the boundaries that we impose on ourselves at any one time: material boundaries in a material time. But the stars also give us a bigness to be big against. They give us the intimation that the consciousness within ourselves is not ordinary; or if it is, the ordinary is cosmic and limitless.

As we try to see into our nervous systems, we have a sense that our carnality, our incarnation in matter, shares properties with the electrical network that we imagine in space. It is as though a single originary idea lies near the center of the Milky Way, where time itself is warped and the hottest and closest fires burn so interconnectedly that everything is ramified in billions of dimensions as soon as it exists.

The complexity of space and the complexity of mind are a single expression of the nervous system. Neutron stars and black holes describe the pressure we feel. On the surface our thoughts flit like dust motes and spit bugs, but we sense the powerful draw underneath, attaching us to anything at all. We know that we cannot concede our existence. We must work at the riddles of creation as they appear in us, and if we do not work at them, they work at us anyway, in the same way that they worked to bring us, and the idle thoughts we tag along, into being. This is why sages in the West practice astronomy. We cannot evade the gravity pulling us to the center. If we build the machines, we must proclaim their counterpart in the sky.

Vastness and complication are properties of the inner organs, not just their organic being but the entirety of space that evolves between them and within them, between them and the overall nervous system and the brain. Mind inhabits density and continuousness as breath and blood travel with it through the body. By the same rule, astral projection is the microcosmic counterpart of astronomical travel. The astral traveler perceives tremendous spaces internal to himself and enters these in exact correspondence, planet for planet and star for star, of the entire universe. It may not be the same universe as the external one, but it is the same universe as his internalized image of the external one.

We are made of our organs and our cells, and it is absurd to think that we can have images apart from them. We do not reflect them in simple literal symbols, the stars as eyes, the bloodstream as the Milky Way, etc., but we impose our collective inherited organ system upon the exterior world. The Milky Way may not be our intestines, but the profound inner experience of such a long winding passage is our basis for imagining the inside of such a spiral anywhere. Small cavities in our bodies create the infinity we imagine in space.

Astronomer Stephen Hawking, who has been a leading cosmologist of black holes and the Big Bang expanding universe, has done most of his work while confined to a wheelchair with a deterioriative nerve and muscle disease. It is almost as though the paralyzing complexity of his own system draws his mind to the center of the universe. He too lies in a "black hole," trapped by an originary force, but he has had the courage to stay in communication both with us and the universe passing through him in this dark phase and to report accurately through the entanglement.

Charles Stein, in a discussion of alchemy, gives a methodology for intuiting the astronomical:

> Our whole going on includes realms that are beyond any possible scale of perception out of which, nonetheless, all of our possible experience is, in some sense, constituted. Since we are also, even in the scientific view, physical beings, we have some primary intuition of that, we feel a connection. When you read about microphysics or astronomical spaces or periods of time calculated in billions of years, that produces a specific reaction in you, that is imaginary in one sense, but is on the other hand, *precisely imaginary.* The world of fantasy that is awakened in you when you think ten billion years is different in a precise way from the world of imagination that's produced in you when you think six thousand years.[2]

To Wilhelm Reich, the spiral shapes of the galaxies revealed a series of cosmic superimpositions in which the collectivity of the starfields surged with sexual energy (orgone) and attempted to unite and breed fresh stars. In looking through telescopes, Reich said, man departs from his inherent humanity and participates vicariously in a cosmic harmony he would express if he were free to carry out his natural human functions. The spasms of sexual intercourse are not only prefigured in the rhythm of galaxy formation; these two events occur at opposite ends of the scale of creation *simultaneously* as aspects of the same pulse. As the galaxies shoot out stars, creatures shoot out their kind. As the galaxies long to superimpose and connect their orgone streams, men and women long to love and connect their orgone streams and either heal by their natural medicine or give birth to new men and women. The streams of energy at large form the universe, the streams within generate cells and thoughts. Man experiences in his mind and in his organs the desire to procreate that is the original desire of the universe to spread and differentiate. The buildup of sexual excitation prior to release is itself the universe surging to continue, to spurt out new seeds and suffuse itself with its own elixir. The passion we feel in lovemaking is thus linked to the formation of stars and systems of stars. That is why the feeling is so powerful and why it is functionally associated with passing the cellular blueprint into history. Above, the spiraling galaxies; below, the seed-bearing creatures of the planets—one stream of energy.

Reich came to see hurricanes, galaxies, the northern lights, cell growth, jellyfish, worms, and orgasm as the same function. The spiral is a spiral of excitation, imposition, and fulfillment on any scale. Even the rings of Saturn are an aspect of it. The blue sky is not light diffraction alone but the color of atmospheric orgone descending on the Earth. Sucked into the yellow resin of bion water from the Sun, it becomes green, as in plants. But plants lose their orgone to the atmosphere in the winter and turn yellow or brown. [3]

In *The Rainbow,* D. H. Lawrence has Ursula emerge from lovemaking under a magnificent night sky to find the magnificence gone: "Gradually she realized that the night was common and ordinary, that the great, blistering, transcendent night did not really exist." [4]

She had found it inside herself, so the stars no longer represented it. She had moved to the center of creation without them.

Things exist for ontogenetic and epistemological reasons as surely as for cosmological ones. The new physics is, in many ways, primarily an inquiry into the origins of Western thought. On the surface, it uses the tools of measurement in the most rigorous manner to make an objective model of the universe, methodically correcting itself when new evidence is found. But still, that model gradually incorporates the contradictions within any attempt to objectify, and scientists are unwillingly included in their own equations. We end up with two overlapping systems: one of them is a cosmology based on the ostensible properties of matter and energy that essentially ignores the disruptive role of the observer and model-maker (this includes the study of stars, atoms, light, gravity, electricity, radiation, etc.); the other is the joint epistemology of the observer and observed.

There is no way to describe reality without acknowledging the participation of human intelligence and ethnocentric categories in the description. Gravity, time, space, and even stars are not absolutes; they are the images that man has from within of a vast unknown creation. Different kinds of beings make a totally different universe, even if they share this one with us. If we were stones on the Moon, it would not be the Moon and we would not be stones. The history of language alone proves that. There is a concrete reality, no doubt, but it is always in flux, and continuously interacts with categories of thought, language, and belief, to generate the universe of any one people or system.

"We have agreed," said John Wheeler in a symposium at Cornell University on the nature of time, "that the world is built according to certain rules. We cannot answer the question why the rules are just as they are, but that they come from our experience we could not deny. We are faced with the problem of man in the small and the universe in the large. The two are not completely disconnected from each other, because for life to exist with its entropy-decreasing biological mechanism, there must exist temperature difference. We could not exist for long without the sun. So from that point of view, man is the tail that is wagged by the rest of the universe. But, from another point of view, the universe is the tail that is wagged by man; when the man observes, he creates a cut between himself and what he sees around him, and this cut is governed by himself."[5]

Man is what balances the rest of the universe and its gargantuan collection of matter. He is the specific counterpart to the stars.

R. Buckminster Fuller explains this insight:

I found myself in 1951 having to write in a book, which I was about to publish, that the mind of man seemed to be the most advanced phase of antientropy witnessable in universe. And if there is an expanding universe there logically is a contracting universe. Possibly man's mind and his generalizations, which weigh nothing, operate at the most exquisite state of universe contraction. Metaphysics balances physics. The physical portion of universe expands entropically. The metaphysical contracts antientropically.[6]

In his Copenhagen interpretation of quantum theory, Werner

Heisenberg reminds us that the way in which classical physics views the universe is the inheritance of both our constructions of nature and reality going back through Greek times to the dawn of man and our ongoing phenomenological interaction with reality. Physics seeks to free itself of bias, but that is impossible. Without bias it would have no history and no perceptual basis in the world. Language itself is prejudiced by clandestine syntactic structures. It is not a neutral tool. It creates reality. The complex structures of nouns, verbs, conjunctions, tenses, and moods, and their equivalents in other languages, compel us into views of motion, time, and relationship that are unique to their own systems. Mathematics may be pure, but it is hardly divorced from the linguistic patterns of the mathematicians.

The linguist Benjamin Lee Whorf gives an interesting case of a non-Western syntactic division of the universe in his discussion during the 1940s and 1950s of Hopi grammatical categories. Hopi verbs, for instance, have many "aspects" revealing the universe implicitly in a state of motion and unfolding that we require semantic changes for. In other words, the transformation is carried unconsciously in the rules for verb change rather than in a conscious decision of meaning. One set of rules involves the punctual and segmentative aspects of verbs. The punctual aspect *ri'pi* (it gives a flash) generates the segmentative aspect *ripi'pita* (it is sparkling). This alone insures that no native speaker of Hopi has ever seen the same night sky as a speaker of English or French. The differences may have been exaggerated by the romanticists who used Whorf in the 1960s, but minute differences make enormous differences in the construction of a science, as Kepler, Newton, and Einstein knew. Whorf offers other examples of punctual and segmentative aspects: *pa'ci* (it is notched) versus *paci'cita* (it is serrated); and *ha'ri* (it is bent in a rounded angle) versus *hari'rita* (it lies in a meandering line, making successive rounded angles).[7] Some noteworthy pre-Whorfian examples can be found in an obscure dictionary at the back of Alexander Stephen's *Hopi Journal* of 1892: *ta'pa* (it gives a snap) versus *tapa'pata* (it is snapping); or *re'ke* (it makes a grating or scratching noise called by the Hopi "rek!") versus *reke'keta* (it goes rek-rek-rek!).[8]

Whorf summarizes the implications:

Language first of all is a classification and arrangement of the stream of sensory experience which results in a certain world-order, a certain segment of the world that is easily expressible by the type of symbolic means that language employs. In other words, language does in a cruder but also in a broader and more versatile way the same thing that science does. . . . Hopi language maps out a certain terrain of what might be called primitive physics. [9]

It is important to remember that it is language which does this *prior* to any conscious attitude about what constitutes nature or the meaning of natural phenomena.

In the first book of his science fiction trilogy, *Out of the Silent Planet,* C. S. Lewis describes the confusion of the character Ransom when he lands on Mars as a kidnap victim. Because he has no language for the phenomena he sees and cannot separate the foreground from the background, he does not know what anything is or even how far away or close to him it is. He sees a purple mass and takes it at first for a heather-colored mountain. It could also be a nearby animal or house. There is a rose-colored cloud that he finds exquisite in tint and shape; it is like a red cauliflower or a bowl of red soapsuds which might be above him and beyond some unintelligible jagged upright shapes. After looking at the "cloud," he turns back to the "mountain" and is startled to see it swaying softly on tall thin stalks like an underwater jungle in the air.[10] This is science fiction Mars, but it helps us to imagine the Hopis first entering Arizona and seeing in the distance sand blowing over mesas; migrating Apaches coming from high ground onto their first herd of buffalo; Tlingits pushing down the Pacific Coast during that "first misty spring" after the Ice Age. We might also recall the disorientation of our first sight of the infrared Sun or the flow and movement inside a cell. Syntax reflects both prior syntax and new reality. In imagining the extraterrestrial now, we are expressing a simultaneous wish to encounter the origins and meanings of our own structures of thought.

"The Hopi," writes Whorf, "actually have a language better equipped to deal with vibratile phenomena [like waves, vibrations, and chemical processes] than our latest scientific technology." The Hopi verb forms oblige "the Hopi to notice and observe vibratory phenomena, and furthermore . . . to find names for and classify such phenomena. . . ."[11]

> In [the] Hopi view [Whorf continues], time disappears and space is altered, so that it is no longer the homogeneous and instantaneous timeless space of our supposed intuition or of classical Newtonian mechanics. At the same time, new concepts and abstractions flow into the picture, taking up the task of describing the universe without reference to such time or space—abstractions for which our language lacks adequate terms. . . .
>
> The metaphysics underlying our own language, thinking, and modern culture . . . imposes upon the universe two grand COSMIC FORMS, space and time; static three-dimensional infinite space, and kinetic one-dimensional uniformly and perpetually flowing time. . . .
>
> The Hopi metaphysics . . . imposes upon the universe two grand cosmic forms, which as a first approximation in terminology we may call MANIFESTED and MANIFESTING (or, UNMANIFEST) or, again, OBJECTIVE and SUBJECTIVE. The objective or manifested comprises all that is or has been accessible to the senses, the historical physical universe, in fact, with no attempt to distinguish between present and past, but excluding everything that we call future. The subjective or manifesting comprises all that we call future, BUT NOT MERELY THIS; it includes equally and indistinguishably all that we call mental—everything that appears or exists in the mind, or, as the Hopi would prefer to say, in the HEART, not only the heart of man, but the heart of animals, plants, and things, and behind and within all the forms and appearances of nature in the heart of nature, and . . . in the very heart of the Cosmos, itself.[12]

What if the whole of classical physics had been developed by speakers of the Hopi language? Would they not have seen everything in manifestation differently from the beginning, and thus come to the dilemmas of subatomic particles, quantum relationships, and quasars on an entirely unique basis, or not at all? Given a billion years each, the Hopis, hypothetically, might reach Andromeda before the American Space Program (though the Americans would beat them to the planets and even perhaps to a few close stars), because space in the universe is the same as time, and the Hopi space-time verbs could eventually create a vehicular gestalt that would make all times equal and simultaneous in the universe, hence allowing an individual to choose his position in the universe. In other words, there are certain distances that man cannot travel unless he is unencumbered by phenomena and mass as we know them.

This is, of course, a fanciful and unlikely comparison. Our attempt to imagine an alternative Hopi physics is also an attempt to disentangle ourselves from the dilemma of our own physics and American Indian linguistic theory, as well as from the moral dilemma of our time with which these are synchronous. The fact that Hopi verb metaphysics lie "hidden" behind tiny farming communities on Arizona mesas, in devotion to corn maidens, dancing kachina gods, multicolored prayersticks and rattles, and sand-painting rainclouds, connects our cosmic projection to our ecological idealization. We cannot help feeling that what is more complex metaphysically is also simpler and more balanced ecologically, which means that the powers we leave to unknown supernatural entities and extraterrestrials are those that we have lost ourselves. The visitations of Hopi priests and Martian wizards are simultaneous in Western culture: they lie in kind with the search for a lost universe. In that sense, we have already been to many other planets without ever leaving our own.

The French anthropologist Claude Lévi-Strauss carries this hypothesis beyond language to primitive systems of ethnoscience and totemic classification. These, he points out, are at least as complex as any mathematics or physics we ourselves derive. Their inferiority to them is based only on lack of simple data, usually about microstructure and infrastructure, knowledge we have gained only gradually through use of scientific instruments. Native cosmology understands the connection, coherence, and transformation by which the natural world is manifested, but it does not usually distinguish between complex information clusters and physically deterministic ones. The principles of interpretation are absolutely in accord with the nature of reality, and they are so potentially useful to us because they reveal aspects

and features of things unknown to us forever. It is no wonder
that we should intuit some latent relationship between the mystery of quantum physics and the mystery of totemism. Our images of things among the stars and within the atom—black holes,
ghost particles, etc.—themselves generate ceremonies and symbols, anthropological and linguistic shapes; and these come to
resemble the totemic categories of non-Western thought as they
emerge from exotic languages and ethnic codes and attach themselves to the simplest and most innocent phenomena: insects,
plants, animals, clouds, constellations, the Northern Lights. This
is why ethnobotanies and myth cycles are implicitly astronomical
and cosmic.

The meaning of any one of these systems is unique, and
though they all relate to some core reality in nature, they cannot
be translated into one another; they share few concrete features.
For instance, in Osage Indian cosmology, animate and inanimate
things are divided into three categories: the sky, water, and dry
land. The sky includes the sun, the stars, cranes, other heavenly
bodies, night, the Pleiades, and has a significant relation to tur-
tles in some rites. The eagle, on the other hand, unlike the crane,
is a dry-land being, along with the porcupine, the black bear,
and the deer. Lévi-Strauss explains:

> The position of the eagle would be incomprehensible were
> it not known that in Osage thought eagles are associated
> with lightning, lightning with fire, fire with coal and coal
> with the earth. . . . The turtle with a serrated tail, an animal
> of no practical use, is often involved in rites. The reason
> for its importance could not be understood without the
> further knowledge that the number thirteen has a mystic
> value for the Osage. The rising sun emits thirteen rays,
> which are divided into a group of six and a group of seven
> corresponding respectively to right and left, land and sky,
> summer and winter. The tail of this species of turtle is said
> to have sometimes six and sometimes seven serratures. Its
> chest therefore represents the vault of the sky and the grey
> line across it the Milky Way.[13]

Stellar affinities are generated from the most ancient and thus
the most layered aspects of the system. In *From Honey to Ashes,*

Lévi-Strauss gives a sidereal transformation from South American Indian mythology:

> Star is an opossum, a forest animal in the first place in its food-supplying capacity and then a savannah animal in its capacity as a polluted and polluting creature, which brings death to men, after bringing them life through revealing cultivated plants to them. . . . From the astronomical point of view, the opossum shows an affinity with the Pleiades since, according to a Rio Negro myth, the opossum and chameleon chose the day of the first rising of the Pleiades to cauterize their eyes with pimentos and to expose themselves to the beneficent action of the sun. . . .
>
> . . . Just as the real opossum, a good wet-nurse, is congruous with bees' honey, so the figurative opossum, who is a bad nursing mother, is congruous with the wasp, whose honey is sour, if not poisonous.[14]

Through further mutual oppositions, involving the origin of honey, bees' wax (the dry, nonperishable part of the nest), and pineapples and plums (which mark transitions between dry and rainy seasons), we come to a transformation in which the opossum becomes a good wet nurse with an udder producing milk as sweet as honey, but with a desire for honey that is so great that it sticks its tongue into the tortoise's anus, which leads to a new set of relationships involved with the origin of the stars, fire in cooking, and disease.

Partially resolved pairs which are simultaneously natural and emblematic parallel the forever unmade cosmology of the universe and space and time. The same pairs map the different tribes and civilizations of men and women as they have spread and been transformed through the jungles and pampas of South America. They are like the stars of the expanding cosmos. The messages and meanings of their myths, which were first distorted by unconscious process and the natural discontinuities in the relationships they sought to express unconsciously, are further distorted by the physical disjunction between groups and the disjunction of any one version of a tale from the many historical versions lying behind it. All of this is inverted through different languages, environments, and interactions between historical groups bearing versions of prehistoric codes. And we have still not begun to touch the real layering and topological displacement. The Indians come to us out of something that looks like darkness, since we cannot see into it by seeing them in daylight; they become the night sky, or their artifacts and customs and tales do, as ours do to them in a different way. We must not shy from the relationship of these intricate patterns to the astrophysics of the modern cosmos, for they are part of the night sky in the same way that the Pleiades and honey are linked through Opossum. Constellations and language patterns are assembled within history, and it is through these structures, arbitrary as they are, that things as remote as other galaxies and quasars begin to reach us from the night sky. We have no choice in the matter: it is one of the natural initiations of the Western world. It laid the basis for the cosmic vision of the 1960s, with its galaxies and lotus plants, its gods and goddesses, and rock music and interior plant wisdom. A tragedy of our culture was that this initiation came with so little guidance and in isolation; our sages who prophesied it fled its raw presence, and it was often squandered in occult fads which lost their archetypal connection, or else it was pumped for a final confirmation that it could not give; mediums and hallucinogens lead neither to the stars nor the archetypes that sustain the sky, though trained shamans and priests do go on stellar and astral journeys with their aid. (Among those who believe in our ultimate transcendence, the battle is between the ones who would have us earn it individually only and those who propose that the human race can be transformed *in toto*.)

Yet, the sixties vision still contains the possibility of guidance from our disembodied and nonpersonal intelligence, as if some collective Western magus were trying to reach us and put us in touch with the joy and wonder that this planet has earned by the courage of incarnation. We can also dance with the stars ceremonially and chant their whale-songs. We can see the way in which we are all stars. It is a terrifying theophany of the cosmos, but it is far less alienating than the Big Bang. Its nakedness and mortality are our nakedness and mortality, and those who experience it fully, like Hopi and Osage priests, never return to the old universe.

14

The Planets
I: The Solar System

WHEN WE THINK of the Solar System, the nine planets come to mind—they and their moons, the assorted comets, asteroids, meteor swarms, and the sea of churning fire they all encircle. In the night sky, the Solar System would seem to be a few needles in a haystack, some of them invisible most of the time, most of them invisible all of the time. It took heroic efforts to discover the outer planets, their moons, and the asteroids, and, for all intents and purposes, these are invisible to mankind without telescopes.

There is another way to imagine the Solar System: it is the gravitational field originating at the Sun. This alone keeps the planets "alive." Without it they would be dead stones, drifting or motionless depending on how one might interpret their inertia through the immensity of space.

The Solar System is mainly empty interstellar space. It is a veil, an almost perfectly transparent veil housing the gravitational field through which we look at the background of the cosmos. If it were not for sunlight and its chemical trail, we would look through a perfect transparency. Light scatters in the atmosphere to produce the blue opaque hood, and the solar wind blows against the gases and particles, creating the faint ionization of night. Even in the darkest of nights, the Sun's radiation creates texture. A sky hangs between us and the cosmos. It may be as fiery as the Northern Lights or as muffled as the twinkling of stars.

———

The planets are infinitesimal compared to the stars, and they have no light of their own. They fill the void between here and eternity by reflecting light from their metallic and gaseous bodies—a fraction of the continuous waves which arrive at their shores. These reflected waves tell us, as they told ancient man in other ways, that the Sun's veil has bits of matter caught in it like gemstones. What the night sky does is to throw the billions of billions of miles of interstellar space in all directions into a single blackness, while the planets, asteroids, and comets stand out as the single moving objects illuminated by the Sun among the stars.

When Galileo and Herschel first looked at the planets through telescopes, they saw surfaces. The stars stayed remote, but the planets swelled into objects. Their features indicated that they were not the source of their own light but rather worlds of varying composition lit by day. Unlike stars, each of which shines with its own discrete light, the planets borrow their visibility from the Sun.

We cannot see a gravitational field, but we infer its existence from the things that are held in it and move strictly by its quantity in the mass of the Sun. With the discovery of Neptune, the Solar System was extended to a field thirty times the distance from the Earth to the Sun (which itself is an average of 92.9 million miles). At the time, this incredible amount was taken as the limit. Pluto carries that to forty times the orbit of the Earth. And we have gradually come to understand that it extends far beyond that, and that the actual gravitational field of the Sun may reach over a third of the distance to Alpha Centauri, the nearest star.

Comets are a striking testimony to the enormity of the Solar System. They come, seemingly, from the depths of space and pass to the heart of the System in eccentric orbits slightly perturbed by the planets according to their sizes and the proximity of their approach. Although some comets do not even go so far from the Sun as Jupiter's orbit, their remote swings can carry them to aphelion somewhere in space 150,000 times the Earth's distance from the Sun. Visually, from there, the Sun is only one more star. Gravitationally, though, it has enough force to hold onto those comets that remain.

The Dutch astronomer Jan Oort proposed that the comets were spewed forth by the same exploding planet between Mars and Jupiter that created the asteroid belt. Most of the material was blown out of the System, while that which barely held on formed an icy cloud at the limits of solar influence from which the comets now originate and to which they return. Although the idea of an exploded planet has generally been rejected, the Oort cloud of remote comets clearly exists, for unknown comets appear regularly, comets that must have last visited this region of the Solar System during human prehistory. The cometary cloud surrounding the Solar System is probably the outermost ring of the original solar nebula out of which the planets and moons were born. The lighter material was blown to these far-away orbits by the radiation of the condensing proto-Sun. As comets approach the Sun again, the fine gas and dust they leave behind is ignited, and debris from the edges of the protean cloud burns anew.

Untold other planets may exist between Pluto and the comets, invisible to us for the same reason that the planets circling other suns are invisible to us: their faint reflected light does not reach us. Their sizes are necessarily limited to a range where gravitational effects would not be readily apparent in the rest of the Solar System. Earlier in the twentieth century, these phantom planets received far more attention than they do now. Astronomers regularly "invented" them from unexplained perturbations in the orbits of Neptune, Uranus, and even Saturn, and from anomalies in orbits of comets. William Pickering, the American astronomer at Harvard, was the most notorious planet-maker. His first planet, "O," was placed at almost 52 times the Earth's distance from the Sun. It orbited the Sun every 373.5 years and had a mass twice that of the Earth's. Pickering derived "O" in 1908 solely from residuals in the orbit of Uranus. A few years later, he announced three more planets: "P" was located at 123 times the Earth's distance from the Sun, with a year of 1,400 Earth-years; it was based on variations in cometary orbits. "Q" was located at 875 times the Earth's distance from the Sun. It had a mass 20,000 times that of the Earth, a year of 26,000 Earth-years, an eccentric orbit, and a sharp orbital inclination. "Q" was big enough to counterbalance the whole System, to operate, gravitationally, as a second, invisible Sun. "R" was located at 6,250 times the Earth's distance from the Sun. Its mass was half that of "Q," and its orbital period was half a million years.[1]

The "planets" that Pickering proposed between the years 1928 and 1931 were bizarre in other ways. "S" was located at 48 times the Earth's distance from the Sun, with five times the Earth's mass and a year of 336 Earth-years. "T" was invented to cover the few remaining anomalies in Uranus's orbit and was placed just outside the orbit of Neptune. "U" was later placed outside the orbit of Jupiter in an eccentric path that sometimes carried it closer to the Sun than the giant planet was; it was only 4.5 percent of the Earth's mass.[2]

Pickering's Solar System is interesting not least of all because it shows that we can imagine an equal configuration to the visible one based solely on the analysis of the gravitational field. The movements of known planets, moons, and comets reveal this field, but they also suggest unseen other influences.

Far from being a scatter of individual sun-stars, the Milky Way is a series of enormous overlapping seas with suns in the centers of them. Except for the suns, the seas are invisible to us, but the universality of gravitation ensures that they are there. They are most likely inhabited by planets, asteroids, meteors, and so on, if our Solar System is any measure. Some of these seas have clouds, both bright and dark, galactic mist of metallic vapors, and universal raw hydrogen. There is also cosmic dust and debris. Occasionally, according to the Newtonian formula, objects achieve the velocity necessary to escape from these waters, and they drift in the void until they enter another sea. Their hyperboloid orbits carry them into the space between the solar systems. They may continue to pass through countless solar systems on a journey through space, they may be perturbed into orbits in systems they enter, or they may be caught and consumed in stars. Most bodies carry only the archaeology of their own solar system and universal chemistry, but wanderers from other solar systems would bring with them messages of the formation of substances from other stellar clouds, and they would no doubt link us in some way to a more ancient common ancestor in the Galaxy. Von Braun and Ordway suggest such an origin for the Moon.

Compared to a terrestrial ocean of water, the solar system appears dry and sterile, but this is misleading and even contradictory. The oceans and seas of the Earth are part of the stellar ocean. So are the Earth's forests and the cells of its living creatures. This ocean of radiation and gravity generates the nurturing climate and chemistry of Terra and maintains them with delicate chords. If it does not seem to do so for the other planets, we must remember that Eden is particular to us, and what may nurture our botanical and zoological garden may be poisonous to other life forms. If the Earth is the only solar planet capable of biology, that capacity is still an effect of the solar sea. It keeps the algae and forests green and feeds them their light, which feeds us and nurtures the visions of philosophers and alchemists. Take this planet out of the stellar sea and the living layer would instantly contract and freeze into a black fossil.

In the early days of the Sun and of the nebula cloud at the heart of which it contracted and burned, there was also an abundance of tiny bodies that did not condense into full planets or planetoids. These are known as planetesimals, infinitesimal planets. Dense as mosquitoes at the beginning, they bombarded the whole of the Solar System. Most of them crashed into planets and moons, and the sky contains only relict meteor showers and comets from its prehistory. The Mariner 10 spaceflight which photographed Mercury in 1974 showed the ancient craters on the innermost planet, evidence that these planetesimals had penetrated to the core of the System. Every planet, asteroid, and moon with a surface was scarred, but on some worlds secondary processes covered the wounds with lava or rubbed them off with winds and water. We measure the age of features in the Solar System by the presence or lack of planetesimal craters.

The meteoroids are the moraine of this ancient armada. Some carbonaceous meteorites bear amino acids and other organic compounds, which suggests that such chemistry may have been present, or potentially present, in the original nebula dust of the System. It is hard to know what this portends in either mechanical or vitalist terms, but it is unexpected. The carbonaceous meteorites might also be carriers of templates from other systems. The Earth could then be showered with life chains that did not originate natively, and we might be strangers and invaders on our own world. Of course, this does not solve the riddle of the origin of life; it transfers it elsewhere.

The original gases of the Solar System were a form of plasma. As the spirals cooled, substance was precipitated out, like ice. We find this substance in various states, ranging from the micrometeors of dust to the gases of the large Jovian planets. Most of the mass is still in the Sun. Only if we looked very closely would we notice the rocks and pebbles scattered about the solar disc. We might well overlook all of them except the four largest planets: Jupiter, Saturn, Neptune, and Uranus. Our own blue-green gem is a very tiny if remarkable pebble.

The larger planets have more of the aboriginal solar material. The smaller planets are almost completely rocky. On Earth, though, the rock has been layered over and incorporated into history. The historical process engulfs us and spawns us, but it is only local. Outside it lies everything else, living and not living. It takes life, biological forms, to weave such a history, and once it is done, it is final, until it is destroyed. The rock on Earth contains the encyclopedic regional histories of our planet, from massive continuous features like plains and mountain ranges to the strata of a single site by a pond over generations and aeons, even when it is uninhabited or inhabited by mute creatures. Rock which is not imbedded with fossils of life contains the prior history of lands where species of animals and tribes of men and women arose later, or did not, and where ecological chains unfolded in accordance with climate and native resources, all of which were incorporated into subsequent systems and technologies. We do not think of the soils of Kansas, the tin of Bolivia, the uranium of New Mexico, the harpoons of Greenland, or even the Arctic ice from which Eskimos build their homes as nebuloid matter, but it is all rock and galactic dust condensed at different points on the loom and then subjected to the rigors and meaning of terrestrial history. The aboriginal corn of Mexico and the barley and rye of Mesopotamia share this heritage.

The kernels of corn are food, not Sun, but they are originally Sun. The solar aspect of ourselves is what finds them edible.

Those sugars and "vitamins" that we assimilate are their solar aspects. And everything else in us and them is a solar aspect of another sort. If the kernel is Sun, so is the husk. If the golden metal is stellar excrement lodged in nebuloid lattices, so is the black lava hot from the cloud. And spiny spidery goldsmith creatures hammer away at ingots in the forge trying to represent something lodged shimmering within the solar archetype.

If the Moon is locally formed, then rocks brought back from it should give us a history of the formation of this entire region, for they are preserved from the first moment. Intense volcanic activity, water, and life have not significantly eroded or altered them, only meteoritic impact. They have sat, as it were, in suspended animation in the deep freeze of space, fossils of primordial cosmogony. The stars are even simpler representatives of a more ancient eon.

All our personal sense of complication, except for the topological and atomic complication of quasars and quarks and their kin, emerges from life and history within a world, more from riverbeds and family genealogies than from galaxies. Take that away and we have only simpler and older events. The history of the universe and the formation of the Solar System are easier to unravel than the migration of the Australian Aborigines in waves across the Pacific or the passage of Indian groups from North to South America. The blood types, languages, and myths of those groups are even more complicated. When Alex Haley worked his way back through the generations of slaves to the Gambian River whose name he had received intact along with the clan name of his African ancestor, and when the bard of his clan's tribal history sang his way back to the moment of Kunta Kinte's capture while out making a drum, a moment at which one face of creation was sundered from another, they had somehow gone deeper and farther than the Big Bang that is behind the universe itself.[3] No wonder Haley wept. He had an intimation of our lost beginning and our broken entanglement in the chain. It was like knowing that we have a beginning somewhere, that we are more than orphans of pond scum and galactic dust. Even the very different discovery of Australopithecus in a South African hill, testifying to the kinship of man with the

wild creatures of this world, is more stunning than the origin of
the Solar System. What Haley found may not even have been
the truth, and if it was, it still stands as less than a candle against
the night that lies behind us. But the real history of the universe
and its complication is unconscious to us, and the part of us that
knows it is unconscious too. So we experience it in replica as
the fragments and roots that can be made conscious and visible.
These claim our trembling and our tears for the whole condition.

The sense of the five original planets as worlds came fairly
late in European history, sometime between, roughly, Copernicus and Galileo. Copernicus demonstrated that it was mathematically simpler to treat the Earth as one of the planets than
as a body in their center; in a sense, this marked the discovery
of a fifth planet, on which we lived. Kepler then showed that all
these planets belonged to a system. Bruno and Cusa had not
distinguished between spirit realms and worlds. Galileo made
it clear: the planets were places that one might go to physically.
Until the meteorological criteria for life were fully recognized,
it was possible to imagine the exotic inhabitants of any one of
these ancient globes. The New World of the Americas, with its
"Indians," was still in the European psyche, and Asia itself was
potentially as foreign as Jupiter or Saturn.

But the idea of the Moon as a world is very old and predates
even any clear sense of the separate hemispheres of the Earth. At
least since ancient history people perceived the Moon as a floating
island, reachable, if not by land or sea, then by some unknown
topographic principle. With the occasional exception of the Sun,
the Moon was the one place in the sky where it was possible to go
without being transformed into a spirit.

For Plutarch, the Moon was a continent, close enough to be
considered part of the Earth's lands. He wrote of great selenean
valleys and shaded areas cast by lunar mountains. The Moon
aborigines bathed in dark oceans whose Latin name we retain in
the dust-bowl *maria* of the present Moon.

There is not so great a difference between the transits that
science fiction writers now pose between galaxies and those
which mages and sorcerors set between Earth and Luna: whirlpools and magical caves that link discontinuous regions become

telepathic tunnels that shoot bodies across physical space.

Kepler's *Somnium* described a journey to the Moon through the northern Polar region of the Earth. It had magical elements but was essentially a secular journey to a physical place. Bruno's worlds could be reached only by sympathetic magic on a cosmic scale: no ignorant layman or lowly astronaut could travel in such a universe. It was a realm of astral bodies ruled by magi and alchemists.

Kepler called his trip a "dream," probably to protect his pagan Copernican vision from the Church hierarchy. It is also a fairy tale that uses the nether elements of seventeenth-century Europe: a female magician speaking Icelandic summons a daemon, and the travelers leave the Earth at the Arctic, near the famed abysses of Mount Hekla. But Kepler looked upon the surface of the Moon and saw countryside, hills and valleys, living creatures. In a few more years, Galileo would peer through a glass and walk in the shadows of lunar mountain ranges. If the Moon was land, then the planets and their moons, after Galileo, were land too.[4]

Kepler's "Moonship" was constructed from the turgor of opiates and the upward rush of unencumbered mass; it was necessarily magical, for no one then could imagine a space vehicle or machine:

> The body no doubt escapes the magnetic force of the earth and enters that of the moon, so that the latter gets the upper hand. At this point we set the travellers free and leave them to their own devices: like spiders they will stretch out and contract and propel themselves forward by their own force—for, as the magnetic forces of the earth and moon both attract the body and hold it suspended, the effect is as if neither of them were attracting it—so that in the end its mass will by itself turn toward the moon.[5]

Kepler spoke of gravity here but did not recognize it.

While the alchemists watched the stages of scorching, whitening, and rainy deliquescence, Kepler dreamed a Moon of storms and seas, swift and sudden alternations of hot and cold. His Moon is spongy, serpentine, filled with "hollows and continuous caves." Life is shelled, long-legged, and serpentlike; the labyrinthine sublunar surface teems with aquatic creatures, rhe-

ostatic, subject totally to the flow of waters and their own somatic wetness—the pull of the Earth bringing them up into the
cold evening, the release of terrestrial weight lowering them into
the deep interior during the hot lunar day. "Growth is very
quick; everything is short-lived, although it grows to enormous
bodily bulk." This is Kepler's compromise between an occult
Moon and its possible physical properties.[6]

The Emperor Rudolph asked Kepler one night as they stared
at the orb in the sky if the Moon were not a mirror in which the
lands of the Earth were reflected; he pointed out Italy. No, said
Kepler, the Moon is a rugged wild land of its own. It is a place
lying to the north of all known civilization, north of North. It
appears in the sky only because air and other exquisite forces
have lifted it.

The seventeenth century did not come to the planets as blank
tablets. They had been astral unities for centuries; and before
that, they were gods, influences, spirits, and myth heroes. Every
world had already been layered with images and associations,
and, in a certain sense, had its peoples and its landscapes. These
were a translation of the astral and astrological influences of
these worlds on the Earth into local planetary sceneries. Mars
was martial from the beginning, red and bloody. There was no
way, after the fact, to distinguish Venus as a world from *primavera*
and the Rites of Spring. Every planet already had a metal, varieties of plants and animals, and an organ of the body. From
these the original planetary natures were drawn.

"Sense experience must become transparent," wrote the modern spiritual astronomer Norman Davidson, "so that an experience becomes a sense organ for what lies behind the phenomenon. ... No-one has ever seen the Copernican system, or ever
will. From the distance of the solar system, the sun would appear
as a star without companions."[7]

On the following pages, I will be concerned more with sculpting imaginal topologies of the planets than with giving the most
up-to-date and scientized versions of their meteorology and
landscapes. In the process, I have drawn on a variety of incompatible sources, mainly to get at the symbolic reality behind them.

It is almost impossible to be true to both the astrological

tradition of planetary images and the later planetary landscapes. The former stretch deep into the past and become richer, with more associations, the further back we go. The latter start as gigantic blankness, dark barges tugged in their orbits. The blankness is there only in our projecting back to the imaginary infancy of objective astronomy. The landscapes were always more sparkly and flamelike than the speculative realms to which we submit their remoteness and wilderness (by the same properties of the same lenses that resolve maria of viral molecules upon their helical lattices). They burn from the beginning. They cannot help but emerge from an astral symbolism.

15

The Planets II: Mercury and Venus

MERCURY is the innermost planet of the Solar System. An eccentric orbit brings it as close as 28.5 million miles from the Sun and then carries it to aphelion at 43.5 million miles. During the "new planet" furor of the nineteenth century, a planet even closer to the Sun was apparently discovered—Vulcan, with an orbit of 13 million miles and a diameter of 1,000 miles. It was named by Leverrier himself, but it is doubtful that it was ever seen. What appeared to some as Vulcan might have been sunspots, and the fate of that world is unknown. It shares a place in history with that other mysterious planet that circles the Sun in the Earth's orbit in such a way that the Sun always prevents us from viewing it—the so-called anti-Terra, long ago dismissed.

Mercury is difficult to see. Not only is it small, but it reflects a mere twentieth of the light that reaches its surface. When it is closest to the Earth, only its unlit side faces us; and when it is furthest from the Earth, it is eclipsed by the glare of the Sun which stands in between. As the two planets inside the Earth's orbit, Mercury and Venus are both morning and evening stars, always closely accompanying the Sun. But Venus is closer to us, larger, and more reflective, and, in fact, very bright. Mercury is seasonally obliterated by the Sun's light, and it is otherwise so dim and elusive that Copernicus lamented on his deathbed that he had never seen it, a bizarre virginity for such a passionate astronomer. Even Giovanni Schiaparelli, the nineteenth-century astronomer who mapped both Mercury and Mars, claimed that he struggled with an almost invisible object. Of the five planet-like stars of ancient cosmology, Mercury is the least visible, and it is a testimony to the perspicacity of the ancients not only that they saw it but that they realized it was on a par with the four more visible wanderers.

Ironically, Schiaparelli's maps of Mercury have held up better than his maps of Mars. They are no finer, but they are less ambitious, and we have not been able to improve much on his basic image. By contrast, his Mars, laced with *canali,* led to a whole mythology of Martians which was later abandoned, and the "canals" were never found. He participated in creating a different Mercurian mythology. After viewing the planet carefully over a long period, he decided that, like the Moon, Mercury had only a captured rotation. Thus, the same side was always turned toward the Sun. This was based on his impression that the surface markings did not change, and it gave Mercury a day and a year each of 88 Earth-days. We might then expect a planet with a parched molten side and a frozen side, with a possible twilight zone in between. If this zone truly existed, it might have temperate conditions. Science fiction writers peopled Mercury with creatures of fire warring against creatures of ice and with tribes of blind cave-dwellers in the central region, underground species who worshipped the Sun and had the same relationship to the surface of the planet that we have to outer space. In some versions, a race of sages dwells in the middle region, bearing, from their proximity to the Solar source, a wisdom that transcends anything else in the System. This is also astral Mercury, messenger of the gods and repository of the knowledge of the Sun.

In 1965, with a new technology of more powerful transmitters, this image vanished from astronomy. The planet was mapped from a radar-radio telescope at Arecibo, Puerto Rico, and was found to have a rotation period of 58.65 days. This creates a totally different Mercurian climate.

Before Mercury's axial rotation was computed, the planet was observed to wobble, a feature predicted by nineteenth-century observers on the basis of the eccentric orbit. Under the old axial period, the wobble would give Mercury as much as a quarter of its 3,000 miles diameter surface in twilight areas that move between heat and cold as the planet revolves around the Sun. On one side of Mercury, a temperature of almost 800° F. would melt lead and zinc, while on the other side, at − 280° F., the potential gases of the atmosphere would be partially liquefied and solidified into pools and slush.

In reality, though, Mercury has such a meager atmosphere as to be essentially airless. Until the Mariner 10 photographs confirmed this in 1974, one school of planetologists created a model for a stormy, poisonous Mercury based on the thin aura that appeared on the planet's disc against the Sun. We now know that the solar wind, combined with the low escape velocity of Mercury, swept this kind of material away long ago, but the model is interesting in itself. It gives an image for picturing Mercury's axial rotation, and it serves as an hypothesis for some planet like Mercury but a little larger.

On this hypothetical planet, the huge temperature differential would cause the winds to blow continuously at hurricane force, solidifying gaseous and molten metals and releasing exotic combinations of metallic gases. The relative thinness of the atmosphere would make the hurricane seem mild by comparison with the same wind velocity on the Earth, but it would still be appreciable, especially given the metallic sleet.

A rotation of 59 days is fast enough to prevent a purely hot side and a purely cold side, but it is not fast enough to balance the climates completely. Although temperatures on the sunward side of Mercury are now figured at a more "moderate" 600° F., it is hotter when the planet is close to the Sun; in regions that have been in the Sun longest, the temperatures may go up as high as 2000° F. The night side never sees the Sun for many Earth-months, and though it is far closer to the solar disc than anything on our own Equator, it may never get above − 50 F. Rock and metal are an effective heat shield.

A 59-day rotation is quite slow, so the Sun in its virtually black sky will crawl across the heavens in 176 days in a slightly zigzag path. Then it will set below the horizon, beginning 176 days of night. Because of Mercury's orbit, the planet actually moves around the Sun at perihelion faster than it spins, so some Mercurian zones will have two sunrises and sunsets in a day, and the Sun will appear to go backwards.

The originally-proposed thin but violent Mercurian atmosphere contained sulphur vapors, sulphur dioxide, krypton, xenon, iodine vapors, and the like, about as poisonous a mix as could be imagined for Earth blood and lungs. These materials would disperse into the atmosphere more and more rapidly as the day reached high noon at 90 Earth-days. As night fell, they would crystallize out of the atmosphere in a dirty rain that would soon become a metallic snow. If the planet's volcanic activity released any of the metal mercury, this would of course vaporize in the daytime, and would be one of the first metals to turn back into silver rain. Thus, dust, sulphur, and metal winds rush toward the dark side, and *from* the dark side come boiling gases as the Sun cuts away the solid edge with advancing daylight.

On Mercury as we now know it, there is probably not enough atmosphere to distinguish the night sky from the day sky; both are black, but the day sky has an enormous Sun in it, with a full corona visible. From this distance, the Sun is an ocean with turbulent waves, and its "wind" will blast most of the lingering or new gas molecules into space. If Earth colonists or scientists were to try what presently seems impossible and set up a habitation zone on Mercury, they would probably have to live underground to escape the Sun's radiation. The trick would be to use the heat of the long day to provide energy for the long night. It would be a solar energy paradise, the epitome of unlimited energy, but with all the dangers of a mammoth atomic energy plant. On Mercury the solar/atomic paradox is fully realized.

Man could do little there anyway except contend directly with the big energy source and make use of it. This points up the absurdity of wanting unlimited energy. Our mental image of Mercury captures much of our present resource greed, as befits the mythology of the planet of Hermes the thief, who steals everything from everywhere. Mercury is also a forge of metals, ready-melted and available in a low gravity situation. If there were a planet Vulcan, it would be an even hotter oven. The sky itself would be tumbling fires.

The Mariner 10 spacecraft came close enough to Mercury to begin photographing it in late March 1974. At first glance, the

planet fulfilled expectations and showed a "lunar" surface with
very old craters and some new rayed craters—streaks of light
new material radiating over the ancient dark. Closer examination
and more photographs showed Mercury not to be completely
moonlike. The cliffs and scarps proved that the planet had contracted after formation and its solid surface had wrinkled. Mercury also has a magnetic field. How this is generated without
faster rotation is still uncertain. The magnetosphere of Mercury
was also without radio signals, and it was generated by the planet
itself rather than by the solar wind.

On a second flyby a year later, the spacecraft passed to within
200 miles of the surface. Mercury was seen to be brighter than
the Moon, with cratered terrain similar to the lunar highlands,
but there were also very ancient plains underlying the craters,
including some smooth lavalike plains crossed with ridges and
cliffs. In the hot area of Mercury was a feature called Caloris
Basin, which is a crater with an unusual lava floor. The biggest
feature on the planet, the crater is 800 miles in diameter and was
possibly formed by an asteroid collision. Its floor has ridges and
complex radial and concentric features, inwardly cracking like
a dried-up pond.

Most notably, the conception of a stormy Mercury was put to
rest by the spacecraft. There was no appreciable atmosphere, so
the metal hurricanes were consigned to myth, or to some other
planet in an unknown solar system. Mercury is now known to
be like the Moon, but denser, hotter, and more disturbed and
complex geologically. Mercury is a dramatic case of Freud's law
applied to whole worlds: "Anatomy is destiny." But we will see
this again, planet after planet.

Pre-planetary Mercury is not only the messenger of the gods
but the late European incarnation of Hermes-Thoth, who carried the magical lore from the ancient Near East and was directly
associated with the origin of language. Hermes-Thoth is a wise
but dangerous sorcerer, bringing things into being too fast for
them ever to be used, like blinding sunlight and rivers of thorium, lead, bismuth, and antimony. In occult tradition, Mercury
represents the intellect and is assigned the color yellow, with
the white of magic bursting through a red robe of sensation in

the tarot card. The card stands for transparent consciousness as a vessel for pure communication, hence Mercury as conveyor of the gods' messages and those of the deeper unconscious.

Mercury "invented" astrology, astronomy, mathematics, geometry, medicine, grammar, and music. An amoral destroyer, Mercury is also a profoundly capable healer. On the psychological plane, it is quick and brilliant, spirited and fragmented, full of merry thoughts, puns, half-words, sounds, phonemes on the verge of meaning but dissociating before it can occur. The metal itself is mobile, forming tiny soft globules. It represents the lungs, which are symbolically a mercury forest of droplets connecting all oxygen-breathing life on the planet.[1]

Venus is the nearest planet to the Earth and also the brightest "star" in the night sky. It reflects twelve times as much light as Mercury and twice as much light as the Earth. Venus is covered with white clouds that shine like a planetwide snowpack. The only way we knew, initially, that we were not looking at snow was that it was far too smooth to be a surface.

Like Mercury, Venus accompanies the Sun from the Earth's perspective and is visible in the dawn and dusk skies. Until the time of Pythagoras, it was commonly thought to be two stars, the Egyptian Tioumoutiri and Quaiti and the Greek Phospheros and Hesperos, the morning and evening stars.

From the beginning of astronomical observation, the Cytherean cloud cover was the most dominant aspect of the planet. Mars and Mercury had surface features, and Jupiter and Saturn showed cloud patterns. Venus revealed nothing. It was simply a gleaming white star enshrouded in mists. Otherwise it resembled the Earth more than any other planet. Its diameter of 7,700 miles is only 200 miles less than that of the Earth. Its year is 224.7 Earth-days. Its distance from the Sun is 67.2 million miles, and it comes as close to the Earth as 27.5 million miles. At the most optimistic, it should be a warmer wetter Earth, and this, in fact, was its image all through early astronomy. The faint bluish light (the aureola) that Venus gives off as it crosses the face of the Sun suggests an abundant atmosphere, a fact that was noted as early as the middle of the eighteenth century. In *The Destiny of the Stars,* published in 1918, Svante Arrhenius, the

Swedish chemist who proposed that life was carried to Earth in spores from other systems (the panspermia theory), wrote that Venus was a warm misty land.[2] Swamps there would resemble those of the Earth's reptilian age. The vegetation would be unimaginably fertile from six times the Earth's humidity. Later in the century, some scientists proposed that Venus was a single planetary ocean covered with vegetation and filled with unimaginable varieties of sea creatures. It was difficult to avoid moving from Venus, the goddess of love and beauty, to a garden planet filled with primal dinosaurlike creatures and civilized fish-beings. These creatures might never have seen the sky, for as far as we know the clouds over Venus have not parted even for a second in all the years we have been viewing it. The creatures would never have seen the Sun, and they would have no explanation for the cycle of light and darkness. There is no starry night on Venus; it is in a different cosmos.

Closer to the Sun than we are, Venus has been taken for our own mythical past, when the Earth was younger and covered with wild vegetation, only its seas inhabited. Cytherean science fiction repeats this image. C. S. Lewis's *Perelandra* is Venus:

> Enormous purple clouds came driving between him and the golden sky, and with no preliminary drops a rain such as he never experienced began to fall. There were no lines in it; the water above him seemed only less continuous than the sea, and he found it difficult to breathe. The flashes were incessant. In between them, when he looked in any direction except that of the clouds, he saw a completely changed world. It was like being at the centre of a rainbow, or in a cloud of multi-colored steam. . . . All sorts of things seemed to be coming down in the rain—living things apparently. They looked like preternaturally airy and graceful frogs . . . and had the colour of dragon-flies.
>
> All day there had been no variation at any point in the golden roof to mark the sun's position, but now the whole of one half-heaven revealed it. The orb itself remained invisible, but on the rim of the sea rested an arc of green so luminous that he could not look at it, and beyond that, spreading almost to the zenith, a great fan of color like a peacock's tail. Looking over his shoulder he saw the whole

island ablaze with hue, and across it and beyond it, even to the ends of the world, his own enormous shadow.[3]

Venus was thought of as a world of rain forests, jungles, towering clouds, gigantic plants like tree-ferns, telepathic tribes, and mermaids. Yet, from the first spectroscopic analyses in 1920, no water vapor showed up in the atmosphere; instead there was an abundance of carbon dioxide. Reluctantly astronomers let their hold slip on this attractive wet world we wanted so much to exist. There were many reasons why water vapor might not be detected, but the accompanying failure to find oxygen was an ominous sign. A new model of Venus began to emerge: a violent desert with storms whipping dust and salt up into the atmosphere.

Scientists differed as widely as possible on the length of Venus's day. Some thought of it as short, like the Earth's; others thought that Venus rotated with one side always to the Sun, and thus that it had a day equal to its year of 225 days. The cloud cover made it impossible to know who was correct until 1965, when Venus's rotation was measured from Arecibo with a startling result that no one had predicted. Its day was found to be 247 Earth-days, longer than even its year. Furthermore, it was found to rotate on its axis in a direction opposite to its motion around the Sun. Several moons in the Solar System are retrograde, but Venus is the only planet. No explanation has been found. The Sun rises on Venus in the West and sets in the East, but, in any case, is not seen at all.

Seven spacecraft, both Russian and American, were flown by Venus during the 1960s, and four of the Russian ships either crashed or soft-landed on the planet. These explorations buried forever the notion of beautiful oceanic Venus. Whereas spectroscopic analysis had indicated carbon dioxide in the atmosphere, researchers felt that 3 percent would have been an enormous amount—100 times the carbon dioxide content of the Earth's atmosphere. Mariner 5 showed that Venus had 90 percent carbon dioxide, producing a greenhouse effect of unimaginable proportions. Venus was very hot; temperatures of 900° F. were measured. The cloud cover was solid and dense, twenty miles thick, extending to forty-five miles above a rocky or sandy surface. The intense heat apparently melted the Russian craft Venera 4. Living on Venus would be like dwelling more than thirty-five feet beneath the surface of a terrestrial ocean, for the surface pressure of Venus's atmosphere is ninety times that which we have. The density of the atmosphere so strongly bent the radio signals sent from Mariner 5 when it passed behind the planet that they circled Venus and returned to the sender, never reaching the Earth at all. Needless to say, clouds, winds, dust, and pressure make Venus an utterly arid planet of deserts with knife-sharp stormy air. Even spacecraft are melted and crushed, some before reaching the ground.

In June 1975, the Russian spacecraft Venera 9 finally parachute-landed a capsule, which then photographed a surface of young irregular rocks. The ship seemed to have landed on a hill on which rocks were rolling down (33° N. latitude and 293° longitude in a region noted as dark from radar mapping). Venera 10 landed in October 1975 on an older plain and found dark soil and pitted rocks, indicating erosion and weathering. The planet was also not as dark as the Russians had expected. At ground level there was at least as much sunlight as on a cloudy day in Moscow in June, and objects and details 330 yards away could be seen.

The surface air was found to be relatively gentle, but the enormous upper atmosphere whipped around the planet in four days, adding pressure to the surface. From spacecraft reports, the clouds seemed to be ice or quartz dust in their middle regions. At thirty miles up, the winds attain 160 miles per hour; while on the surface just below, they blow at a mild 1⅓ miles per hour. Meanwhile, the uppermost clouds move at 260 miles per hour. Mariner 10 showed a specific polar hood and complex circulation patterns forming a planetwide complex; there was a particular stormy region at the point of direct sunlight. By 1973, new photographic techniques in the infrared range revealed the upper clouds as 75 percent sulphuric acid and the rest water. With fluorine also present in the atmosphere, this leads to corrosive clouds of fluosulfonic acid. The entire process is extraordinarily complicated, with sunlight heating the upper clouds, and surface and chemical reactions heating the lower ones.

Venus also showed no magnetosphere but a tremendous solar wind wake.

Although heat and chemistry alone had done away with the Garden, it was still surprising when radar mapping showed enormous craters, seemingly planetesimal markings billions of years old that had not undergone erosion or volcanic flow. However, some mountains, chasms, and very long lava flows appeared on the maps, and one huge cratered volcano. James Maxwell has the distinction of having his name on both the tallest mountain (Maxwell Montes rises 35,400 feet above Ishtar Terra, a northern hemisphere highlands) and the Maxwell Lava Flow, hundreds of miles long.

An American Pioneer satellite equipped with radar entered Cytherean orbit on December 4, 1978, and it proceeded to map the planet's surface. No distinct plates have shown up in the crust of Venus—hence no grinding collisions to produce earthquakes and volcanoes. It is one continuous continent. The surface rocks are much thicker than Earth's, and the hot plastic material beneath them is unable to break through. The satellite has also mapped a rift 1,400 miles long and 9,300 feet deep cutting across Aphrodite Terra.

Venus seems as though it should be like the Earth, but it isn't. If both started with the same amount of carbon dioxide, the Earth reassimilated its supply in the carbon of the rocks in the planet's crust and in the oxygen of the atmosphere. Also, aboriginal sea creatures and water itself took carbon out of the air and put it into the ground. Since the carbon cycle apparently never took place on Venus, perhaps because of the greater heat keeping the carbon in the atmosphere, the same chemical endowment could have led to carbon dioxide remaining a gas, which would have increased the planet's heat even more. Life-giving on Earth, where it formed the central node of protoplasm chains, carbon was life-smothering on Venus. Perhaps the oxygen lost from boiling water vapor on Venus combined with carbon that was not bound into the crust of the planet to form more carbon dioxide.

On Earth everything went right, at least for us: hydrogen and oxygen went into water; carbon went into limestone and other rocks. On Venus carbon dioxide remained gaseous; heat increased; and water vapor reached the upper atmosphere, where the molecules lost their hydrogen, giving rise to a hydrogen corona. The Earth loses water this way only fractionally, but

Venus, which is almost baked dry, still loses another million tons a day. The greenhouse effect is a vicious cycle; yet it could have begun from only a slightly warmer temperature in the beginning. Such is the subtlety of planetary chemistry.

In current times, Venus has been anything but a Garden of Eden. It is a warning of the possible fate of Earth if industrial waste products continue to pour into the atmosphere, adding to the carbon dioxide while the carbon-removing forests of Africa and South America are bulldozed away. On one side we may be threatened by another ice age, but on the other we are fore-warned by Venus that whole oceans can boil off and that this begins with a subtle temperature difference.

Some planetologists have suggested seeding the atmosphere of Venus with carbon dioxide-consuming algae that thrive in high temperatures. If these found Venus tasty, and if there were no native life (at least in the upper atmosphere) competing with them, they would multiply and cover the Cytherean sky, turning it green and working their way down in the atmosphere. Since they thrive in hot springs, these algae could perhaps survive the temperatures on Venus. Photosynthesis would release oxygen, and great millennial rains would begin. For thousands of years it might rain on Venus, and we would get our garden after all.[4] Maybe. The idea is perhaps more symptomatic of our condition than a realistic response to another world, but who is to say of people who have come this far down the path?

Immanuel Velikovsky, an often discredited scientist, inter-preted the conditions on Venus very differently.[5] Long before the present spectroscopic and radar discoveries, Velikovsky theorized that Venus was not a sister of Earth at all but a comet that had been torn out of the planet Jupiter and arrived in the vicinity of the Earth three thousand years ago, reversing our magnetic field and causing global cataclysms. Velikovsky specif-ically traces this comet to Athena, born from the forehead of Jupiter and Astarte with her two tails. He also cites other myth-ological evidence from cultures throughout the Earth.

Such an origin might explain the climate and composition of Venus, its dissimilarity from the Earth, its retrograde motion, and its nonexistent magnetic field, none of which are satisfactorily handled by present theory. Velikovsky died embittered that, as new scientific evidence appeared to cry out for a revised model of Venus, his was summarily dismissed. The scenario of planets as moving actors jumping out of one another was too outlandish and radical, and this far outweighed any circumstantial evidence.

His comet Venus had a violent history after it emerged from Jupiter. It disturbed Mars in its orbit and showered both Mars and the Earth with radioactivity. Part of its tail was captured by Mars, another part was torn loose by the Earth and became petroleum clouds which settled into the ground. Velikovsky assumed that the petroleum came from the decay of a species of vermin that inhabits Jupiter and Venus. This would mean that our wealthiest oil sources are not terrestrial but Jovian in origin, carried here by a comet that became Venus. Stealing some of the Earth's oxygen, Venus set its own petroleum on fire, and this continues to burn, giving off the white carbon clouds. Velikovsky's followers have created a whole theology out of this planetary event. Note the following from a pamphlet handed out in New York City in 1964:

> None have sinned, not one. No one is to blame for *any* of the atrocities of the past 6000 years, nor for any that are to come. There was no sin in Sodom and Gommorah. The flames came down from a comet. It was nobody's fault that the flood came down. The water came from a comet, not a god.
>
> It was a comet, not a person, not a hand, not an eagle, not a snake, not a demon, not a holy father, not a holy mother, not a witch, not a cat, not a wolf, not a ghost, not a vampire, not a dragon, not a sword, not a bull, not a cross, not an angel, not a phantom, not any of these things.
>
> It was a blind unthinking and unhearing comet. It was sent by no one. It intended no evil and no good. It had no intentions at all relevant to the human species. It listened to no prayers and accepted no sacrifices. It made no promises and chose no special people. Those who were destroyed were destroyed by chance alone. Those who were spared were spared by chance alone.
>
> . . . It was a comet, not a god.

This is the modern prejudice anyway, though not on the basis of Venus's origin as a Jovian comet.

In the traditional occult, Venus is the goddess of love and ripeness, tranquility and charity. It represents the desire within nature to grow and spread and become wild fields of plants and herds of beasts. It is subconsciousness, generating ideas, creating form out of Mercurial fragments. Even minerals are spawned by the archetypal intelligence of Venus.

The metal of Venus is copper, which is associated with both water and plants—water by its ability to absorb fluid, and plants by its green color. Venus the goddess emerged from the ocean like copper in foam.

Venus was once cohesion and beauty, creation through eros. But now we have a twentieth-century inferno. Traditional symbols do not lie. Is this the disappointment of industrialism mirrored back in the enigma of radar Venus, which still lies beneath a white mist?

16

The Planets
III: The Moon,
the Earth,
and Mars

NO BODY IN THE SKY has been more devalued in the modern transition from the spiritual heavens than the Moon. Luna was once an equal partner to the Sun. Sol ruled by day, Luna by night. Alchemically, the Sun was gold, the Moon silver; the Sun was the King, the Moon the Queen. Together they bred the metals. The Sun brought fiery intelligence and conscious seed; the Moon brought memory and unconscious growth. Between them, they made man. From this throne the Moon has tumbled into a replica of crude inert rock hammered by meteoroids.

To ancient astronomers, the Moon seemed to be the same size as the Sun. It is actually only a quarter the size of the Earth, with a diameter of 2,160 miles. Its proximity to us, not its size or brightness, gives it a central place in our mythological and physical systems. As a satellite, the Moon is an anomaly. No other planet has a moon even close to a quarter of its own size; in fact, the Earth and Moon comprise a double planet system, with each having substantial influence on the other.

The Moon's overbearing mass leaves the Earth vulnerable to a powerful lunar internalization. The engagement of these two is carried out in the one way possible for bodies in space: gravitationally. Our surface seas, biological waters, and molten metals are tugged back and forth by the Moon. Inanimate materials record this force through their own mammoth structures on the Earth, transposing lunar rhythms into grand topographies, selenean grottoes and palaces. Caves are hollowed out by the Moon's tides, and sediments are built up in lunar cycles. Glaciers accumulate the icy tides. Animate materials "remember" the Moon and store it in cellular and psychic phases that go on for the lives of organisms and the histories of species even when these are broken from the rhythm of the actual Moon. Inanimate tides can only respond to the Moon as it is. Living things can record the lunar music, dance to it in other phases, and pass it on through chromosomes to their remote descendants, so that *they* will embody both the ancient Moon and the Moon of their own moment in time. Between the old and the new phases, complex lunar patterns emerge. And the visible Moon is taken into folklore and myth, where it finds itself again, symbol against biological rhythm, and reemerges with new myths, deeper and more remote lunar music, and the traditional chalices, coins, goddesses, and temples.

Lunar effects are so scattered and so imposed and reimposed on each other, melodically and amelodically, that we can no longer find them, but there is a Moon present in every one of us, and in every natural event, in every stone and piece of dust—a Moon of some significance. The Moon leads subtle psychosomatic currents through our waking and sleeping, our consciousness and unconsciousness. Passing overhead, the Moon lightens the ocean by one ten-thousandth of its mass. The entire waters are lifted together in a single coherence, and the tides slide out. Organic liquids are molecular, and the lunar response is intensified in their high-pressure capillaries. Lunar sensitivity is excruciating. The tides may seem like raw neutral events when we regard waters on a bare rock ledge, seas receding to show long tidal flats and shellfish beds, but every internal shift within us releases profound sensations, images, and shapes, transforming the most basic aspects of what we are. The Moon stirs creatures with unintentional movement, endless aimless activity or wandering. The Solar System is a medley of tidal effects, but the Moon's are the most powerful on us because they share our solar orbit. The two bodies are in constant interaction and interference, and their gravitational waves form a complex Earth-Moon field. If the Earth is animate and the Moon is dead, surely this is only part of the picture—the Earth must share in the Moon's deadness, and the Moon must share in the Earth's life. The first photographs of the Earth from the Moon remind us of an original indivisibility.

The occult Moon stands for the stream of consciousness that flows between the manifested world and the hidden world. As spiritual silver, it is the source of regeneration and reproduction: in crystals, as cellular somatic material, and as thoughts, numbers, images, ideas. It embodies the colloidal basis of life and mind. The use of silver in photography reminds us that the Moon itself is like a photograph of the cosmos. Sunlight, starlight, and meteorite obliteration fall on it, and it is a perfect mirror, a photograph of everything that has happened. The autonomic Moon functions in the personality as instinct, desire to touch, and also as fear and flight. These are quick silvery gestures. Astrologically, the Moon draws out of the other planets their strongest tendencies. It is a mirror, and the mirroring is an eternal deepening of their own individualities.[1]

There is an old hermetic/astrological belief that the Earth is bound by the Moon, imprisoned by it. Occult practice demands the making conscious of blind responsive and reactive movements. The counterlunar disciplines are the most difficult, yet crucial, for men and women to master. They include meditation, awakening within dream, precise choreography, prescribed ceremony, poetics, the martial arts, and all those other disciplines that seek to break with the Moon by imitating it and imposing it back on itself. An infinitesimal amount of being is made conscious, and through that man adds directionality to his life.

Luna stands for the enslavement of man's will in blind, meaningless, destructive activity, mechanicalness, and habit. The Moon sustains life, but unchecked lunar flow becomes simply an agony and a spasm. William Faulkner writes of being born, trying to act, and finding all these other people and their arms and legs in the way, and one's own arms and legs in the way, and all of them animated as if by puppet strings.[2] Although he did not intend it as such, this is a description of the negative astrological Moon in the collective personality of the Earth.

In Gurdjieffian philosophy, the Moon sucks people's souls into its body at the moment of death, and this endless transit is the living link between the Earth and its dead animator. It is the ultimate basis for the association of the Moon with death. The souls are living electric things, built up by the transformation of stellar matter through digestion and breathing into thought and spirit; they can be attracted magnetically and physically by a proximate body. That body need not be sentient; it can be as oblivious of dreams and fantasies as a comet is, but it will eat souls as we eat the animals we kill. Perhaps Gurdjieff's Moon is the devouring Eagle of Juan Matus' cosmology, a ravenous, all-seeing giant past whom only masters can flee. As the sorceror warned Carlos Castaneda, we will be a gift for someone else, even as the rabbit in our trap must, in the economy of nature, be a gift for us.

The Moon is the first obstacle to be overcome by the soul after it has been separated from organic nature, for it must recognize that it will be sucked into its own habit, into automatic response, and thus into oblivion of any individuality it has developed. The Gurdjieffian dances hammer away at lunar subjugation and teach the dancers single free movements from among the Moon motions they defiantly mimic back. Freedom is formed of lunar activity made conscious. Otherwise all bursts of freedom are illusory, mere sublimated lunar gestures.

Gurdjieff was a ruthless and severe guru because he felt that the chances for preserving any of this after death depended on absolutely unswerving training, to break down the Moon's habitual pull on Earth life. Action had to be made conscious. Men had to see their true situation in the universe. "The earth," he said, "is a very bad place from the cosmic point of view—it is like the most remote part of northern Siberia, very far from everywhere, it is cold, life is very hard. Everything that in another place either comes by itself or is easily obtained, is here acquired only by hard labor; everything must be fought for both in life and in the work." [3]

He had no pity for those who suffered. Pain was a means of waking people up, momentarily startling them out of lunar tyranny. Those who suffered needed not sympathy but training to make the suffering conscious. Pain located them in the real universe.

Everything consumes and transforms. Man must convert elemental material back into spiritual substance if he is not to die unredeemed.

But perhaps there is also a Boddhisattva function in the universe; perhaps there is one who does not himself enter paradise until all the other souls have gone before him. So he has a long wait. The cows are sentient as they stand in the field, carrying in the heat none other than their own heavy bodies, their tails swishing the flies. He will wait for them. Pine needles, maple leaves, catkins of momentary flowers; he will wait. Three men in a car in L.A. shoot a child on the sidewalk for kicks. He will wait. "In every particle of dust," we are told, "there are present Buddhas without number."

The astronomical Moon clearly stands for the beginnings of this present system. Some say that it came out of the same nebula cloud that formed the Earth. Others say that it was captured from deep space. It is slightly less dense than the Earth, so either it got the lighter material out of the swirl or it originated elsewhere.

"The Moon is more than our lamp of night," wrote Rudolf Thiel, "more than the generator of our tides, more than a frozen, lifeless satellite. It is a surviving document out of the first day of Creation, from a day that perhaps even antedates the birth of light. It bears upon its face a runic script that tells us of how in the darkness of earliest genesis the heavenly bodies of the solar system, moons and Earth, and all the rest, emerged out of the primal nebula and grew great under a hail of meteorites." [4]

In the captured Moon scenario, the original Earth was roiling with radioactive fires; water from underground steam was beginning to collect in pools, and the primeval ocean was formed. It rained and rained and rained, eroding rocks, producing clay and mud and swamps. Shorelines emerged. Mountains built up in the sea. Enormous cumulus and nimbus clouds sparked lightning in the deluge, ultraviolet light rained down from the Sun, and the first amino acid chains came tumbling through the broth. The fertile water washed up on the clays, where new elements were incorporated into the DNA strands. Then this runaway planet swept into the Earth's field, swallowing the original moons in tremendous explosions. Gravity grabbed it and tore it, and continues to hold it with one face on the Earth. Tides stirred and volcanoes burst under the stress. But the runaway was caught. And so were we. Fiery stones showered the Earth. Hot lava spewed from the belly of this dead thing and spread across its primal craters. Now two planets were locked into orbit around one another 93 million miles from a sun-star, circling each other at a distance of 240,000 miles and orbiting the sun in 365¼ days.

A local origin for the Moon as the Earth's twin is far more likely, as we shall see. In either case, our satellite is an example of what happens to stellar material when it is cooled and exposed without an atmosphere. Nothing keeps the meteoroids out and nothing erases their marks. Trillions of tons of rock have been added to the Moon since its birth, leaving a world of craters-within-craters. The biggest one is 800 miles in diameter, now filled in with lava and called a "sea." The impact must have nearly fissioned the Moon. The next biggest craters are 185 miles in diameter, and the smallest can be found in beads of Moon rock viewed through an electron microscope. The seas (*maria*) are actually old impact craters covered with lava. One-third of the Moon's hemisphere that faces us is made up of these and of the lakes (*lacus*) and marshes (*paludes*). They are all lava, with a layer of dust.

The fact that man went to the Moon in his ships, collected stones from its actual body, and returned to tell of it is a great tale, one that a Pawnee priest with his ancient medicine rocks would appreciate. We are committed to artifacts by our history. We value the oldest things: coins from the tombs of Egypt, the jade of the Confucian emperors, and the gold and silver pots of Asia Minor. Archaeologists have sifted the dusts of the Earth looking for relics of past civilizations and the early peoples of the New World. It is no longer a matter of rubies and gold, and it never really was. More valuable are the chipped pebble tools and molar teeth of creatures who lived and died millions of years ago, whose thoughts we cannot imagine, yet who began thought and so must be contained rudimentarily and fundamentally in our own thinking. We have scoured the Great Plains, Borax

Lake, Frightful Cave, and Five Mile Rapids, looking for clues to migrations that took place following sacred constellations across whole continents. We have collected Clovis points, manos, hammerstones, scapula bones, Thule harpoons, medicine bundles, praysticks, and Mandan poles. So we have voyaged to the "Moon" before, or to aboriginal sites that give our succession meaning. Because of the history of science in the West, the Moon rocks have a meaning they could never have in Pawnee or Hopi culture. They are the actual Moon. They are the completion of a question asked over thousands of years.

In analyzing the lunar artifacts, we are the same people who recreate the sequence of Indian cultures in the Great Basin from their broken tools. We accept that matter is never created, never destroyed, at least in our time. The Moon is an alternate version of ourselves, with a different destiny. In the Moon rocks we see the mark of the beginning of time—the formation of our own world and the other worlds in this System. And we have fulfilled the consequence of that kind of logic by going there to get them.

Several different types of rocks were brought back. Igneous rocks, mainly of calcium and aluminum silicates, were evidence of a once-molten Moon and the planetesimal and meteoroid deposits that began at birth more than four billion years ago. As the Moon's crust was forming, meteorites fell into its glowing red ingot. Although the Moon is not volcanic in the sense of having eruptive cones, it is volcanic insofar as igneous material breaks through cracks in the lunar surface. Basalts and rocks of potassium, phosphorus, and rare earths were formed in the following billion years from deep lava flows working their way to the surface. The oldest basalts have high percentages of titanium, a fact still unexplained. The glasslike and beady rocks also indicate some unknown agency. Despite this, and despite the Moon's lack of an iron core, the chemistries of the Earth and the Moon are remarkably similar, suggesting that these two worlds originated in the same whorl of the cosmic nebula.

As a lifeless, airless world, the Moon has been consigned to the planetary junkheap, but then fair Venus has proven to be a wasteland of another order, and the Moon has other redeeming qualities. Those who advocate space stations point to the Moon's low gravity, unimpeded diurnal solar energy, and abundant metals. Material mined on the surface of the Moon could be tossed directly into space by machines; there it could be smelted by raw sunlight and constructed into enormous dwelling and research units in the virtually gravityless void. With far less energy than on Earth, millions of people could be housed and fed. Using the Moon, we approach the life-giving Sun. And we begin to imitate the supercivilizations of our science fiction, who engineer great wheels and tubes about their planets, intricate cosmic mandalas dwarfing the original world.

But when we reduce worlds to mines, we reveal our ultimate prejudice toward ceaseless resources and expansion. We are callous capitalists, even the communists among us. We will use anything we can claim. This is our brilliance. If there are no Selenites or Martians to dispossess, our job is all the easier. But that does not mean we will look long and hard for them, and in places where men would not go. Once again, we will shoot first and ask questions later.

Is space construction the next step of cultural evolution? Or is the industrial age a false trail that contains the terms only for its own reduction to entropy? Can the Earth's biosphere, down to the subtlest life-chains, insects, and critical traces in soil and bacteria, be duplicated on artificial planet-moons? Has it already been duplicated by agribusiness in its monocrop farms? Or are these another mistake that risks ultimate famine for temporary plenty? Gurdjieff argued that we cannot mine even the Earth without disrupting our psychospiritual life, for all the deposits of minerals and metals have vital counterparts in the balanced personality of the planet. Global derangement comes exactly from dismantling the Earth's mineral psyche. It is clear, in any case, that industrialism, and the collective salvation that it proposes, can expand only into outer space. And if it can't go there it can no longer lead us, and another prophecy awaits our coming.

We cannot defile the lunar imagery that we have accumulated in our being. We can no more change what the Moon is by spaceflights than we can hide the real nature of the Earth by factories and cities. The old nature myths and gods remain, hidden within us and in sacred regions. The Moon goddesses remain, and the Moon itself in the sky continues to mold and initiate us.

Some 7,927 miles in diameter, slightly oblate and inclined on its axis, 8⅓ light-minutes from the Sun, the Earth is a living planet, geologically and biologically. Like the other planets, it was formed in a molten ball, and its solid parts developed as plates floating atop the original incandescence. New magma continuously erupts within, moving the plates and spreading the continents to new locations. They crash together, raising mountains and sinking coastlines. California and Egypt are temporary lands on a world that has seen Atlantis and Lemuria come and go thousands of times.

Biology and its consequent chemistry make the Earth what it is. Plants capture sunlight by photosynthesis and create a living layer above the stone. The oxygen they release may have been poisonous to the earliest life forms, but later creatures used oxidation as a means of releasing energy from substance, which led to complex animals of many cells. These then created another level interpenetrating the plants.

Water is the key to the chemical cycles which occur above the lithosphere. Water covers three-quarters of the Earth's surface, and most of that is ocean water filled with salts, metals, and dissolved gases—sixty of the ninety-two natural elements. Less than 1 percent of the planet's water is fresh; 2 percent is frozen in glaciers and ice caps. Some of it is contained in the atmosphere in complex cloud patterns that are integrated into cohesive weather systems by temperature zones and the ocean streams and currents. Water has a continuously moderating effect on climate, cooling hot areas and warming colder zones.

The oxygen in the atmosphere is critical to most living beings, but it is mixed with three times as much inert gaseous nitrogen. In the upper layers of the atmosphere, the oxygen becomes ionized, forming an ozone layer which protects the surface from radiation.

Blue oceans, white clouds, and brown-red land masses dominate the Earth that is seen from space. For all that we do in our divided nations and philosophies, we create this one lovely coherence and survive within its nurturing. One gets the illusion, said the astronaut Michael Collins, that there are somehow many worlds, many possibilities of this one world, if from nothing else than from the number of photographs there are of the world and the number of different ways in which it is referred to and discussed. But it is neither arbitrary nor multiple. Collins saw a single globe sitting there, once, uno, primo, in space, as its clouds and oceans changed.

To enter the Earth by metal craft is a vibrating, shattering experience, and this is how it should be. Gravity protects this special place, a zone removed from its surroundings by more than simple space and the invisible fields and belts that issue from it. It is a wet hole in a desert trillions of miles long in all dimensions. And within that larger moistness are billions of moist bodies, jellies held together by hydrostatic tension and their own tough cellular networks, impermeable by simple water. Within them are still tinier bodies: eggs, spores, genes. Being born into the Earth through this chain of matter is also a vibrating, shattering experience. The newborn infant crawls as a pagan newt from its mother, choking on its own blood. It is also an astronaut reaching this world in a ship made of the finest materials: earth, air, fire, and water. For us, the Earth is where incarnation and creation meet. We lie here watching shapes form and dissolve as the cumulus clouds blow in from the ocean and out over the hills.

Every day, we can try to see our celestial habitat as Collins viewed it from outside. The Sun sets, and its bent rays scatter blue particles across the zenith while multicolored particles dance at the horizon. Then the air is quiet, and stars pop through the darkening veil, the brightest ones first, until night is complete and there are thousands of them. Meanwhile, the Earth itself is rotating, so that the ocean of sunlight continues to wash against a new tinted edge of dawn, crashing through the last shadows with brilliant morning light.

Two millennia earlier, Lucretius described this realm from the old Empire:

Showers perish when father ether has flung them down into the lap of mother earth. But the crops spring up fresh and gay; the branches on the trees burst into leaf; the trees themselves grow and are weighed down with fruit. Hence in turn man and brute draw nourishment. Hence we see flourishing cities blest with children and every leafy thicket loud with new broods of songsters. Hence in lush pastures cattle wearied by their bulk fling down their bodies, and the white milky juice oozes from their swollen udders. Hence a new generation frolic friskily on wobbly legs through the fresh grass, their young minds tipsy with undiluted milk. Visible objects therefore do not perish utterly, since nature repairs one thing from another and allows nothing to be born without the aid of another's death.[5]

Stars mold the universe in three dimensions of space and one of time. The original nuclear fires have been subsumed in the atom, and a thin smoke blows off the loom of gravity, leaving behind bright, tinted worlds; fields of wild clover; snakes and barnacles and flies; and seas of liquid and air. The flight of the space shuttle *Columbia* demonstrates the complexity of the star rhythms. We cannot flood space with our cities and fly off to other worlds yet. A barrier prevents such extension. We must train ourselves in the exactitude of gravity, progressing through its labyrinth one step at a time. The resolution of *Columbia* lies hundreds, perhaps thousands, of years beyond; but, if we do not infinitesimally creep into the star net, those who follow us will be disinherited. There is no shortcut, and no one can do it for us. What the space program demonstrates, the master of *t'ai chi ch'uan* has known for generations: there is only one form, one axis, one center; after each move has been internalized, a deeper move follows, and then another, endlessly, all in precise and absolute attention to gravity—whether it be rolling a ball of energy from the *tan t'ien* up the spine or re-entering the windy world in a giant glider. We scrape the surface of perhaps a fourth dimension whose naked force could place us in another galaxy or shoot an opponent forty feet into the air. We can no more touch it than an amoeba can swim out of the tide, but we can allow its current to carry us zone by zone across the sea.

If we could travel fast enough, in ships powerful enough, at close to the speed of light, we would actually be able, within our lifetimes, to reach the most distant galaxies imaginable. We are twenty-one light-years from our own Galactic center, twenty-eight light-years from another galaxy. If we built a ship that ran on interstellar particles and radiation and traveled at close to the speed of light, we could end up in cosmically remote regions that our birth in this part of the Milky Way would seem to have denied us forever; we could experience water dripping in a cave on another planet around a Sun in another galaxy. Upon returning to Earth millions of years later, we would find the constellations twisted out of shape and nothing at all on our home planet, even archaeologically, remaining from our time of birth. Yet we ourselves would survive.

This may not be possible after all, but if it is not possible, then that is so for technical reasons, and we can always imagine another technology that could accomplish it, and we can project it years into the future or to people in other galaxies who ostensibly visit us in UFOs. The point is that it is cosmologically possible. And so our imprisonment in matter is open along at least one subtle arc. The universe is somehow made up of present time distended and stretched out to eternity. We are not just clay and not just vibration. We are their alchemical wedding. The Earth likewise.

Daniel Statnekov recently described for me a quest which began when, at an auction in Delaware County, Pennsylvania, he bid successfully on an old piece of South American pottery. One day, without premeditation, he blew into its spout; the resulting tone shot him into a body of light which sped across a universe of luminous bodies and black clouds. From that moment he sought the shaman behind the sound. Initially, he searched museum storerooms for companion pots; he oversaw experiments on the acoustics of the whistles; he visited Peru. Ultimately, he apprenticed himself to a moldmaker in Los Angeles and there recreated the jugs. Then he drove across the desert to a wilderness area of Southern New Mexico to the New-Age Rainbow Family's annual sacred gathering. That night, under a blazing Moon, he handed the whistles to those present and instructed them how to play, until a eerie chant filled the forest. In my own first-person account of his experience:

Pulses of energy coursed through my body. Something else was awakened within me. It was a voice I had heard before, many times in fact during this quest. Now I could hear it for what it is. It was the voice of the mind that goes on imagining despite anything and despite everything.

"Perhaps *I* was the shaman behind the whistles, flowing backward against the weft of time. No!, there was my arrogance again. Perhaps the shaman of the whistles existed outside of time and combined moments in remote civilizations to weave the long body of the Earth: the Earth, the single animated planet Earth, which was just one big whistling vessel, the single tone of which merged with the Rainbow Gathering of the Solar System.

Of course, Temple of Sun and Moon—of course, ancient shaman potters casting *us* in the vibrating clay.[6]

As surely as Venus, being closer to the Sun and younger, became the Earth's mythical past, so Mars became our legendary future—a dying civilization on a planet grown old, a planet whose magma had cooled sooner, whose life had formed earlier, which had civilization when the Earth had only one-celled animals, which expended its air and water sooner, and now is in the last throes of existence after millions of years of history. Our hypothetical Martians were alternatively wise and peaceful, expansive and invading. Some of them were like Earthlings, others were based on the chemistry of silicon because of its bonding affinity with carbon and its ostensible abundance in the Martian sands.

From the time that Schiaparelli saw the lines in 1877 and Percival Lowell drew the waterworks and imagined an ancient civilization trying to preserve itself by drawing water from the polar caps, Mars has, to our minds, been inhabited. The Martians were our cosmic neighbors whom we strove one day to have the pleasure of meeting.

It has often been pointed out that the idea of Martian canals arose first in a mistranslation of Schiaparelli's term *canali* as "canals" rather than "channels." Lowell, conceiving these as artificial structures, published two provocative books: *Mars and Its Canals* and *Mars as the Abode of Life.* The Martians, he speculated, not only built these canals to irrigate their increasingly dry planet; they also launched two large satellites, the moons Deimos and Phobos. In Lowell's own words:

> . . . The lines start from points on the coast of the blue-green regions, commonly well-marked bays, and proceed directly to what seem centers in the middle of the continent, since most surprisingly they meet there other lines that have come to the same spot with apparently a like intent. . . . The lines appear either absolutely straight from one end to the other, or curved in an equally uniform manner. There is nothing haphazard in the look of any of them. . . .
>
> A mind of no mean order would seem to have presided over the system we see—a mind certainly of considerably more comprehensiveness than that which presides over the various departments of our own public works. Party politics, at all events, have no part in them; for the system is planetwide. [7]

Lowell's Mars spawned the "mediæval" desert civilizations of Edgar Rice Burroughs to which John Carter, his fictional hero, astrally projected. This kingdom gave way to the more peaceful telepathic sages of Robert Heinlein and Ray Bradbury, but Lowell lay behind all of them. His image was that compelling.

Until the first space probes, Lowellian Mars was still a possibility, though analysis of the density and composition of the Martian atmosphere during the 1950s seemed to all but do away with it. The later version was perhaps not exactly as Lowell had conceived it, but was rather a combination of his conception and Bradbury's and those of hundreds of other science fiction writers. If the red planet did not hold intelligent beings, at least it must have life—a fact which would be almost as stunning in its actuality as the imaginary monuments of long-dead civilizations. From the beginning, Mars betrayed us, almost exactly in the way the whole second half of the twentieth century has, which is the way in which we have betrayed ourselves.

Mariner 4 reached Mars on July 14, 1965. It took twenty-two pictures, covering about 1 percent of the surface. The part photographed was heavily cratered and not unlike the Moon. Mariner 4 also showed no magnetic field to deflect the solar wind and an even more minute atmosphere than was feared, 0.4 percent that of the Earth.

In July and August of 1969, Mariners 6 and 7 reached Mars. Although they showed some evidence of more complex terrain, including mountains and deserts, they in essence confirmed the earlier message: Mars was covered with craters. There was nothing to explain the dark features on Earth-based photographs except dark crater bottoms. The atmosphere turned out to be 90 percent carbon dioxide and a little heavier than previously thought. There was some water vapor fog. Temperatures near the South Pole went as low as − 189° F., while a hot equatorial day reached 68° F., sweltering by Martian standards.

Mariner 9 arrived in November 1971 to find Mars covered in its entirety with a dust storm that had arisen in the southern hemisphere a couple of months earlier, when the ship had been partway to Mars. A yellowish cloud emerged in the desert and crater region of Noachis, just west of a mountainous zone called Hellas on early maps. With Mars at perihelion and with trapped heat increasing the winds, the storm reached 100 miles per hour and required a month to settle as the planet slowly traveled further from the Sun. When the dust cleared, there was a totally new world. Now that we had lost Lowell's Mars for good, a strange nonlunar landscape began to emerge. Four dark areas, with deep circular rings of craters, stood above the sand. But they were not impact craters, they were volcanic craters—the biggest volcanoes seen anywhere on any world. The largest, Nix Olympica, was three hundred miles wide at the base from its lava flows and stretched eighteen miles in the air. Its name was accordingly changed from "Snows of Olympus" to Olympic Mountain (Olympus Mons). Another volcano, seen in the clearing dust, was 910 miles wide across its base cliffs.

And these volcanic caldera were not all. Mars was covered with channels and complex lined geography. Something had lifted the crust in some regions; in others there was erosion. And there were things that looked suspiciously like dried-out riverbeds, meandering and feathery. Later spacecraft saw more. Mars had a canyon so vast that its tiny tributaries were larger than the Grand Canyon. It stretched across the equator as long as the Mississippi River. The icecaps were found to contain a significant amount of water on top of a layer of carbon dioxide permafrost. (The water ice evaporates seasonally.) And there was clear evidence of water erosion in the canyonlands beneath Olympus Mons, dendritic patterns stretching for 3,000 miles and in 450-mile-long channels that seemed to deepen and widen downstream. These were ancient Martian rivers, now waterless, reminiscent of Lowell. Mars was an arid land shaped by water, filled with gulleys and canyons like the American southwest.

As the whole surface was photographed, the old craters were in abundance too, but there is a large amount of surface area on Mars, the same amount as there is *not* covered by water on the Earth; thus there is land for many distinct topographies, climates, and regions. The North Pole was surrounded by a gigantic dune field, probably wind-shaped. One area was filled with inexplicable "pyramids." Extensive clouds of water ice capped the volcanoes. There was even a mackerel sky one day over Labyrinthus Noctis. In some areas, the clouds were very complex, running from cirro-cumulus to cumulus with fog and mist beneath, or in cyclonic spirals from which volcanic shields dramatically emerged in the dawn as the spacecraft raced across sun and darkness. The southern polar region showed ledges and wind erosion of the ice. Mars was not an eternal photograph like the Moon; it had days that were different from other days and for local reasons, not because some new meteorite had fallen.

The cloudiness in such a thin atmosphere actually indicated an incredibly high humidity, with the atmosphere almost saturated and ground fog everywhere. Water was found in all the rock samples tested by the landers. But most of the potential Martian atmosphere was trapped in the polar caps.

Mars is roughly within the Earth zone of temperatures: at perigee it is 35 million miles farther from the Sun, at apogee it is 60 million miles farther away. It is somewhat smaller than the Earth and Venus, 4,216 miles in diameter. Schiaparelli and all later observers saw Martian seasons, with dwindling and expanding polar caps. But seasons need not mean great poppy fields or irrigated grains. On Mars, seasons are apparently dust-storms, reflecting climatological change with movement through the yearly cycle, intensified by the inclination of the planet on its axis. Because of the thin atmosphere, the temperature plummets swiftly after sunset. On a warm summer day, the Martian night is well below zero. This means that any life form would have to sustain this temperature range. Since the polar caps should be able to refreeze at night, their rapid seasonal shrinkage indicates that they are quite thin.

The first Viking lander rested on a desert in Chryse Planitia strewn with boulders of all sizes and small ridges. Sunset over the summer plains was a brilliant magenta, the color of our first alien sky. The topographic contour lines on the picture gave the illusion of a jewel-filled geode, radiating in concentric circles of delicate pinkish, violet, and magenta shades until the last ring disappeared into the ebony Martian night. The redness of the ground was from a relatively thin coating of hydrated limonite. The iron oxide influenced Mars's image from the beginning. In 1644, when it was newly imagined as a planet, Father Athanasius Kircher described it in his book *Mundus Subterraneus:* "The surface is extremely hard, rough, sooty, and sulphurous, but incombustible, sweating tar and naphtha, surrounded by poisonous vapors. From mountain gorges brownish flames burst with a frightful stench; the seas are viscous sulphurous mud." [8] Mars does show a hundred times as much sulphur as the Earth.

The second Viking lander rested on the more northern tundra of Utopia Planitia among rock-free channels. The test for life had ambiguous results. The spacecraft drew some of the Martian dirt into its laboratory and reported that Mars was virtually teeming with microorganic life or minute insectoids. After the previous disappointments, this was almost too good to be true. We had come to terms with a barren Mars; then a new mystery arose. Of course, "life" was only an interpretation of broadcast codes, and later interpretation was that some substance in the Martian soil "mimicked life," to use the words of planetologists. How can something mimic life? Were they saying that the experiment was flawed? Were they saying that they had found something neither dead nor alive?

Ultimately the experts concluded that Mars did not have even the organic compounds found on some meteorites. It was as dead as dead can be. As for the activity, they decided that some aspect of the Martian soil seemed to digest Earth's offering of organic molecules for unknown reasons.

However, not everyone shares that point of view. Richard Hoagland, for one, in his discussion of anomalous artifacts in the Cydonia region of Mars, touches on the possibility that Viking's "positive" results could reveal a "fossil echo" of relatively recently extinct life. In dying, that biology had gone about "oxidizing every available material.... [which] in fact could be the explanation for the bizarre results of the so-called biology experiments—that they are *indicative of a previous biological epoch.*" [9]

The moons of Mars were discovered during August 1877 by the American astronomer Asaph Hall, who had previously complained about the planet's moonless condition. Deimos was found on August 10, and Phobos a few days later. Both are extraordinarily faint, and Phobos (alone of all the moons in the Solar System) whips around its planet in less time than it takes the planet to rotate on its axis. Hall named them after the god Mars's attendants (Panic and Fear), and Lowell later considered them satellites launched by his intelligent civilization. Mariner showed the moons to be objects composed of one of the darkest materials known, heavily cratered, irregular in shape, and very old. They are utterly different from the Earth's moon, and they are probably captured asteroids made of dark carbonaceous material.

Still, we got to another planet, stood by proxy on its plains, watched its pink or blue sky, and saw its sun set. John Carter and the "Martian Chronicles" were not dead, but evidently they belonged elsewhere, or they belonged to this Martian world in another, supernatural way. The fragments of different Martian novels rush by: the computers of Deimos; ice-skating home along the canals in the subzero Martian night; furry balls of creatures bounding across the desert; colonies by the dead sea; the windships, the wonderful windships, like great Phoenician vessels, one after another across red sands; the metal books with raised hieroglyphs; the electric spiders; the palaces; the battles in dry sea bottoms; the poisonous showers that the Martian dictators made Flash Gordon take; the freezing dawns with twin moons; the theft of Phobos; the ruins of stone on vast deserts; the hypnotists who created Illinois towns there; the remaining jewels of the Martian dynasties; the invisible telepaths in the atmosphere; and finally, the abandoned Earth colonies falling into ruins like those of Lowell's Mars, and then all of them covered by sand and craters and boulders, and never having existed, so that we come to Mars ourselves in the sixties of America and the West all differently.

In the words of John Carter:

> I am of another world, the great planet Earth, which revolves about our common sun and the next within the orbit of your Barsoom, which we know as Mars. How I came here I cannot tell you, for I do not know; but here I am, and since my presence has permitted me to serve Dejah Thoris I am glad that I am here. [10]

But this was another America, before World War II, just as it was another Mars. John Carter's intrigues sound as impossible as the heroism of the CIA in the sixties. And the more ancient Mars has died at the hands of post–World War II space science.

But some of the Viking photographs show "land forms" that might be artificial structures. Hoagland imagines visitors to our Solar System hundreds of thousands of years ago, who built cities under the Martian surface and visited Pithecanthropus at the dawn of our species; one of their monuments, a Sphinx staring upward at the heavens, hauntingly and inexplicably resembles a human face.

> Long before men looked at Mars and dreamed of going there one day, someone may have looked and Earth and watched it rise, green and sparkling, before a Martian dawn. We have seen the evidence—a collection of enigmatic artifacts lying in the reddened Martian sands—and it is staggering: the possible ruins of a city, crumbling for all too many years back into the windswept wastes of the fourth planet of the sun.
>
> And lying to the east of this collection of eroding "structures," something even more extraordinary—a likeness of a human face—etched perfectly into a mile-wide mesa where no human face has any business being.
>
> On Mars. [11]

In occult terms, Mars is transforming and regenerative. It is
certainly the bloody planet of war—not war for war's own sake,
but war as the inevitable conflict of forces involved in change.
Mars has a vigilant and a processional quality. It is a lawgiving
force that structure must obey; Mars is unrelenting. If it relented
to save a single sparrow outside the law, the structure of matter
itself would cave in and all would be lost.

Mars is rhetoric as well as law—social order, personal property. It is a planet of embodiment whose metal is iron, which
gives shape and structure to substance and generates spherical
and radial forms. Iron is simultaneously associated with blood
and magnetism, with the dodecahedron-pentagon shape of pyr-
ite crystals and the iron will. It forms very strong chemical
bonds. In the martial sphere, these are implemented as weapons
of iron. This may be incidental to Mars the planet, but it affected
the imagery that Burroughs gave his world—chivalry and battle—and it served the implacable designs of the Martian invaders
who appeared on the radio suddenly on October 30, 1938, as
War of the Worlds was broadcast:

> When I came in my son said, "Mother, something has come
> down from Mars and the world is coming to an end." . . .
> I heard 40 people were killed and there was gas and every-
> body was choking.[12]

The enormous gulf between Mars and Jupiter is filled with
thousands of small airless rocks, the biggest of which, Ceres, is
450 miles in diameter. In one sense, the asteroid belt is like the
lost continent of Atlantis. Some great world may have been here
and exploded. Or the asteroids may be the remaining planetes-
simals, embryos kept from forming their own world by Jupiter's
bulk. As such, they would be an exposed cross section of the
origin of the Solar System, as Olduvai Gorge is for the history
of Africa and the origin of man. They cluster in groups, some
highly perturbed by Jupiter, like the Trojan asteroids which developed colinear libration points with their giant neighbor. The
asteroids might contain relics of the prebiological chemistry of
the nebula, or they might hold the barely recognizable remains
of a civilization which destroyed itself or was destroyed. It would

be a sad and shocking moment to realize that the first solar empire was here and that something cataclysmic befell it before we were born. We would wonder: are we its survivors? More likely, we will find only rocks and badlands, as in the science fiction image of the asteroid belt as a kind of scrub outpost of mining villages where outlaws hide.

As we pass beyond Mars and the asteroid belt, we leave the golden age of science fiction and the Terran planets, and we enter the true center of our System. Mars and Venus represent the myths of a previous generation. The outer Solar System stands for the 1980s and beyond.

17

The Planets
IV: Jupiter
and Its Moons

O<small>F ALL THE PLANETS</small> , Jupiter is the one whose image has deepened most in the last decade. For a long time, its sheer hugeness dominated every other sensibility, and, in a Solar System where we were looking for delicacies like the Earth, Jupiter was a monster, an insensitive bully, indiscriminately capturing moons and crushing everything that got in its way. Our Martian imagery was so developed that Mars actually seemed vaster, though Jupiter is thousands of times the size of Mars. There was little to say about the giant planet except that it was an ocean of cold poisonous gas.

Through telescopes, Jupiter shows up as richly colored bands: brown, light orange, amber, and reddish. The red spot itself is a single persistent feature, unexplained scientifically. It alone could hold more than three Earths; three times the diameter of our whole planet, our whole world, could fit in this one feature with room to spare, and more than thirteen hundred whole Earths could fit into Jupiter itself.

The fact that it is gaseous, with helium and hydrogen dominating, has come, in itself, to be interesting. Mars, like Mercury and the Moon, seems sterile and lifeless. After becoming worlds in our imagination, these bodies have lost much of their worldhood and hang in space as huge metallic shields bombarded by random stones—virtually skyless, and without the interesting softness of liquid or the subtle blendings of distance against a rich sky. Venus has an atmosphere and a sky, but they are hot and dry.

Jupiter is at least wet. If we could sit inside an imaginary house with windows, at the point on Jupiter where there might be a surface, the windows would be whipped by brilliantly colored liquids moving at terrific speeds. The storms would splatter and interact, and the light from this weather would be a constant variance of auroral sparkling and faint rainbows of bent sunlight. Photons rushing onto the Earth smash into the blue sky, fall into the oceans, and some are drunk by green plants. Photons falling onto Jupiter are swept into a continuous 300-mile-per-hour storm that has stirred everything up from moorings nothing ever held and by these many millions of years has found an equilibrium in which everything, torn in chaos, is actually sifted into precise belts of affinity and order. The light enters and is torn into colors and food for this pattern.

We also know now that Jupiter is not quite so cold as we had thought appropriate for its distance from the Sun. It gives off more heat than it receives, and in some images it is a miniature Sun, not large enough to burst into incandescence, but large enough so that something like solar heat is coming from the planetary body. The Sun itself is fire, and Jupiter is liquid and air, which is a big difference. On the Sun everything is obliterated and simple. Jupiter plays with the complexity of matter right down to its core. In a wild chemical dance, Jupiter keeps substance on our own side of Sunhood, exploring it in methane and hydrogen alchemy, spinning it around in mirrorings of solar storms. We cannot imagine a furnace as a world, but we can begin to accept a storm, for we have seen how Earth itself can terrifyingly turn colors and stir up hurricane winds and blow chemicals upon ships and houses and begin to twirl everything into funnels of liquid, wind, and light. After it quiets we look at its debris, the littered planks and torn rags. What repose could we promise the Jovian debris in unceasing gale?

With Jupiter we are entering a different realm of meaning, for this is not a planet with a surface; it is a sphere of contained swirling gases that may get thick enough to form a ground only at the bottom of an enormous dense sea. Nothing could have prepared us for the tumultuous tapestry of cyclonic movements visible at all levels of Jupiter as it was photographed by Voyager. We saw a land of ceaseless churning activity, each minute pattern of it larger than the Earth, with an eerie coherence of internal movement. From the "Whole Jupiter" perspective of Voyager, we could see these maelstroms as connected streams of an intricate meteorological system; yet each of them contained patterns as complex and coherent as the whole system, and each of those patterns contained patterns. The visible swirls were knitted by invisible swirls, right down to the size of an Earth ocean, a mere pond by Jovian standards, and, from there, down to minute pools. All of these were fused in the magnificent ikon glowing at night's distance.

White blobs passed in and out of the red spot, dissolving and reforming. How? Currents circulated in circles and countercircles, like paint in whirlpools. Some of the waves seemed almost ornate and cushiony in their splotches of foam and scrolls 50,000 miles long, bearing gentle Jovian wombs in their centers. Brilliantly blue and green, their counterwaves rushed out behind them. Red and white and greenish storm spirals with dark interzone channels thundered against and through the scrolls. Viscosity tore out the top of the red spot, its last layer of yolk, turning yellow, blue, and white in doing so. Then, over a space the size of whole planets, it splashed down into a brilliant white flood beneath a white oval cast off by a similar painted wave.

Billows and swirls crashed against each other, and each interference produced a dominance of one or another design, or dissipation into some totally different pattern.

And this is just one area of the planet around the red spot. The complexity of chemistry defies description. If we could survive an entry of Jupiter, Arthur Clarke seemed to be saying at the end of his *Space Odyssey,* we would pass through an endless undulant rainbow in which lands would come into being, surfaces shimmer, all to be swept away into deeper and deeper mirages and distortions until time and space were turned into something else.

The new images of Jupiter emerge from a sixties counterculture, though, in fact, they are far older and more archetypal. They include "inhabited Jupiter," "Jovian resources," and "Jupiter, gateway to the outer worlds."

Inhabited Jupiter came into being as we let go of the prejudice that this simian shape of ours is the one intelligent symmetry that nature can make. In prior decades, we had imagined humanoids maintaining the canal systems of Mars, nursing their dying civilization. UFO encounters were usually with beings of human or semihuman shape. And, whether we believe in the ancient astronauts or not, our prejudice has been to see them as beings like ourselves, their hominid images cut on stones of the Sahara and in the temples of South America: Erich von Daniken's great white gods.

But as we observed other species on our own world and noted man's less than glorious behavior in the local ecosphere, we became more objective about "destiny's angel." The whales and dolphins of the Earth's seas are intelligent beings of another kind. Why might not intelligent water-beings arise on another planet?

Evolution of the mind has been placed back at the feet of the raw cosmic materials: hydrogen, oxygen, nitrogen, carbon, and silicon. The toxic whirlwind of Jupiter has become a bloody and fertile egg. Methane and hydrogen and ammonia gases are now understood in terms of their resemblance to life, to the crystalline matrix of living cells, rather than in terms of their deadly consequence if inhaled by terran lungs.

"We cannot imagine that Jupiter is inhabited," I wrote in an essay on the planet in a book of ecological thoughts in 1968. "Yet we imagine the ancient desert cities of Mars, as though Oaxacan or Egyptian, the canals bringing water from the polar icecaps to a dying empire. We can embroider Venus with dense jungles, an age of seeding ferns and lizards, rain forests and quaking bogs. But what creature breathes ammonia and swims under tons of icy atmosphere?"[1]

This is the old prejudice, the boastful certainty of our privileged real estate in the temperature range of the solar sea, our rightness as a species. But it was necessary then to begin to speak for Jupiter, not for the Jovians, but for the dangerous simplicity of our images of ourselves.

On Jupiter the universe is hardly getting down to something interesting; it is getting down to itself, what it is at this distance and pressure, as on the Earth. But we believe our own melodrama, hence the Garden between fire and ice, between water and stone, between jungle and desert. Jupiter is a Garden also. Life breaks like a crystal, grows outward, a bud shedding protective hairs, knows itself in sexual feedback; life is methane and ammonia, for methane and ammonia are children of the sun as oxygen and carbon, and are conscious but to other ends. Jupiter is now in the middle of its ammonia and methane history. . . . The map of Jupiter, belted in colored latitudinal zones like the forests and tundras and deserts of phytogeography, is an historical puzzle, a map left by unknown sea-kings of another world of which we are dimly and always conscious, a map we cannot deny by reducing it to literal chaotic vectors. . . . Jupiter's history is as tragic as our own, as uncertain, as needy of saviors and wisemen, these ammonia-hydrogen life-forms assuming crystalline bodies as flesh but their own flesh.[2]

This image softens us and puts us back in a living universe. We are no longer astronomers first; we are creatures, and our astronomy is as much a living protuberance as the cartilege of the shark or the feathers of the owl. If it has something to say about Jupiter too, all the better, but it is Earth looking back at Earth through the Jovian possibility.

Looking out at the inhabited planet, we must realize that from any particular ring of consciousness, any other, based on different chemical chains, will look like a chemical hell, as Earth does from the Jovian laboratory on Io. They claim that no one could live in hydrogen, oxygen, and carbon; no one could live on such a light world; everyone would float to the sky. . . .

Jupiter leaves on Kodachrome a signature of history, of use, of conscious dreaming to undo the enigma. And, as we, the Jovians softly breed, and listen within for the voice of their planet, listen from the North Polar Regions, yes, and in the North North Temperate Belt, listen from the nations of the Equator and the schools of the South Tropical Zone. They are not Esquimaux and Polynesians; they are creatures of ammonia, and breathe ammonia and love ammonia bodies, the curse of flesh albeit, and their dreams are the eternal dreams contained in ammonia crystal and ammonia nerves.[3]

If we were gracious, we would extend to the unknown inhabitants of eternal Jupiter the same desires for peace and honor that we wish "them" to extend to us, the same humane curiosity that we, as Westerners, failed to use in Africa or the islands of the Pacific, turning the peoples into less-than-humans and pretending that we had a Biblical injunction to enslave them and steal their bounty. The Jovians should be so warned. And we should be warned too. This is the Air Force fear of UFOs, that they might actually be great galleons carrying conquistadors, the first vessels of an army larger than ours, to which we are vulnerable and naive. Is this a projection of an ancient cosmic terror? Are we so embarrassed for what we have done that we must continue doing it? Should we not find our own cosmic sympathy first and regain our dignity on Earth before we even imagine who goes thither among the planetary spheres?

The idea of "stealing" Jupiter is not as remote as it may seem. It is outside our present capacity but not outside the conceptualization of our technology or the scope of what seems to be our greed. For instance, in the 1960s, Freeman Dyson suggested that we could completely vaporize Jupiter and use its materials to create a shell around the Sun. We—i.e., the human species, the people of the Earth—would dwell on the inside of this shell, with a surface area one billion times greater than that of the Earth, utilizing every single photon emitted by the Sun.[4] This is certainly the present supertechnology writ large and applied to the two major potential sources of energy within our reach: Jupiter and the Sun. If not build an immense shell, then perhaps we could maintain a gas pipeline directly from the ammonia-hydrogen atmosphere. These images are fever symptoms. Whether we are astronomers, space physicists, or simply citizens, our feeling for twentieth-century Earth leads us not only to look back to simpler, more pastoral times (whether there ever were such), but also to fantasize endless windfall profits from new strikes. Our peoples seem too many, our bombs too big, our oil too depleted, our planet in general too small. For what, we do not know.

But Jupiter's size and composition speak to our Terran identity in another way. Jupiter is not just a collection of different storms, cloud layers of different colors, internal energy sources, and interphases, any of them many times bigger than the Earth. It is a single planet, and it gives us a sense of our own size, not in its largeness of resources or its dwarfing of our volume but in the way that any planet coalesces as a single system within the limits of its space and materials. The creatures of Jupiter, Arthur Clarke's science fiction medusas and mantas, no doubt face the same population pressure we do:

> It did not resemble a tree at all but a jellyfish—a medusa such as might be met trailing its tentacles as it drifted along the warm eddies of the Gulf Stream.
>
> *This* medusa was two kilometers across and its scores of dangling tentacles were hundreds of meters long. They swayed slowly back and forth in perfect unison, taking more than a minute for each complete undulation—almost as if the creature were clumsily rowing itself through the sky. . . .
>
> High intelligence could only develop among predators—not among the drifting browsers of either sea or air. The mantas were far closer to him than was this monstrous bag of gas; and anyway, who could *really* sympathize with a creature a hundred thousand times larger than a whale?[5]

We pretend that if the Earth were the same volume as Jupiter, we would still have millions of years left before expending our resources. This is not true. Material and volume expand at the same rate inwardly. We would be at exactly the point we are now, for all worlds are finally the same size. In seeing Jupiter as big, we see the Earth as a big world too. Volume is a law of space, girth of matter. It is how we inhabit and appreciate our volume, not sheer number or amount, that determines the depth of our existence.

Looking at Jupiter through the photo-satellite, we know that this is a space into which 1,318 Earths would fit, though the conception is meaningless. Our experience cannot be multiplied that many times. Nor are any resources limitless. Something else determines our crisis. We have already envisioned the mortality of the Sun, which is the mortality of all free energy.

The true Jovian image is not poisonous gas, ceaseless gales and whirlpools, or monstrous size. All of these lie beyond our comprehension, beyond both infinity and zero. Jupiter stands inside us as a ceaseless unconscious process and as a radiant unity. Jupiter is the self that prevails, clear of any threat of death and destruction or diminution—and in the center of this Sun System. We stare into it, single mind by single mind, each one of us a unity, an image of creation. Jupiter is not thirteen hundred and eighteen things; it reflects back our own mind, as if it were a mind itself.

When the planets were formed, King Jupiter claimed a full 70 percent of the material made available in the nebula cloud around the Sun. So it continues to hold much of the mass and angular momentum of the Solar System. Its diameter is 86,000 miles, but, big as it is, it rotates rapidly on its axis, once every ten Earth-hours.

Jupiter maintains a mean distance of 483 million miles from the Sun, which it circles every 11.86 Earth-years. It is quite cold in the outer atmosphere, − 184° F. on the average, which is one reason its storms last so long: their energy dissipates slowly. Another is the lack of surface features to modify tempests. Jovian storms have deep roots.

Jupiter has retained a large amount of the basic gaseous materials that the planets, moons, and Sun inherited from the Solar nebula in their formation. It is very young in the sense that it hasn't aged and very old in the sense that it is a living dinosaur, a planet in the primeval state. Its immense mass has held the lighter gases that escaped from planets with weaker gravitational fields, so Jupiter has an abundance of the "life" compounds: methane, hydrogen, water, and ammonia, as well as helium. By comparison, the Earth is made up of metals and minerals, with extensive deposits of iron and silicates. Dead or alive, Jupiter is an impressive nursery for natural selection and mutation to play in for a few billion years.

The center of the planet is very hot, 54,000° F., or five times the temperature of the surface of the Sun. The pressure on the planet is the equivalent of a hundred million Earth atmospheres, quite possibly enough to turn the hydrogen metallic. This may, in fact, be the Jovian surface.

However, as cloud layers are heated from beneath and transmit heat, a moderate zone fluctuates through the planet at different depths and in irregular currents. There is enough internal heat and external cold to produce intermediate climates, both tropical and temperate, poisonous by our standards but not by the standards of the organic compounds which would form on such a world. There are potentially hundreds of millions of microenvironments in the Jovian swirls-within-swirls in which life could develop. The atmosphere is strafed with lightning from end to end, and this could well jolt organic molecules into existence throughout the Jovian sea. It is indeed a strange birth for cells among the clouds, but all births into the world of light are strange. All are a sort of fire of waters. The "photosynthetic" brightening and darkening of the red spot in thirty-year intervals suggests a biological pattern, a thicket of vegetation in a cornucopia of edible molecules.

Jupiter has an extremely large and complex magnetosphere and intense radiation belts, some of them caused by the metallization of liquid hydrogen under great pressure. Visible Jupiter is enormous enough, but the magnetosphere extends 450 million miles around the planet. Some particles in the vicinity of Jupiter are so charged that they are hotter than the interior of the Sun. All of this is invisible in the Earth's sky, but if we could see it, it would be just about the most dominant feature of our cosmology; it would outshine the Moon and rival the Sun.

The immense radio noise of Jupiter was first heard in the mid-1950s and was thought to be associated with the rotation of the planet itself because of its ten-hour phases. It was later discovered to be the rate of rotation of the magnetic dipole field, which is inclined 10° from the physical axis. Each burst is at least the equivalent, in energy terms, of an earthquake or a hurricane. The broadcast cycle is linked in a doubly periodic system with the rotation of the magnetic field of the planet and the 1.77-day revolution of the satellite Io around Jupiter. As Io is bombarded continually with Jovian radiation, it emits an invisible torus of charged particles, so that it passes around Jupiter in a doughnut-shaped tunnel. At the same time, Io connects to Jupiter directly by a horseshoe-shaped flux tube of five million amperes. This makes Io and Jupiter a complex system of magnetism, radio noise, and radiation unlike anything else in the Solar System. The gigantic planet and its miniscule moon generate more energy between them than all of the Earth's electrical generators. If Jupiter is the chief god of the Solar System, Io is the radio and the forge; it is the immediate receptor of the Jovian power, which it transmits to the universe.[6]

Jupiter has a fantastic system of worlds encircling it as planets encircle a Sun. It is, in that sense, a second center to the Solar System, named appropriately after Zeus (Jupiter), who overthrew Cronus (Saturn) and the old gods, and who now presides as king over the present millennium. The Sun may have nine planets, but Jupiter has at least fifteen moons, the last two of them discovered by Voyager on the edge of a thin Jovian ring system. The four large moons are the Galilean satellites, formally discovered by Galileo but seen by sharp-eyed shepherds and sailors for millennia, and hence known esoterically from the dawn of time. The four large Jovian moons have become the mystery worlds of the 1980s, holding the promise of exotic realms despite their low temperatures and high radiation.

These satellites were visited by Voyager in 1979 and photographed one by one. Suddenly the Earth was showered with images of four "planets" that most people had never heard of. Their landscapes were stunning, though our survival on them would range from a matter of seconds on Io to barely longer on the other Galilean moons.[7]

Io is the closest large moon to Jupiter, at a distance of a little over 227,000 miles. It has a diameter of almost 2,000 miles, or 90 percent that of Mercury. Only tiny irregular Amalthea and the two unnamed 1979 Voyager moons (one within Amalthea's orbit and one outside it) are closer to the planet itself. Europa is a third again as far away as Io and slightly smaller. Ganymede is 36 percent larger than Mercury and over 500,000 miles from Jupiter. Callisto is slightly larger than Ganymede and a little less than twice as far away from Jupiter.

The other moons of Jupiter are very tiny. A second group, made up of Himalia, Elara, Lysithia, and Leda, revolve around the planet at between 7.15 and 7.27 million miles out. Their diameters range from 12 to 37 miles. A third group circles the planet in retrograde clockwise orbits at distances from 12.86 to 14.73 million miles away. None has a diameter larger than 18 miles, and the smallest has a diameter of 9 miles. Pasiphae, Sinope, Carme, and Ananke are so highly inclined that they are virtually leaning on their sides. They are perturbed in their revolutions about the planet by the other satellites, by Saturn, and by the Sun itself, with orbits so eccentric that they defy Keplerian ellipses. In fact, these moons change their orbits regularly like a mime of electrons. They may well be captured asteroids. The other satellites are tiny and unnamed.

Io was the first Jovian "planet" visited by Voyager. Its surface was the biggest surprise of the space program. It could have come from another galaxy. Mars and Venus had been pondered for decades in advance. But there was nothing to prepare us for Io. Instead of the expected craters, there were curious erratic zones and splotches of dark and light material, some obviously liquid flows, bright patches of color in sharp, irregular patterns, and regions where it was impossible to tell figure from ground or which way a current was flowing. Active volcanoes were shooting plumes 200 miles in the air. Here was the first geologically alive body and the first visible uncratered surface in the Solar System other than Earth's. Who would have expected the honor would fall to Io?

It is now assumed that Io's climate and topography are created by the intense relationship between it and Jupiter and the simultaneous gravitational pull between Jupiter and the other nearby satellites. This twisting back and forth causes tidal bulges and a crust that rises and sinks more than thirty feet per Ionian day (or Jovian revolution). There may also be a sulphur ocean within Io feeding subterranean sulphur lakes, or pure sulphur springs from aquifers. Io also has very black crescent shapes on its red hot surface, and blue clouds. The former may be lava flows.

This world is so continuously bombarded with Jovian radiation that it is a ceaseless crucible of lava, lightning, ions, and flares. Gas and ice clouds form everywhere, as over an imaginary industrial city. Io may be geologically alive, but it clearly has forfeited creature life as we know it.

Mythological names are automatically given to features on celestial bodies, with the difference that they now come from international culture and with a particular sensitivity for non-Western terminology and Third World divinities. So the first map of Io represents the global culture that photographed its surface; the volcanic paterae are Persian, Mongolian, Egyptian, Celtic, Iroquoian, Incan, Nicaraguan, Zambezian, Quechuan, Pawnee, Babylonia, and Hopi. One is named after the Japanese sun-goddess Amatersau, who reemerged from a cave to restore light to a darkened world. The volcanic peaks, shield volcanoes, and vaporous fissures are named specifically after fire gods and goddesses: Marduk (Sumero-Akkadian), Masubi (Japanese), Maui and Pele (Hawaiian), Prometheus (Greek), Surt (Icelandic), Loki (Norse), Amirani (Soviet Georgian), and Volund (the Germanic blacksmith god).[8]

Europa was only distantly glimpsed by the first Voyager, but the second photographed it closely. The pictures showed an enormous frozen ocean streaked with dark wiggly lines. The surface was as smooth as that of any world ever seen. The dark areas had so little relief that they might have been colored stains on the ice, but were probably fissures filled by material oozing from the Europan interior. Io was found to be a world of black lakes and riotous sulphur geysers. A walk across it would take us through intermittent yellow, orange, and blue snows. Europa would bombard its visitors with huge ice pellets shot up from geysers. If we crossed the entire planet, we would never leave the ice age; only the color of the crust would occasionally change from brown to white and back again. Some scientists proposed an active worm life beneath the ice.

Ganymede turned out to be an enormous meteor-ground glacier with primordial brown ponds, muddy and frozen for eternity and themselves pocked with craters. It may have been entirely covered by ocean earlier in its history. Part of the surface consists of long crosscutting and interfering chains of ridges. Twenty miles of such valleys are followed by thirty-foot-high shelves. An explorer might abruptly leave one such system and enter another going off at an angle or find the pattern interrupted by a crater but continued on the other side. Scientists have referred to these as possible tectonic plates, so that Ganymede is a frozen picture of continental drift.

There is probably no more pocked body in the Solar System than Callisto. It has recorded so many millions of years of meteorites in ice that it looks more like a chunk of conglomerate than a world. One impact basin is more than 100 miles across and many miles deep, with a smoothed-out bottom. Concentric circles run out from it for miles. It is one of the biggest collisions registered in the rock of the Solar System. In this case the rock is ice. Callisto froze early and deep. At the moment of impact, this world had an instant ocean, but almost immediately ice poured in and the ocean began to refreeze, creating the hundred-mile long ice castle of frozen splashes, eerie towers, and twisted ice shapes, with crumbling ancient ice renested in new ice formed of ancient ice melted and refrozen. This is probably a dead museum, but who knows? Who knows if man will ever walk here and shine his lantern through the colored ice and stand within this gargantuan monument.

Of these satellites, the three innermost, Io, Europa, and Ganymede, seem almost synchronized with each other. The sidereal rotation period of Io stands in a ratio to that of Europa of 2.0073, almost exactly the harmonic; and Ganymede's sidereal rotation has a ratio to Io's period of 4.0441, almost exactly double the first ratio. When Io and Europa fall on the same line passing through the center of Jupiter, then Ganymede also falls on the line or stands at a right angle to it, and this is true of any combination of the three: either all three are in a line if two are, or the third is at a right angle to the other two. The line of this conjunction rotates gradually around the planet, completing a cycle every one and a third years.[9] This would obviously be a focal point for any Jovian astrologers, and, in fact, Arthur Clarke seemed to use the lining up of the Galilean satellites to mark a moment in Earth-Jupiter time in *2001* just before the astronaut's descent into the giant world. The Galilean rebus discloses the entry into the Jovian temple.

Clarke's story begins when a remnant of intelligence is found on the Moon.[10] It points outward to Jupiter. The Moon is the base, the watchpost and signaling area for outer space peoples involved with our species, perhaps even ancestral to us. An enormous computerized spaceship is sent on an odyssey to the Jovian center, but, even from the beginning, there is the implicit problem of what to do when it gets there. Will the mission be self-evident? Surely it cannot land there. The whole voyage is undertaken within this unstated mystery, as if man is compelled to answer the summons, compelled genetically and astrologically.

After various disasters en route reduce its crew to one, the remains of the ship are sucked into the gravitational field of Jupiter. The moons line up. The ship, it seems, could not have arrived at any other time. Even though millions of years lie between the initial message to man (in the bestowing of intelligence on early hominid forms) and the arrival of the ship, this is a matter of seconds in the timing of planets. Imagine just one sailor alone on the stormy Pacific. This astronaut is flung into the unknown whole of Jupiter, thirteen hundred and eighteen times as big as Earth. He must fall through the layers of storms and colors buffeted like a feather in a hurricane until he is crushed and the small fragments of his ship and his own body enter, on about the level of a bug, the Jovian vastness. It is more than death; it is the whole cosmic history that lies behind each of us (in our coming to be at all) and before each of us in eternity.

This is not what happens in the film. Space and time change. The astronaut enters a room or is lying in a room. He has become a spore. He is an old man. The Earth and Jupiter are breeding together; a heavy cosmic sexuality hangs over the bed. As flesh and intelligence, these worlds spawn an infant who is returned immediately, in a bubble, to the whole of the Earth. He is the child of the astronaut-Earth and the Jupiter system; and he is the avatar of Jupiter-Earth connection. The astronaut is killed but not killed; he lives through his whole life in the density of Jupiter's seconds. The meaning of his experience is wrung out of his flesh, but it stands clonally for all of Earth, as raw material for this new being, equally formed from the unknown system of Jupiter, which was linked to the Earth aboriginally and unconsciously. This is Jupiter as guardian of the secrets, key to the Solar System, but also willing magus to the Earth, as willing as those on Olympus once were to make this

world, from a mountain which dwarfs even the mountains of
Venus and the volcanoes of Io.

In January 1981 I dreamed of Jupiter and its moons, no doubt a
consequence of writing this chapter. The astronomical image
released a hidden archetypal layer:

Returning to the village in Vermont where I once lived, I am
wandering toward the river at night. I learn from an undisclosed
source that I am now in the Solar System. Immediately I begin
to look about for planets. I do not know what region I am in.
Suddenly I see a huge bright object spinning in the front yard
of a house by the river. I recognize it instantly from its markings
as the moon Ganymede of Jupiter. It is radiant, enormous, and
intricately engraved, and, as it spins, I see all the features of the
Voyager photographs. Yet, it is somehow contained in this front
yard. Now that I know where I am, I begin to look for Jupiter
itself. I suspect it must be over the large hill that rises out of
town to the mountains. In fact, I am drawn in that direction by
an immense gravity. I try to look through the trees, but the
forest is as dense as lead, and I can only feel the presence of
Jupiter beyond.

I start at once to climb in darkness, and I am very careful. I
feel that at any misstep I can stumble and fall into Jupiter. The
climb is perilous, as if I am walking along a mountain ledge
overlooking the sea. I wonder if there are any other moons
about, and I turn to see a tiny ball spinning rapidly in a bush in
front of a house. I think, "How cute. That's the tiny fifteenth
moon." It is minute compared to Ganymede, but just as fiery
and radiant. I realize that dozens of these moons might be scattered in the bushes all around here, and I feel as though I am
a child in an Easter Egg Hunt.

The heaviness pulls me up the hill, and, suddenly, through
the trees, I see an enormous limb of brilliance. It is so overwhelming that it seems literally to blow me back. But I push on,
as if I am floating in space. I see the broad bands of the planet,
and I struggle to get out of its way.

A voice is suddenly telling me that I don't understand gravitation at all. "These are not the real planets," it says. "They are
painted balls." I understand that it is speaking about the actual

planets in space; it is saying that they themselves are only painted balls and that these replicas of them are mere symbols of the internal planets. There is another gravity, inside gravity, which is the real core of substance. I feel a wholeness and a bigness, as if all that cannot be connected or realized in a lifetime is joined in a unity of self for this one moment.

Astral Jupiter is clearly the king of the present Solar System. He enters roaring, filling people with terror and laughter, solemnity and pomp. The metal of Jupiter is tin, which is involved in coagulation, condensation, and the formation of cartilege. It is bony, or grey like the matter of the brain. Tin stands opposite the fluid breath of Cytherean copper.[11] The Jovian contribution to personality is justice and interpretation, with an emphasis on prosperity and growth, completion.

If Jupiter is the new order, Saturn is the old dying forces. Outside temporal wisdom, says bearded enigmatic Saturn, lies ageless wisdom. Inside my temporal system, says mighty Jupiter, is magic and splendor and ceaseless procreation. For the present, anyway, Jupiter symbolizes the end of possibility. Saturn begins something that is beyond us. It will be a long time, in any case, before we see past the bigness of Jupiter in ourselves.

18

The Planets
V: Saturn, Uranus,
Neptune, Pluto,
and Their Moons

As WE MOVE FURTHER OUT in the Solar System, toward other stars, our information about worlds dwindles. We have sharp images of the Moon and Mars, but Uranus and Neptune are faint and fuzzy. We see only shadows of their grossest surface features. For the outer moons and Pluto, we have no images at all. They are bare tincture stains on the black illusory curtain of night. Beyond these, there may be other worlds in this System, and there are surely countless other worlds among the stars, but those we do not see at all.

The night sky sits as an almost weightless cap upon the heavy Earth. Its meanings have been stretched thin over billions of years of time-space, the photons barely reaching us despite their capacity for long-distance travel. All of the sun-stars and all of their worlds shower the Earth with not even the energy of the creatures in a droplet of pond water. At this distance they are mere ghost-selves. But the thin skin of their collective image is an impregnable wall of cosmology—cosmology which locates all real weight and mass at enormous distances from our center. We are dependent upon light. Without it, we are blind and ignorant.

But most light does not reach us. Most objects are unimaginably far away. In our own Solar System, neighboring planets only a few orbits away are virtually invisible. There is distortion in our atmosphere, and we and they are continuously moving in relation to each other, blurring long exposures. Even our most powerful telescopes strain to see out beyond Jupiter, much as fish in the mesopelagic zone do to see the Sun itself.

Detailed information about the outer Solar System must come from space probes because we cannot "see" far enough into it to gather any but the most meager information. Pioneer 11 and both Voyagers have now completed photographing the Jovian and Saturnian systems and Voyager 2 engaged the Uranian system in 1986. In 1989, as the first Voyager heads out of the Solar System, its twin will encounter Neptune and its moons—like Uranus and its moons, worlds unknown until relatively recent times. Small and fragile as these robots are, they are transmitting to the collective consciousness of the Earth visualizations of the worlds they skirt.

The night sky has always been a source of our deepest visions. It has provided, from aeon to aeon, in conscious and unconscious forms, the images that have changed us. These new worlds—planets and moons—are being seeded among us at the end of our cosmic summer. No scientist or seer can begin to predict the crop they will yield early next cosmic spring. None of us will be around to see it, but the seeds have been planted, and whatever they are to become has already begun to form inside us.

These space probes seem absolutely necessary for some unknown reason. Their rich and even generous images stand against a paucity that we have not yet recognized. And it is not only a paucity of resources in the ground or of funds for the space program. It may have something to do with the record of ourselves that we have placed on the vehicles for creatures who may cull them from the cosmic debris. Our world is an overpopulated armed camp, and yet we are lonely, we seek someone to talk to, even after our death. We kill off sentient species even as we seek sentient species to learn from and to teach. As Voyager courses the dark space between Uranus and Neptune, we struggle against minimal, almost arbitrary violence and cruelty. All the various faces of terrorism ask us to deny them, and so far we have been unable, except for a collective moment here and there in North Africa or the Philippines. We have worn our civilization to the bone. Soon enough, our probe will stand in the presence of Neptune, seeking revelation. But Neptune can speak only to our descendants; its images will be too vast and obscure to interpret in modern times.

Long after it sends us images, Voyager will carry one curiously precious (and ethnocentric) record of who we are. We will be somewhere else entirely.

What all this suggests is that somehow we should know better. And I cannot even say what it is we should know better, or why.

For better or for worse, we are different now. And we will change even more. But perhaps we have become so utilitarian that our leaders and so-called representatives would be quite willing to trade these visions in for a new line of missiles or a percentage point or two against the national debt. Future space probes to the outer moons may never be launched with the present prejudice, but fate decreed that we should fire these babes into the night before our minimality prevented it. Now we are at their mercy and the mercy of the images they send. A moment in our own technological development coincided with a window in the heavens: a satellite lofted through it would go on a grand tour of the Solar System. Historical factors almost blocked the mission. Thousands of meteors, asteroids, and fallible parts on two delicate machines still stood in the way. Yet, both Voyagers have survived, perhaps miraculously, to send back close-ups of Jupiter and its system of moons. Clear images of hazy, ringed Saturn arrived immediately following the election of Ronald Reagan—an event the ancients would have ascribed to Saturn anyway. Literally hours after our close encounter with Uranus and Miranda, the space shuttle *Challenger* exploded, driving us out of the heavens—a vintage Uranian response according to modern astrology. Who knows what events will coincide with our images of Neptune?

And what will be the ransom of the image of a humanoid face sculpted into the surface of Mars? Such an artifact has the unique potential to redefine who we are and what we are to become. More than the work of a thousand archaeologists and historians, it virtually screams:

Rewrite Earth history. Look beyond the forgotten past. You are someone else entirely. You are not who you think you are. Act now, before it is too late.

Obviously the meteors and asteroids that let our machines through mean to leave us no choice.

Traditionally, we have known that Saturn, Uranus, and Neptune are Jovian planets, massive, gaseous, and primitive. They retain the primordial planetary environment: hydrogen, helium, and other light gases blended in thick atmospheres with no surfaces in the usual sense. By contrast, these gases have escaped from the smaller worlds, leaving thin auras upon the secondarily formed rocky cores. On any gaseous planet, there is uncertainty about how deep the visible features go. Are we seeing just the outermost layer of the atmosphere, or are the features sustained with some profundity? Are we seeing clots of gas at the tops of convection currents and the anti-cyclones they form with the upper air, or are we seeing eddies in the tops of swiftly rotating clouds? This question can be asked separately of the bands and the ovals on each planet. Though they are written literally in the wind and in gas, they may persist for hundreds of years.

The history of these worlds, since the birth of the System itself in the galactic cloud, has been an increasingly entangled engagement of storm layers and their effects. The bright pungent bands and ovals of weather lines stand out, but there is no archaeology cut in fossils or stones. The differences among these worlds come from their sizes, their distances from the Sun, the local endowments of original gases, the random patterns of development that each zone on each world has followed, and the delicate and complex interaction of all these things for millions of years. One ecological gradient surely dominates: as we move outward, the temperature drops rapidly and the Sun comes to look like an extremely bright star. Day sky and night sky, from Neptune, are virtually the same.

Before Voyager reached Saturn, it was difficult to imagine how it would be different from Jupiter. But right from the earliest images, it was revealed in light as a unique never-before-seen landscape. Saturn's face appeared iridescent yellow, almost golden in the sunlight, with storms twisting and swirling across it in ribbons and bands of yellow, tan, orange, and darker brown. It is the familiar Jovian turbulence, but with its own zones and patterns and peculiar hues. Jupiter looks like the bloody innards of a beast or a richly colored oynx. Saturn looks like the unformed yolk and albumen of a young egg or like an ancient gold coin rusted from seawater. Beneath these cameos, no doubt, lie profound differences of nature and character.

The winds across the lemon cloudtops were measured by Voyager at speeds as high as 900 miles per hour. Tan and dusky ovals were seen, as on Jupiter, marking the deep churning eddies of gaseous material from below. The Saturnian cold no doubt slows down chemical reactions and storm interaction, which accounts for some substantial differences from Jupiter. Saturn also seems to be less dense, with a greater abundance of lighter gases. Its radiation belt is twenty times weaker than that of Jupiter. Saturn's seasons are also likely to be longer and more intense than those of Jupiter—longer because of Saturn's year (equal to 29.5 Earth-years), and more intense because of Saturn's greater inclination on its axis. Regional effects would probably develop more distinctly than on Jupiter. Perhaps these factors lead to Saturn's larger quantity of ammonia haze, the golden clouds, and the displaced bands.

On Jupiter, the bands and currents seem to move across the planet alternating from west to east and east to west in a manner consistent with one another and with the upwelling zones. Voyager 1 showed Saturn's currents displaced ninety degrees from the upwelling zone, atmospheric jets extending to higher latitudes than on Jupiter, and local storms erupting into regional eddies that became entrained in the jets. Saturn seemed stormier than Jupiter, more variable and chaotic. However, Voyager 2's visit allowed scientists to view storm centers and atmospheric currents longer, and they turned out to be predictable and symmetrical despite the irregularities. Because the seasons were changing on Saturn, it is possible that we were viewing mainly the equivalent of March winds.

In the southern hemisphere is an oval anticyclone akin to the large red spot on Jupiter. This "Great Brown Spot" is neither as big nor as differentiated, but it probably originates from the same kinds of climatic conditions.

Other features of Saturn were known before the Voyager passage. The planet circles the pale Sun at a mean distance of 886 million miles. The Saturnian day has recently been recalculated to a length of ten hours and thirty-nine and a quarter minutes. Saturn's diameter is roughly 74,500 miles, and its volume would hold 815 Earths. Mostly composed of light gases, with some ethane, acetylene, and water, Saturn—like Jupiter— may have a tiny core of metallic hydrogen. Its low density, only 70 percent that of water, gives it a surface gravity barely more than that of the Earth. If one could find an ocean large enough, Saturn would float in it.

Although they are incidental to internal planetary dynamics the rings have been Saturn's distinguishing feature since Galileo discovered them. He never saw them clearly enough to discern their nature, and so he imagined that Saturn was a double or triple planet. Then, as the angle of the rings to the plane of the Earth changed, they apparently disappeared, and an astonished Galileo wrote in December 1612: "Has Saturn, perhaps, devoured his own children?"[1]

It was Huygens, in 1659, who disclosed their separation in a treatise upon Saturn: "A thin, flat ring, nowhere touching, and inclined to the ecliptic."[2]

Some early astronomers interpreted the rings as an aeromantic sigil, speculating, for instance, that ethereal Saturn was composed of gem material with a golden aura about it. In general, however, the rings were discovered too late for traditional magic to incorporate them in the astral planet before the Newtonians were well on the way to a gravitational solution. Continuous reexamination during the next two centuries showed that there was a system of rings, some of them faint and some of them dark. The rings were not a fixed crown; they were the cumulative effect of matter in motion. They were an orbital phenomenon like moons. This suggested, to the nineteenth-century astronomers, that the possible source of the rings was the fragments of a broken moon that had approached too close to the planet and shattered. From the slight differences in their orbital speeds, these fragments would follow a path; and as they collided with each other, the path would distribute into a ring. Maxwell showed mathematically that the rings could not be solid but must be made up of "an indefinite number of unconnected particles, revolving around the planet with different velocities according to their respective distances."[3]

From our new knowledge of the history of the Solar System, we have considered other possible sources for the rings: a wandering planetesimal or asteroid torn apart, a stillborn satellite, or the nebula cloud of the System itself. We have also found that rings are not unique to Saturn. Rings of a different and dark material were found around Uranus quite recently; amost invisible from Earth, they circle the poles of the planet rather than the equator. In 1979, very thin Jovian rings were discovered by Voyager. Clearly, then, rings betray a rather commonplace natural phenomenon and are not a special endowment of Saturn, though the Saturnian rings are a particularly glorious and complete demonstration of the phenomenon. From radar mapping, we now consider that their componential chunks are less like dust and more like boulders and stones covered with ice, or snowballs and hailstones, tumbling in their eternal circle, one behind the other. Inside the rings, we would not experience the smooth collective phenomenon. Instead, we would be pelted by irregular pellets of snow and ice as though we were standing in a cold meteor shower. The rings we see from the Earth are the same underlying Newtonian circles we find everywhere, whether on a supergalactic level or in the phases of the Moon.

From telescopic observation, we have been able to establish certain aspects of ring topography. For some time we have known that the rings of Saturn have an outermost diameter of about 171,000 miles while being only a few miles thick. Individual ring sections are visible, ranging in width from the faint Crêpe ring's 10,000 miles to the bright B ring's 16,800 miles. As early as the seventeenth century, one clear division was discovered between the B ring and the outer A ring. Later measured as 1,860 miles wide and named after its discoverer, Cassini's Division was assumed to be an empty space, a zone swept absolutely clear of fragments between rings. Other smaller rings and divisions were assumed as well. In fact, Pioneer 11 was originally charted to pass through Cassini's Division. Closer observation corroborated by satellite photography forewarned scientists: Cassini's Division was not a division at all, but an additional zone of rings. Voyager later found at least twenty distinct bands in the "Division." There are small gaps in the rings, however, and these are ostensibly regions swept clear by resonance from the satellites.

Although Pioneer did not approach the planet and take the dramatic close-ups that Voyager did, it managed to discover two new moons, and it began to disclose the complication of the rings. By measuring where the trapped particles of Saturn's Van Allen belt were blocked, Pioneer found a thin outer ring later named "F." Meanwhile, ground-based observations through the late 1960s and the 1970s had shown that Saturn had more than the traditionally assigned ten satellites and that there were a number of small irregular inner moons, intricately connected to the dynamics of the rings. In fact, if we add the Voyager discoveries, Saturn now has at least fifteen moons. Although it is presently impossible to attribute all of ring dynamics to planetary satellites, certain specific relationships other than gaps have been tentatively proposed by scientists. For instance, Jupiter's ring may be held in place gravitationally by the irregularly shaped satellite Amalthea. The F ring, only sixty miles across and 50,000 miles above the golden cloudtops of Saturn, appears to be held in place by the thirteenth and fourteenth satellites operating as Newtonian sheepdogs. One of the jagged moon fragments orbits the planet just inside the ring, and the other orbits just outside it. Since the inner moon is faster, a gravitational tug between the two of them develops, making it impossible for any of the "sheep" fragments to escape. Furthermore, the mutual gravity of these moons forces particles together in clumps. Six of these internal F-ring features were photographed by Voyager. Since they are not discrete bodies with separate orbits, these clumps cannot be called moons; yet they and the thirteenth and fourteenth moons show that the distinction between moon and ring particle, between sheepdog and sheep, in the formation of the ring and moon systems is a subtle and changing one.

Close-up photographs of these moons, taken as Voyager passed through the ring plane, showed them to be not only oblong but jagged in such a way that they could have once been a single body. The destruction of the single moon, perhaps by a meteor as big as the one that almost split Mimas, created not only the twin co-orbital satellites but the entire F-ring system.

The two satellites perhaps explain the F ring and the gravitational accretion of particles within it, but they do not explain one of the most extraordinary features of the Saturnian system discovered from the initial raw pictures. The F ring has three ribbons that are braided and seem to cross over each other in different planes like a helix. These twisted rings also become thinner and then thicker and are knotted in spots, indicating some totally unknown force. From the early days of the Newtonian renaissance, it was clear that multibodied gravitational systems are very difficult to describe and understand. The Saturnian rings are the most elegant local statement of that problem. So many bodies are caught in so many gravitational fields— Saturn itself, the moons both near and far and large and small, and the ring fragments of varying size and distance—that gravitational interaction cannot be predicted in terms of the collective outcome of systems.

One scientist remarked on television that these braided helices were certainly the only example of life viewed in the Saturnian system, implying ironically that gravitational complexity was mimicking biological complexity. "In this strange world of Saturn's rings, the bizarre becomes commonplace," said Bradford Smith, the photography section leader. "Those twisted rings seem to be defying the law of orbital mechanics as I understand it. They must be doing the right thing, be we just don't know what laws of physics they're following. . . . It all boggles the mind that it even exists. It's just weird."[4]

As Laurence Soderblom of the imaging team said, "It's the unthinkable that we're looking for—the unimaginable."[5]

The surprising conclusion from Voyager 2 is that the resonance is most effective on the outer edge of the B ring, apparently distorting its boundary into a giant ellipse that precesses in space every 22½ hours (one orbital period of Mimas). The push-pull action of the rotating ellipse pumps energy into the rings, and the images show that the major axis of the elliptical edge points 90 degrees away from Mimas—exactly opposite the sense of tides in the Earth-Moon system![6]

Voyager gave us our first pictures of the ring system as a whole and characterized it as an actual topographical entity. What scientists once described as half a dozen ring systems with divisions became five hundred, and then a thousand, individual rings and ringlets as Voyager approached. The rings spread out from Saturn on a vast flat plane like an enormous phonograph record with extremely fine grooves. The flat ornament had become a three-dimensional landscape in stone, its actual bigness revealed in perspective as Voyager soared above its plane.

Inexplicable spokes appeared across ring sections, moving as the rings moved. They were dark as they spun between Voyager and the Sun, bright as the probe flew past their eclipse. These spokes were perhaps ice phenomena among the particles of the rings, forming on the night side of the planet, apparent as the rings emerged from shadow into their respective mornings, and fading as the ring "day" moved through "noon" into late afternoon. Additional freezing may occur in spoke patterns at night; the Sun then melts them back into slush.

Voyager also reported other ring phenomena. The C ring seemed to be made of looser assortments of particles, and to be semitransparent. In photographing the small thirteenth and fourteenth satellites, Voyager 1 discovered the shadow of another tiny ring, perhaps also held together by still tinier satellites. In the faint glow of Saturnshine, Voyager 2 recorded spokes even on the underside of the B ring, perhaps the result of electromagnetic forces originating in the planet itself. Saturn also emits an unexplained periodic radio pulse.

Recording 256 different degrees of relative light and dark, as well as nonvisible bands of the spectrum, the probes are simultaneously blind and far more sensitive than we are. As the grooves in the rings show up and the spokes turn from dark to light, we realize that we are looking at the infinitesimally fine detail of light itself. Intricate texture leaps forth as the angles of the camera, the Sun, the planet, the rings, and the moons change. We might think of ourselves driving through the terrestrial fields at sunset. Tinted shadows fall across the hills. The cows seem made out of rich brown mud, the lakes out of sky. The spiders' webs are soft mucous from the creatures' bodies, each morsel strung in taut geometry. The houses are arcs of energy, their walls ginger and transparent. Each smudge and leaf vein stands out, and the myriad insects above the field to the horizon are distinguished as ring particles. The blue ions of air seem molecular in their collectivity. Then we pass over the cusp into night.

Saturn has ten named satellites. From inner to outer, these are: Janus, Mimas, Enceladus, Tethys, Dione, Rhea, Titan, Hyperion, Iapetus, and Phoebe. They are named after Father Saturn's cohorts in the old world of the gods. Titan is the largest moon in our Solar System, but the rest are quite tiny. In fact, before Voyager, they were assumed to be mere dirty snowballs, more ice than rock. Voyager gave us our first chance to view planetary objects in the range of 750 miles in diameter in the cold reaches of the light gaseous planets. These bodies are far lighter and of different material than the ostensibly captured moons of Mars. The large Galilean satellites show obvious evolution and historical complexity, but some of the Saturnian satellites show surprisingly similar features.

Tiny Janus, 100 miles in diameter, was discovered by French scientists in 1966. Very little is known about it, and it is even unclear whether the present Janus, confirmed by Pioneer, and the original French one are the same moon.

Mimas is a little more than 200 miles in diameter, and it orbits Saturn 115,000 miles from the cloudtops. It is only slightly heavier than pure water ice, and probably contains some silicate material. What is notable about Mimas is that it survives at all. A quarter of its diameter is filled by an impact crater eighty miles wide and many miles deep. A steep rim surrounds it, and a giant mountain rises to a sharp peak in its center. Other large craters, including some that are twenty-five miles wide, cover the Miman surface. Mimas looks like a big snowball that gathered cold out of nebula material and then was bombarded by planetesimals into a field of craters. It is a relic of the early days of our System.

Mimas was discovered by Herschel, as was Enceladus, the next moon in sequence orbiting Saturn. What is surprising is that a body about the same size as Mimas (Enceladus is 150 miles larger in diameter) and about the same distance from the primary planet is so different. From the remote pass of Voyager 1, Enceladus showed no large craters and only some faint stripes reminiscent of the internal evolution of the larger moons in the Jovian system. Voyager 2 recorded more classic aboriginal cratered plains but also relatively smooth, craterless sections that could probably be no more than 100 million years old, suggesting continued geological activity. Both Mimas and Enceladus may house water volcanoes and methane geysers. As it is sheared between Saturn and Dione, Enceladus may be specially subject to tidal heating similar to that on Jupiter's Io. It is also the likely guardian of the faint E ring.

Tethys, Dione, and Rhea, the next three moons in sequence, extend from orbits of 183,000 miles to 327,000 miles. All three were discovered by Cassini, who also found the next to outermost moon, Iapetus. These are the most complex of the small moons viewed by the first Voyager.

Tethys, 635 miles in diameter, is a block of ice like Mimas, and also heavily cratered. But there is other highly unusual topography on Tethys, including a lambda-shaped twisting canyon or fault valley running for 250 miles along a north-south axis and approximately fifty miles wide. There is also a huge white spot on the surface that may be a hill or just very bright ice. These are not crater mounds. They represent distinct geological processes local to the moon. Although topography in ice is rare, the ice was fluid once, and was melted and remelted by materials churning up from the interior.

As Voyager approached Saturn from the distances of the inner Solar System, Dione showed a bright spiderlike marking in its center, giving it the appearance of a star sapphire. This and other ropy patterns imply internal evolution from molten material, as on our Moon. There are "lunar" craters too on Dione, but this world recalls most the cracked surface of Ganymede. Rhea even more strongly resembles Ganymede, except that its surface material is brighter, indicating that something from very deep within the core of the moon is emerging. Rhea has complex streaky glowing areas and swirling patterns, which intimate not only impact craters but also rearrangements of fields of ice and ice cliffs. The surface has been sheared and torn apart. Dione is somewhat bigger than Tethys, and Rhea is almost 1,000 miles in diameter, but this is still remarkable geologic upheaval for such small icy moons.

The Saturnian and Jovian systems emerged from their seg-
ments of the nebula cloud somewhat differently. Saturn got
lighter material; it developed a much fuller ring system; and its
moons seem haphazard in arrangement. Jupiter has a small
amount of moon and ring "debris" close to its surface, but for
the most part the large dense moons are inner moons, and both
size and density decrease as one moves away from the planet.
This may or may not indicate the way in which the primordial
material of the system was distributed, but it does strongly suggest a clustering of matter toward the center of the cloud. However, we cannot simply carry this model over to Saturn. There
are many small inner moons around Saturn, as well as the rings,
and there is only one moon of planetary size, Titan. This is four
times larger than the next largest moon, and it is followed by
three more of the Mimas to Rhea variety. It is also further from
Rhea to Titan than it is from inner Janus to Rhea. That enormous
gap of more than 400,000 miles is filled with a gaseous disk of
squashed torus shape containing a very thin distribution of hydrogen atoms, probably blown off the surface of Titan, which
continues to lose its original endowment at the rate of about a
kilogram per second.

Voyager missed Mimas-size Hyperion entirely, as that moon
was on the other side of the planet from Titan when Titan was
photographed. There is a relatively small gap between the orbits
of Titan and Hyperion. The next moon, Iapetus, has always been
known for its odd appearance, indicating either extreme irregu-
larity of shape or discoloration. From Earth, one side of this moon
is six times brighter than the other, as though it were shaped
more like a cylinder than a ball. Voyager 2 captured a splotch of
extremely dark terrain on the forward side of Iapetus's orbital
motion. Even on the bright side the floors of some craters were
stained by this blackness, as black as any dark material in the Solar
System. It is possible that substance from the interior of the moon
has burst through a surface of frost.

From all the moons except Iapetus (and perhaps Phoebe), the
rings of Saturn would be only barely visible at the "razor" edge,
for they would be seen along the same plane in which the moons
themselves pass. Iapetus strays sharply from the plane. Anyone
on this body would see the whole surface of the rings, like the

wings of a butterfly, as the moon soars over the plane. Iapetus is 800 miles in diameter and more than 2,200,000 miles from the surface of Saturn.

Phoebe, discovered like Hyperion in the late nineteenth century, is six million miles further away than Iapetus. Only 800 miles in diameter, it is also retrograde and eccentric in its path. It may be a late addition to the system, perhaps a captured asteroid or comet.

The water of Saturn's moons is primordial—not later rain but original H_2O from the solar nebula. Since that ancient freezing in the darkness of space, the ice has been twisted, melted, re-frozen, and pocked with meteorites, but it is cleaner than any mountain brook on Earth will ever be again. The moons of Saturn are cosmological water, planetary glaciers. They are frozen replicas of cosmogony, attending the god of time. That same nebula water on Earth remained liquid; and after aeons of chemical interaction with other substances, it became contaminated with life—life that returns, through Voyager, to view some frozen blocks of the original spring.

Titan is the largest moon in the Solar System (but see Neptune's Triton, below) and the only one with an atmosphere. More than 3,600 miles in diameter, it is bigger than Mercury. Even a decade ago, we could not have discerned the full significance of this moon. In some science and science fiction books, it was mentioned parenthetically that Titan might have life on it. But what brings Titan newly to the forefront is our recent appreciation of the uniformity of the Solar System—in particular, we have become aware that all the planets and moons evolved from relatively similar beginnings. Although Titan is a distant moon of a faraway planet, it is as much a sister of the Earth as of Saturn. With Saturn it shares distance from the Sun and the same ancient patch of elementally enriched star debris. With Earth it shares the conditions of surface and terrestrial-type gravity. In any case, the star debris was probably little different in the vicinities of Saturn and the Earth.

Titan's importance to us is also a direct reflection of the decreased organic potential of Mars and Venus. We have moved, in a sense, away from the old inner Solar System into a new system of hydrocarbon action and primeval atmospheres. Suddenly, we

must search among the unfamiliar Jovian worlds for our likeness
and origins instead of among the familiar Terran planets. The
ancient plains of Mars show only traces of river valleys that dried
up long before the forerunners of men lived in the Old World
jungles. But Titan is covered with photo-organic smog, and
organic compounds likely fall to its terrain and drift across it like
snow. If Mars is our long, bright visual plains and hard rock
surfaces, Titan is the dirty and salty intimacy of our cells.

After Mercury and Mars, scientists were prepared for disap-
pointingly thin atmospheres, and Titan's bounty surprised them.
Voyager found that the Saturnian moon, despite a relatively
weak gravitational pull compared to that of the Earth, held an
atmosphere extending to three hundred miles above the surface
(three times higher than the Earth's) with a surface pressure one
and a half times that of the Earth. Telescopic observation had
shown an atmosphere, but had not prepared scientists for its
extent or its high nitrogen content. This photochemical smog,
with thick clouds of methane and other hydrocarbons, apparently extends right down to the surface, with nitrogen rain and
snow falling through it. The atmosphere totally obscures the
face of the moon, and it will take a Titan landing to learn what
it is like on the surface. One scientist said: "We might find nitrogen icebergs in a methane sea." There also might be oceans
of liquid nitrogen. Probably, though, Titan is too warm for these
exotic topographies.

Although this is a ghastly environment for human survival, it
is a rather promising environment from the point of view of
universal organic chemistry. Titan might abound in the kind of
swamps in which complicated hydrocarbons form. Carbon, oxygen, and sulphur have all been identified in the atmosphere,
and a large amount of water is likely—as on the other Saturnian
moons—to be locked in ice. If all this material is bombarded by
the general cosmic radiation and by the pale Sun through a red
hazy sky, then many of the more complicated hydrocarbon
building blocks may be forming in seas and swamps, materials
familiar to the water oceans of the ancient tropical Earth. Hydrogen cyanide and acetylene both appear to be present, and
there is an unknown abundance beneath that smog.

Chemically, Titan appears to be a very cold and somewhat

small primeval Earth. It retains a great deal of hydrogen in its atmosphere—witness the torus between Titan and Rhea. As on the gas giants, there are large amounts of helium, methane, and ammonia. But there is a surface. It may well be a surface of pure water ice.

Titan's distance from us is negligible in cosmic terms, although it is crucial in terms of a fragile life form such as we are. But it may well have its own fragile life forms. Severe cold is the most extreme problem. At the time of the first Voyager visit, Titan was just emerging from a deep winter, with temperatures recorded by Voyager as low as $-300°$ F. Creatures born during Titan's spring and summer, a period of five or six terrestrial years, would have to be able to survive the winter, or at least pass on genetic material that could survive it. Otherwise, all of the evolution of the chemistry of life would be crammed into a ridiculously short period, and new creatures would have to evolve each summer.

There is, however, some reason to be optimistic, from a human standpoint, about the summer climate on Titan. The moon shares Saturn's orbit around the Sun, and thus its long seasons. The $-160°$ F. now estimated for the height of summer is considerably more than was once thought. It is also possible that Titan's temperature rises even higher regionally from internal heat sources. In addition, there is a greenhouse effect from the smoggy atmosphere. Distinct seasonal changes seem likely, even from brief viewing of the upper atmosphere. There is a dark northern pole obscured in haze, and the entire northern hemisphere is darker than the southern hemisphere. Even at its brightest, the Sun does not shed any more light on the Titanian surface than the Moon does on the Earth's surface.

There is a remote chance that in areas of extended summer and internal heat, perhaps underground, ammonia and water lakes have formed. If these survive the winter, there may be a hydrocarbon paradise on Titan.

Saturn stood at the end of the old Solar System, an aged king with a long white beard. Beyond him was nothing. He was organization, completion, age—the final and frozen arrangement of things. Even as revolution and radical and unconscious actions change things, Saturn still stands as a great rock fortress, within custom, within society, within matter, and within mind, holding to the original and eternal truths. The strength of the Saturnian gesture is overwhelming, but its invocatory images may be fleeting and misleading. There is a coldness and sadness to Saturn because it is eternal, hopeless, unremitting. In electing a Saturnian, we, in a sense, turn to and acknowledge our own inner darkness and the hold the remote and unconscious past has on us. Even the later Galilean rings fit the sepulcher image: Saturn is a ringed planet, the only one as seen from Earth. It is a closed tomb. Something has died there, and the spot in the sky is marked in such a way that it could not have been missed by the Earth's first telescopes. The Jungian psychologist Charles Poncé, describes the creative potential contained within the Saturnian tomb:

> The function of Kronos/Saturn is to instruct us in the nature of limitation, depression, and the dryness of a wisdom that seeks to make all things equal....
> Uranos, the one totally and purely involved in mater/matter, has his genitals thrown into the ocean by his son Kronos. Hesiod informs us that the castrated member floats upon the ocean for a long time, foam gathering about it, bearing inside it the immortal being who shall soon be spawned—Aphrodite, goddess of love.... What is implied is that behind every compulsive act, there is a seed of love that can emerge if one can cut oneself off from impulsivity.
> ... What is born of water and defunct genitals is the first image of soul. The message is: the way to soul comes only after putting an end to the concretizing of instinct and the casting of all our energy "out there" into the world. But Kronos does not see or know of this, for Hesiod tells us that he threw his father's genitals behind him. In short, he failed to see the value concealed in both instinct and compulsion.[7]

The finality of Saturn is both its virtue and its curse. Mythologically, Saturn is the creator of time, which makes him a healer, a guardian, a shield. He protects the inner Solar System from the infinite chaos. In the body, he both creates density and disintegrates used materials, including the skeletal frame itself ultimately. His wisdom is like the oldest Buddhist teaching— the wisdom of suffering. Because Saturn guards time, he alone contains the wisdom outside of time. The encircling ring has come to represent, in modern times, the protective function of lead, the boundary around a boundary, so that something more remote and complex, cosmic in its sigil, stands on the ancient edge. Lead is heavy, sluggish, impenetrable, but also of a rich depth. When it is combined with the tin and copper of bronze, we can hear its profundity in the tone of the bells. That sound is not the wisdom of the copper or tin.[8]

From Janus and Mimas, the incredible golden planet fills the whole sky, drifting up as a buoy in the void. If the Gurdjieffian Moon steals souls, what must Saturn do to the poor creatures in its system! A night of full Saturn is brighter than the solar day. To the astrologers dwelling on the Saturnian moons, the planet itself is so dominant as to be meta-astrological. The other moons and the thin ring line would make up the local "zodiac" for the astrologers of Titan and Dione.

Ringed Saturn is the passageway both into and out of the modern world. And it is the gate in time to the ancient kingdoms of the Earth. Outside its orbit are only the radical occult planets, discovered in modern times, which represent different cosmic forces entirely.

Uranus is the next planet, though a 300-mile-wide object was discovered in a planetary orbit between Saturn and Uranus in 1977 and named Chiron. It is probably doomed to become a moon of one of the two planets or to be caught by one and bounced to some other part of the Solar System.

Mythological Chiron was half-animal, half-man, the offspring of Kronos (Saturn) in the guise of a horse, and Phylria, a sea nymph; he married a water goddess, and his daughter was Thea, one of the first astrologers. Contemporary astrologers immediately addressed the new "planet":

Once a planet is sighted by astronomers, its energy manifests on Earth. Chiron rules healing with the hands, crystals, initiation alchemy, actual alteration of the body in some way by the mind or spirit.... It rules all issues of making Saturnian form on Earth and then bringing—[through] Uranian white light—higher consciousness and energetics into form. The energy is now present on Earth since Chiron's sighting. The only question left is how quickly we integrate it.[9]

Uranus circles the Sun in about 84 Earth-years, making its astrological circuit the measure of a long human lifetime. Its diameter is about 32,000 miles, and it is 1.78 billion miles from the Sun. From Uranus, the Sun has hardly any disc left, but is still a brighter star than any other.

The Uranian atmosphere of methane clouds reflects back 90 percent of the light that falls on it. Ammonia mists probably lie beneath the methane. The overall appearance is blue-green, or greenish with whitish belts in the equatorial region. At − 360° F., it is still fairly warm for its location and may have internal sources of heat. It is heavier than Saturn: 1.2 times the density of water.

Uranus rotates rapidly (10 hours, 48 minutes), but it does so on its side. The Uranian axis of rotation is almost parallel to the planet's orbital plane, so its North Pole faces the Sun for half a year and outer space for the other half. There is no terrestrial diurnal-nocturnal cycle. Day and night are forty-two Earth-years each, but daytime is distinguished only by the fact that the Sun prescribes a ten-hour circle in the sky. Other variations in this cycle come from the alignment of the planet's axis and orbit.

Voyager 2 was not given much of a chance of reaching Uranus, so by the time it arrived there nine years later, it was already an antiquated and erratic craft. Yet, scientists back on Earth were able to reprogram the satellite from a distance of millions of miles so that it brought late 1980s technology to the Uranian system. Even so, the obstacles in sending information back to Earth were daunting. Uranus is so far from the Sun that sunlight there is 370 times weaker than that on the Earth and radio signals from there take almost three hours to reach us. Also, because of the tipped axis of the whole Uranian system, Voyager had only a few hours while traveling at ten miles per second in which to record images of the planet and its moons. The stunning pictures belie a combination of a damaged spacecraft, dim lighting, a rapidly moving camera, exposures of longer than a second, and a whole heavens of static through which to pass a barely audible signal.

Even closeup, Uranus was little more than a blue spheroid. Voyager measured high temperatures in the upper atmosphere and traced the rotation of clouds always westward around the planet. It discovered a powerful magnetic field, twisted by Uranus's extreme tilt into a kind of corkscrew. The nine rings discovered in 1977 showed up distinctly as fine dark edges, and a tenuous tenth ring also appeared.

It was the five moons of Uranus (plus ten previously unknown and very tiny satellites) that provided remarkable planetary images. Scientists already knew that the moons of Uranus orbit the planet oddly. Over 21-year cycles (quadrisecting the complex Uranian numerology of 84), they move from equatorial to polar orbits, circling the planet alternately around its center and then above and below it. Titania and Oberon, the outermost moons, were discovered by Herschel. Lassel found Ariel and Umbriel in 1851 while searching for the first two. Innermost Miranda was found on a photographic plate by Gerard Kuiper only in 1948. Because of Uranus's tilt, the five moons are retrograde even though they seem disposed to normal prograde orbits. The largest, Titania, is only 1,000 miles across.

After Voyager sent us its report of five bizarre terrains, scientists were inclined to believe that there was a single tale behind the Uranian system. Perhaps some primeval encounter with an asteroid or other body had thrown Uranus onto its side and at the same time forced its moons into inclined orbits. One collision led to a series of collisions, a spectacular billiard-ball effect destroying some moons and battering and dislodging those that survived.

From the outskirts of the Uranian system, Voyager first encountered Oberon. Not only did it show impact craters with brilliant rays but dark material, perhaps dirty water, lining their basins—evidence of volcanic activity. Titania's crust was cracked into valleys that ran across a substantial portion of the world's 990-mile diameter. Umbriel was a uniquely dark moon (for Uranus) with a highly cratered, geologically inactive surface and a single bright ring that contradicted its otherwise primitive appearance. Since its spectrum revealed high percentages of water, scientists presumed the ice must have become covered with a powder or contaminated with methane from the moon's interaction with charged particles from Uranus's magnetic field.

Because of its small size (only 725 miles across) no one would have been surprised had Ariel turned out to be a crater-pocked iceball that cooled before any significant geological activity could alter its surface.... No one was quite prepared for the spectacular landscape that Voyager revealed.

Vast rifts stretched completely across the visible face of

Ariel. At first glance it seemed that the moon was simply a more vigorous replay of Titania. But as Voyager flew over Ariel's terminator it captured a scene that brought to mind the winding arroyos of Mars. A network of broad, smooth-floored valleys branched from one another; it seemed possible that ice, not water, had flowed within them.[10]

Enceladus's volcanic surface is likely the result of the tidal forces among Saturn and its other moons. But there are no Uranian moons in resonance with Ariel; only in the past might a differently-orbiting Umbriel and Miranda have generated enough force to melt their sister satellite.

Miranda turned out to be even more shocking. This minute world of only 300 miles in diameter (of which we saw but one side) was a patchwork quilt of distinct, sharply-defined landscapes that appeared only artificially connected to a single environment. In fact some scientists surmised that Miranda had been split asunder once and then reassembled willy-nilly. Others felt that the anomalous landscapes might represent different phases of the same process. In one area juts gnarled, irregular cliffs; in another are smooth parallel tracks of ridges and grooves. One extremely jagged cliff actually breaks clear through the crust of the "planet" and out the other side. Stretching from the equator into the lower hemisphere is a design of light and dark terrain (called "the Chevron") so compellingly patterned that at least one occult author (the originator of the Harmonic Convergence) considered it a supernatural signal linked to the humanoid mesa on Mars. What a cosmic treasure hunt that would be if extraterrestrials who placed their first clue in Cydonia Region, Mars, hid the next one on an obscure inner moon of Uranus!

Occult Uranus has strong magical affinities. Its discovery is associated with its message—i.e., its actual body became visible when man was able to respond to it. Insight into the hidden secrets of nature, fantastic inventions, elaborate machines, and unemotional thought are all Uranian functions. Uranus rules astrology because it generates cohesive laws of whole systems. It is an astrum of lightning and fast-striking change. Although its rearrangements are necessary, it can tumble lifetimes of work as it rotates topsy-turvy on its axis with its erratic interacting moons. It looks like an atomic nucleus, and it is the archetypal

creator of atomic power. Its magnetic field has the oblique periodicity of a pulsar.

Since Uranus always destroys the old order and initiates a
radical new one, even as it did on its discovery, it is the enemy of
Saturn, guardian of the ancient Solar System. Saturn tries to hold
the throne for the inner kingdom of traditionary planets; Uranus
leads the astrological revolution. The Uranian either seems to be
amoral or to act from motives that lie beyond the understanding—even the imagination—of ordinary people. Eerie, dis-
loyal, electric, Uranus is a ruler of Aquarius.

Except for its more normal inclination, Neptune is similar
enough to Uranus to be a twin. It seems to have more methane
and less ammonia. 2.8 billion miles from the Sun, its year is 165
Earth-years, and it rotates in 15 hours, 48 minutes. Its diameter
is 30,760 miles, and it is 1.67 times as dense as water. If Lassel's
satellite Triton is as big as it seems (3,700 miles in diameter),
then it, not Titan, is the largest moon in the Solar System. Triton
also circles the planet in a very tight retrograde orbit of 5 days,
21 hours. Nereid, discovered by Kuiper in 1949, is tiny (300
miles in diameter). It behaves more like a comet than a moon:
its 360-day Neptunian year carries it from less than a million
miles away from the planet to more than six million miles away.

Piers Anthony uses Neptune as the central planet in his science fiction novel *Macroscope*. As the spaceship approaches the
green gas globe, this is what the travelers see:

> Its roiling atmospheric layers were horrendously evi-
> dent. The great bands of color hardly showed now; instead
> there was a three-dimensional melange of cloud and gas
> and turbulence suggesting a photography of a complex of
> hurricanes.
> . . . [He] felt as though he were peering into a cauldron
> of layered oils recently disturbed by heating. . . . Gray blue
> bubbles a thousand miles across seemed to rise through
> the pooled heavy gases, while slipstreams of turbulence
> trailed at the edges. In one place the recent passage of a
> bubble had left a beautifully defined cutaway section of
> gaseous strata, yellow layered on green on pink and black.
> In another, masses of whitish substance—hydrogen snow—
> were depressing the seeming ocean beneath, ballooning
> downward in a ponderous inversion.[11]

Piscean Neptune is magical like Uranus, but more mystical than electric. In the personality it sometimes seems motiveless but with dreamlike visions of a hidden unity. If Uranus is a scientist and magician, Neptune is a dreamer, mystic, and prophet, more concerned with the hidden shape than the high-energy forces. It will create a vast work of art or philosophy rather than a machine or a technology. If Uranus invented the radio and the telescope, Neptune gave both a planetary and cosmic meaning. The global European migration and the spread of Western civilization is Neptunian; so are the airlines and multinational companies. Neptune is a medium and a musician associated with Venus. Uranus is a mechanic and an inventor associated with Mars.

Neptune is also dangerously unbalanced, tending toward schizophrenia, involved in drugs, hallucinating. Alcohol, opium, and cocaine are its astral flowers. "Normal perception is a jail," writes the poet Gerrit Lansing, "from which [Neptune] wishes to break out." He adds that the Neptunian dissolves to create. He is attracted to "the watery powers of the underworld," the "criminal, the forbidden, the untasted, always seeking to unveil, though not through the rational mind."[12] Neptune is a planet of mirage, rapture, enchantment, holy places, arcane speech, the relationship between sex and blood, communion, and communalism. Neptune was discovered in 1846, and the *Communist Manifesto* was published in 1848. This is the astrological basis of the latter's planetwide effect on the modern world.

The search for a ninth planet in our Solar System began in the manner of the search that led to the discovery of Neptune. But it was an exhausting, fruitless obsession over three decades, with an ambiguous resolution in 1930. Percival Lowell began the quest at the turn of the century from his observatory at Flagstaff, Arizona. Working with unexplained residuals in the orbits of Uranus and Neptune, Lowell calculated the probable orbit of Planet X, and he and his staff proceeded to search for it throughout the likely regions of the sky. But Lowell recognized "that when an unknown is so far removed relatively from the planet it perturbs, precise prediction of its place does not seem to be possible. A general direction alone is predictable."[13] He died in 1916, well before the discovery.

The man who would eventually find Planet X was Clyde Tombaugh, a self-taught astronomer who worked on his family farm in Kansas during the day and studied the heavens at night with a 9-inch reflecting telescope that he made himself. He wrote repeatedly to the Lowell Observatory for a job; Vesto Slipher was impressed with his drawings of Jupiter: "fairly good for such a chap working all alone."[14] So Tombaugh was hired. He was twenty-two years old, with a high school education. Slipher gambled that his raw intelligence would be more useful in the search for X than the usual submissive university type. Tombaugh was twenty-three years old when he became the last person to discover a planet.

Tombaugh worked by exposing plates on good nights and then "blinking" successive exposures of the same area on different nights in a special machine to see if any "star" moved. Searching down to the 17th magnitude, he found innumerable difficulties in exposing the plates and producing blinkable pairs. Gradually, he worked toward resolving the fundamental problems. The most serious obstacle was the thousands of asteroids moving through the zodiac. Searching at this level of magnitude, he was plagued by their blinking. "The key strategy," he concluded, "was to take the plates within 15 degrees of the opposition point, so that the daily parallactic motion of the earth would cause all bodies external to the Earth's orbit to retrograde through the star field—the more distant the object the smaller the angular displacement during the interval between the dates the plates were taken. This solved the asteroid problem beautifully."[15]

After months of working with Lowell's orbit, Tombaugh began an exhaustive search of the entire zodiac in September 1929. He moved from Aquarius into Pisces, from Pisces into Aries, and then into Taurus and Gemini. In eastern Taurus and western Gemini, the average number of stars per plate increased from 50,000 to 500,000. By early November, Tombaugh was in Scorpius and Sagittarius and was encountering a million stars per plate. Disappointed thus far, he returned to western Gemini in January 1930. Blinking two good exposures of the delta Geminorum region from January 23 and 29, he saw the shifting star, Planet X.

Since it was found at Lowell's observatory, under the auspices of his search, by an astronomer using his tables, Lowell was given credit for having discovered the planet along with Tombaugh. But Pickering claimed that the new body was his Planet "O." Then, when he heard of its small size, he felt it should be discarded immediately as the perturbing influence on its neighbors. The perturbation on Neptune's orbit requires a planet of 50,000 miles in diameter, and Pluto is, at most, 4,200, and more recently has been mapped at 1,500. In fact, as recently as 1979, it was suggested that Pluto is no bigger than Ceres. The astronomers doing the photometric research on Pluto at the University of Hawaii, Dale Cruikshank, Carl Pilcher, and David Morrison, concluded that Pluto's mass was a few thousandths that of the Earth. This is "much less than would be required to perturb the motions of Uranus and Neptune measurably. . . . If this train of logic is basically correct, it appears that Tombaugh's discovery of Pluto in 1930 was the result of the comprehensiveness of the search rather than the prediction from planetary dynamics."[16]

But then, where is Lowell's predicted trans-Neptunian planet? For all intents and purposes, Pluto has been used to save the appearance of Lowell's discovery. Even the choice of the name, Pluto, instead of the more popular Minerva or Cronus, was partly based on the lucky accident that the first two letters of the name of a major available god also happened to be Percival Lowell's initials. The *PL* symbol for the planet could thus honor Lowell. But clearly it is no more his planet than Pickering's. And even Pickering was satisfied with the name, which he read as standing for Pickering-Lowell.

The minute Plutonian satellite, named Charon, was discovered by James Christy and Anthony Hewitt in 1978. This allowed measurement of Pluto's mass by Kepler's third law and confirmed the extraordinarily small size of the ninth planet.

Prior to the discovery of Charon, astronomers favoring Pluto as the perturbing influence on Uranus and Neptune had a number of explanations for the ostensible small size. Some hypothesized that it is such a black frozen planet that we see only a 3,000-mile-wide glint of its 50,000-mile-wide sphere, like a sparkle on a black Christmas ornament. Another suggestion was that

Pluto is a white dwarf or a black hole, a burned-out cinder from the other half of a twin Sun system of which our present Sol is the remaining half. Pickering suggested that it might be a stray white dwarf picked up from another star system and thus the only body in the Solar System with an origin outside it. This would give it the necessary mass for the perturbations. For a planet so far away, we can imagine almost anything.

From this supposed one-time sun, the Sun we know is just another star in a black sky. Pluto is 2.7 billion miles away from the solar disc, and takes 248 Earth-years to make its annual orbit. We know how fast light travels. The 186,000 miles per second is beyond conception. Yet, it still takes the Sun's light 3.22 minutes to reach Mercury. That same light takes five hours and twenty-eight minutes to reach Pluto. If we imagine a beam of light whipping off the Sun's surface at 186,000 miles per second, zooming down the corridors of interminable darkness and space so fast that it opens shafts of light that disappear into the distance even as they come from a remote darkness in another direction— then we can understand how long is that five-hour-and-twenty-eight-minute passage to Pluto. The temperature at Pluto, -369° F. or lower, would freeze any atmosphere. If it is truly a child of the primal nebula, it should be water, ammonia, and methane ice, with occasional haze, for these are the last substances to condense from the other rings in the cold of deep space. Pluto perhaps has a water ice core, a methane and ammonia mantle, dead methane seas, and a frozen methane crust and atmosphere.

A Plutonian day is, of course, hard to fix without knowing its surface features, but variations in brightness suggest a possible 153 hours. Pluto is perhaps 88 percent the density of the Earth, in this respect being more like the inner than the outer planets. It might even be an escaped moon of Neptune. It is the only planet that lies outside of the ecliptic that makes up the zodiac, so that Pluto is at an angle to the whole plane of the Solar System. Its orbit is eccentric compared to Neptune's almost perfect circle, and, on December 11, 1978, Pluto moved within the Neptunian orbit. The small world will reach its closest point to the Sun on September 12, 1989. Neptune will be the remotest planet until the year 1999, when Pluto will swing out beyond it again, en route to aphelion in 2113.

Occult Pluto is a realization of hidden inner forces that have been operating secretly and suddenly burst into being. It rules transformation, but also regeneration, metamorphosis, and even reincarnation. Uranus marks the beginning of atomic power in the natural element uranium. Man-made neptunium follows on the elemental chart, and then the most dangerous of the artificial elements to be released into the oceans and the life cycle, plutonium. Hitler was said by astrologers to have brought negative Plutonian influences to bear following Pluto's discovery, i.e., the most horrendous aspects of buried human consciousness.[17]

Pluto also represents a bringing back of the least expected: the ghoul, life after death. This is the appropriateness of the name: Pluto, lord of the Underworld, with his boatman Charon. "With his queen Persephone he held sway over the other powers of the infernal regions, and over the ghosts of the dead. The symbol of his invisible empire was the helmet that made men invisible."[18] The black hole is a perfect image for Pluto, but so is the frozen debris of Solar System beginnings. Pluto's whole discovery was an enigma in a Plutonian way. Pluto is also, mythologically, the source of wealth and grain, both of which come from the earth. His cruelty and inexorability are part of the cosmic order. An eccentric planet, slightly out of the zodiac, passing slowly through the signs, is the appropriate agent of millennial and cataclysmic change. The astrologer William Lonsdale says:

> The force of Pluto is like a force from a vast vast vast desert way way way out there. Pluto is there to draw us into a greater universe. Like it's the last outpost that keeps reinstilling us with a cosmic perspective and keeps taking away our materialistic assumptions.[19]

Pluto also dispenses earthquakes, epidemics, world wars, and magnetism; its magicians are fakirs and yogis. From its Underworld association, it bears the horror and gloom of images so deep in the unconscious that we cannot reach them, or else we receive them only as nightmares. They are shapeless and shadelike, akin to death.[20]

Pluto's astral allies are the amphibious animals, the poison-bearers, ants, spiders, and hairy plants. Black diamonds and deep purple-blue stones—or anything undergoing metamorphosis (cocoons, stalactites, stones changing color)—are Plutonian.[21]

But there is another interpretation of occult Pluto, one that more clearly represents the conjunction of the visible planet with world history. Pluto's real message is neither World War II nor the planetwide deployment of atomic power, though these are Plutonian conditions. It won't be a mind-matter ray or psychic electricity either: these are other passing manifestations.

The psychologist James Hillman writes:

> Hades [Pluto] was of course the God of depths, the God of invisibles. He is himself invisible, which could imply that the invisible connection is Hades, and that the essential "what" that holds things in their form is the secret of their death. And if, as Heraclitus said, Nature loves to hide, then nature loves Hades.
>
> Hades is said to have had no temples or altars in the upperworld and his confrontation with it is experienced as a violence, a violation. . . . He is so invisible in fact that the entire collection of Greek antique art shows no ideal portrait of Hades. . . . He leaves no trace on earth, for no clan descends from him, no generations. . . .
>
> All this "negative" evidence does coalesce to form a definite image of a void, an interiority or depth that is unknown but nameable, there and felt even if not seen. Hades is not an absence, but a hidden presence—even an invisible fullness.[22]

Pluto's real mystery is unknown, and it will apparently remain unknown for eons to come. Then there is my dream of March, 19, 1981:

I am with Spock and Kirk in a small spacecraft, having to escape from our exploding mothership; we are also using its energy to propel us to the other end of the Solar System. The damaged ship turns out to be wedged in between my father's old house and a grove of trees. I run into the house and discover a control panel. The sky on the screen is a model of the Solar System with all the planets and moons. Then it changes. Suddenly I am at the edge of the Solar disk looking down. I notice innumerable planets and moons, though I can't even locate the known ones. I am supposed to find Pluto for us, but I see all sorts of other configurations, including stars among clouds. Something tells me that I am looking at new unknown patterns, objects that have no names yet. I locate the tiny whirling outer planet, but it is called Oedipus not Pluto even though no one has seen it yet—meaning not that astronomers have prepared a name in expectation of it but that there is a planetary form out beyond our senses already named Oedipus. I realize it is a revenge on Freud and his symbols, labelling this new planet with his most obvious primary symbol to indicate that it is *totally nonsymbolic*; if it is actually Oedipus, and if its dream identity is a subterfuge, then there is nothing left it could stand for. It is very small and whizzing along, throwing off particles of sparkling dust in its orbit. I can see the whole complication of the inner Solar System back through it. It is an absolute product of the Sun's gravity. It is the proof that the dream is autonomous and that its symbols come to an end in the twentieth century at the limits of the stars.

19
Science Fiction
I: The Origin of
Celestial Worlds

AN OLD COMIC BOOK shows a Martian orchestra with its snouted players. An alien audience attends while they "play" the standard Earth instruments, but intricately colored shapes arise from the openings and blend above them. Elsewhere, hives of intelligent insectoids go forth in armed vehicles for a bulbous queen who hatches the generations of her centurions. Beings of mist evaporate into the atmosphere of their planet. Crystal creatures lie sessile across the lands of an entire world, assimilating moisture and accumulating a vast philosophy. Another planet's terrain is the organs of a giant beast, its tubule sensoria "mimicking" fields of flowers. Runaway planets intersect the Earth's orbit. Some of them are uninhabitable; others contain sixteen-eyed pyramidal creatures and their cyborg aides. Giant reptiles ride horselike beasts somewhere in the universe. The planet of telepaths eludes our astronauts; they cannot find the landscape, for the inhabitants project only the phantasms they want them to see. These planets exist at the other end of this Galaxy, or in another galaxy. They have their coliseums and cities, their "Homers," "Shakespeares," and "da Vincis."

True science fiction began late in our history as a complement to the infinite universe of the astronomers and mathematicians. Imaginary worlds formed in the debris of mythological ones— all located hypothetically among the stars and dimensions of the night sky. Planet zones were generated throughout Newtonian space, and the Darwinian algorithm filled them with life forms.

Ancient myths tell of stellar forces and the supernatural beings who arise in the sky and on other worlds. Even *Genesis* is the tale of the creation of a planet, and the works of Dante and Milton carry this extraterrestrial theme. Aristophanes, Apuleius, Aesop, and Plato are all considered proto–science fiction writers, for they deal with imaginary cities, extraplanetary travel, and talking beasts. The most famous of these writers, in a science fiction context, is Lucian of Samosata, a Syrian Greek stonemason of the second century A.D., who wrote *Verae Historiae* (True Stories), which suggest the twentieth-century *Amazing Stories* and *Astounding Science Fiction*. In one of Lucian's stories, a Greek sea vessel is swept to the Moon by waterspouts and winds. There the crew witness preparations for a war with the King of the Sun, who is disputing possession of Jupiter with the Lunar King. A huge double wall is built as protection against the Sun. Finally, both sides agree by treaty to colonize the Morning Star. The Greeks continue on their journey through the Zodiac and visit a city in which talking lamps dwell. Their adventures take them to realms of giants and monsters, cities of gold and gems, and an Isle of Dreams with a dream palace.

This is not really science fiction, nor does it lead to science fiction. Until the secular sky had broken free of the astral heavens, there could be no stellar adventure that was not equally occultism and mythology. Lucian's planets and creatures are simply supernatural Earth realms and spirit beings. Even the Lilliput of Jonathan Swift's *Gulliver's Travels* (and other imaginary lands of the seventeenth and eighteenth centuries) are not so much science fiction "worlds" as intentional allegorical extensions. Science fiction is at once more ancient and more modern: it is a projection of our unconscious boundaries into an infinite cosmos at the same time that it is a self-conscious attempt to invent replicas for the degrees of limitlessness itself.

Science fiction bears the last embers of our former astronomical grandness and of the cosmos that we imaginarily and sympathetically inhabited as we came out of prehuman darkness. It wasn't science fiction then, but it was at least as cosmic as anything that the modern interstellar writers have come up with— the deep shifting cycles of lotus-within-lotus universes we could not know linearly and thus knew radiatively, intuitively. Strangers came then, too, from strange lands, but they were astral strangers, demonoids, daemons, and angelics; they dwelled in cacti and lizards and butterfly-moths and burst suddenly from the Moon and planets onto the Earth, where they initiated our ancestors under the shadow light of the spirit sky.

The stellar epic is as old as our species. The nether worlds and the empyrean sky were discovered by Ice Age shamans and sages stretching from primeval Africa to the islands of the Pacific. Over millions of years of study of the visible heavens and the fact of their own being, they came to an understanding of the invisible truth. Great worlds lay hidden far away, but they impinged on this one through our human nature. We could enter these worlds only after dangerous journeys and in other shapes.

Neither the Platonic nor the Ptolemaic universes represented the complexity and profundity of this mundus The mediaeval cosmos, which science finally eroded, was not the ancient mythic cosmos. It had man in the center for reasons of academic and religious liturgy rather than divination and vision. Copernicus and Galileo did not destroy the sacred cosmos; rather they made it possible for us to regain it by laying a new basis for star exploration. When we come "back" to science fiction, it has elements again of Ice Age consciousness. That is why it sparkles with the newness and hope of unknown worlds and at the same time haunts us with the relics and intimations of worlds long forgotten.

Long before the planets and the stars became places to go to, they visited the Earth in other shapes. We have not inherited documents detailing these matters in the Stone Age, but we have heard tales of similar import among non-Western tribal peoples, tales which are no doubt reflections of the old stellar fiction. Among the Sherente of Brazil, Venus was a masculine being, Jupiter a woman:

> One night [the Jupiter] Star came down from the sky to a young bachelor who had fallen in love with her. The young man hid the star in a gourd, where she was discovered by his brothers. Star told her lover and invited him to accompany her to the sky. Everything was different from its equivalent on earth. Everywhere he saw smoked or roasted

human flesh, and when bathing he saw horribly mutilated shapes with open body cavities. He escaped by sliding down the bacaba palm up which he had climbed; and when he got back to earth, he related his adventure. But soon after he died, and his soul went back to Jupiter, and now he is a star beside her in the heavens.[1]

The sense of the sky as a place is incipient in this myth, but the creationary elements predominate. In a Winnebago Indian legend cycle, a powerful space-being visits the Earth and impregnates a maiden who dies bearing quadruplets. The firstborn, Manabozho, attacks the one born last, Chokanipok, and, after cutting enormous chunks from his body, scatters them about as flintstones and turns his intestines into "long twining vines." Then, the one born third, Wabassa, flees to the north and is transformed into a shaman rabbit.[2] This is not a story about the objectified heavens as a place; it is an attempt to explain the Earth in terms of the germinative principle of the sky. The birth of each of the Greek gods is likewise a quasi-stellar event:

Aphrodite, Goddess of Desire, rose naked from the foam of the sea and, riding on a scallop shell, stepped ashore first on the island of Cytherea; but finding this only a small island, passed on to the Peloponese, and eventually took up residence at Paphos, in Cyprus. . . . Grass and flowers sprang from the soil wherever she trod. . . .

Some hold that she sprang from the foam which gathered about the genitals of Uranus, when Cronus threw them into the sea; others, that Zeus begot her on Dione, daughter either of Oceanus and Tethys the sea-nymph, or of Air and Earth.[3]

The arrival by scallop shell might bear the mark of an extra-terrestrial vehicle, but this is clearly not what Aphrodite is about. She represents, in the minds of those who imagined her collectively and over time, the emergence of beauty from the debris of creation, its original personification in a sentient creature.

Contemporary science fiction has its episodes of exotic love between aliens and humans, but, in these matters, Aphrodite's visit to Anchises, leading to the birth of Aeneas, is primal and indicative of an intimacy we still seek:

So speaking, [Anchises] caught her by the hand. And laughter-loving Aphrodite, with face turned away and lovely eyes downcast, crept to the well-spread couch which was already laid with soft coverings for the hero; and upon it lay skins of bears and deep-roaring lions which he himself had slain in the high mountains. And when they had gone up upon the well-fitted bed, first Anchises took off her bright jewelry of pins and twisted brooches and earrings and necklaces, and loosed her girdle and stripped off her bright garments and laid them down upon a silver-studded seat. Then by the will of the gods and destiny he lay with her, a mortal man with an immortal goddess, not clearly knowing what he did.

Anchises' first realization of the nature of his lover comes when she awakes him and stands before him by the couch: "Her head reached to the well-hewn roof-tree; from her cheeks shone unearthly beauty such as belongs to rich-crowned Cytherea."[4]

It is no wonder that several contemporary authors, under the spell of science fiction and secular astronomy, have imagined that these visitors were real extraterrestrial beings, perceived by our ancestors as gods. Robert Temple associates the Babylonian fish-tailed Oannes with amphibious beings from the star system of Sirius—beings who, the Dogon say, founded their society: he imagines an intelligent creature "resembling a kind of cross between a man and a dolphin."[5] The literature of our planet abounds with possible spacecraft and extraterrestrial travelers. Von Daniken, Temple, and others have cited references to such things in written and oral tales, in petroglyphs of saucerlike objects, and in inexplicable archaic objects that resemble clocks and computer wheels. Temple relates a Dogon description of an alien descent. The vehicle sounded like large stone blocks being struck in a particular small cave near Lake Debo. "The ark landed on the Fox's dry land and displaced a pile of dust raised by the whirlwind it caused. The violence of the impact roughened the ground."[6] A flame went out from the ark and touched the grass.

Temple finds another "landing" in the Sumerian tale of *Gilgamesh* from the third millennium B.C.: "There appeared stars in the heavens. The host of heaven fell down toward me. I tried to lift it but it was too heavy for me; I tried to move it, but I could not move it."[7]

If extraterrestrials came here in the Pleistocene, their contributions have already been incorporated in our civilization as the deeds of gods and the visions of shamans. The gods exist for other reasons too; and if spacemen were momentarily synchronous with them, this may change aspects of their message, but not their meaning as divinities: they still speak from beyond the stars through the human psyche. Von Daniken is unintentionally accurate when he cites "our human past which somehow is bound to become our human future some time or other,"[8] for this is true already in his assumptions that Thor, Ra, Quetzalcoatl, and Rama were space visitors, not gods; that Ezekiel saw extraterrestrial machines, not divine orbs; that Enkidu was a spaceship in *Gilgamesh*, etc. He has made the shadow over our origins into our destiny, but he has also distorted our relationship to the early high civilizations and made it impossible for us to distinguish any true extraterrestrial relics that might be camouflaged on this world. Von Daniken insists that we were bred from aliens and are their children—which makes us gods also. But the universe is so big and complex that this claim has no more meaning, even if true, than the profound mystery of DNA itself in the bowels of the nebulae.

The World of the Dead was the most visited "planet" of antiquity, and although it was a realm entered through a state of "spiritual" transformation, it was also a literary forerunner to space-travel:

> When ghosts descend to Tartarus, the main entrance to which lies in a grove of black poplars beside the Ocean stream, each is supplied by pious relatives with a coin laid under the tongue of its corpse. They are thus able to pay Charon, the miser who ferries them in a crazy boat across the Styx. This hateful river bounds Tartarus on the western side, and has for its tributaries Acheron, Phlegethon, Cocytus, Aornis, and Lethe. Penniless ghosts must wait forever on the near bank; unless they have evaded Hermes, their conductor, and crept down by a back entrance. . . . A three-headed or, some say, fifty-headed dog named Cer-

berus guards the opposite shore of Styx, ready to devour living intruders or ghostly fugitives. . . .

The first region of Tartarus contains the cheerless Asphodel Fields, where souls of heroes stray without purpose among the throngs of less distinguished dead that twitter like bats, and where only Orion still has the heart to hunt the ghostly deer.[9]

The kingdom of Osiris, known to the Egyptians, is a different world of the dead. Humanoids there have hawk, jackal, and lion heads. A hare-headed being holds a knife. A hippopotamus goddess and a squat dwarf stand beside each other, bearing knives. Beside them is a ram-headed ghoul. The hawk of Horus, wearing two crowns, is poised on a sepulchral building. The Sun and Moon are replaced by the Eyes of heaven.[10] Some contemporary archaeoastronomers find Egypt exotic enough to be a possible extraterrestrial outpost on the Earth. The Sphinxlike visage on the Martian tundra flanked by five-sided pyramids certainly encourages that speculation. In fact, if truly artificial, the site is old enough (by crater count) to be a lineal ancestor of Egyptian civilization.

The visitor to the Tibetan land of the dead is prepared for fantastic and terrifying creatures:

O nobly-born, from the north [will dawn] the Blue Wolf-Headed Wind-Goddess, waving a pennant in the hand; and the Red Ibex-Headed Woman-Goddess, holding a pointed stake in the hand; and the Black Sow-Headed Sow-Goddess, holding a noose of fangs in the hand; and the Red Crow-Headed Thunderbolt-Goddess, holding an infant corpse in the hand; and the Greenish-Black Elephant-Headed Big-Nosed Goddess, holding in the hand a big corpse and drinking blood from a skull. . . .[11]

This is a world of dull, smoke-colored lights, unabated storms, beasts of prey, deafening sounds, and bands of pursuing monsters. The *Book of the Dead* advises that these specters are the actual consequences of anger, greed, fear, violence, indifference, and other negative emotions and attitudes. It is not that the Bardo realm (into which souls first pass) is merely symbolic; it is that emotions are physical facts that dissolve into inhabited topographies when the corporeal aspect behind an individual disintegrates. These are not biological beasts or geological landscapes, even though they have an origin in creature existence; they are psychic representations.

Realms of the dead are not the only archaic planets. Fairy tales are filled with Earthlike worlds inhabited by weird and magical creatures. In the Irish accounts, there are trooping fairies, changelings, ghosts, leprechauns, giants, demon cats, spook hares, bewitched butter, banshees, and waking dreams. A four-leafed clover captures the suddenness with which this world becomes another. In the Germanic tales of the Brothers Grimm, a prince is entrapped in the body of a frog, a sentient crow is nailed to a palace wall, a flounder grants wishes to a fisherman upon being thrown back, witches dwell in the center of every deep forest, and Beauty is visited each time by the Beast. Mary Shelley later calls that monster back to life beneath flashing stars with stirrings of odd memories. The tinder box that brings the dogs from the sky and the lamp that summons the jinni from another dimension are now electronic devices. When the American Indian shaman Coyote climbed a thread into the sky, he found aged spiders sitting in a meadow; and during the day he spent with them there, a year passed in the world below. It is no wonder that time between planets now is dilated and other worlds are inhabited by telepathic savages, thinking rocks, mermaids, and disembodied voices. We have suspected such "places" from before the days of Phoenicians.

The Irish *immrama* and the Norse *Sagas* are fragments of a vast oral science fiction that pervaded Europe from ancient times through the middle ages. Odysseus took one of the earliest extant "space" voyages; he went into an unknown cosmology among lotus eaters, the Cyclops, and the witch Circê; a bag full of winds—living creatures in a leather sack—was presented to him by Aiolos. We cannot reduce those adventures to the Aegean, but we can expand the Aegean to include the stars.

Then there are the sea journeys of Brendan, a mediaeval Irish monk who was perhaps a Neolithic shaman. He was attacked by a giant spitting fire; he saw a floating crystal column; he came to a place where light passed through the water to the cities beneath. The giant spitting fire could have been a volcano on an island off Iceland. The crystal could have been floating ice. Perhaps Brendan and his crew turned to the south, coasting Vinland, and looked into the transparent coral sea.[12]

The Icelandic seaman Erik the Red sailed to the Americas four times; on one of his voyages, he encountered an aboriginal race, probably Eskimos or Beothuk Indians and named Skraelings ("little people") by the Norsemen. These swarthy, stubby folk looked like trolls. They came in nine skin-boats, whirling their bull-roarers "in the same direction that the sun moves, and they made a noise like flails," according to *The Saga Tale* of A.D. 1005. Freydis, Erik's daughter, suggested an attack upon these puny-seeming beings, but the Skraelings drove back the iron-bearing strangers with slings and arrows and with weapons made of sea-mammal floats which crashed on the ground among the Vikings, giving off horrendous noises. (No doubt our species has met itself elsewhere on this planet as strangers, but this one recorded case stands for thousands.)

When Erik the Red left the Western lands, his ships full of ivory, oil, and hides, he sailed north looking for new worlds. He wintered at an unknown place that he called Eriksholm; the men built homes from driftwood that had been carried by currents from Siberian rivers. At the end of a hard winter, they continued north.

Then Erik came to the end of the world: giant icebergs, half a mile in length, crashed from the face of ice, sending out tidal waves for miles and yet still visible at the distance of Erik's ships, the greatest glacier face on this interglacial Earth. Here Erik looked north into a mirror of continuous blinding daylight, uninhabitable as the Sun or interstellar space in a way that made Baffinland look like paradise, for Baffinland was at least a continent. Here he floated among the peaks of sunken mountains, the fragments of olden worlds, the glitter so bright that he could not see, where all the languages and landscapes and directions mixed in the polar scramble of atmosphere and solar wind, closer to Thor than he had ever been, closer to Middle Earth.[13]

Centuries later, Marco Polo went among the Tartars and to the courts of Cathay. The Portuguese brought Africans, their beads, ostrich egg cups, and wood carvings back from the interior of another continent. Early sixteenth-century voyagers returned from the New World with coarse-haired red "savages" who spoke unearthly languages. Were these the lost tribes of Israel? Were they even our human kin? In the late eighteenth century—that recently—the returning ships of Captain Cook reported unknown species of plants and animals, exotic kings and chieftains, southern ice, and immense statue heads on Easter Island. Legend, theology, and early anthropology merge here.

We sense the power of the unknown West in Shakespeare's late plays. The tragedies of his kings have ended; the pranksters, fairies, and buffoons of the comedies are put to sea. The European theater is shipwrecked on what seems at first a tiny isle but is actually a gateway between aeons and worlds. It is as if Shakespeare knew that only something totally different could follow him. He had enough of Galileo and John Dee in him for that foresight.

Through Ariel and Caliban, he tells us that there are lands on the Earth inhabited by beings who are not like us and who share neither our history nor our Christian tradition. If they work magic, it is by their own native arts.

"This island's mine, by Sycorax my mother," says Caliban.[14] There are not even Egyptians lurking behind his claim. There are only local gods and wilderness. The isle is filled with wild and wondrous sounds and voices.

The Tempest is not itself science fiction, but it is a direct forerunner. Magician and daughter become scientist and daughter a thousand times over, marooned on the planets of other suns. And the handsome spacemen, like the shipwrecked nobles of Shakespeare's play, come to reclaim the lady both from her possessive and powerful father and from the native spirits. The Mirandas of outer space look back at the Earth as a star and say, "O brave new world. . . ."[15]

Some things have never been found: mermaids, winged tribes, Amazon women, the white Christian kingdom of Prester John in Africa, the continent of Atlantis, the antipodes who live upside down, and so on. Their meanings have been transferred to historical episodes, as when the Mormons decided that the American Indians were the lost Hebrew tribes; or they have been assigned to the less glorious things that *have* been found, as when mythical Brazil was abandoned and the name given to a vast tropical wilderness. No Fountain of Youth, no telepathic races, no two-headed humanoids or underwater cities have ever been discovered. Some of these things have been transfused directly into science fiction, and they are found again imaginarily on the planets in that tradition—they and far stranger races and creatures.

It would take the European mind many generations to realize the wonders that were disclosed by early ethnographers and travelers. The Australian Aborigines lived in a dreamtime landscape that was almost supernatural. Their Earth was the bones and blood, genitals and semen, of a collective being of which they were the living members. And they received news of the dead over great distances without visible messages or messengers. They had a science of the interwoven families that challenged any social system elsewhere. The American Indians visited plants in their minds and charmed animals, and if they weren't weird and multicolored by birth, they painted themselves into bizarre spirit-figures and did dances no one had imagined, raising elements of consciousness not yet broached in the West. The actuality of kachinas and medicine men and buffalo dancers and sun-priests was stranger than any fantasy of them. Where they fell short in teratology and supernatural powers they made up in *actually being* and in living in full regalia and commitment as those alien creatures.

Carlos Castaneda is very late for one going out among Indians to seek a fierce and unknown universe. He did not travel to a planet in Andromeda or even to one of the nearer stars like Sirius. He simply crossed the border into Mexico. There he discovered things as incredible and inexplicable as anything science fiction fantasizes for peoples of vastly superior technologies and psychokinetic powers. In the universe of Don Juan, which stretches to the ends of the cosmos, Castaneda is a waif. Perhaps because we already suspect that this vital shamanism abounds on our world, and because we intuit such powers vestigially in ourselves (and cannot get at them), we invent more simply attainable wonders in interstellar space. Our imagination tries to justify our troubled lives.

Mystics of all religions have told us that mind can shape matter, that we can make whatever we need. But to do this we must take our incarnation seriously and not play at being alive. Science fiction pretends to let us eat our cake and have it too. We get the great power of mind over matter not through personal rigor and training but as the result of a collective exterior adventure or a technological invention. We set these wonderful planets apart in the heavens so that we might not pollute them with our arrogance and our error, and so that they may outlive us and our Big Bang universe and continue to exist even if we finally fail them in ourselves. Our shaman hero inherits the stars, but we must fight for every clump of dirt.

Castaneda describes speaking to animals in unknown languages, entering the psyche of a passing bird, being in two places at the same time, growing new organs in his body, and jumping into a chasm to sure death, only to rematerialize in a marketplace elsewhere. Not only is this the stuff of quasars and black holes, but some people claim that Castaneda has written science fiction disguised dishonestly as ethnography. [16]

In his *Billion Year Spree*, Brian Aldiss locates the beginning of true science fiction in the genre of the Gothic novel: strange worlds set in remote lands, ghosts, vampires, giants, castles, sultans, treasures, supernatural visitors, isolated villages in which the laws of nature shift. [17] Aldiss then traces the Gothic novel to Horace Walpole's *The Castle of Otranto*, published in 1765. And where did *Otranto* come from?

"On a June night in 1764, Walpole had a nightmare in which he saw a gigantic hand clad in armour, gripping the bannister of a great staircase. When he woke, he began writing his novel." [18]

Much science fiction also originates in visions, trances, and psychopathic incidents, so the beginning of the genre is as bottomless and untraceable as the stars.

The first science fiction novel was Mary Wollstonecraft Shelley's *Frankenstein*, which also had its origin in a dream and was written before the author was twenty, in 1816. Even if the monster is a partial projection of the dark side of her poet husband, the resulting creature is clearly not a ghost or a golem in the usual sense; he is fictionalized as a "machine" created by a scientist. He ponders his obscure origin and unhappy lot as science fiction robots will for millions of hypothetical years in the future. Mary Shelley, suggests Aldiss, gave birth not merely to a monster who lay sleeping just beyond human ken but to an entire genre.[19] Soon after, Jules Verne invented the machinery, and H. G. Wells sent rockets into the Solar System.

Other modern literary genres, like the Western and the detective story, have *cinema verité* landscapes. Science fiction landscapes tend toward the surreal and ornate, but they must be the landscapes of some thing. Most likely that "thing" is the imprisoned psyche of science itself—of astronomy, physics, chemistry, and biology as they were stripped of their interior component and wrested into the service of progressive society. Science fiction comes into being with technology and industrialism and reflects their epistemology. That is why Mary Shelley's robot is the first. The true science fiction creature must be artificial and industrial, or it must be discovered (or discover us) on a journey arising from technology.

Science fiction worlds are proposed as other things, so they capture that aspect of ourselves that wishes to propose an Other even as they carry meanings that we no longer have access to in spiritual inquiry and thus have cast into the unknown dimensions of time and space. They may originate in *our* science, but when *its* potential realms are externalized, they seem the products of other intelligences. From a stochastic imagination, alien shapes and exotic terrains emerge. When they work, they startle us, for we have succeeded in putting a dark and compelling crack in the natural world. We have dressed the imposter so well he could replace us, right now.

Science fiction also requires the ingredients of the romantic Western novel: adventure in exotic lands, transcendence of social limitations, and the development of a unique personality and soul. "There may be trillions of galaxies, and billions of billions of stars in those, and billions of planets orbiting about those stars," Dr. McCoy tells Captain Kirk during a *Star Trek* episode, "and who knows how many races and individual beings—but only one Kirk in all of that." Without this element of human uniqueness, fiction merges with allegory, as in *Pilgrim's Progress*.

As long as each of us is a discrete being, and each alien world and creature is novel and original, there is reason to visit all of them. If they go on forever, then we must go on forever too, as writers and explorers. They cannot be categorized or generalized. They do not form a zodiac. We must approach them in their regional and infinite diversity, and experience them palpably, with their indigenous colors, scents, and sounds.

Poul Anderson's novel *The High Crusade* is not particularly rich in texture or complexity, but in its simple tale, the vastness of the science fiction possibility is imposed on the unsuspecting mediaeval world. Through a series of remarkable twists of plot, the entire history of science fiction and UFO encounters is rearranged. [20]

The story begins when, in 1345, Sir Roger, an English baron, is in the process of raising an army to join King Edward III in France. However, a spaceship lands in his village. Its occupants are five feet tall with blue skin and short tails. Though everyone is terrorized at the sign of actual devils, and exorcism is the first strategy, there is no time to weigh alternatives. The invaders hurl fire from a weapon, scorching to death one of the locals. The soldiers respond without thinking. To their amazement, their arrows penetrate these blue demons. Hundreds of arrows are fired, and three of the invaders fall over as easily as popinjays.

Sir Roger is a modern thinker. He has no idea who these invaders are, but he is impressed with their vehicle, and he wants to use it against the French, and then, if successful, against the Infidels in the Holy Land. After taking Jerusalem, he can return heroically to England. He is unfazed by the concern that it is a satanic ship. Enlisting the aid of the crew members still alive, he learns how to operate it. To the objection that they are devils and the ship is cursed, he simply replies that they are sorry devils indeed if they can be killed so easily. Instead, the idea is put forth that they are from a place beyond Cathay, a land which already had elusive precedents in Plutarch, Brendan, and Pytheas.

Sir Roger piles everything into the spacecraft—men, women, children, horses, cows, pigs, chickens. They levitate rapidly. The clouds turn out to be mere mists; the Earth is round, the Moon pocked. The Earth disappears beneath them like a stone "down a great well."

They expect to be taken to France, but their captive pilot has betrayed them and set the ship on automatic controls to return to the home planet, part of an expansionist interplanetary empire that intends to conquer the Earth too.

Sir Roger is undaunted. He imagines that in such an enormous empire there will be great booty, and the creatures themselves do not seem powerful in combat. He succeeds not only in capturing the planet upon landing but in taking over the entire empire. It is his descendants, having organized the many worlds into a feudal kingdom, who meet the first spacemen from Earth.

These English knights in interstellar space who retain their mediaeval world-view and yet conquer a vastly complex civilization form a powerful image of a moment in time and space that transcends the book and demonstrates exactly how science fiction works through the integrity of single nonallegorical lives. Sir Owain's courtship of Lady Catherine beneath strange stars and two moons is the central heart-chakra image. Are we not the descendants of peasants and fishermen even when we go among the stars? Is not any technology we use to escape the Earth also a myth we project ceaselessly outward?

For generations, the offspring of this English army spread their empire, in the course of which they search the suns, right into the center of the Galaxy, for the Earth and the Holy Land. When the first Earthship arrives, they are deeply moved. Their origin in a sacred faraway land turns out not to be just a legend. They offer the Earth crew an astrologer to guide them to the court of the King; there the terrestrials hear about the royal expeditions to promising Sagittarian star clouds.

Science fiction is somewhat of a misnomer. We are actually creating stellar mythology. We are projecting every imaginable aspect of the present world frame into the unknown problematic basis of reality, and we are seeing ourselves reflected back ever more remotely and relativistically, until it might seem that our existence in the universe could be anything at all. For lack of a coherent cosmology and a fixed world axis, we have come to hard times, and we have no quadrants or clepsydras with which to realign ourselves or sky. Adjustments hardly last a year now, let alone a generation or an aeon. We tilt cosmogony every which way, and change the dimensions and moral basis of the universe likewise, and this has become more acceptable to us than passively waiting for our destiny. We have come to prefer Shakespeare's pre-modern existential Hamlet to the ancient Scandinavian prince who attempted to keep the constellations in place and on whom the latter one was incompletely based.

If we cannot fix a single reality and a coherent universe, we will invent every possible one. The madness may once have been in the stars, but we have taken it down into our lives. We are the only prophets and the only heroes left. Our illusion is that we have escaped the fate of cosmic unity, but we are now that fate, and we alone betray what the cosmos can become.

20

Science Fiction
II: Self and Cosmos

THE KEY TO SCIENCE FICTION is not the exotic nature of the worlds visited in outer space or the interstellar distances covered. Varieties of planets and creatures can go on forever in these books without our even intuiting a cosmic meaning. The true key to science fiction is the passage of our minds and spirits, and sometimes even our bodies, to other dimensions and realms of consciousness. This may happen on a starship voyage to faraway solar systems and other galaxies, but it also may happen without our ever leaving the Earth. A place is not automatically "cosmic" because a writer tells us it is on another planet. The strange creatures in the Earth's oceans are cosmic, and even the butterflies and grasshoppers in the fields are cosmic. Science fiction does not create the cosmic by astounding us with bizarre machinations; it does not find other worlds only by exaggerating the unearthly.

"There are far too many worlds in this desert alone," the shaman Juan Matus tells Carlos Castaneda, "for us ever to know them all in the pitiably short time of a man's life."[1]

The ordinary novelist must portray the human condition within the terms of a particular century and social milieu. He can imply cosmic forces, but he cannot introduce their raw nature into his books. If he does, they become science fiction. A science fiction writer can move his characters through the stars and can move the stars themselves; he can even have stars think and communicate; he can throw an entire culture into an alien condition. However, we must not be fooled by the landscape. Dostoevsky and Faulkner revealed as much about man's fate among the stars as any science fiction writer; by not bringing the stars into the foreground of their work, they showed their subtle and intricate presence everywhere.

A book such as Charles Dickens's *Great Expectations* actually contains the mystery and texture that a writer like Poul Anderson then projects thinly across outer space. Could anything we invent for another world be stranger than Miss Havisham in her faded wedding dress, the wedding cake rotting on the table with spiders running in and out, the clocks stopped, the cobwebs covering the walls in candlelight?[2] Is this Mars ... or Andromeda? The classic science fiction quest is to get to the bottom of things, whether these be the shadow of Self on the Cosmos or the reflection of Cosmos through the Self. Neither space travel nor visitation of aliens can change the grail.

Ursula LeGuin's character Ramarren (*City of Illusions*) awakes in darkness without memory and is given the name Falk by those around him. His green eyes mark him as an alien. Through the course of the novel he travels across the United States of some future century seeking an explanation of who he is. Even the Prince of Kansas, using geomancy and an abacus-ephemeris of precious stones and junk, cannot find him, for Falk has come from Eltanin, the eye of the Dragon, by starship—a light-speed journey of 142 years. But he does not know this, for the enemy Shing blasted his ship out of the sky, killing all the other envoys and leaving him memoryless.

At the climax of the book, in the Shing city of illusions, Ramarren recovers his original self only at the expense of Falk: the Shing perform an act of mind-razing to keep him from guessing the truth. However, on Eltanin he was spiritually and telepathically disciplined, and he has left a single obscure clue at the seventh level of his training to lead him back to Falk. Then, at the moment he recovers Falk, he becomes two people and almost loses his sanity, for the identities have grown as equally mature adults using different brain cells. His double-self suddenly sees two suns:

... the orange gold of Werel's sun, the white gold of Earth's:
he could hold them now side by side as a man might hold two
jewels, comparing their beauty for the sake of heightening
their praise.[3]

As long as Falk and Ramarren survive together in him, he has
the opportunity of saving both their worlds from the Shing.

In the Dickens novel, Pip finds out that an escaped convict
whom he met in a graveyard as a child and for whom he smuggled
food out of his house has been his secret benefactor ever since.
Pip's bounty came not from the stepmother of the unattainable
woman (as he hoped and suspected) but from a hunted outlaw.
When he discovers this, he seems to fall entirely from grace, but
there is another twist: the convict is also the woman's father. This
second turn of the wheel allows him to recover everything. He
wrests his lover from the darkness with which the story is enshrouded, tearing open the curtains of the old house to let daylight
through the cobwebs. A single innocent act of the heart in childhood becomes his entire destiny—the same destiny he could not
force through affectation or pride. The story begins with a meeting in the graveyard, seems to abandon it, and then finds its
redemption through it. Science fiction takes this moment and
spreads it across universes—which doesn't make it any bigger, but
transfers it into a modern frame with a sense of how big it always
was.

There *is* a convict and a graveyard at our beginning, and our
very existence throws light through a previously blackened
room. This is our inheritance. In a universe of stone and fire,
the convict himself is a prince. The rich woman and her daughter
are a fantasy of better worlds and how things would be if we had
not been born ignorant and poor. We seem not to deserve the
cosmos at all, and then we become its actual salvation. The
ancients knew it as destiny too and placed it in the stars by a
different method.

Science fiction writers take the cosmos itself as a figure for
our origins and our destiny, a figure writ large and projected out
away from us where we seem to see it as a mammoth unity. It
is not any particular shape that gives cosmic overtones; it is the

fact itself of an eternal enigma in a star-filled night. We cannot
evade it or disarm it, so we must enter and reveal it. But mostly
science fiction fails. The bigness is corrupting, and the writer
ends up with a minor theme ornately decorated with stars,
bizarre landscapes, trivial monsters, and other baroque creatures.

During the ominous years before World War II, Olaf Stapledon
tried to invent the bigness and blackness of the whole universe in
his book *Star Maker*. In the beginning, a single Earthling is
contacted and induced up into the heavens:

> Rubies lay behind me, amethysts ahead of me. Surrounding
> the ruby constellations there spread an area of topaz stars,
> and round the amethyst constellations an area of sapphires.
> Beside my course, on every side, the colours faded into
> the normal white of the sky's familiar diamonds. Since I
> was travelling almost in the plane of the galaxy, the hoop
> of the Milky Way, white on either hand, was violet ahead
> of me, red behind. [4]

His speed increases, and the stars and galaxies fly past in a
blizzard. Instead of moving outward into an eternity, he approaches the source, the Star Maker himself. This supersentient
being puffs out trial universes, observes them in a wink, and
then devours them to try again. Against such a sterile creationary
force, the horrors of war should seem trivial. After all, the Star
Maker consumes war and peace equally:

> As he lovingly, though critically, reviewed our cosmos in all
> its infinite diversity and in its brief moment of lucidity, I
> felt that he was suddenly filled with reverence for the crea-
> ture that he had made, or that he had ushered out of his
> own secret depth by a kind of divine self-midwifery. He
> knew that this creature, though imperfect, though a mere
> creature, a mere figment of his own creative power, was yet
> in a manner more real than himself. [5]

But the Starmaker can do nothing to improve the quality of
this universe:

> He had seemingly outgrown all desire to save them from
> the consequences of their finitude and from the cruel im-
> pact of the environment. He loved them without pity. For
> he saw that their distinctive virtue lay in their finitude, their

minute particularity, their tortured balance between dull-
ness and lucidity; and that to save them from these would
be to annihilate them. [6]

With such a figure for the cosmos itself, Stapledon can arrive
only at a kind of astral nihilism. But the unacknowledged shadow
of Hitler across this book is more horror-provoking than a star
maker who idly destroys whole universes. Scale alone does not
make an idea big or an image deep. The local darkness outbid
Stapledon here.

In contemporary science fiction we are less involved with
trying to personify the cosmos and less occupied by the creation of
ulterior worlds. As we attempt to integrate Hindu and Buddhist
themes, we are moving into a literature of self-revelation and
reincarnation. The astral and astronomical universes approach
each other once again and intertwine, even when writers are only
superficially aware of the relationship.

In *Lord of Light*, Roger Zelazny creates a world of god-figures
who are not actually deities but ruling-class members given divine
attributes and virtual immortality by a technology of engrams and
mind-transfer. Karma now measures the debt of creatures bio-
electrically, enacting cycles of disembodiment and reembodiment
based solely on political power; it is used, even as computers are,
to maintain an existing order. As in much science fiction, reincarnation has become a tyranny extended beyond lifetimes.

Zelazny's decadent nobles have taken on the names and metaphorical powers of the gods and goddesses of the Hindu Vedas.
Warring with one another and changing bodies and sexes, they try
to enjoy the sensual pleasures of eternity. They elevate the few
and banish their enemies to bestial or imperfect bodies. The bulk
of mankind remains savage and dispossessed, while these lords—
as Mara, Yama, Vishnu, and Brahma—make beautiful bodies for
themselves, subjugate harems, and accumulate wealth. They have
even forgotten that they are not the actual gods, because they have
been these entities for so long.

The one renegade, Siddhartha, the binder of demons, has been
banished to the eletric field about the Earth, but his engram is
taken back and reincarnated by the rebels. Unwilling at first even

to reassume his flesh (as Ramarren was unwilling at first to reintegrate Falk), he finally relents and leads a revolution against the corrupt gods.[7]

In the actual Hindu universe, karma simply is; it cannot be corrupted by technology developed by a being on any world, no matter how advanced. Karma is even more final than gravity. But in this science fiction universe, it is perverted into a form of electricity by biological engineers.

The advanced yogi does not need matter or starships to find his way to the ends of time, and he creates his own "black holes" with that other fine material inside him. He can see from before it all to beyond it all, or at least he can see to the limits of all desire, and no other seeing is possible. He sacrifices his life in order to be a mutation, but what he leaves behind cannot be inherited in the cells of his offspring.

In *Star Trek,* many of the more notable episodes are spiritual or mental, as when Captain Kirk is split into his polarized halves by a transporter malfunction, or when Spock enters alien minds and sees the universe they see—from Hortas of rock and silicon to creatures of sparkling lights. Other beings and intelligences flicker in and out of the universe through which the starship *Enterprise* assiduously travels. They are part of the larger creation. From meetings with them the travelers are changed, and the voyage becomes a cosmic initiation.

"Space: The Final Frontier!" we are told at the beginning of each episode. But it is not space, of course, that is the final frontier. It is ourselves. We are traveling across a layer of the cosmos in an illusion of space and time. The first *Star Trek* movie is an epithalamium of our species with its own creation. It is a machine-age Gnostic tale: an old Earth-made satellite (V'ger) returns from the remote reaches of time and space; now it seeks something more than just data, more than just new planets and landscapes. In the end, a man and a woman and the V'ger merge in a metasexual fountain of lights, auras, and atoms, and they clone a new species, just as dreaming children do in Arthur Clarke's *Childhood's End,* or the transmigrating Hopi ancestors do following the spirit of a great bird. The willowy androgynous-looking beings of *Close Encounters of the Third Kind* may be visitants from outer space, but their manipulation of time and dimension implies that man has come into contact with something new in the cosmos, thus something new in his own nature. The spaceship over Devil's Tower may be pure machinery, but an underlying mantra and cosmic melody are used to make the connection, and the object closely resembles a fully manifested mandala mushrooming into our realm from another space.

There is also a real literature of reincarnation: individuals suddenly awaken to other lives within them and discover the self evolving across lifetimes. Even an astronaut finds himself on a much longer cosmic journey than he suspected.

In Paramahansa Yogananda's *Autobiography of a Yogi*, the author's teacher tells the tale of his own teacher, Lahiri Mahasaya, who was summoned unconsciously to a meeting with the avatar Babaji. This avatar was his teacher in previous lives, but Lahiri does not remember him. With a single touch of the hand, Babaji enlightens his old pupil. He brings the other lives back into his consciousness until he realizes what this all is. Then the deathless one speaks:

> "For more than three decades I have waited for you to return to me.
> "You slipped away and disappeared into the tumultuous waves of the life beyond death. The magic wand of your karma touched you, and you were gone! Though you lost sight of me, never did I lose sight of you! I pursued you over the luminescent astral sea where the glorious angels sail. Through gloom, storm, upheaval, and light I followed you, like a mother bird guarding her young."[8]

In the Tibetan novel *Mipam* by Lama Yongden, both Mipam and Dolma are reincarnated century after century until they see each other back at the beginning according to the vows they took then. At the end of the novel, Mipam "remembers." Dolma, the woman he would have married, is returned to the astral sea so that they can complete the episode begun aeons earlier:

> "Because I refused thee the gift of what I possessed of the Doctrine [he tells her], I remained for centuries unable to understand it wholly. Be thou delivered from the desire for vengeance that has brought thee back into this world

for numberless sorrowful incarnations, and may I be delivered from egotism and pride, the primal springs of that
desire.

"Take thy rest for a brief space in the Paradise of the
Great Beatitude, then, having chosen honourable parents
in a neighboring region, and having been born with a male
body, come to me in ten years' time and rejoin me here at
Ngarong to be my pupil and my well-beloved son."[9]

Man is in exile from something. Mankind has been driven out
of the stars, and each individual has lost his or her roots. The
race has lost its origin and its destiny. Perhaps all the sentient
beings of all the planets are in exile.

Outer space is perhaps one aspect of our passage through
"numberless sorrowful incarnations" until we return to the
source of our desire, which, according to karmic law, brought all
this into being in the first place, including the starry night.

Philip José Farmer has created two imaginary universes in
which planetary and biological engineering have become so advanced that beings are kidnapped from their worlds and their
bodies, put in new bodies, and whole artificial planets are created by Lords who then rule them as tyrants. In the World of
Tiers series, the Lords have each created a planet as his or her
private paradise, using synthetic bodies of real beasts, mythological beasts, and beautiful humanoids. However, the Lords
have lost touch with their human roots and have become cruel
experimenters, warring on each other and trying to destroy each
other's worlds simply for amusement because eternity has become tiresome. They delight in trapping each other on their
own worlds or invading planets and dislodging the resident Lord,
who may be their own father or son or daughter, but from so
long ago that it has lost meaning.

In the first novel of the series, *The Maker of Universes,* Farmer
creates a cosmos based partly on mythological Greece (including
pools of nymphs and naiads), with adjoining regions from modern Germany, the American plains inhabited by Indian tribes,
and a South American jungle, all on the tiers of one planet,
inhabited by reembodied souls stolen from the Earth.[10]

The leading character is Robert Wolff, a discouraged, chubby, middle-aged classics professor who has a nagging wife and is looking for a retirement home in Phoenix. He opens a closet in an unoccupied house, hears a horn, and finds a whole new world:

> Sunlight flooded in through an opening. . . . Vegetation that looked something like trees—but no trees of Earth. Through the branches and fronds he could see a bright green sky. . . . Six or seven nightmare creatures were gathered at the base of a giant boulder . . . of red quartz-impregnated rock and shaped roughly like a toadstool.

A man in a buckskin breechcloth summons him into this world with haunting words: "So you finally came!"[11]

When Wolff does not accept the invitation to enter, he is thrown a horn by the stranger. That night he sneaks back into the Hohokam Homes Development, and just as guards are closing in on him, he blows the horn and finds himself on the grass of that other world beneath a moon two and a half times the size of Earth's moon. Birdcalls fill the air, and orange-yellow fireflies with ellipsoid wings and 10-foot wingspans dart by. It is more than just an adventure: his relationship to this place is not arbitrary.

Wolff starts out in this world as a misfit, the one unbeautiful and "sick" creature in paradise. He can feel sorry for himself only so long, for, soon enough, paradise turns out to be deadly. Everyone has been kidnapped into this world and implanted in a body, each from a different epoch and country of the Earth. Only Wolff seems to have gotten here by some other means. Over time, the strange world has its influence on him, and he grows younger, healthier, and stronger. With the woman Chryseis, whom he meets on the first day, and Kickaha, an American man in an American Indian body who alone travels easily between the tiers and cultures of this planet, he sets out on a mission to reach the top of the tiers, the laboratory and control room. Alternately harassed and aided by the harpy-eagle Podarge, at times separated from and at times rejoining Kickaha, his trickster ally, Wolff is eventually able to storm the great laboratory and free the world— but not before he discovers that he himself is the Lord who made this world, who imprisoned Chryseis, Podarge, and the rest in their bodies. Driven by a rival Lord onto the Earth, where he falls victim to amnesia, he in fact lived a whole second life, begun *in medias res* in Kentucky—his position as a classics professor dimly reflecting his more ancient and immortal heritage—until the sacred horn was used by Kickaha to summon him, even as Aslan summons the children to Narnia in the C. S. Lewis novels.

Wolff has taken a journey into the meaning and origin of his own life. As he overcomes the trials and traps, he also confronts his prior ruthlessness and cruelty, his own inner nature, for he is the one who set the traps, who made this world. He returns to the throne as an enlightened Lord, a new being, to replace not only his corrupt successor but also the shallow hedonist that he himself was when he was first immortal.

This is our own dilemma as a race: to get to the bottom of the thing that has made this technology through us, that has made us make this technology and so enslave ourselves by it, and then to transcend it, to return as good kings rather than as the tyrants and despoilers we have been. For Wolff, once the Lord Jadawin, it takes a trip to the Earth in another body, memoryless, to restore humility and to give life back its texture and its meaning.

No doubt there are secret unwritten texts on which the manifest books of science fiction are based. This is their message: "We will be found to be the makers of this whole thing—we who now pretend to be mere impotent and innocent bugs actually project the starry fields to beyond the imagination or powers of even the most Olympian gods. We are the makers of universes. The tyrant we seek to overthrow is ourselves."

Such a discovery will restore our youth and our power, but it will be a terrible reckoning, for we have evaded it so long. It must bring a final unavoidable responsibility for our misdeeds. This is why Farmer's version of serial immortality is so appealing. As banal as his fictional worlds are, they leave open the possibility of finding our place downriver, or in the next star system, the next incarnation. This is the ultimate promise of the stars: that we will get to the bottom of this somehow, that there is world enough and time and someday we will find out—in person—who we are.

In his epic series of novels centering on the planet Dune, Frank Herbert invents a female lineage in which each adept is trained to recover the collective memories of her ancestors. The discipline is maintained through a strict breeding program in which males are barred from the actual priesthood. The excretion (spice) of the giant sandworms (Shai-Hulud) is the order's consciousness-expanding catalyst. However, the Reverend Mothers also await a single male—the Kwisatz Haderach (Shortcut)—who will be able to see further than any of them.

The first novel turns on the initiation of Paul Atreides as Muad'Dib, the prophet, the priesthood's genetic solution. Muad'-Dib becomes the single male seer by swallowing and transmuting the poisonous "Water of Life," the death sweat of the sandworm, and he leads a revolution of the original inhabitants of Arrakis, Shai-Hulud's native Dune world. In the archetype of this role he is also Jadawin, Siddhartha, Pip, and Falk:

> This was what his grandmother and the Sisterhood sought! He knew it. His awareness flowed on a new, higher level. He felt the past carried in his cells, in his memories, in the archetypes which haunted his assumptions, in the myths which hemmed him, in his languages and their prehistoric detritus. It was all of the shapes out of his human and nonhuman past, all of the lives which he now commanded, all integrated in him at last. And he felt himelf as a thing caught up in the ebb and flow of nucleotides. Against the backdrop of infinity he was a protozoan creature in which birth and death were virtually simultaneous, but he was both infinite and protozoan, a creature of molecular memories. [12]

Paul's son Leto is ultimately transformed through spice-addiction into a massive, immortal worm who then attempts to rule the universe forever. In fact, he becomes the universe, i.e., the social body, and survives as such 3500 years, a benign dictatorship of the memory of the past:

> . . . [He] held the multi-thread reins, balanced in his own vision-lighted view of time as multilinear and multilooped. He was the sighted man in the universe of the blind. . . . A thought as yet undreamed in the farthest future could reflect upon the *now* and move his hand. [13]

Over such a long span, however, Leto loses his humanity and

connection to life; ultimately this worm/polis is murdered, closing the Golden Path. The difference between Herbert and other
science fiction writers is that, instead of summarizing universes,
he actually created this one, composing five volumes, from before
the Kwisatz Haderach to millennia after the death of Leto, giving
each tribe and philosophy and creature a name and integrating
their histories with one another across a whole cosmos.

In Piers Anthony's novel *Macroscope,* four people steal an advanced machine from a space station and flee the global military.[14] The machine, the macroscope, is primarily known for its
ability to receive a gravitational product of the radioactive decay
of objects, and thus make events throughout the Galaxy visible,
even those blocked by enclosures or within substances. But it
also receives a form of "information rays" that evidently cross
the Galaxy and contain instructions from higher civilizations;
and, most important of all, it receives an extragalactic ray sent
by a supercivilization in an unknown part of the universe, with
information exponentially beyond anything in the Milky Way.
Unfortunately, this ray merges with a mind-destroying vector,
and only one of the four people who now possess the machine, Ivo, can survive its destructive force and draw information
from it.

Borrowing technology from this extragalactic ray, the crew
reduce themselves to protoplasm to withstand great acceleration. Then they travel rapidly to Neptune, where they recon-
struct themselves and establish an Earthlike base and garden on
the moon Triton. The Earth, whose armies pursue them, recedes
from the rest of the book, and the four are engaged in an extragalactic riddle which also holds the destiny of their planet.

They drive Triton into Neptune, forming a black hole
through which they explode into the Milky Way's depths, back
through history to before the birth of the Earth and the Solar
System. En route, as they pass backwards in time, Ivo visits
Phoenicia, and through the macroscope they see their planet
covered with jungles and inhabited by dinosaurs. With the temporary aid of Schon, a criminal genius who is jailed for life inside
Ivo's personality, they are shown the formation of the Solar System, and they view the Milky Way Galaxy from the outside:

The pallid white of the stars and nebulae deflowered by Earth's atmosphere existed no more; the colossal fog of interstellar gas and dust had been banished from the vicinity of the observer. The result was a view of the Milky Way Galaxy as it really existed—ten thousand times as rich as that perceivable from Earth.

Color, yes—but not as any painter could represent, or any atmosphere-blinded eye could fathom. Red in the center where the old lights faded; blue at the fringe where the fierce new lights formed. A spectrum between—but also so much more! Here the visible splay extended beyond the range for which nomenclature existed, and rounded out the hues for which human names did exist. A mighty swirl, a multiple spiral of radiance, wave on wave of tiny bright particles, merged yet discrete. . . .

. . . The great spiral arms, coiling outward from the center, doubled bands of matter beginning as the light of massed stars and terminating as the black of thinning dust. Not flat, not even; the ribbons were twisted, showing now broadside, now edgewise, resembling open mobius strips or the helix of galactic DNA.[15]

Self stands equal to cosmos here.

Eventually, the crew discover that the destructive ray was intentionally attached to the extragalactic information source, and they find the station generating it. There Ivo picks up an instrument like a flute and begins playing it. It brings ultimate reality into being, beyond mind and body. The last vestiges of concrete existence in time and space evaporate, and each of the characters is transported to a place in the stars where physical destiny merges with astrological destiny. Under the influence of this instrument, a person stands instantaneously at the unique spot in the universe where his sign and his being are the same.

The older scientist Groton and his wife find themselves on exotic planets in dangerous situations. Groton discovers that the Destroyer was set in place as a means of protecting the Galaxy from young bellicose cultures that had ravaged it many times by misusing technology from the ray. But he cannot return to Earth. He meets the Horven people, who tell him that his destiny lies outside their astrological charts, for he exists ninety-eight million years in their future. This is essentially what Gorolot the

Phoenician had told Ivo: "Either you have never been born, or you come from so far away that you are not truly under any of the signs I know."[16]

The science of astrology in this book measures the basic coherent force of the universe. Interstellar civilizations are the ones that will develop such a science as they naturally seek the origin of personality and event among the twisted space-time frameworks of the stars. It is the only system that pinpoints a concrete event in the entangled cosmic oceans. Without an intrinsic astrological connection, time and space would become unbundled and flow everywhere; substellar destiny would be arbitrary.

Ivo and the young woman scientist Afra meet their destinies at exactly the place where the star music is played. The flute has made Schon indispensable, and he takes over Ivo and confronts Afra, who has spurned the Ivo personality behind which he lay trapped. Schon and Afra then engage in a psychic battle of signs, with Ivo as the only possible judge; it is a battle between their absolute planetary aspects, in which they are equal as incarnated individuals (otherwise Schon would win easily despite Afra's brilliance).[17] In this contest, the victory goes to the one who is able to face his or her own true nature. The planets of their birth are then drawn from the cosmos, and, one by one, engulf them.

Afra's haughtiness and fear of her own nature put her way behind, but she wins the contest under the more radical outer planets, from Saturn on, with the denouement at Pluto, where she forces Schon into confrontation with the Destroyer itself, which his arrogance cannot handle. Schon and Ivo finally merge and become a single being. With the macroscope, they return to the Earth, hoping that one day they—or their descendants—will be able to direct the ray beyond the Galaxy and contact its wise and magnanimous senders.

Frank Herbert's books are filled with clones, cyborgs, and artificial intelligences. In *Dune Messiah*, there is the ghola Hayt, spawned from a few cells of the body of Duncan Idaho, who died while defending Muad'Dib. This ghola, germinated in secret chemical tanks by the Tleilaxu, the inhabitants of a renegade planet, is bestowed upon Muad'Dib as a gift by the Space Guild.

The ghola presents a complex danger, for it clearly comes from the enemy and it freely acknowledges that its purpose is to destroy Paul, and thus that its makers do not fear his knowing this. It is a decoy, but it is also such a haunting likeness of Idaho it is irresistible to Paul. To destroy it is as dangerous as to accept it.

The ghola also experiences flashes of imagery, brief unretainable memories as if of another life as someone else. "Aren't you curious?" he is asked.

> Of course [he replies cautiously]. Curiosity urges me forward, but I move against a heavy reluctance. I think: "What if I'm not the one they believe me to be?"[18]

Our own perceptions are all the dimmer, but we also live lives in flesh made of ancient cellular blueprints. What if . . . we are not? What then? And whose memory is it, if not in our cells then in our psyche, that sustains all this from the beginning of time?

"I think," says the ghola, "what a joy it is to be alive, and I wonder if I'll ever leap inward to the root of this flesh and know myself as once I was. The root is there. Whether any act of mine can find it, that remains tangled in the future. But all things a man can do are mine. Any act of mine may do it."[19]

Later he tells Paul: "When the Tleilaxu first awakened me, I had visions. I was restless, lonely . . . , not really knowing I was lonely. Not then. My visions revealed nothing! The Tleilaxu told me it was an intrusion of the flesh which men and gholas all suffer, a sickness, no more."[20]

"I was there," the ghola dwarf Bijaz tells him. "I was there when they put your dead flesh into the tank and I was there when they removed it, alive and ready for training."[21]

So Hayt should have no claim to the original, no claim to the life of which he is just a clone. Yet, at the turning point of the book, when the whole future lies in the balance, Hayt reclaims the dead life:

> A sensation of living two lives simultaneously spread through his awareness: Hayt/Idaho/Hayt/Idaho. . . . He became a motionless chain of relative existence, singular, alone. Old memories flooded his mind. He marked them, adjusted them to new understandings, made a beginning at the integration of a new awareness.[22]

With terrible pain that wants to refuse it all, sleep forever, with delicious ecstasy that wishes to swallow again and again, as many times as possible, the bright and haunting images stored forever in the cells, Hayt embraces Idaho—and the sand that flowed through Idaho's hands, the songs that passed from his lips, the memories that he had at all times of other times, the overwhelming passion to encompass them all, and his own.

Thereafter the whole universe could be crushed in the Big Bang, and somehow we would have known all there was to know, been all there was to be. We would have survived.

21

Science Fiction III: Jesus of Nazareth

THERE ARE TWO WAYS for man to achieve his destiny in the stars: externally, by going out in ships; and internally, through a transformation or transmigration. Ultimately, the science fiction "conquest" of outer space is in direct conflict with the spiritual goal of inner development. From a theosophical perspective, the materialism of the stars (from whence we derive not only the Big Bang but all space colonies and extraterrestrials) is precisely the addiction which traps our species in its cosmic infancy. Space-frontier advocates vehemently disagree, arguing instead that it is *only* our expansion beyond this world that leads to our maturity as a species. So, on one side we have space migration and life-extension; on the other, evolution and reincarnation. It is an old battle between politicians and Rosicrucians, scientists and yogis, but its terms are so complicated and incongruous that sides and roles change from generation to generation, and often individuals maintain totally inconsistent positions. There are some science fiction writers who use the irreconcilability of this issue as their focal point.

In his novel *Childhood's End*,[1] Arthur Clarke imagines an internal, evolutionary passage into the space of the stars and planets. As the premise of this event, overlords come from outer space to guide human development and steer our species from self-destruction. The overlords understand inner transformation, but they cannot achieve it themselves, as they are trapped in a biogenetic cul de sac. Even though they establish a peaceful regime, many terrestrials consider them conquerors and tyrants because they explicitly forbid exploration of the universe. Additionally, the guardians can never show themselves in the flesh, because an earlier appearance so terrified mankind that their likeness is preserved only as a figure of darkness, the Devil with tail and horns. The rebellious humans feel robbed of their cosmic destiny, but the aliens know that the only way to achieve real space travel is by turning away from rocket ships and going through a waking dream. This requires not individual spiritual discipline but a biological transformation of the entire species.

Eventually a generation of children matures without ever becoming adolescents or adults. They are the next phase of the mutant foetal apes who prematurely gestated into hominids. Clarke is using a model of the neotenous and paedomorphic mutations that catalyzed our evolution from the other primates in order to project equally strange offspring from us. Just as the weak, slow-moving humanoids that fled the forests of Pliocene Africa might have looked hopelessly fragile to their flourishing simian uncles, so the children of "childhood's end" seem defenseless runts to our fictional descendants.

But the children develop radical new capacities. They are able to dream in such a way that their minds pass out of the Solar System, then out of the Galaxy, then into the corridors of unknown space. This is not internal astral space; it is stellar geography as the overlords map it:

> "I have searched all our records," said Rashaverak. "We have no knowledge of such a world, or such a combination of suns. If it existed inside our universe, the astronomers would have detected it, even if it lay beyond the range of our ships."[2]

The aliens tell the fathers the truth about their dreaming children: where they go, their predecessors will not be able to follow them. Man will have his transgalactic journey finally, but not in spaceships. He will evolve back through his own quintessence, transforming space and time and escaping the speed of light. The industrial planet will be abandoned, an empty cocoon.

In his trilogy, *Out of the Silent Planet, Perelandra,* and *That Hideous Strength,* C. S. Lewis portrays an Earth cut off from the rest of the Solar System and imprisoned by a malign angel. This creature desires control of all the worlds in the physical cosmos, and the Earth is his fortress and throne. He is, as we have always suspected, the Devil.

Surrounding himself with wars, bureaucracy, and machines, he isolates the Earth and cuts its peoples off from the communion of beings on other worlds. This, in fact, has gone on since the beginning of history.

The Devil's ultimate plan is for an army from this world to go out into the cosmos and subjugate it for him, planet by planet. He trains Terrans to recognize only the material aspect of things so they will overlook the spirituality of Mars and Venus, and he encourages xenophobia so that they will attack alien creatures of those planets. This is who we are, Lewis is saying. Spaceflight may be our next natural stage, but it is a sterile and self-destructive gambit unless we confront our ethical and spiritual exile. After all, the heavens are a potential battleground too, of bleak unending matter.

In the first book, the Devil's plan is disrupted when a corrupt scientist named Weston and his associate kidnap an unsuspecting philologist named Ransom and force him to accompany them on a journey to Mars. The purpose of this expedition is to offer the philologist as a sacrificial victim to the great angelic lord of Mars, Oyarsa.[3]

But Mars is part of the enlightened community of Solar worlds, and Oyarsa is a spiritually advanced being of light who primarily wishes to meet creatures from the imprisoned neighbor world. In the course of the novel, the kidnappers murder many trusting Martian creatures, imagining themselves as frontiersmen opening up the West. Oyarsa traps and punishes the invaders according to their karma, and he enlists Ransom as an ally to free the Earth.

In the second volume, Ransom is sent by Oyarsa to the planet

Venus (Perelandra) at a time when its beings inhabit the local equivalent of the Garden of Eden. He arrives just before Weston, whose body has now been taken over by the Dark Lord and who has become an Un-Man. "Weston" will proceed to tempt the "Eve" of this world to disobey the commandment of the local lord not to sleep on the fixed land. Ransom must prevent the "original sin" from repeating here. The confrontation must be direct and physical, since these are flesh-and-blood creatures in a planetary sphere. Ransom must literally destroy the human vehicle of the Devil in order drive him from this new innocent world.[4]

In the final volume, Ransom has become a magus on the Earth, though he bears a dangerous wound on his heel from his defeat of the Un-Man. Working with the lords of the other planets, he is now ready to redeem the Earth. The confrontation is joined at a scientific institute where researchers are developing advanced techniques of brain research and mind control while destroying the surrounding forest that still bears Druid magical forces. The Dark Lord is physically present at the institute, and he uses experimental parapsychology to bind ancient demonic energies. But the lords of the rest of the Solar System appear at last in full astral-physical attributes, a joyful liberating army. The Earth's destiny is restored, and the Earth is given its rightful seat at the council of the Sun.[5]

Lewis's books are a direct attack upon experimental physics and biology as well as the science fiction and night sky they have bestowed on us. They are a rebellion against the cybernetic immortality of the computer. The universe might be better than this, Lewis is saying. We might be in exile (just about forever) from the Golden City.

On his first trip to Mars, Ransom is startled to discover that the nightmare of dark and empty space engendered by modern science is "blasphemous libel." Instead of "the black, cold vacuity, the utter deadness," he finds the universe a great "empyrean ocean of radiance. . . . He felt life pouring into him from it every moment. How indeed should it be otherwise, since out of this ocean the worlds and all their life had come? He had thought it barren: he saw now that it was the womb of worlds, whose blazing and innumerable offspring looked down nightly even upon the earth with so many eyes—and here, with how many more! No; Space was the wrong name. Older thinkers had been wiser when they named it simply the heavens. . . ."[6]

This could be Giordano Bruno speaking, except that the vision takes place on a spaceflight, not by astral projection.

In *Perelandra,* Lewis describes Weston as possessed by a deadly idea:

It is the idea that humanity, having now sufficiently corrupted the planet where it arose, must at all costs contrive to seed itself over a larger area: that the vast astronomical distances which are God's quarantine regulations, must somehow be overcome. This for a start. But beyond this lies the sweet poison of the false infinite—the wild dream that planet after planet, system after system, in the end galaxy after galaxy, can be forced to sustain, everywhere and for ever, the sort of life which is contained in the loins of our own species—a dream begotten by the hatred of death upon the fear of true immortality. . . .[7]

It is the same fear on which Robert Silverberg bases the immortality quest of *The Book of Skulls:*

"You have been subtracted from the universe, LuAnn. No, the universe has been subtracted from *you.* Forget what's going to happen to your body now, the worms in your gut, the pretty blue eyes turning to muck, and just think about all you've lost. You've lost it all, sunrise and sunset, the smell of broiling steak, the feel of a cashmere sweater, the touch of my lips that you like so much against your hard little nipples. You've lost the Grand Canyon and Shakespeare and London and Paris and champagne and your big church wedding and Paul McCartney and Peter Fonda and the Mississippi River and the moon and the stars. . . .

"Death may have been good enough for Beethoven and Jesus and President Eisenhower, but, meaning no offense, I'm different. I can't just lie down and go. Why is it all so short? Why does it come so soon? Why can't we drink the universe? Death's been hovering over me all my life."[8]

We imagine countless other blue-green worlds we might still live on: their untouched algae oceans with strands of motley seaweed meters long and wrinkled in the insignia of another

DNA; their moist virginal forests covering continents, inhabited by nothing more complicated than soft orange newts; or their tens of thousands of plump fearless birds screeching in one unbroken column from horizon to horizon across a sea of bearded flying fish they feed on in an eternal mandala as they drop to the surface and return. We dream of green fields we could not explore in a lifetime, rich in exotic clover and fruit, lit by a young alien sun. So many worlds replace this one in our psyches, so many second chances lie before us. A soft rain falls in the summer of a different year in a different orbit, a rain so naturally medicinal it will heal not only us but our whole race, heal us by gentle voodoo of everything and forever. But these birds may be our unexamined lives whose calls echo through our deepening coma; the fields may be our precious mortality. We consign them to fantasy and science fiction only after all other paths and philosophies have failed us.

Our cosmic imperialism is a joke. We are still strangers to our own planet and to ourselves. We are in no position to conquer other planets, let alone galaxies, and immortality leads to the Un-Man or a foetal ape. We cannot force our way into those green fields by a life-extension narcotic or a starship. Our "meaning" already lies in the cosmos, and our youth is an eternal return.

The antidote to "the sweet poison of the false infinite" comes from another dimension of the universe. It is the Great Dance, which we have met many times in occult literature, but which appears for the first time in science fiction at the culmination of Ransom's trip to Perelandra. He sees a loom as complicated as the universe might actually be:

> It seemed to be woven out of the intertwining undulation of many cords or bands of light, leaping over and under one another and mutually embraced in arabesques and flower-like subtleties. . . . He could see . . . wherever the ribbons or serpents of light intersected, minute corpuscles of momentary brightness: and he knew somehow that these particles were the secular generalities of which history tells—peoples, institutions, climates of opinion, civilizations, arts, sciences, and the like—ephemeral coruscations that piped their short song and vanished. . . . Some of the

thinner and more delicate cords were beings that we call short-lived: flowers and insects, a fruit or a storm of rain, and once (he thought) a wave of the sea. Others were such things as we also think lasting: crystals, rivers, mountains, or even stars. . . . It did not surprise him then to find that these [universal truths or qualities] and the persons were both cords and both stood together as against the mere atoms of generality which lived and died in the clashing of their streams. . . . The whole solid figure of these ena-moured and inter-inanimated circlings was suddenly re-vealed as the mere superficies of a far vaster pattern in four dimensions, and that figure as the boundary of yet others in other worlds: till suddenly as the movement grew yet swifter, the interweaving yet more ecstatic, the relevance of all to all yet more intense, as dimension was added to dimension and that part of him which could reason and remember was dropped farther and farther behind that part of him which saw, even then, at the very zenith of com-plexity, complexity was eaten up and faded as a thin white cloud fades into the hard blue burning of the sky, and a simplicity beyond all comprehension, ancient and young as spring, illimitable, pellucid, drew him with cords of infinite desire into its own stillness.[9]

What about the spaceman Jesus Christ, who came to the Earth in the womb of a woman? It is not enough to say that Jesus had the divine spirit in him. So do we all by the same Gnostic proph-ecy. We are all the sons and daughters of God.

But Jesus was the offspring of an extraterrestrial—not a cosmic astronaut but the Star of Bethlehem. That is, He was a child of the night sky and the alignment of the heavens. Even if He didn't come here by ship (like Superman from a dying planet), He came with a message from outside our system. The Christmas carol speaks as much to the Ice Age as to the Church:

> Silent night,
> Holy night.
> All is calm.
> All is bright.

Even on the streets of modern cities, with the stars obliterated, the snow shimmering in headlights, and the glitter and tinsel stars on Christmas trees, *Silent Night* seems to play as much to the galaxies of eternal time and space as it does to mortals. A virgin and a holy infant sit huddled beneath the stars. The supernatural agency is secondary to the fact.

We stare at mangers in store windows and village squares and are transported into a science fiction landscape—another planet, somewhere else, yet here, here all the same.

We don't understand Christmas, and our present celebration is particularly barren. But we do feel something gathering, something akin to the starry sky and its darkness we cannot probe.

"Tell him to stay away," screamed Herod. "This is my world. I will not share this kingdom with a star."

His subsequent decision to kill the firstborn in the area around Nazareth was a massacre of potential invaders, astronauts who at the same time were astrological life forms introducing Pisces, entering the Earth not by metal ship but from inside the blood. Star, embryo, and God overlap.

Whether He could have come to this world directly by manifestation or in a ship from another creationary zone is a matter we shall leave to Gnostic speculation. The Christian mystery and the transubstantiation are based on the fact that He came by the womb of our species. He incarnated in the flesh, or an aspect of Him did. This was called His Son, and, later, the Holy Ghost.

It is the incarnation that makes Christianity something more than an extraterrestrial religion carried by a space preacher. Christ was not like an astronaut who might arrive tomorrow, go to the United Nations, set up solar energy stations, tap geomantic power sources, and teach telepathic and telekinetic arts. There are some who no doubt would have preferred this sort of *tour de force*. The faithless rabbis, for instance. But this would have delayed man's ultimate confrontation with his own nature, his date with himself inside time. Such a being would have come from outside our biology and history and would have treated them as manipulatable things rather than as shapes emerging of their own intrinsic nature. That would have been a denial of the inner world. Of course, an extraterrestrial Christ may still come. And he may not. But at least so far, we must earn our own grace.

Christ arises from within our history and biology, and his acts are those of an Earthborn. He comes as we do, from the egg, the flesh, the genes, the continuity of tissue from the first cell. He is shaped of everything which man is, and the fish are too. His ecstasies, his insights, his tears are expressions of the flesh. Those tears took thousands of millions of years of biological evolution to occur. They do not pity us from some superior position. Christ cries as well for the frog and the mouse, in whose cells the tear ducts were primordially fashioned.

The Son of God is the Son of Man. We are all travelers on a ship braided of the same material; hence, we are all natives of the same place, though our spirit or protoplasm may originate in bean or seed elsewhere. No astronaut, no matter how learned and well-traveled, could come to us from such a cosmic place. He might come from outside our history, but he could not come from outside of time itself, from outside the universe. He might not be human, but he would share in the cosmic biology. We would still have to decide whether to believe in him or not, trust him or not, on the basis of his program.

The Christian visitation has an impact that UFOs cannot, for it recapitulates the embryogenic passage of our own spirits into flesh. Christ is tempted by the same passions and apostasies that tempt us. His life is generated by chromosomes and must blend with both historical Israel and Rome.

Outer-space rescuers have no business forgiving us, and they cannot rescue us finally because they are not us. Yet, from a spiritual standpoint, our technological culture is little more than an invasion from outer space. The machines may stall things for a while, but they will not change the basic issues. Even if spacemen should come and distract us from the karma of our history and our own nature, it would delay things only a while—a few hundred years, a thousand years, even a million years. Ultimately, we would be faced with the consequences of our original situation. We could play with new toys, spaceships, lasers, etc., for millennia (if we are lucky); but in the end, we would come to the same dilemma of an incarnation among stone and fire.

Because karmic law is written into Buddhism and Hinduism from the beginning, these religions, unlike Christianity, do not require a son of God. The cosmic consequence is already embodied in the flesh. All incarnation is *re*incarnation. Radio as-

tronomy has merely verified, for the educated Oriental cosmologist, the suspicions that he inherited about the night sky
and that his ancestors intuited before him—namely, that it is an
exact map of the actual and potential universe, of matter and
energy, and of the extension of that karmic law to the ends of time
and space.

22
Astrology

WHAT WE THINK OF AS ASTROLOGY is a system of star divination inherited by Near Eastern civilization from the prior ancient world and passed on through the Greeks in Alexandrian Ptolemaic cosmology to mediaeval Europe, where it was combined with local star mythologies and general Gnostic science. Zodiacs and star divination were common throughout the ancient world. Very old systems appear at the dawn of Chinese and Egyptian civilization, and there are equivalent Mayan and Aztec constellations. It is possible that some Stone Age system underlies all of them, and that the Old World star sciences share a relatively recent root (from ten to twelve thousand years ago) from which the New World systems diverged.

Neolithic man built Stonehenge, Woodhenge, the Caracol, Monks Mound, the "akus" of Eastern Island, and various menhirs, cairns, and astronomical temples throughout the planet. The starry night was the original sacrament and government of our species. Ancient cosmologists noticed that on the Earth things changed swiftly and irregularly—a sudden gust of wind in the trees, a crumbling wave, a burst of rage or laughter, a passage of birds, a fever. Peoples gradually moved across continents and seas, floods wiped out landmarks, tribes vanished, but these skymarks remained, changing infinitesimally. In the sky, things progressed according to profound cosmic rhythms and numerological codes. The stars were a deific reflection of terrestrial activity, for they returned in sequence, either with the seasons or according to esoteric mathematical formulae. The sky was a palace and a kingdom where deities acted out eternal roles. It was also a dark crystal in which the Earth's landscapes revealed their essence.

How the gods and planets came to be the same is a meaningless question. They were one almost from the beginning. The mythical deeds of the gods, including acts of treachery, heroism, compassion, and lust, are personae, but their lives in the sky, i.e., their actual movements as planets are fixed and predictable. They pass through the houses and holy spots, setting the boundaries and conditions for all the events in our sphere of Earth, which lies inward and subordinate to their zodiac. The rest is folklore. It is clear that there are too many people and too few gods for the latter to be busy interfering in all our lives at once. There must be some other way. Mercury and Jupiter are occupied in the heavens; if they manifest as Earth-beings, they are subject to one location at a time. However, if they are formed within us, within our very personalities, then a single god may simultaneously bring his aspect of things to bear not only on many people's lives but on all people's lives and the lives of all things.

The zodiac we know and have built upon in Western culture was inherited from the Chaldeans and the more ancient Sumerian and Accadian peoples of Assyria and Babylonia. The Egyptian and Chinese systems have substantially different constellations and astromancies. The astrological symbols of the West are basically Babylonian. We inherit their intuitions of darkness and light and their twelve-stage cosmic season. We inherit their gods in their planets.

Astrology represents a synchronicity between the ancient calendars of the farming communities of the Near East and a theory of cosmic or celestial influence. From our point of view, it may look like two systems, and it may well have been two systems at various times, even originally, but in practice astrology treats the two systems as one. As long as the heavens are divine and the planets are destiny-bearing gods, the units and "houses" they measure are identical to the archetypes they sow.

The measurement of time does not require a theory of celestial influence. Calendars became astronomical tools during the Stone Age quite separate from any system of astral cycles and rhythms.

But astrology maintains the measurement of time as sacred, or, in present-day parlance, psychic and archetypal, and it assumes that measurement as a basic harmonic linking microcosm and macrocosm. As civilization moved out of liturgical and ceremonial space into days, months, and years that were purely political and scientific, the sacred sense of time was occultated.

The theory of celestial influence *does* require calendars and ephemerides, for they are the mathematical representation of the wholeness and interrelatedness of the cosmos. Without them the "idea" of celestial influence can be honored, but there is no rigorous method for recording its degrees and variations. So astrology evolves as the statement of the synchronous relationship of all events in creation and the means of predicting and understanding fragments and cycles by their relationship to the whole. The stars, as the projective background of the creation, stand for the functional unity.

Astrology is a millennial science; that is, it has existed from unknown origins in prehistoric times up to the present, changing its form by culture and by aeon. It is an archetypal science: we cannot say what its ultimate form is, for we know it only by the aspect it reveals at any one time. It is a mistake to stereotype astrology in the form of the daily horoscope or in any of the antique variants of it that we have from ancient, mediaeval, and Renaissance cultures. Each of these, as well as each of the contemporary philosophical and psychological astrologies, attempts to reconcile temporal and local images with the cosmic ones that lie behind them. Thus, we have innumerable astrologies, all of which share a core of thought and each of which is adapted to its particular occurrence.

In calling astrology a "science," we do not mean that it is a science in the same sense that chemistry and physics are. It is a science in the old etymological sense of "a system of knowledge." It is also a science in the mathematical sense of measuring quantities. Modern physics might take issue with the cause-and-effect postulates behind the measurements, but it could not challenge the basic algebra of chart-making and planetary relationships. Millennial sciences help give rise to the modern sciences that are often their partial namesakes. So astronomy shares something of its origin and mechanics with astrology, but it is basically a separate development, not requiring astrological thought. It is misleading, then, to think of astrology as ancient or primitive astronomy. There *was* an ancient and primitive astronomy, but it is more accurate to call it archaeo-astronomy or ethnoastronomy. There are also archaeo-astrologies and ethnoastrologies which parallel and interact with their astronomical counterparts but which are also essentially a different system of inquiry. Archaeo-astronomy generates calendar systems early and astrophysics late. Archaeo-astrology leads to astral astrology, Qabalistic magic, and the contemporary astrology of personality.

The most obvious other millennial and archetypal science is alchemy. Alchemy is presently more obscure than astrology, but components of laboratory and elemental alchemy were taken directly into chemistry, physics, and astronomy. In fact, alchemy is far more relevantly a forerunner of astrophysics than astrology is. The adaptation of physical alchemy to modern technology has legitimized its role as early historical chemistry. However, it is exactly those elements which alchemy shares with astrology that were *not* incorporated into modern scientific thought: the vital source of the elements, the transmutability of matter, and the astral body.

Medicine and botany are millennial sciences in the same dilemma as alchemy: their mechanical features laid the basis for their industrial counterparts, and their traditional and vital features were abandoned as primitive magical thought. Herbalism was looted for its allopathic pharmacy, but its role in holistic native medicine was ignored. When medicine became a training in concrete anatomy and pharmacy, it abandoned the shamanic art. Yet, millennially, herbalism and healing retain their "primitive" features, and these will no doubt return in other guises in future times. Even today, certain of their aspects are recognized but are called parapsychological to distinguish the seeming laboratory effects of mind over matter, which have not been proven scientifically, from the ancient arts and rituals that used such ostensible effects to heal the sick and bring rain. This is how millennial sciences are renamed and rediscovered. If astrology is ever adopted by a mainstream scientific community, it might not be called astrology anymore. In fact, some current attempts to redefine it call it "astro-biology." (Our other modern response to the occult is to reduce raw clairvoyance and spiritual practice to cosmic philosophy and clinical therapy.)

In a holistic civilization, the millennial sciences would blend with the current technologies and, to a certain degree, with each other. The medical applications of astrology would merge entirely with herbalism and psychiatry, even as astrophysics would unite with the theories of celestial influence. The present age is a dark one in this respect, for everything is fragmented and knowledge has become a chaos of useless data. But if anything survives a dark age, the millennial sciences do. They have no allegiance to the transient forms, so they reemerge on the basis of their universal and archetypal principles. Either they are guided by the old texts or they are intuited anew. Some vitalists might decry the present order, but the millennial sciences helped bring it on by their corruption and superstition throughout the Middle Ages and the Renaissance. They allied themselves with religion and occult orthodoxy in a way that trapped humanity in useless orders of authority and fantasy. If vitalism is able to return after the aeon of mechanics and technology, it will be a far tougher and more powerful vitalism, and one that will use the lessons of physics and chemistry to reestablish a harmony of man on the Earth. The prior vitalism could not have done this.

The present nihilism of which astrophysics is king has certainly cleaned house. It may have killed a lot of priests and made the Earth virtually uninhabitable before it is through, but physical determinism and the power derived therefrom will have scraped bottom. Revolutionary gangs will not be able to lead mankind so easily back—especially if vitalists alone can grow a garden again and draw energy from the cosmos, restore the ozone layer and rainforests and pay the medical bill.

Goethe may have intuited this when he put the torch in the hand of botany and asked it to carry the flame through the coming winter of mechanism. Kant had failed him, and himself, and had not provided the basis of a moral order in the universe. The stars reflected an increasingly *amoral* order, and the progressive industrialists unknowingly served this guise. Blake saw this too and addressed the readers of a future time, not immediately thereafter but after that, when the thing would have happened and been done.

Esoteric astrology takes the present "Aquarian" revival as a remote echo only of a distant age yet to come—perhaps its remotest echo into our age darkened by machines and acid rain. It was hardly a whisper, but every succeeding tremor will be deeper and more resonant—fair warning to those who claim pretentiously that the "hippie era" is over. The "hippie era" may be over, but the Aquarian Age has yet to come; and when it does, we will not be able to tell the scientific from the occult. What happened was shadow before substance; the big medicine awaits our descendants. According to tradition, it will crest around A.D. 2376.

Astrology is patient and long-standing. It tries to coordinate large dynamic blocks of time, space, and personality. It is an attempt to say the impossible, a system for measuring the immeasurable. If it fails, it fails in the biggest task of all: to define the simultaneity of life, thought, creation, and space-time. It is better to attempt such a measurement than to pretend it could have no relevance at all.

Once the movements of the planets and the Sun and Moon in the zodiac are transcribed, the astrologer need no longer have reference to the actual night sky. In millennial terms, this is a severe failing of modern astrology. The present shining night does not engage the astrologer as much as his ephemeris. Yet, the original inspirations, psychic or emotional, came from viewing the sky by night. The deep understanding that made astrology a philosophical system more than a puzzle of personality types came from its daily and direct connection to the cosmos. Without that, astrologers like Copernicus and Kepler would not have discovered the location of the Sun and the orbits of the planets. Without the devotion of Herschel, Adams, Leverrier, and Lowell to the night sky, astrologers would not have the Uranian, Neptunian, and Plutonian factors that are so important in their charts today. As astrology changes with the eras, it always makes use of the new stars. The specific discoveries are unpredictable, but each of them—quasars and pulsars included—is in the universe somewhere, or in man's model of the universe, and so must be included in the dynamic chart of the whole. Astronomy has always fed images directly into astrology, and astrology has interpreted them in its own traditional terms. At the same time, astrology assumes that the stars speak to us directly— themselves at night, as symbols, and in the lives of our friends, lovers, and kin—and that we pick up such star wisdom quite apart from any knowledge of the system. Because astrology is the "science" of the whole, it is free to assume the basic unity of all events and images and their reference to the cosmic field.

The "moment in time" is critical in astrology, for it is the precise measure by which the connection of events is established. Events are synchronous because they lie simultaneous to one another across the axis of creation. At the moment of an individual's birth, the heavens are also "born" anew; they form a unique configuration, and in that can be read the potential of that individual, the aspects of the universe he or she reflects in miniature. A being is, in some primary sense, a replica of the heavens at the moment of birth. One is not absolutely condemned to a linear pattern of development, but the potential contained in that moment of the cosmos is incarnated in a discrete life.

Rudolf Steiner, the twentieth-century German mystic scientist, claimed that if we knew how to interpret and read the brain tissue, we could see the constellations of the sky written into the delicate flesh below the skullcap:

> If one photographed the brain of a person at the moment of his birth, and then photographed the sky as well, exactly as it stood over the place of birth, this picture would show quite the same thing as the human brain. . . . Man bears within him an image of the heavens, and this image is different for every person, depending upon the place and time of his birth. This is an indication that man is born out of the whole universe. [1]

Like the eighteenth-century Swedish theologian and scientist, Emanuel Swedenborg, Steiner believed that all the planets and stars are inhabited: Mercury, Venus, Jupiter, Saturn, Uranus, the Sun, Rigel, and the planets of Rigel and Canopus. But, he pointed out, they are not inhabited in this plane.

Although some systems argue for the direct telepathic or gravitational influence of the planets, this is not necessary. It is only necessary to find an instant in absolute time from which to locate discrete events in the cosmos. The stars—and, in particular, the planets in the zodiac—provided that for ancient man. In theory, though, the same image could be taken from the cells inside a leaf or the imprints on brain tissue. Astrology is simply a system of birth charts set against the heavens, and the symbolic meanings have been worked out through those images from the beginning. It is the only historical record we have of the application of such a symbolic system, but the actual functioning of the system generating the symbols is far deeper than our perception of it.

Birth charts are not the only astrological instant. Conception charts can be made if the moment is known. Death charts can be cast to know what a person's death potentially takes back into the collectivity of the heavens, what the universe has "learned" from that person's life and thus will pass on to the unborn that come from its field. A chart can be cast for the potential of every moment; according to Marc Edmund Jones:

> The universe is orderly because it holds a place for anything at all, according to the particular time and space requirements of whatever general and specific relations are brought together in experience; that is, given a focus in an identifiable situation. Horary astrology takes the moment of an event in the ordering of the universe, which is provided quite literally for all human beings by the celestial motions of the earth, and measures the relations of these heavenly movements with that horizon on the earth's surface which, in its turn, is established by the place of the event. [2]

We no longer imagine the stars touching people with invisible rays or holding them by magnetic reins, but the connection of circumstance between Earth and heaven is fundamental and sufficient. Carl Jung, both on his own and in collaboration with the physicist Wolfgang Pauli, attempted to make a model of "synchronicity" as a law equal to causality. Events would be linked by simply the chance or concurrence of their happening. The synchronicities would not be experienced by us directly, only their coincidence in time and space, but their effects would be enacted continually on an unconscious level where life is in psychosomatic unity with the cosmos.[3]

This is how clinical use of the zodiac and constellation symbolism is justified by analytical psychologists. The symbols themselves not only are synchronized to lives and constellations but they represent collective historical recognition of the underlying unconscious process of the universe. The order and intelligibility that are visible in the night sky and the world of nature arise spontaneously, psychogenically, often without connection, as forms pass from the unconscious into images and ideas. "Animals pay no attention to sun, moon, planets or stars," writes Norman Davidson. "They are ruled by them."[4]

In *Perelandra*, C. S. Lewis quotes the ancient hermetic prophecy that "there is no such thing as chance or fortune beyond the Moon." The name of the space voyager, Ransom, though it originated aeons earlier when his forgotten ancestors received it in its etymological root form, becomes the clue to his trip to Venus, his ultimate role there as a "payment that delivers." His sudden recognition of that unlikely connection saves his life, his mission, and, in a sense, the spiritual evolution of the Solar System. But how could it have been any different? "Before the world was made," Lewis writes, "all these things had so stood together in eternity that the very significance of the pattern at this point lay in their coming together in just this fashion."[5] It is as though the primordial cloud in which the physical atoms were united was also a psychic nebula which has since spread to encompass time and space without losing its original connections.

If we ask, what does astrology mean, we are really asking: what is meaning itself? Dane Rudhyar writes:

> It matters not whether such symbols are dreams or mystical visions or omens or occult "signatures," or any one of the forms of life-interpretation and even divination that have been used for millennia. The point is that all life-encounters become endowed with significance. Man becomes thus Interpreter and Seer. He lives in a world of souls, in a world of significant wholes, because wholeness, or holism, operates through his consciousness. . . . When the operation becomes perfect, there is in the intuitive interpretation of the symbols of the moment the same certainty that exists in the biological instincts; a certainty which the intellect can know only in logic and pure mathematics—the certainty of a tautology; a certainty that comes from *evident identity*. . . . The perfect intuition is the result of an identification between the perceiving individual whole and the perceived whole situation.[6]

Contemporary astrologers and astro-biologists still attempt to uncover the concrete basis for celestial influence and the birth chart. For instance, some reason that the gravitation of the Sun, Moon, and planets could affect the different organs and hormonal center of the human body, unmasking genes and hierarchicalizing the underlying rhythm for the combination of centers of anatomy and embryonic tissue into elements of personality. But this would have to be gravity working with unimaginable specificity and subtlety.

Before dismissing celestial influence, we should remember that many astro-biological relationships are axiomatic. The Earth with its biosphere is solar material. It is precisely the ongoing interaction of particles of solar light with cells of plants in photosynthesis that generates all biological and psychological activity on Earth. Furthermore, the Sun holds the Earth in an orbit in which our world receives only the exact measure of light and heat needed for our survival. That's why we incarnate here in the first place.

The Moon, which actuates the ocean's tides, equally produces tidal effects in the liquids of the body and the brain. Since our cells are composed mainly of water, they are profoundly susceptible to lunar influence. Watch the waves moving onto a beach. Though these swell and discharge with great explosions, they are set in motion by the lightest touch, the same touch that is applied within us and causes "waves" in our protoplasm. With its monthly (= "moonly") cycle, the Moon triggers a series of rhythms around which biological fields are organized. There might have been another biological clock that life could have used to organize itself, but since the Moon was there, it was the loudest voice, and it is too late now to disentangle our biology from the lunar cycle.

For instance, experimenters found that oysters removed from Long Island Sound opened and closed them themselves in Evanston, Illinois, "at the time the tide would have flooded Evanston, had the town been on the seashore—that is, when the moon passed over the local meridian."[7] During October and November, in the last quarter of the Moon, the Palolo worm of the Pacific coral reefs begins reproduction. The back half of the worm with the genital material rises to the surface while the rest perishes on the reef. Eggs and spermatozoa float together and mix at low tide for several days. The sea is transformed with bright material, and the event is celebrated in Samoa on the sacred calendar. In Florida, eels swarm with the quartering of the Moon. Insects, newts, worms, crabs, and seaweed have all been shown to respond to extraordinarily minute changes in gravitation, electrostatic fields, and magnetism, changes imperceptible especially compared to the information with which they are continuously flooded. The only explanation is that living beings become sensitive, through millennia of evolution, to the exact microrhythms they require for survival. These rhythms are established in them embryologically and exist not in the nervous system but in some infinitesimal colloid. The influences are as fragile and holographic as protoplasm itself.[8]

Although responses to the planets of the Solar System cannot be demonstrated experimentally in the way that patterning by the Sun and Moon can, we cannot overlook how much electrical, magnetic, and gravitational material is supplied by them, especially those that are particularly close to us (like Mars and Venus) or particularly large (like Jupiter and Saturn). Each of these bodies helps to maintain the overall equilibrium of the Solar System, and each of them gives off varying forces as it passes nearer to and further from the Earth. Jupiter cannot be seen by a bird in flight, nor can Mars be heard by a mole in its tunnel, but these planetary bodies generate resonance, perhaps of a discrete and profound sort not yet discovered, and that resonance makes up part of the overall environmental background in which the Earth occurs. Unquestionably, the influence upon us of Jupiter is small, and the influences of Uranus and Neptune are respectively smaller still, but they are not nil. And it is not their present resonance that matters so much as the repetition, for millions of years, of the same complex pattern in watery mirrors on Earth.

The zodiac is a path along which the Sun, Moon, and planets *appear* to move because the Solar System lies in a single plane. The images and meanings of the signs are aligned with twelve star-groups as if the latter were of equal size and duration, though they are in fact of vastly disproportionate span (Cancer is small, Pisces enormous). But the explanation lies in the synchronicity between a system of archetypal psychology and a

seemingly arbitrary grouping of star patterns. Once the system
is established, people are able to think in terms of it, and layers
of meanings envelop the original ones. All of these continue to
interact until the system's mytho-historical bigness resembles,
on our scale as a species, the bigness of the sky.

When critics attack one or another aspect of astrology, they
miss both the absurdity and the grandeur of the whole proposition. Zodiac astrology treats every constellation as the same
number of degrees, i.e., as occupying the same size area of the
apparent sky, and it describes only the exact match-up of actual
star-groups and calendar periods (signs) that occurred thousands
of years ago, once. Debunkers have satirized astrology as something like an apartment house in which every occupant has
moved to the apartment directly above him, with the penthouse
occupants closing the cycle by occupying the groundfloor suite.
The only trouble is that no one has changed the names on the
door, and the mail goes to the wrong people, visitors enter the
wrong apartments, and everyone seems or pretends not to notice the difference. It is business as usual. If astrology were to
change in accordance with the sky, it would lose its association of
birthdates and signs and, equally, its seasonal correspondences.

Astrologers have an interesting resolution for this problem,
one very much in keeping with millennial science. The traditional
arrangement is assigned only to a branch called zodiac astrology,
and the corrected system of signs and constellations is given its
own territory, constellation astrology. Constellation astrology
specifically corrects these two errors, but, in so doing, it does not
negate zodiac astrology. The zodiac is fixed within Earth history
and thus expresses realities and potentials as they occur exactly
within that history, i.e., within the Earth as it resists its connections to the heavens and maintains a local order. The meanings of
zodiac astrology are social, occupational, artistic, political, etc.,
most of the things that people consult astrology for. Modern
society *is*, in fact, out of touch with the sky, and although it sees
that the constellations are no longer in their old places, it is hardly
interested in them anyway. It is more concerned to maintain its
meanings from day to day. But then there is revolution in Iran and
a volcano in Washington State, events which are literally
zodiac-crashing.

The zodiac stays within Earth history and tries to hold onto its meanings, but the sky rushes ahead into new time. Eventually, though, the Earth "adjusts" to its actual place in the heavens, and the two astrologies pull together. The continuous pattern of pulling away and pulling together produces a moiré pattern of effects, so that the truth of any situation lies somewhere between the two, depending on how true a given culture or era of history is to its absolute meaning in an objective perspective in the stars.

Constellation astrology describes the cosmic potential of the Earth in relation to remote stars and galaxies. It has little to say about secular or historical fate; its information predicts the adjustment of the Earth to real conditions and the resulting global changes. Its art and psychology are radical, suggesting the birth of new forms rather than development within existing ones. These forms are in alignment with the present panoply of the heavens and not the Earth's ever-rushing to catch up. For instance, the boom of oil cultures and their resulting political and social systems are considered, by the zodiac which attends them, in terms of the events which actually occur within those cultures. But the constellations read them only in terms of the limited supply of oil on the Earth and their ultimate contribution to an Earth that is adjusted to its entire history and destiny in the cosmos.

Esoteric astrology, like relativity theory, does not stop once it has discovered the first distortion of two simultaneous times. If it is hard to imagine events within constellation astrology, the new heliocentric astrology is almost inconceivable. By moving its point of focus from the Earth to the Sun, where the center of the Solar System is, gravitationally, it charts events which have the Sun for their center and the Earth as simply an influence (there could be any number of differently centered astrologies in the Solar System alone, including one for every planet, moon, asteroid, comet, etc.). According to contemporary astrologers, heliocentric astrology addresses the basic and concrete reality of matter down to a subatomic level. Its horoscopes are of relations between the planets over millennia, perhaps communications between sentiences spread through the Galaxy. It is corrected according to the gravitational reality of the Solar System, so it cannot be pegged to the scale of an individual life in a country on one planet. But that life must still intersect the plane of the Sun somewhere, whether or not the person ever comes in touch with the moment.

If we were to discover a galactic center and use that as our astrological reference point, we would be able to talk only of galactic potentials, which would be deeper than subatomic quarks on the physical scale, or of such fine intelligence as to be unrecognizable, except as pre-material, pre-sentient measure for all which is now material and sentient. Such a center exists, of course, and we have known, since early in the twentieth century, that it lies out in the bright Sagittarian direction of our viewpoint of the sky. Virgo looks directly opposite it. The Sun circles the galactic center every 250 million years.

No doubt the Milky Way and its sister galaxies circle a supergalactic center, presently guessed to lie in exactly the opposite direction, fifteen million light-years out through Virgo. The astrological mesh here would be all the finer, all the more exact at every infinitesimal point of location. It is beyond experience, but it is not beyond imagination. Ancient astrology intuited this. Modern astrology uses the material of relativistic physics and radio astronomy to say this again. Our lives are tied to an unseen harmony and rhythm; the zodiac is the coarse terrestrial duodecimo of that rhythm derived from local Babylonian time and sky, and for the purposes of daily divination it suffices. In the words of the Taoist astronomer:

Heaven's net is wide;
Coarse are the meshes, yet nothing slips through. [9]

New Age astrology, which avoids astrophysics and even astronomy like the plague, is out of touch with cosmic astrology, which stays in tune with the changing world aeons and evolving views of the stars. Astrology today has become therapy—pop therapy in the newspapers, psychic therapy in the parlors, and depth psychology in the office of clinicians.

The greatest danger for astrology [writes Charles Poncé] is to be found in the Kronian tendency to spiritualize the person—to make of his chart a thing without soul. It would be a great pity if astrology were to become just another psychology of consciousness, for it is only in astrology where we find the Classical representations of Gods and of the soul unabashedly presented as powers residing beyond the control of ego, as mysteries whose movements and effects might be clocked and predicted, but whose ulterior motives may never be understood....

If there is any one idea I am trying to put forward, it is that we must resuscitate a forgotten function of astrology that allows the reunion of the personal with the imaginal, the creation of a subtle body, and the continuance of Genesis.[10]

Elsewhere he adds, quite unambiguously:

...the purpose of engaging with the imaginal realm is to become active participants in the transformation of nature. Not *our* natures, but nature itself. This is the real meaning of transformation—it is not person-centered, it is archetypally centered....[11]

The zodiac itself is the systemization of a twelve-aspect sequence of transformation—from the moment in Aries when the universe bursts into being to the absolute destruction of everything at all in Pisces—after which the cycle begins again in Aries. This repeating evolution describes not only any region of the universe but our calendar year which begins truly in Aries (March) and ends in Pisces (February). "Out of Pisces," writes the astrologer Walter Sampson, "which is the limbo of decayed worlds, the scrap-heap of former creations, that chaos of disembodied entities, dissolved, disintegrated, lost, the creative fire and shock of Aries, burning away the dross, fusing the remainder into its original elements, makes fresh substance, which is Taurus." [12] Another astrologer, William Lonsdale*, says:

Aries is conscious only of the self in the moment of action which is exactly when nobody else is conscious. Everybody else falls asleep for a split second and that's where Aries was awake. All the rest of the time Aries is asleep and everybody

---

*Lonsdale's comments are edited from a series of unpublished talks on the zodiac he delivered in conjunction with my course on the night sky at Goddard College in Vermont, 1977

else is awake. Nobody knows what Aries is trying to do.…
"What's happening, man!" is the question of Aries. And the
answer is, just what you see in front of you.… The other
Aries question is, "Are you destroying beautifully, are you
doing a good job of destroying?"

There could be no more definitive figure for the Big Bang
primordial nebula itself.

Taurus conserves the stuff of Aries and grounds it in structure.
Like the Pyramids, the Bull makes a defiant stand: "I am every-
thing, I will last forever, without diminution or deterioration."
Lonsdale paints a Taurean picture:

The Bull is the creature who comes down to earth and who
makes himself a space here, a pasture, and who proceeds to
ingest the materials of this earth, to chew them, and in the
process become one with earth stuff, earth substance. So the
Bull is "he who is here." He who has arrived.…

The mystery of Taurus is that Taurus is not unto itself.
Therefore getting lost in oneself in the center of springtime
one gets lost in a dream. Taurus self-obsessed is a dream. It's
a fantasy, an illusion. The whole nature of the sign of Taurus
is the process of externalizing, of bringing forth the fruits,
making things available, making them accessible, making
them beautiful, making them present. Suddenly the whole
manifest universe looms before us.

With Gemini we begin to descend into the realm of
duality, of loss of the heavenly light, the realm of pain, loss of
contact, loss of touch. And the first way that we experience it
as a loss of touch with "the other." The great tragedy of
Gemini is the sense of not connecting with other people, the
sense of not making that connection, and of that connection
not really being possible.

The twinlike reflection of things is that all of us are
mirrors to one another. Every one of us is a perfect mirror to
every other one of us. Every one of us directly reflecting back
exactly what we send out. We can't help but do that on the
Gemini level. We're very good at it. We're so good at it we
don't even notice.…

With the sign of Cancer you have this experience of
fullness, of everything being right there. That's kind of
definitive with Cancer, wanting to be permeated with sense

experience and with emotion and consciousness and a sense of belongingness and the continuity of existence, wanting just to be flooded with the feeling of being part of one's immediate sense world.

Then Leo the Lion, representing the Sun, strides out of Cancerian collectivity and incarnates. He rebels against the oneness of nature and declares his individuality and freedom. Lonsdale describes this sign as being very like his own Uncle Leo who repeatedly asked, "What's my name, what's my name?" and delighted in the same answer each time. He goes on to describe more highly developed Leonine aspects:

The natural impulse of a Leo is to renounce the fruits of your own labors, is to give everything over, to say, "Yes, I've attained this, and now I release it because it was not me that attained it, it was the I Am in me, the Christ in me.... The way we redeem anything is by overcoming it. If we really fall for our experience on its own terms we can't ever overcome anything.

At Virgo we yield, we do work, we take up a trade, we begin the inward journey. Culture and civilization follows. Virgo is chaste and unspoiled because at this phase the creation is virginal and sweet. It can still be made into Paradise.

Libra, a set of Scales, marks the marriage of the Lion and the Virgin; it brings equilibrium and serenity—the conviction that all this is somehow okay as it is. Lonsdale says:

We seek endless imitations in love with another person, in artistic expression, in care for a family, in all kinds of distractions and diversions, hedonistic or otherwise. We seek endlessly to try to reproduce what this experience is about. We try to get out of ourselves in every way but the one way that actually works.

Then Scorpio comes in Autumn bearing Antares on its spine, exactly counter the Bull—he is destroyer, resurrector. To Taurus, Scorpio answers, "Nothing is forever." The quintessential Scorpio characteristic is to fall into utter gloom and despair and then, at the moment of greatest hopelessness, to rebound with tremendous energy, to transform everything that was dark into light—

but ultimately to descend back into the abyss. Lonsdale describes three ways we contact Scorpio:

> In the best love experiences we ever have, in the best relations with other we ever have, and in the deepest darkest crannies of our psyche that we've ever explored. The usual way that Scorpio manifests itself is outwardly through very amazing experiences with other people whether sexually, powerly, lovely, any-ly—those things that happen with other people that really send us behind ourselves. Inwardly it usually manifests as the things we cannot tolerate anymore in ourselves where we have to go through a total purging experience.... The world of Scorpio is the solitary individual in a kind of interior reflective relationship with all of being.... It takes us through total total underworld experiences and then there's a moment where we emerge and we realize that, oh, there's a whole other side, there's a whole other way....

Sagittarius begins the last phase of the zodiac and the year, the collective phase. The bow-and-arrow-bearing Centaur is the sum of all truths and all human wisdom regardless of culture or perspective. It marks the breakdown of self-interest and the multicenteredness of Gemini—the beginning of selfless love and collective responsibility. Sagittarius wants to make everything work, wants to get everybody involved and entice them them with fresh possibilities and potentialities. In their impulse to create everything, Sagittarians also make lots of junk—useless toys and banalities. But they are breakthrough individuals, ultimately pushing humanity to the next phase.

Capricorn is a head-trip sign, a thinker; the Goat is collective knowledge as the source of authority, representing science, technology, and government; it is "final form forbidding further growth."[13] Lonsdale contrasts Capricorn with Cancer:

> The positive Cancer stage would have to do with becoming receptive to the heart aspect of life. The positive Capricorn stage would have to do with being capable of experiencing a spiritual reality and allowing it to have its effect without trying to do anything with it. Cancer is fulfilled by feeling, Capricorn by the true depths of intuition. Cancer is defiled by

emotion, Capricorn by intellectualization. Now this kind of intellectualization that goes on at the Capricorn stage is the most evolved there is. The Capricorn intellect builds fantastic cathedrals of the mind on purely theoretical foundations. The Cancer emotionality immerses itself in extraordinary depths of passion that carry it away from its own real feeling.

There is also the negative Capricorn, the Anti-Christ; Lonsdale says:

I believe that this being will probably be the most impressive human being that has ever hit history. He will be capable of bringing peace to all nations, extraordinary peace. He will have great power, and he will be a master of many arts. His outstanding characteristic will probably be that he is all things to all people and in a sense he shows people exactly what they want to see. He will be a master of the occult arts, and he will bring a new kind of magic to the scene, a magic by which, without much effort at all, any one of us can experience clairvoyant visions and in which we all can enjoy our private inner fantasy world.... Now there's only one price that we will have to pay for all this, and the price is that we must leave behind us any traditions of spirituality and admit that this is the best of all possible worlds and that this is where it's happening, where the action is. And it will be a very small price to pay because people will feel like that was just there in order to reassure us before this happened and really this is the only thing we ever believed in to begin with, this world.

But no one sign can ever take over the zodiac. Aquarius the Water-Carrier follows Capricorn, bringing planetary oneness, the end of all authority in creative intelligence. Lonsdale says:

If Leo is the sign of involution, Aquarius is the sign of evolution. Aquarius means in some sense getting it all out here, but it's very difficult to talk about the possibility of manifesting all kinds of new consciousness and so forth when the main focus of that new consciousness is its own transcendence, which is exactly not dealing with the negative Aquarius reality that we find. In other words, what we have is a transcendent impulse in humanity, and then we have this grisly, anything but transcendent reality....

Aquarius has been seen in astrology as the sign of the millennium, the new age, the most dramatic potentialities for growth and new developments, not just in this time but always. Aquarius is like a pure desire for something to happen. Aquarius represents the dissolution of old forms. This is absolutely axiomatic, absolutely essential to any concept of Aquarius, the final stage at which old forms dissolve before something new wishes to happen.... The Aquarian type of world that calls to us doesn't just knock saying, "I'd like to come in." It says, "Let me in or I'll let you out!"

Then just when we're thinking it would be nice to live in an Aquarian lodge forever, Pisces the fish arrives, and with him, the destruction of everything in universal unconsciousness, in forgetfulness, in the space that exists between any two universes. Sampson writes:

It is a place of shadows, strange shapes, monsters, dreams of unearthly beauty and haunting poignancy. It is a dim indefinite region, opalescently lighted, in which forms come and go, across which mists float, through the veils of which nothing appears sure. . . . It is the place of vanishing, where all things melt and merge into the universe, return to their Maker. . . . It symbolises the final decaying processes by which things are resolved back into their primal elements, disintegrated, scattered, their identity completely vanishing. [14]

Lonsdale tells us:

This is the last sign of winter. It's the next world. This is the sign that says, "I am nothing" so that Aries can say, "I am what I am and just that and nothing else." But first we have to have an "I am nothing." And it is very hard for anybody, least of all people with strong Pisces, to give full credence to something called "I am nothing." But when you're inside of the Piscean experience, it's a whole other dynamic. It's like reaching into a world where in actuality all that doesn't matter anymore, all those concerns, all those preoccupations, all those continual endeavors, because the only thing that counts is something very hard to get at but that's either there or not there. And it's not a matter of explaining, justifying, defining, pursuing, making sure of anything....

Pisces is a very difficult sign to fathom mainly because it's not really a sign at all. Sort of like the other eleven signs are busy just being signs, fulfilling their own little zodiacal niches, and Pisces comes along and blows the whole thing up, relativizes the whole zodiac, says I'm the whole zodiac in a microcosm.

In the end the path obliterates itself. In the end what you come to on the path is that there is no path. What you come to at the end of the zodiac is that there is no zodiac, what you come to at the end of Pisces is that who ever heard of Pisces, what is this Fishy stuff here? You come in the end to the extinction of it in something so much greater than it that we can't even begin to fathom it but we can only love it and give ourselves to it and be glad and that's the end of our story.

Astrology is our rune on the hollow surface of infinity, or we are the shadow play of astrology upon the dream of cosmic night.

23

Star Myth

Astronomy has never been a neutral objective science. Once man developed systems for decoding the obscure patterns of the heavens, he was subjected to an ongoing flood of messages and meanings. No one man or woman developed these systems, so all men and women were subject to their collectivity.

The changing shapes of the constellations and the movements in the sky, as an independent feature of nature, have a dynamic effect on the peoples who observe and study them. Generation by generation, the stars are transformed, but so are the species and the planet. Our great battle, after all, has been with meaning, not with nature. The stars do not visibly control destiny or, by strings attached, cause floods and invasions. They do, however, control meaning, and meaning controls these cataclysmic events, for meaning alone can justify and explain them. This is the intimation of planetary motion, solstice, and Moon phase. It is as though the universe were trying to speak to us from the depths of its being, to tell us what it is and what is happening to us. An eclipse or comet seems to scream warning and transition from the mute heavens. Since there was no known script, tribal man made a hieroglyphic alphabet for the stars.

It is not just a matter of primitive society being influenced by sidereal divination. Johannes Kepler's "solution" of the orbit of Mars led, by its algebra, to the industrial revolution. Albert Einstein's resolution of matter and energy led to Hiroshima and Three Mile Island. Star knowledge is literally and always brought down to Earth, where it has a profound effect on the condition of our life. Admittedly, it is our *interpretation* of the stars' behavior that has the impact rather than the stars themselves. But they have a primacy in that, and their natural continuity carries our meanings from aeon to aeon.

We and the night sky are truly indistinguishable partners in cosmology and creation. We give the sky an identity which is, in fact, our own. Each society that has sought pure knowledge of the heavens has imposed on the heavens the meaning of itself, and thus taken back a certain truth about objective nature simultaneous with its self-fulfilling prophecy about what all this is. We are initially embryos in an embryological expansion of matter. And we are internal forms within an internalization of images and forms. We cast against the remote and eternal heavens something from the depths of our unconscious process as well as the conscious bias of our institutions. We do it to all of nature, but the sky is the most remote and mysterious feature of our world, so it takes on the deepest and most unconscious expression of our hidden agenda.

We tend not to question the mythical basis of astronomy when it is applied to the god-inhabited skies of native peoples or to the astral skies of astrologers and theosophists. "Of course, these are projections," we think. "They are the results of prescientific ignorance, and they have nothing to do with the sky itself." Some ultimate court may decide so, but since there is presently no such court nor the likelihood of one, we must accept that divine, astral, and astrological skies remain coexistent with the series of increasingly refined skies discovered by astronomers of the last centuries.

What may be harder to accept, especially for some of these astronomers and their contemporary advocates, is that their own skies are also cultural projections. The Big Bang, the expanding universe, neutron stars, and even gravity are finally ethnic and provincial notions. None of these things really exist. They are approximations—compromises between what nature is and what society is—even as primitive myths are. Both were equivalently brought into being by cosmogenesis and embryogenesis, and each expresses an aspect of that process. The very rapid shift in theory among astronomers, even from decade to decade in our own time, should tell us that none of these present maps is absolute. In a hundred years, they will seem quaint period pieces. In a thousand years, they will be all but forgotten. Another universe may come into being, one that we cannot presently imagine, which will be as different from ours as ours is from the Babylonian.

Alfred North Whitehead spoke of the "background" of civilizations. Any given culture exists in the foreground of its beliefs, its institutions, its mysteries, and even its self-criticisms. These are all the things it knows. There is also a background of which it can never be aware and which will define it. Even as we look back on the Egyptians and know what they could not, the people of a future time may be able to look back and see who we were and in what sort of heavens our cities stood. But they will not know the truth of their own cities and skies. Even if they are only hypothetical, we are still trapped by the fact that our attention must be on our actions and intentions and not on their definition against time.

In both a physical and a mythical sense, the sky is the background to all of civilization—on other worlds: other skies. Ancient myth is originally stellar myth, cosmic philosophy. We have emerged out of it, and its meanings and directives are now unconscious in us. We carry out aspects of their societies that the Phoenicians and Celts could not know. Much of our hidden background is ancient and archetypal; some of it may lie in future worlds, but even these, the old stories tell us, are the eternal return of original worlds.

Star myth is virtually as old as consciousness. It originates in the Pleistocene epoch, before the dawn of writing; and by the time it is written down, as *Gilgamesh, Gawain,* and the *Kalevala,* it is already a relic of a million dead peoples.

As historical remnants, myths are attuned to the oldest aspects of somatic consciousness. Their chthonian affinities and basic impenetrability make them finally transhistorical. The profundity of Pleistocene consciousness, removed from us in linear time, is similar to our cellular codes, from which we are not separated at all in time (since they are inside us) but by the hierarchical branching of tissue in our bodies. And it is this that myth has always tried to remedy. It has tried, by a strangeness and a discontinuity equal to the fact, to recover impossible treasures, our origin in time-space and our kinship with ancestors whose offspring we are and whose care and blessing we have by the direct bonds they formed, generation by generation, with their own children, until we too were born.

The night sky is the bedrock of myth, and it remains so today, providing us with astrophysical and science fiction myths, "star wars" and "close encounters" to give voice to those things deep inside us that nothing else can pretend to express.

In their epic work on star myth, *Hamlet's Mill,* Giorgio de Santillana and Hertha von Dechend portray cosmic beings which are strung on the stars in the same way that we now string time itself on the speed of light:

> These personages are unmistakably identified, yet elusively fluid in outline. They tell of gigantic figures and superhuman events which seem to occupy the whole living space between heaven and earth. Those figures often lend their names to historical persons in passing and then vanish. Any attempt to tie them down to history, even to the tradition of great and catastrophic events, is invariably a sure way to a false trail. Historical happenings will never "explain" mythical events. Plutarch knew as much. Instead, mythical figures have invaded history under counterfeit presentments, and subtly shaped it to their own ends. [1]

These are the archetypes, and they are virtually our only convincing version left of the gods behind history. For the Egyptians and their ancestors, they were true gods, star-beings and creators. Plato saw their elemental geometry and passed it on as number. Galileo Galilei exposed the corporeal robes of the planets, and the gods were driven out of history. We now find their fragments and reflections in psychology and political ritual, where they vary with unconscious process, and in a realm of so-called matter, where they vary still between matter and energy.

"To be sure," write Santillana and von Dechend, "mythical beings are born and pass on, but not quite like mortals. . . . They have been before, or will be again, in other names, under other aspects, even as the sky brings back forever its configurations. . . . If one respects their true nature, they will reveal that nature as *functions.*" [2]

Now we are simultaneously in the world of ancient totem beings and topological algebras. Star myth embraces both.

Functions of what? Of the general order of things as it could be conceived. These figures express the behavior of that vast complex of variables once called the cosmos. They combine in themselves variety, eternity, and recurrence, for such is the nature of the cosmos itself.[3]

The real night sky is revealed not by science or "by the poet's conscious thinking, but by the power of the lines themselves, so utterly remote, like light coming from a 'quasi-stellar object.'"[4]

We may be deprived of the ancient stars, but we are not deprived of their remnants. They lie dormant in our geology as much as our astronomy, in TV soap operas and rock and roll songs. The ballplayers on their arc-lit diamond at night and the flashing stars of the disco palace may be pale reminders of real cosmology and myth, but they are still given power and beauty by the old gods. Because these are so far away and we have none as great as they were to replace them, the current sparkle is also tinsel before the real night.

From the perspective of ancient man, though, birth in this zone and clime is no accident, and we are not innocent. We are the secret perpetrators, in the mind of matter, of the conditions in which we find ourselves. On some utterly primary level that we no longer experience because it is beyond even the shadows of memory or the old wisdom, we chose and created this. We put ourselves under this sky and sealed its lot upon us. Not only are we destined, but we can view the track of that destiny in the sky.

A survey taken in urban American ghettoes at the time of the first Moon-landing in 1969 showed that a majority of the people interviewed believed it was a hoax.

"Man on the Moon. That's just crazy," said one person.

"The American government and the stuff it makes up. They must think we're pretty dumb to fall for that."

Modern man no longer knows what the sky is, let alone what's possible technologically in the continuum of his automobiles and heated homes.

He does not know the planets or the constellations, and he

has been shown so many fireworks and strobes—so much electric gaudiness—in this century that he regards the stars as decorative, or simply as extensions of this exploited world. People are generally busy with other things, or with what they think are other things, and their idle thoughts do not take a cosmic bend. They prefer matters of relationship or finances. The stock market and the Equal Rights Amendment are more burning issues. If they get really cosmic, it is about patriotism, a great comeback in a sporting event, or sex. People do not like the dark hole in reality that nighttime discloses. Neither did the Sioux warriors, but they studied it and they inhabited it within their means.

Native man was privileged in that regard to be able to stand under the full conflagration of the heavens and not know or pretend to know what they were. They were dazzling and superior; they were above him; and they contained enduring meanings and destinies. Their luminosity and mysterious motions suggested intelligence and hidden dimensions of reality. They were a far far greater thing than he could ever hope to be. Yet, in another sense, they were exactly who he was.

Star loss is not a trivial matter, for, in the breaking asunder of cosmic wholeness, there is a severing of psychic unity. We now suffer a "mental" disorder so vast and general that we do not notice it anymore. But every day we are troubled by upsurges of unconscious cosmic material that disrupt our fragile identities. Behind the little anxieties lies the big one of the sky. And the thing we call schizophrenia exists unknown and collectively in mankind. We are disreputable and self-contradicting by nature. We are born at best into a partial reality. Robert Temple diagnoses it in *The Sirius Mystery:*

> Our modern civilization does not ignore the stars only because most of us can no longer see them. There are definitely deeper reasons. For even if we leave the sulphurous vapours of our Gomorrahs to venture into a natural landscape, the stars do not enter into any of our back-to-nature schemes. They simply have no place in our outlook any more. We look at them, our heads flung back in awe and wonder that they can exist in such profusion. But that is as far as it goes, except for the poets. This is simply a "gee whiz" reaction. The rise in interest in astrology today

does not result in much actual star-gazing. And as for the space programme's impact on our view of the sky, many people will attentively follow the motions of a visible satellite against a backdrop of stars whose positions are absolutely meaningless to them. The ancient mythological figures sketched in the sky were taught us as children to be quaint "shepherds' fantasies" unworthy of the attention of adult minds. We are interested in the satellite because we made it, but the stars are alien and untouched by human hands—therefore vapid. To such a level has our technological mania, like a bacterial solution in which we have been stewed from birth, reduced us.

. . . The numbers of people in insane asylums or living at home doped on tranquilizers testifies to our aimless, drifting metaphysic. And to our having forgotten orientation either to seasons (except to turn on the air-conditioning if we sweat or the heating system if we shiver) or to direction (our one token acceptance of cosmic direction being the wearing of sun-glasses because the sun is "over there").

We have debased what was once the integral nature of life channelled by cosmic orientations—a wholeness—to the enervated tepidity of skin sensations and retinal discomfort. . . . We are causing ourselves to become meaningless body machines programmed to what looks, in its isolation, to be an arbitrary set of cycles. [5]

Life is so brief and fragile in the context of the durable and awesome scenery of night, and we have so little contact with the inner sky, that we do not dwell there long in our attentions. One turns away from the stars, fixes a meal, calls a friend. The lesson would be electrifying, refreshing, but we are not in the mood for such lessons. Instead we experience a kind of cosmic loneliness, and we put the stars aside to live our lives. But is this cosmic loneliness a result of the present infinite view of the ruthless stars and galaxies, or are they themselves a symptom of the cosmic loneliness we already feel in a society which has lost spiritual and ecological direction and which already has nothing to offer man for this trip except, as in the beer ad: "You only go around once and you'd better grab for all the gusto you can get!"? No one could seriously believe this as stated; and yet all

of us do in some way, and pay a terrible price. The alternative
would be to express our own cosmic dimension; yet we have
forgotten how, and it is taught almost nowhere.

We proclaim, rather haughtily: "It *should* be sunny at this time
of year!" without realizing the bigness we could have if we knew
and accepted the cycles themselves. Like existential waifs, we
never get to the bottom of our psychological mysteries and mal-
aises, and move from incident to incident without real connection. We postpone and buy off the cosmos until death itself.

In the introduction to *Hamlet's Mill,* Giorgio de Santillana
and Hertha von Dechend take up this issue from a different
perspective. They first acknowledge that the ancient star-wisdom tells us something of cosmogonic beginnings, of "the breaking asunder of a harmony" and the tilting of space. Then they
add:

> This is not to suggest that this archaic cosmology will show
> any great physical discoveries, although it required prodi-
> gious feats of concentration and computing. What it did
> was to mark out the unity of the universe, and of man's
> mind, reaching out to its farthest limits. [6]

Life attempts to express its own innermost truths, and these,
if they are not expressed, will lodge more deeply in unconsciousness to make themselves known in other ways. If we ignore the stars, we ultimately feel the loneliness and mortality
even more deeply, for the sky is a fact. The stars are there, like
them or not, and though we can hang out in a covered city all
night and greet the Sun as a kind of electric light in the morning,
we must ultimately come to terms with who we are and the
nature of the scenery here.

Just because we are no longer archaic does not mean we no
longer require a cosmogony or that we have solved the problems
of the ancient priests. Our position is more tenuous than we
realize. De Santillana and von Dechend continue:

> Einstein said: "What is inconceivable about the universe is
> that it should be at all conceivable." Man is not giving up.
> When he discovers remote galaxies by the million and then
> those quasi-stellar radio sources billions of light-years away

which confound his speculation, he is happy that he can reach out to those depths. But he pays a terrible price for his achievement. The science of astrophysics reaches out on a grander and grander scale without losing its footing. Man as man cannot do this. In the depths of space he loses himself and all notion of his significance. He is unable to fit himself into the concepts of today's astrophysics short of schizophrenia. Modern man is facing the nonconceivable. Archaic man, however, kept a firm grip on the conceivable by framing within his cosmos an order of time as an eschatology that made sense for him and reserved a fate for his soul. [7]

In the beginning of stargazing, the universe was a flood of sacred matter, set in harmony and regulated by the deep rhythms and cycles of nature. If man was a spirit, the stars were sentience floating in a spiritual medium, a cosmic music beyond time, but carrying time through its eternal return of individual entities and constellations. This movement was grounded in the world itself. If history seemed a series of enfolded cycles, repeating and changing, the sky was the visible and orchestral arrangement of the series. Human cycles were part of larger cosmic cycles. The slipping of the seasons from the precession of the zodiac was understood exactly as a progression in the cosmic order. The oscillation of the Earth on its axis, which caused the precession, became the simple aeonic metric because it changed gradually and irredeemably, while the major cycles (of daily rotation and annual revolution, and the waxing and waning of the Moon) remained the same. Of course, the oscillation gave rise to a cycle too, but it was well beyond the life span of men or civilizations and was recognized only perhaps in the great World Ages of some systems—for instance, in the present Hindu *Kali Yuga,* which comes close to the actual span of the precession cycle we now know as 25,725.6 years. The precession of the equinoxes was a cosmic guarantee that the gods required millennial change on the Earth and a succession of civilizations. And this omen of the Great Year stood against Rome as it had stood against Persia and Egypt, and then Christianity adopted its apocalyptic message within its own set of meanings.

The original sky was a cosmic harmony, unreachable in essence by man, but from which he derived mathematics, music, divination, and law. He had a direct internal experience of the movements of the heavens, an almost telepathic kinship with the things he called the stars or with that essence for which he thought the stars stood. If man suffered under such a sky, he also found redemption in it, for its movements were subject to universal karma. He could hardly complain, for he was spiritually and psychically one with the heavens. That experience, as a collective activity, is gone.

The River Eridanus, later identified with the Nile, the Po, and the Danube, was a river in the sky, a constellation of hundreds of faint stars flowing out of the heel of Orion toward Cetus, then meandering back toward Lupus. The faintness of the stars was not as important as the existence of the river itself, a river on whose banks gods walked and which carried traffic to the land of the dead. It is in that starry river that the body of Phaëthon lies, and the sparkling waters flow over him on their continuous journey to the other world. The Eridanus is the river whose confluence with another river—not the Nile, Tigris, or Euphrates—marks the birthplace of civilization. That other river is either the zodiac or some faint tributary leading into the Galaxy itself, a torrent of light that the Greeks called a helix and that we still imagine rushing simultaneously over and under us to the center.

The alchemists thought of their work as literally capturing part of the sky. The planets and stars moved again in the constituent chemicals and their interactions. The alembic itself enclosed the experiment in a sphere, and a local sky formed, often twinkling with "stars" or arched with a fine rainbow. The sixteenth-century alchemist Edward Kelly called his work "the theatre of terrestrial astronomy," and he raised a golden Sun and a green lion which bit the Sun, causing it to bleed red into the waters.[8] Norman Davidson imagines the primeval aurorae:

Sweeping across the sky with unearthly light, they are the vestments and shields of the Norse gods, heroic in battle. Who could live beneath them without being aware of power in higher regions?[9]

The first philosophers and astronomers are now almost as remote from us as those we invent on the planets of Aldebaran. We inherit their blind collectivity within us and some fragments of their star myths, but that is all.

Our species conceived a single frame to which Heaven and Earth adhere. The "modern" destruction of that frame began at least a millennium before the birth of Christ. With the wobbling of the Earth on its axis and the subsequent precession of the equinoxes through the zodiac, the celestial aeons were transformed, one into another. The Sun abandoned its scorched trail in the Milky Way, and the flow of waters to the Underworld was diverted from the Galaxy into the Eridanus. The cosmic unit was challenged, then disassembled, and the sky against which our species was born became disjointed from the Earth's axis. Some three thousand years later, that sky was already adrift without a single original deity, and it settled—infinite, directionless, and outside time.

Homer was probably our last living link with Ice Age cosmology and the mythic heavens. All the rest of our "data" is archaeological and ethnographic. But even Odysseus's voyage was nostalgic—a return to the fading vestiges of an Atlantean kingdom that swept once simultaneously across the Earth and Sky. It is fitting we know Homer as a voice rather than a man.

Dante spoke the truth for our whole tribe of wandering, faithless Indo-Europeans when he wrote:

I woke to find myself in a dark wood,
Where the right road was wholly lost and gone. [10]

That road had been lost long before the Church schisms, and Nazareth was a surprise and premature flash of its connection to all of space and time before and after. Dante's astronomy was more savage than Jesus's, and it invoked a star for which Bethlehem was one cycle of an eternal return.

Dante sent Odysseus on a final voyage into cosmogonic space. He sailed to the outermost West, beyond Spain and the Pillar of Hercules. Five times Odysseus watched the Moon fill with light and then wane. The known stars failed to rise from the ocean, and new stars filled the sky. Then he and his men reached a mountain surrounded by a whirlpool, a pinnacle rising from the sea to the heavens, Purgatory. His ship was swept up in the current and spun three times around. Then the hollow above it closed, and Odysseus's wanderings were at an end, though ours had barely begun. The whirlpool that swept up Dante's Odysseus was found in the Southern sea only by the displacements of an exiled civilization that no longer saw the gods or knew where they lived. It was originally in the sky, beside Rigel, and it led directly through the sacred Eridanus to the Land of the Dead.[11]

The charisma that attends myth is still, in part, the charisma of the superior lands of the sky. To the Indians of the Plains, the Milky Way was dust kicked up by the Buffalo and the Horse—the original Buffalo and Horse who prefigured the ceaseless herds of the daylight. Imagine the moonlit dust across Dakota, and how it sparkled against its stellar counterpart. The difference between Alexander and Napoleon was that Alexander was the last of the old kings. When he attempted to conquer the world, his image was the Cosmos, the Sky. There was no clear map for such a conquest, but it was intimated in his taking over the temples and texts and priests of the peoples of the world and in the prophecies of the Heavens he sought and summoned as he moved across their terrestrial reflection. Napoleon simply sought lands and territories; his military strategy was secular and without a supernatural element. Both men died with their goal unattained, but Alexander's failure was different from the other. He was already at the dawn of the modern world, when the sky had changed so much that it could no longer hold his deed or those of the Persian kings he supplanted. It was astonishing to him to find that the cosmos could not be conquered. He arrived after the twilight of the gods, when the center had fallen out of the sky and the constellations had shifted from their ancient homes.

In a mythic sense, Alexander's campaign was to restore the old sky, to bring meaning back through cosmic adventure. He failed, and history washes over him as Eridanus washes over the body of the fallen Galaxy. The oracles, in the words of Plutarch four centuries later, were no longer true; they no longer spoke of the cosmos; the telepathic star-priests heard nothing, and they have heard nothing since, though we have probed the heavens from the electromagnetic to the psychic bands. A pilot at sea during the reign of Tiberius, in the first years of the first century A.D., heard the last cry of the ancient world as his ship drifted near the island of Paxi: "Great Pan is dead!" A voice from nowhere speaking words that were utterly clear. The gods were leaving us, and we would have to follow them into the night.[12]

Alexander and Plato had come too late. Napoleon was a forerunner of the modern darkness and the malignant world wars. By then the sky had descended to the Earth and been divided, and we have come to speak of quantity only, no longer unity and cosmos. Space rockets now mark our promised connection to the golden civilizations of the sky, civilizations in our future whose sources predate the inhabited Earth. We have almost completed a cycle, it seems. Its origins are invisible because they have been buried, and its destiny is invisible because it is yet unborn. We may never recover the star myth, but, at this point, we must go either back in time, into the depths of collective unconsciousness, or out into the undiminishable heavens.

The early scientists did not give up the divine sky all at once, but it came to resemble a mind, a puzzle, a cryptogram, more than a myth. Neither Kepler nor Newton foresaw the implications of the modern linear sky they helped to create. For both of them, the sky remained an otherworldly mystery and a reflection of a more perfect geometry beyond it. Motion and gravity were visible forms of invisible forces. Still, they had dislodged the spiritual underpinning of heavenly movement; they had reduced the cosmic basis to numbers and geometries. Gradually, even the riddle and the mind of God disappeared, even though, well into the twentieth century, astronomy books continue to discuss, almost nostalgically, the place where God might fit into this eternal collection of stars and galaxies.

The City of the Sun was mapped by the revivalist hermetic movement of the sixteenth century but was more fully conceived by the science and astral magic of the following century. Tommaso Campanella, the Italian philosopher, was the transitional figure. He wrote the book *Città del Sole*. If the correct stellar influences could be drawn into the habitat of man by the proper talismanic figures and perfect circles, the celestial order would begin to shine in the houses and streets. The city might itself light automatically by divine sympathy. Angelic light would be drawn numerologically into its lanterns. In such a place, there would be no criminals; laws could not be disobeyed.[13] Fantastic as this may sound, it stands directly prior to Newton in the tradition that gave us electricity. Electricity would have satisfied Campanella too; it was stellar and geometric enough. But he would have been appalled to know that natural forces did not guarantee universal justice, plenty, and eternal brotherhood on Earth. His goal was to rule human society not by the sympathetic and synchronous magic of the heavens, as in astrology and the occult sciences, but by the mathematical and structural laws of the heavens applied to human society. Where else would justice and harmony reside but in the night sky? Where else could we seek the end to the discord of nations and the slaughter of man and beast?

By now we have grounded our stellar formulas, and we have tried parliaments, democracies, and capitalism. The industrial and socialist states of the modern world derive from this vision. And if we have not found what we were looking for, we have certainly learned the contents of that particular night sky.

The early hermetics and Rosicrucians, however, saw only the initial benign face of science. Hermes was an ancient Christ to them, a healer and a wise king. He was also the original star magus. If the great puzzle of motion in the astrum could be solved through mathematics, that same mathematics could show the way for troubled and unjust society. The old wars may have been Martian or Jovian, as man sought astrological explanation and legitimacy. The new revolutions, in the eighteenth century, were specific attempts to drive the lineage of kings from their thrones in the heavens down onto Earth, where scientific and rational man, common terrestrial humanity, could transpose the actual order of the stars. This is not the way history or the chronicles of the times describe it, but it is a possible way to understand the simultaneous evolution of astronomy, which describes the background against which man acts, and his moral order and society. A couple of centuries later, the task would be given to the proletariat, and Marxism would replace stellar law.

After the European revolutions against monarchy, with science providing a thousand promising paths to utopia, these ideas were secularized in the writings of the eighteenth-century *philosophes* and were embodied, in fact, in the Constitution of the United States. The idealism of America is, to a large degree, the idealism of the hermetic enlightenment, containing its belief in symmetry, the balance of power, and the harmony of the parts: a judicial, legislative, and executive system that mirrors the astral and elemental balance of forces. Thomas Jefferson was unintentionally a proxy Rosicrucian sage. We have long ago departed from the idealism, but it remains the clandestine optimistic image in American society. The pyramid on our dollar bill recalls its quasi-Egyptian origin.

The historian Carl Becker captures what this process meant to the eighteenth century, and what the United States inherited:

> The new heaven had to be located somewhere within the confines of the earthly life, since it was an article of philosophical faith that the end of life is life itself, the perfected temporal life of man; and in the future, since the temporal life was not yet perfected. But if the celestial heaven was to be dismantled in order to be rebuilt on earth, it seemed that the salvation of mankind must be attained, not by some outside, miraculous, catastrophic agency . . . but by man himself, by the progressive improvement made by the efforts of successive generations of men. . . . Posterity would complete what the past and the present had begun.[14]

The eighteenth century was no longer involved with astral magic, but it was far more aware than we are of the consequences of astronomical theory on society and vice versa. Enlightened government was a transposition of "the regular and constant order of facts by which God rules the universe."[15] Man had inherited God's logic, so he could be like God. Furthermore, he would *have* to be like God, for he was subject to the same universal law. And man had looked through a telescope into the workings of the upper spheres, the operations by which creation was held together. Gravity, light, and molecular structure had shown how God works. If He could keep order in His kingdom, containing such enormous objects and vast realms of space, surely man could derive regional laws from the cosmic laws and create a workable society.

One is uncomfortable thinking about nuclear war; yet the stars are nuclear war writ large—enormous fires whose death throes will destroy planets and whose ultimate compacting (if true as proposed) will mark the end of the material universe. People who carry skulls and dress in death costumes throwing ashes to indicate the consequences of humankind tangling with this energy are enacting, on the one hand, a profound truth about something that has gone wrong in our time (the sloppy use of crude stellar energy in short-term schemes), and, on the other hand, a satire of what is shown in space: death of suns and stars too, death of the universe, which has been offered in place of religion, in place of internal process, and in place of life methodology. Our own age is threatened by a holocaust of man's own making (unless there be accomplice wizards and demons or extraterrestrial intelligences behind man himself), and it is no accident that scientific theology of this age proposes a cataclysm that will obliterate everything and what everything is—things which were ostensibly once brought into being by just such a cataclysm. We have hardly been less arbitrary and cruel to each other.

The "starring of the Earth" is now complete (if we may call it that by parallel with Charles Reich's 1960s fantasy of the "greening of America"). The explosion of nuclear weapons, imitating the Sun's own fueling process, is finally the epitome of relocating stellar law on Earth. The locomotives and early automobiles share something with Kepler's vision of the orbit of Mars and Newton's mathematicization of the gravitational force. Man thought he saw a retrievable being in the sky, but when he captured it, it was an unknown intruder and the sky became incidental. In fact, the sky, in the sense of original forces of physics, is everywhere, and it is no longer necessary to have reference to the actual radiance. The preference for social programs instead of the space program is a symptom of this dislodgement. Some want more bombs, others want more welfare checks, but they don't want the sky unless it serves them directly, either as a weapon or a controlled weather system. Our societies pretend to sit by themselves on their own terms, though the same universal laws, whatever they are and however we interpret them, hold everywhere.

Looking down on the Earth from space, Michael Collins understood our dilemma. We are like ants, digging up trifles from under the surface, oil and coal, as if they were limitless and as if this behavior were enlightened or even sane.[16] The only future that man can have at this rate must be set imaginarily in future worlds of outer space. In terms of the Earth, man has failed to grasp in any economically or politically viable way that it is a planet, a single planet. There are no others; to imagine them does not create them.

Meanwhile, science has given us another sky with the seeds of a new ecological morality. The fossil fuels are solar energy, altered by photosynthesis and aeonic chemical activity. The winds are also solar, or gravitational, in their origin. The tides are lunar gravitational energy. Life is stellar chemistry. All the rivers flow into all the seas, and all the clouds arise from the whole and stand against it atmospherically. The lightning and the radiation of the ionosphere are aspects of a single field. It is one boundaryless chemical droplet, steaming from its seas and lapping up into ice, with clouds strung through the invisible winds. "Brown-red is the color," wrote the poet Charles Olson, "of the brilliance of earth."[17]

This was the first gift of Whole Earth consciousness. We were allowed to see a unity directly, and it was a unity expressed throughout mankind: in other ways in the writings of the alchemists and Taoists, in Zuni creation myths and the *I Ching*. Nature is a one, a harmony of diverse elements, and it acts as a one: the clouds, the Arctic ice, the open seas, the Sun penetrating the whole thing, making its radiance in the guts and giving it a blue aura that separates it from the surrounding space as a fine engraving is different from the unmarked jade around it. If it were not for our fearful greed and fatal existential doubt, we could almost come home in this century.

Solar energy is atomic energy too—not the direct explosion in imitation of the star core but its medicinal by-product passing through space. We can call it medicinal without fear of metaphor or sentimentality because the process of photosynthesis is the protean medicinal process. It weaves the strands that become the self-healing replicating cells. It creates the flesh and blood of the nuclear scientists and engineers and the antinuclear demonstrators counterposed in the atomic sunlight. The problem of the sources of matter and energy is a far more complex one than the pros and cons of any politicization reveal. We are the products of explosions, we contain explosions, and we keep ourselves going with a tinder box.

To accept solar energy and reject atomic energy may seem a contradiction, but it is a practical strategy. It also relives an ancient mythology. Solar energy is what the universe gives us of itself at this distance: Take this and you will be enlightened, take this and you will be healed. And we have not been wrong yet. We have waited to be born, and the seas have filled with life. We have waited while life crawled onto the land and established itself, and we understood that we were born already, and then we came more fully into being and built our farms and manors, our astronomical observatories and our cities. In these we understood the Sun again, the measure of our place in the cosmos—as simple as units on a sundial, the fields of barley and bulgar in the Near East, the vast rainbow corn of the New World. Our solar society existed for millennia. It was a society of flowers, grains, fish pools, tonics, mirrors, and delicate parchment. All of this came from the stark abyss of fiery hydrogen gases a mere stone's throw away. Gravity covered it, and light dispersed through the sky into colors which formed eyes to see them. It couldn't have been a better universe. It couldn't have happened to a better universe. It said: wait and I will happen. And it did.

The new atomic universe of radio astronomy and particle physics is a terrifying one, and we have become its dull-witted targets. We are blind to the particles we are meant to avoid, radioactivity and decayed nuclear matter, and we cannot see, even with our finest telescopes, the chaos and violence that is destroying the cosmos. Its warnings and prophecies are all about us, yet we are somehow spared and allowed to go on living in what is essentially a Greek city.

The two terms of the paradox must go together: death by too much energy, panic from too little energy—panic and starvation.

The physicists have given us nothing. They have failed us. The very sound of radio noise in the sky is the crackle of our own anxiety, and it is also the crackle of our present cosmological insufficiency. The great violence we perceive in space may be more than our own destructiveness; it may be the suppression of our creative abilities to harvest inner space, a perception that the inner spaces are in turmoil and we are cut off. But what if we are not? How dread the responsibility then to make a decent world and recover our birthright.

We stand before an incredible task. It would be something for even a planet of supermen who could fly into space. We must, if we too are to survive, avert the destruction of the universe. We must reverse the Big Bang. Which is to say, we must prevent the destruction of our own planet and its systems of meaning. We must pass through the Big Bang, even as we must pass through existentialism, Marxism, capitalism, materialism, and all the other tricks of the atomic age, and we must make a new universe, something like the Ionian and Hindu ones but without exactly those features that lead inevitably and rightly back to the present condition. The darkness is not something that we can go back on. Its riddle itself is our destiny.

Unquestionably, the space program is mechanical and external, but even machines are born after long incubation in the unconscious processes of our planet. The space program expresses the destiny of those machines in a way that psychotropic drugs and bailing out automobile corporations do not; it expresses *our* destiny within this dangerous technological adventure. The machines may be dumb and inanimate, but through us they struggle toward humanity and articulation. By their mute agency, men stood on the Moon and watched the rising of the radiant blue Earth against the infinite black. They stood outside the sphere of all human operations, looking back at the entirety of what they had been. Machines made this possible; machines from our minds placed our collective mind beyond the Earth. If they are mere technology, then such technology holds magical powers.

Abandoning Mars and Saturn voyages in favor of mental hospitals and MX missiles consigns our future to exactly those things, the ones we have chosen. We can use technology to turn our planet into an armed camp or a social drug center, and we can use it to explore the oneness of life against the infinity of the cosmos.

Astronomers were once our priests, and, whether they know it or not, they still interpret the moral as well as physical structure of the heavens. And they have shown us a universe that would seem to devour without rhyme or reason: stars crushed, galaxies of stars destroyed, stars devouring other stars, black holes devouring everything; they have shown dying suns swallowing their solar systems. Where ancient astronomers found a divine whirlpool, modern ones received the news that the whole of matter was created once in a giant explosion from a space perhaps no bigger than a dime, and they said: there is no moral structure; in fact, there is nothing at all.

Our ability to transform scientific information has been far outweighed by the amount of that information and its very gloomy implications about our species. Even our local Solar System is disclosed, planet by planet, as a sequence of hellish environments in which our potential survival, if we should suddenly be transported there, would range from a matter of milliseconds to a matter of minutes at the most. The rest is explosions and radiation. The beauty of space is overshadowed by the sense that it is nothing but a noisy brute. It explodes galaxies and worlds in the way that we build and put out campfires. The planets in our vicinity are not neighbors; they are fires, storms of poisonous gases, and dry meteor-pummeled stone. The Martians and Venusians of the 1930s and 1940s, even of five years ago, now seem fantastic wishful follies. Their "remains" are strewn on bouldery plains and around 500° carbon dioxide volcanoes. The old mythologies, whether they be of Ice Age man, the mediaeval astrologers, or science fiction writers of the rapidly passing twentieth century, serve a crucial purpose we may only dimly understand. And it is not enough to say that they explain us instead of outer space; it is not enough to reduce them to projections of our own habitation into the uninhabited void.

We were shown shapes of awesome capacity, perhaps safely in the distance for now—these ferocious and relentless beasts—but also hot upon us because the expanding universe cannot hold them at bay forever. It was not just a case of being consumed by these creatures but of having our whole universe consumed. Excited atoms scream like geese in slaughter when galaxies collide. No doubt the geese or quasi-white-feathered-birds of these other brilliant worlds are slaughtered too.

The vast explosions of space dwarf anything imaginable, though on our scale they seem to represent the downfall of vast civilizations, like the decline of the West, the dismembering of the Roman Empire, or the overthrow of Aztec and Inca Kingdoms. Perhaps that is what they are intended to mean, their esoteric nature showing through their material guise. But for now, mankind has been asked to be present at its own funeral, a funeral which took place billions of years in the past and perhaps billions of years in the future. It is an atomic nightmare.

Where were the gods now? Where were the divine power and the perfect geometries that ruled in its stead? Where were the uncompassionate but just laws of nature? They seemed to have vanished from a universe in which everything had suddenly become possible.

Dreams and the psychology of the unconscious had shown man that his instincts and desires were limitless beyond his will and that every failure to express them would express them anyway. They would generate his societies, his laws, his art, and his international crises. But at least they had meaning; at least they shared with man his inner nature. Even the cruelty in them was the cruelty in his destiny, or the cruelty and resistance through which he had to pass to achieve his destiny. Whatever in them was alien would be made familiar by internalization and cathexis, even if it changed his nature by becoming familiar. He knew that he would experience his destiny and his meaning as part of himself, and that he would arrive at it by the continuum of association and consciousness in his own mind.

We have achieved the same proposition that the hermetics espoused for entirely opposite reasons: that Heaven and Earth are reflections of each other and the same laws prevail in each. We have made the sky our bedfellow and have put ourselves to sleep in the starry night. It is a coffin, and we no longer look because it is too horrible. The sky is our midwife and our interrer. It is our placenta but also our ashes. Unity is inescapable. The same elements and forces are everywhere. On the one hand, the meaning of the sky is reduced to a human scale, which makes it less mysterious. On the other hand, the scope of the sky and its possible moral structure are put utterly beyond men in a circumstance that is far more terrifying than even the old gods.

Unquestionably, the new sky set men free; the old sky had been a tyrant, ruling men's fortunes, taking away their rights, and setting corrupt priests and kings on their thrones, all in the name of cosmic myth. But it also kept the cosmos sacred and intact. Now we are treated as a speck in a puddle that must be influenced by whatever raindrops, detritus, or lines of force happen here. Coherence has become accidental and random, even if it still exists to hold solar systems and galaxies together, as well as the interior of the atom. We are free men and women, free of the tyrannies of the stars and of those who interpret their will into repressive kingdoms and castes. We are now subject to vast amounts of meaningless information about bigger and bigger things. The sky used to set an example for moral structure. Now it seems merely to permit amoral freedom in line with the principle of shapeless creative hydrogen fire and universal entropy.

Because the sky is so big, it becomes a blank, a zero. Beside it we feel we are innocent and wonder why all this misfortune has befallen us. We feel we are decent people. "Why were we not born in a better place at a better time? Why this planet, this world, this violent history? Why should we be subject to wars, earthquakes, revolutions, famine?" Since we feel we did nothing to cause these things, since they are an interpolation of stellar material into a terrestrial frame, we become isolated and alienated. We connect to nothing.

Isaac Bashevis Singer, the twentieth-century Yiddish novelist, has Asa Heshel wonder about the universe on the eve of Hitler's invasion of Poland. "Meteors shot across the sky, leaving fiery trails behind them. Silent summer lightning quivered in one corner of the heavens, foretelling a hot day. Fireflies shone and were extinguished; frogs croaked; all kinds of winged insects came fluttering into the room and dashed themselves against the walls, the windows, and the bedposts."[18] This is the modern empty universe. John Donne never would have seen it this way. "Asa Heshel thought about Hitler; according to Spinoza, Hitler was a part of the Godhead, a mode of the Eternal Substance. Every act of his had been predetermined by eternal laws. Even if one rejected Spinoza, one still had to admit that Hitler's body

was part of the substance of the sun, from which the earth had
originally detached itself. Every murderous act of Hitler's was
a functional part of the cosmos." [19]

Passive acceptance of the morally unacceptable is the lot of
modern man.

Galaxies and stars blow up from internal forces. No wonder,
then that societies do too. Hitler's ovens are the moral equivalent of a neutron star in a system which once held life. Starvation in Cambodia is the equivalent of a supernova. Why not
invade Afghanistan? Comets invade planets; galaxies invade other galaxies, killing a possible billion billion billion people. Why
not put the people out to sea in dinghies? That's what gravity
does. That's all that planets are anyway. That's how life was created from the trillions of chemical compounds in the original
sea.

In another Singer novel, another character views the starry
sky, wondering if there are concentration camps and starvation
out there too, or possibly some spark of hope. When he realizes
that modern astronomy proclaims the same universal struggle,
he is overcome with despair: "A rage against creation, God,
nature—whatever this wretchedness was called. I felt that the
only way of protesting cosmic violence was to reject life. . . ." [20]

In the last fifty years in particular, we have done away with
the remaining vestiges of public morality. The sky stands as a
moral lesson only to thugs, looters, and terrorists. It expands ad
infinitum; it explodes without caring for the innocent victims;
and it enjoys itself without thought or fear of tomorrow. It has
no plan for the future. How strangely like ourselves!

Our own economies expand, and the value of money dissipates with the galaxies of the night sky. Inflation and the expanding universe may be light-years apart in terms of their apparent origins in the modern system, but they share a realm of
thought. They indicate equally the inability to set value, the
sense that all value is relative. As we find nothing but violence,
relativity, and destruction in the sky, we find ourselves surrounded by depravity, rioting, starvation, and advanced weaponry. The
"starring of the Earth" is right up to date. Family structure crum-
bles with the stable Solar System. What is there to live for if the
stars no longer care? Why even try to behave decently, with such

a ruthless bandit on display every night?

Our knowledge has snowballed, and our means for dealing with nature have put us in an environment mostly of our own making. Yet the basic mysteries are as impenetrable as ever. Our civilization sits beneath the same sky as uncomprehendingly as Stone Age man stood beneath it in his own loneliness. And by the clock of the heavens, a brief second has passed from then till now.

It is not a case of primitive wishfulness or lack of appreciation of the harshness of the cosmos. Archaic cosmology was just as fierce and merciless as our 250-miles-per-hour Jovian clouds and black holes swallowing light itself. The Hindu gods retain some of the original clarity of that mythic universe. Shiva is the sentinel of both love and death, the devourer of life and the source of life. As Shiva dances, the whole cosmos shimmers as his reflection. His throat is blue from a poison that he drank in order to save mankind. And then there is black Kali, goddess of disease, murder, evil, wisdom, revelation. "It was a prodigiously vast theory," according to de Santillana and von Dechend, "with no concessions to merely human sentiments. It, too, dilated the mind beyond the bearable, although without destroying man's role in the cosmos. It was a ruthless metaphysics."[21]

Anu fulfills his promise to scorned Ishtar by flinging a Bull of Heaven onto the Earth, a bull whose every snort eradicates hundreds of warriors. Enkidu rips the right thigh out of the animal and hurls it back in Ishtar's face. Disease itself is sent to punish this brazen despoiler. The body of Osiris is shredded through the cosmos. Triton blows back the flood with his radiant conch shell. Marduk shoots the Hyades into the squadron of cosmic monsters, dispersing them into the heavens. Isis flees Typhon, sprinkling the ground with ears of wheat. Odin sends a storm through the Milky Way. Samson pulls the house of the Philistines down on himself. Surt bursts from the divided heavens with a sword of fire. Phaëthon drops the reins of the Sun's chariot at the sight of the Scorpion, and the zodiac is shattered, the forests scorched; the body of the usurper lies in the Eridanus. King David sings to bring the waters up from the Abyss. Quetzalcoatl disappears into the great sea. The ancient Shah Kai Khushrau fades from the mountaintop into the sunless sky while the five paladins sleep. He is the last of his kind. "Farewell for ever!" [22]

It is no accident, in a mythical view of things, that an aroused Islam tries to drive the Western World out of the Near East, i.e., out of the sacred sky of ancestry and myth. Revolutionary Islam, in Iran, old Persia, virtual homeland of astrology and the Kings of the Sky, now attempts to break through the meaningless marketplace static and peg things again to a holy event. Public beheadings are acceptable, but eroticism and hallucinogens are not. If the Ayatollah Khomeini seems utterly rigid and unyielding, it is because he imitates that old sacred political way of doing things. His rules make no sense for human beings as we conceive them in the modern world, but they make total sense for planets and stars which must guard absolute orbits. In exile in Paris, he had no power to take over Iran, but Iran chose him as a figure for itself. The people, the Revolution, chose him, not apparently because he was eloquent on their concerns or educated on the type of society they wanted, but because he represented the old gods and the strength of ancient times. He brought back the unyieldingness of cosmology that preceded this modern tumult of races and values and marketplace politics. From the point of view of Islamic revolution, Big Bang Theory and pornography and crime are sworn accomplices in the Western World. The ostensible neutrality of astrophysics and international law merely obscures that.

It is not simply a matter of spiritual development and personal meaning. If we were more star conscious, we would be ecologically more astute and politically and economically more cross-cultural and wise. The false boundaries and passing meanings of decades and ways of life would be guided by something more central and enduring. It would help our energy crisis if we thought more clearly and profoundly about how energy itself originates in the stars and finds itself located on the planets.

We may not wish to take the Shiite path ourselves, but we can see where contemporary science and morality have taken us. It is not even certain that any of us, or any living thing on this planet, can survive them, despite the billions of years that were put into getting us here. We live now with the knowledge that our civilization will be buried even more deeply than the temples of Rome, and that we will be showered by more than just the dust of winds and human forgetfulness and ignorance. Our heavenly city must be covered with the debris of an exploding Sun and the electric dust of a dissolving universe. We can no longer pretend to be making unlimited progress, so we war and murder in the cosmic void. No hope and no place to go; such is our disappointment and rage. Denis Diderot became deeply troubled by a forerunner of this notion in 1765; what got into his brain like a tiny insect that he could not dislodge until it threatened to topple his entire encyclopedia was the possibility that an unnamed comet, tearing out of the random blankness of the cosmos, might destroy the Earth in a cataclysmic collision. It did not relieve him to think that it was not likely to happen, certainly not in his lifetime. It bothered him that he could not put away the worry and that he could come up with no simple solution to such a pedestrian and almost light notion. In its sheer simplicity, it must mask something terribly profound.

It did. What was a whisper to Diderot would become a gong in the center of another city only two centuries later. It was no idle thought; it was the forerunner of a madness, an obsession in which man would become trapped.

Diderot feared that knowledge of this comet would take away all mankind's reason for noble activity and self-development. "No more ambition, no more monuments, poets, historians, perhaps no more warriors or wars. Everyone would cultivate his garden and plant his cabbages."[23]

He got the details wrong, but he certainly captured the mood. When the implication of universal Darwinism became clear to George Bernard Shaw, he wrote: "If it could be proved that the whole universe had been produced by such Selection, only fools and rascals could bear to live."[24] And such is the case, though we do not think of ourselves as fools and rascals; instead we are the mutants and accidents of directionless turmoil.

Without initially being aware of it, man severed one thread that held him to the sky, and then followed the other into the future; by now it has expanded to replace the original cosmos with new blueprints from the heart of matter. Since we are born and die within this technological nexus, and since we could not survive without it, many of us may laugh at the idea that the old magical sky held anything true or important in it. But we are biased, being the very interested partisans of the present order and not having lived any other way.

It is not simply that we have moved into spiritual darkness. By learning natural laws and creating a technological society based on them, we have become more humane and gentle in many ways. We have broken the tyranny of some of the cruelest of the old gods. Persian and Incan societies may have been in touch with the heavens in ways we are not, but those paths led to star-justified wars, slaughters, slavery, and sacrifice. In any case, even the last of the old human magi emphasize that this was the path that man was meant to travel, and he could no more evade the current transition, the initiation into the conscious knowledge of matter, than he could evade being incarnated in the first place. The dream is still that we can keep the best of the new order, and, through long painful discipline and meditation, reexperience the basis of the ancient wisdom—not recover it from texts and magical lineages, though these will always be clues and guides along the way, but create it anew in terms of the actual condition of the present Earth in the cosmos. This means that the next hermeticism and astrology will have in them aspects of astrophysics and microbiology. And they will not be initiated in pop images of black holes and extraterrestrial intelligences. These may come into play in totally unexpected ways, or they may wither into period pieces of our troubled times.

We have reached a turning point. It is a priority of the new consciousness—the society emergent in the occultism, radical politics, and Whole Earth philosophy of the sixties—that only a breakdown of the current technocracy, with its laws of time and space, will lead to a greening of America and a new heavenly city on Earth. It will be a nonnuclear city, a city derived from Zen, telepathy, perhaps the vital power in pyramids, and old-fashioned solar energy (it will be Città del Sole). It may even get energy from black holes and quantum physics. It will be a science fiction city which may speak to other intelligences, though not necessarily by radio telescopes. It will restore the botanical and healing power of the Earth. It may be all of these things, some of these things, or none of these things, but these alone as images stand for the new heavenly city, the new order.

It cannot happen any longer as pure astral magic and with disregard for the laws of the universe we now know from physics and biology. But these sciences must give birth to occultism and religion anew, borrowing something from a past golden age of which most has been lost and most had already been lost by the time of Plato, presiding over the birth of a new star-wisdom, a new music both arcane and modern, so that the fields of flowers and grains and the body of man and woman can once again be a primordial reflection of the starry firmament. In these fields, greening and starring can be the same thing.

Where we stand today is in need of a theory of the heavens, complex enough to contain all we know, yet beautiful enough to encompass all we are, cosmic enough to include modern science, yet true to all we are and have been, including Pawnee star maps on buffalo hide, space probe photographs, notches in bone of Moon phases, and replicas of the Scorpion and the Scales.

24

Flying Saucers and Extraterrestrial Life

THE NIGHT SKY is like Homer's sea—vast beyond measure, mysterious, dangerous, but still navigable, and also inhabited by unknown, perhaps nonhuman beings. The prospect of interstellar civilization changes the very nature of the sky for us. The stars become ports in space; our own world is also a potential port in other people's skies, and a fair target for anything else which nature has formed in its diversity and extent.

The sea can be entered by simple beings in handmade vessels, like the Polynesian "astronauts." But a raft cannot be slipped into the interstellar medium. It requires a boost to beyond the home planet's gravitational hold, and also, at the very least, strong materials and an artificial atmosphere on the ship. These were impossible feats for the tribal cultures that have dominated most of human history, and for their primitive equivalents on other worlds. Civilization, however, progresses by exponential degrees. It was not so long ago that Leonardo da Vinci's "aeroplanes" were science fiction art, and not so long before that that the distances of the sea were too great for those who sailed them and perished when their ships were shattered or their supplies ran out. Rocket launchings follow the first flying machines by less than a human lifetime. Gravity and distance are fundamental, but they are also relative. We face a night sky that may hold magnificent worlds beyond number, but it is also an emptiness of inconceivable vastness with high levels of radiation and widely separated suns.

We have yet to encounter beings from other worlds. Despite all the UFO reports and supposed close encounters of the second and third kind, the extraterrestrials remain unknown. Their existence has been proposed on hundreds of thousands of occasions, but it has neither been demonstrated nor proven. Like the various spirits and disincarnate entities sighted throughout history, they are an overwhelming presence on our world, but they have not moved from the shadow regions to an upperworld of political and scientific visibility.

From the depths of the Stone Age, we have had intimations of intelligences not our own, of visitations, but these have always been, in one way or another, internal concurrences: the allies of shamans, the deities of myth, the visitors from astral realms, the various demons and angels, and the ghosts of the dead. Even if these should turn out to have objective external existence, they are not beings who emerge in the universe in the same way that we do. They are not embodied as we are, and they are not our counterparts. Spirits are not informed in the way that we are, and they are not uninformed in the way that we are. Encounters with them change our sense of reality and of our own nature, but they do not broaden the physical and biological context of our species.

We have come into being in a cold and secular place without any guideposts or references to what lies outside it. Only those who have come into being in the same way can give us a reference for our human existence. Spirits do not share the flesh with us, and they apparently do not share the billions of years of evolution that are incorporated in our process. They clarify incarnation only as it relates to their different form of existence.

The potential impact on us of extraterrestrial life is unimaginable. We are misled by scientific supposition and science fiction into thinking that we have already gauged the possible aliens. We have not. The most conventional extraterrestrial would affect us more profoundly than even the exotic insects and crystal intelligences of science fiction. These latter are projections of ourselves, while the real aliens come from outside the entire biochemical and psychosomatic chain in which we have developed.

Whether we fully appreciate it or not, biology (life science) means to us the living forms on this planet only, the sequence of life originating in protoplasm and carried from the first cells into multicellular organisms whose interdependent fusion is embodied at the primordial levels of our own existence. It is only a single continuity of life forms. It does not include, for instance, life forms on Mars; even the simplest of these creatures, if they exist, are not protozoas in a terrestrial biology. They are something else. Biology does not subsume the life forms on any other planet orbiting any other star, even if that planet is blue, watery, and oxygen-rich, and its star is a replica of our own Sun. We would be most shocked to be visited by spacemen who resemble us, for if this did not indicate that matter has in it a template leading to the human shape, it would mean that the combination of environmental, pregenetic, and genetic conditions leading to man is duplicatable (and perhaps the only chain capable of intelligence); that we did not originate on this world; or that we are the lineal ancestors or descendants of people on other worlds. Unless there is some unknown quality in matter, life forms evolving elsewhere must have unique biological histories; they must originate differently from inorganic matter and non-living compounds, and they must continue to evolve differently every step of the way. Even the most minute differences in the original amino acids and DNA material would have profound consequences. Such differences would affect one-celled animals or their equivalents, and they would be incorporated at every level of plant and animal life, including intelligent beings and their societies. All the underlying biological strata would contain the structural components they inherit from their evolutionary predecessors; these structures would be ramified at each level of increasing complexity with new differences and unique variations. At the level of sentient beings in a society, the differences between us and any extraterrestrials would be inconceivable. We would share only the raw star debris.

But scientists assume that extraterrestrials would have to know the same laws of nature that we have discovered either to communicate with us or to travel here, since the intrinsic physical properties of the cosmos are universal. For this reason, astronomers broadcast mathematically meaningful messages to the stars, and listen for such broadcasts passing among the stars. One message we send and seek is a series of beeps marking the prime numbers: 1, 3, 5, 7, 11, 13, etc. Such a sequence is not produced by any known natural process, yet it apparently expresses a design which is fundamental anywhere in the cosmos: integers divisible only by themselves and by one. If we located such a prime number "broadcast," it would corroborate not only the existence of extraterrestrial civilization but the commonality of our scientific path.

In one optimistic scenario, beings from another world send or bring us useful information that speeds our progress and improves our planet. But even the bare statement of the existence of others, without any ensuing data, would transform us. It would demonstrate that technology is survivable; it would show scientists that they were on the right track. A mere series of prime numbers originating elsewhere would indicate that technocrats can lead us into a future that has already happened somewhere—unless, of course, the message comes from others in the same turmoil as ourselves when they broadcast. Then they might no longer exist.

It is also possible that life might take on such a different form that we would not recognize it, that thought itself might develop along such unfamiliar lines that we would not be able to communicate with it. The prime numbers and the spectral lines of the elements seem universal to us, and we presently take it for granted that they are known by any civilization able to send messages to the stars. But this could be a provincial assumption.

Unquestionably, the universe from our vantage reveals a uniform physics and chemistry, but even if this universality should hold up with travel to the remotest regions of the creation, it does not guarantee that anything resembling that uniformity is sustained in the biological, psychological, and social levels that have built upon the physics and chemistry. We already expect sex types, languages, and basic social institutions on other planets to be foreign to us, perhaps undefinable in our terms. But we might not even be able to tell that the living are alive, that intelligent creatures have minds, or that a certain feature is a civilization. The boundary between organism and environment, as we know it, might not apply elsewhere. The objects of conscious thought might not be communicable to our biological line.

There are perhaps only two ways of avoiding such a final cosmic isolation, and the dice are already cast: it is up to us to see how they have fallen. One way is for matter itself to contain a predisposition toward certain forms and archetypes. Despite random variation throughout the cosmos, ultimately the same basic structures would be expressed. The second, and possibly related, way would be for higher systemic levels to bridge the differences of content and of structure from world to world by similarities of function and of adaptation to the macroenvironment. Intelligence, as the apparent final layer, would bridge the greatest differences. Ideally, when intelligence is applied to the deciphering of nature, it generates commensurate images everywhere. If this is true, science would fulfill its own prophecies and become the galactic language. Through science, we might transcend terrestrial culture and enter a cosmic civilization. Then all of the years from the first walking apes to global technology would be understood as an early and primitive stage of our species. The next phase would be something like the coming of the Europeans to the Plains Indians, but it would occur all at once, as though Chicago, Detroit, and Indianapolis simply landed, fullgrown and operational, at their present sites, and the local inhabitants were immediately enrolled in schools and given movie tickets and taught to drive cars. Something exponentially larger than what happened here over centuries would happen almost instantaneously.

We should be prepared for the impossible. Even if the impossible never happens, the practice of it will sharpen our sense of the cosmos. The meeting with extraterrestrials would be different from a meeting with spirits, for we cannot bypass or belittle the physical cosmos. If there are extraterrestrial beings, they have their own spiritual life. But the physical fact of different creatures throughout the cosmos transcends spiritual issues on this one level: in the bigness of physical creation, there might be others formed like ourselves. They would have emerged from the enriched star debris along a totally different line; they would understand universal law differently. All our customs and beliefs would have to be reexamined in the context of their behavior. The meanings of our actions would never be the same. Key concepts would need to be rethought in terms of other types of intentional sequences and philosophies: justice, compassion, harmony, peace, love, power, and morality would have new applications. No government or religion would stand unchanged. These other creatures would have come into existence just as we did, by natural law. The differences between nations will be trivial beside the differences between life forms. How do you develop a commensurability of value systems when you are not even made out of the same material? Men cannot agree, and they virtually share a collective mind.

Christianity and Islam would face beings arising from cells or cell-like clusters, not our cells but cells of the same fundamental elements. Could the priests and imams tell these beings what they tell humans about creation and incarnation? Communists would have a similar dilemma with extraterrestrial social orders. These would not reflect the sequence from patriarchy through feudalism to capitalism and socialism. What would theorists who searched even the atom and its particles for the dialectic have to say? They could reject the extraterrestrial orders as alien and irrelevant, but to do so would be dangerous, for it would deny the same natural law on which they claim communism rests. By their very presence, the extraterrestrials would be subversive.

Having come this far through science, which we derived from universal laws in the heavens, we are in no position to reject the natural origin of thinking and acting creatures from those heavens, or the things they make and do.

If we even find someone to talk to, our isolation is over. We then experience a thing in matter and psyche that is larger than ourselves: even two orphans of star debris can hold an elegant conversation in these vast and hollow halls. We suddenly exist among the stars and their incomprehensible vastness and emptiness in a new and brighter way. We come as a species, collectively, to such a moment, but each one of us also becomes a different person.

Until then, we are alone. We are devastatingly lonely, and have been even since our gods were driven from the heavens and the night became an alien infinity.

Meanwhile, science stands at least a century short of examining the depths of its own psyche. The true Earth scientist who will ultimately speak for us to those in the stars may be wiser and more compassionate than those who presently stand in his place. Hopefully, he will represent a multicultural planet, social and sexual justice, economic and ecological harmony, and a unity of spirit and matter. Perhaps he will also embody such virtues. Until then, we are asking our radio mechanics and some clever computer technicians to speak for us, with all their ethnocentrism, untested humanitarianism, and political naiveté.

And this is only on a matter of prime numbers and a civilized scientific dialogue. It ignores some of the more Gothic science fiction scenarios. What if the beings out there are represented by something more like the Mafia, the Rosicrucians, or some combination of those? What if we are wise and peaceful and they are bellicose? We could end up in much worse trouble and more lonely than before we began to look.

The shapes of our cells and brains and those of extraterrestrials might keep us forever and inalterably strangers, different freaks formed by random undirected processes of selection among stars. In transcending our differences, in overcoming the injustice done to both of us, in facing the cosmic joke together, we may meet sympathetically and discover our true biology and humanity.

Thus far, the entire literature on flying saucer contacts has underwritten the enigma of our own identity and shadow selves more than it has told us who the extraterrestrials are and what they are doing here. The messages ostensibly received from alien spacecraft have been diverse and contradictory. There have been thousands of such reported transmissions since unidentified flying objects became legion in the terrestrial skies at the end of World War II. In 1954, while flying a military aircraft in pursuit of unknown spacecraft, Mel Noel was contacted over a high-frequency VHF channel: "Our crews are made up of individuals from planets known to you as Venus, Jupiter, Mercury, Mars, and Saturn. . . . Life does not and cannot exist on these planets; it's all inside the planets, it's all in the interior, just as the house of the Lord. This is the house of the Lord we live in, the interior of the planet."[1]

He was told that our planet was entering a new cycle in 1958, that there would be earthquakes and erupting volcanoes in the 1980s, "that there would be mass geographical, spiritual, political, economical change as a result of this cycle, and that the planet would be moving from the third to the fourth dimension."[2]

Among the more recent transmissions is a sequence of messages received from spacecraft passing over Sweden in 1975; the occupants of these UFOs claimed to be from planets in the Pleiadian star system. These communications are particularly interesting because they are sensitive to the diplomacy involved in one biological line contacting another within this large physical cosmos. "It is very important," they tell the Earth-beings, "not to think of yourselves as the only case of matter reaching sentience in this creation." A "cosmonaut" identified as Semjasse goes on to say: "We, too, are still far removed from perfection and have to evolve constantly, just like yourselves. We are neither superior nor superhuman. . . . In no case do we come on behalf of anybody, since creation, by itself, confers no obligation on us. It is a law unto itself, and every form of life must conform with it and become a part of it."[3]

Flying saucers, or unidentified flying objects, express the quintessential puzzle of the sky. Their problematic existence combines the various celestial paradoxes in one epiphenomenal event. Occult heavens and astronomical night are brought together, not at one level but at all the different levels on which they are confused. Strange orderly lights and patterns of light streak across the sky. Enormous vehicles land in remote places, and humanoid or alien beings emerge. The vehicles look like two dishes with their tops stuck together, cylinders with chandelier protuberances, gyroscopes, vortex wheels, silver derbies with torus rims, radiant light bodies, or some combination of these. They appear suddenly and disappear just as suddenly. They often register on radar. They have been sighted by experienced pilots, Air Force personnel, and nonbelievers. Occasionally they have seemed responsible for the loss of aircraft. Some individuals claim to have taken trips in UFOs, either willingly or through molestation. Some visitations involve trance states, loss of memory, and sharply divergent reports from two people having the same experience. The whole mystery defies explanation. On one level, it would seem that the saucers cry out for a simple technological resolution, probably an interstellar civilization. On another level, there is no simple explanation. As long as we do not know what reality is or where exactly we are in the dimensions of the universe, things will break in; and this includes not only UFOs but all sorts of psi phenomena, ghosts, and outrageous coincidences. A resolution of the flying saucers may have to wait for the big resolution, of everything.

If the saucers are mechanical spacecraft from other worlds, then they are not visions and are not, per se, of spiritual interest. They are of spiritual consequence only to the degree that the mere existence of alien beings affects our cosmic destiny, or to the degree that the beings who pilot them are spiritually developed or carry authentic prophecy. The planets of the zodiac have clear occult status. They are traditionary transcendent entities. UFOs may yet be, but they have no such standing now. Ultimately they could turn out to be messengers in an astral or supernal realm, creatures of other dimensions, or energies related to the aura. Wilhelm Reich proposed that they are flashes in the orgone envelope of the Earth, and his adherents have stood atop buildings at night to watch the planet charging itself in the bisexual field. But these "phenomena" are still only interpretations in a possible uninvented parapsychology. They have no established spiritual identity.

Because the saucers do not have a firm place in either scientific or spiritual traditions, they necessarily fall in between and exploit the territory between the two. Science cannot accept them as natural phenomena or artificial creations of scientists elsewhere, and the esoteric teaching does not recognize them as divine or astral. But isn't this begging the question? There is, after all, just one creation, and if science is true to its mission, all events that actually happen are finally its responsibility. It may choose to call some things hallucinations or projections, but then it is responsible for an explanation of these. If there are gods or extradimensional forces of any sort, science must find out what these are and place them in its system.

The problem with flying saucers is not their failure to fall into either the spiritual or the physical tradition. It is that they have arisen this late in history, after the religious-scientific division, so they do not have a position already assigned to them. Instead they prey directly on the spiritual-physical split that we have imposed on the present world. That is a most basic feature of their nature. They are no more confusing or uncertain than any other phenomenon in approaching this dichotomy, but they exploit the profound split in our own belief system and thereby receive its full impact. They do not give rise to the split, but the way in which they occur is a symptom of it. They are crude forerunners of a new theory of the universe, and we should consider them with that expectation.

A quick survey of possible interpretations shows the range of the flying saucer phenomenon:

> They are spaceships of beings from another planet, perhaps around another sun or in another galaxy.

> They are vehicles or creatures from another dimension interaccessible to ours. This same explanation has been given for the Yeti and Bigfoot.

> They are clandestine military craft or experimental weapons of terrestrial nations.

> They are local spirit forms or life forms made of energy and light.

> They are psychic phantasms caused by human telepathy or telekinesis.

> They are the visible aspect of an unknown energy.

> They do not exist at all; they are imaginary projections.

Other hypotheses are possible, but these are a diverse assortment to start with. Let us see what their most immediate implications are.

The spaceship hypothesis presumes that the UFOs are mechanical objects powered by some form of energy. They are real vehicles, like our own rockets and planes, only much more advanced. We have pretty much eliminated every planet in this System as a source of humanlike life, with the possible very remote exception of Saturn's moon Titan. Thus, spacecraft most likely must come from beyond the Solar System, or they must also be conceived and operated by an utterly alien life form.

If they come from beyond the Solar System, their technology exceeds ours by more than ours exceeds that of Neolithic man. We can begin to conceptualize interstellar ships, but we are far from being able to construct and launch them. We have no energy source that would carry us to other solar systems; nor can we attain the speeds necessary to get people there in a time even reasonably within the scale of the human lifetime. If the UFOs come from another galaxy, the marvelousness of the technology necessary increases exponentially again.

But what if the saucers do not come from outer space at all, but originate in another dimension outside our perception? It is hard enough to imagine how a universe of three dimensions plus gravity and time came into being. It is impossible to conceive how dimensions themselves came into being. UFOs from other dimensions would make the sky incredibly dense and complicated, with knots and invisible holes. Our existence in what seems to be real physical space would become an hallucination of temporary contingent space, interruptible by laws we do not begin to know.

Already we have an identity crisis over who we are, as individuals, as countries and races, and as a planet. Our problems are complex and usually fatal: nihilism, Nazism, world war, resource depletion, global madness. Any one of these is as all-engulfing as the universe itself. But what if the physical and biological yardsticks are altered? The shock could be either fatal or evolutionary. Mankind could find itself far crazier yet, or it could find itself, period: it could find its cosmic destiny. Perhaps this is what the radical journalist Hunter Thompson meant when he said: "It hasn't gotten weird enough yet." The cosmic is comic. If we survive long enough to laugh, our laughter will be a deep expression of the universe within us, of accepting the creation as it is—despite the very obvious deficiencies we have and the seeming paltriness of life against the whole of matter and the whole of time.

We do not know what UFOs are, so we only dip our feet in this dark cold water. We think about it or we create stories about it. *Close Encounters of the Third Kind* was so powerful a cinematic experience because it tried to put to rest all previous imaginary civilizational contacts and to posit a single real one. But we were cosmic virgins trying just a little bit harder to make our fantasy real.

(At a UFO meeting that I attended in the basement of a bank in Hamtramck, Michigan, in 1966, the gathering was told that it was honored by visitors from Venus and Saturn. I looked around the room, and suddenly everyone appeared strange and extraterrestrial. Everyone was a candidate. Someone said to me that his friend came from Venus. "How do you know?" I asked. "He drives with his eyes closed," he told me.)

Close Encounters was only the latest vicarious experience of the simultaneous realness and unrealness of the aliens. Remember how they looked at the sky without blinking in *It Came From Outer Space*. That was them! They weren't us! Those were the others.

We seem to know that we are in a crisis of meaning and a concurrent moral crisis, and we are ready to risk quite a lot on the hope of new perspective from outside where we are. We are willing to go outside of history in order to get outside of this present historical dead end. We are, at the same time, willing to postpone the debate of whether these epiphenomena are more mortal threats than godsends. We do not even ask ourselves if we are ready. The very shallowness with which we imagine the contact, in various films and other works of planetology and science fiction, suggests that we are not ready. Perhaps this is why it does not happen while it continues to seem to happen. Perhaps this is why the aliens always land in West Virginia or rural Argentina and never on Red Square, the White House lawn, or the United Nations Plaza.

Semjasse, the visitor from the Pleiades, ostensibly told us: "General public contacts are not in our own best interests at this time, and besides, they would not convey a correct significance for the state of mind in which we now exist."[4]

If this sounds mysterious and almost inexplicable, it is probably meant to. The explanations always sound strained, but then we are led to assume that we would not understand the real reason.

Enemy UFOs change the sky into a military zone, the aerospace of the Pentagon—pointed outward toward infinity in terms of the possible source of attack and the nature of the weapons. Or the sky becomes a camouflage for cosmic intrigue. Seeds fall, seeds disguised on meteors landing indistinguishably in the night. But this too is a projection, for so far *we* are the supercivilization developing outer-space weapons. Flying saucers themselves followed World War II and its bomber technology. As we became more cosmic, the threat to us became cosmic. No sooner than the movie *Star Wars* provided us the image of a whole planet annihilated by a "laser" from space, we passed the name on to our own proposed array of Earth-orbiting lasers. We have seen this explosion so often in comic books by now that we are almost inured to its danger.

There have been many science fiction "invasions" of the Earth by antipathetic expansionist peoples, H. G. Wells's *War of the Worlds* being the prototype. *The Invasion of the Body Snatchers* presents a more sinister strategy. What if the aliens should invade from within, like viruses or mental aberrations? If they could invade by spores, they could invade by anything. Some people have even suggested that DNA came to Earth as a spore, accidentally seeded or consciously planted by beings across the Galaxy attempting to spread life. It affects us not at all this far into the "invasion." The situation is like that of a child who worries his own parents are the kidnappers. What recourse is there at that point? And who could have seemed more "Martian" to the residents of Hiroshima and Nagasaki than the Yankee fliers? *The Invasion of the Body Snatchers* expresses mainly our anxiety that we are susceptible to such an invasion and that there is no defense. If we are not safe from one another, then we are not safe from ourselves. And if we are not safe from ourselves, then who are we?

There is also the possibility that flying saucers are illusions or projections of another kind. In the late 1950s, Carl Jung explored the UFO phenomenon and concluded, with some misgivings, that the most important thing about the mysterious craft was not the concrete fact of their existence but the nature of the human projection onto whatever thing (or non-thing) was there. Jung did not dismiss a physical source, but he felt that a great number of sightings were individual projections. Others, involving many viewers, were collective hallucinations. He concluded that something was happening in the human psyche that required Unidentified Flying Objects, and he sought their explanation in that. If they should turn out to be metal ships with sentient passengers, we would still have to work out our projection of things seen in the sky, in this instance in the context of real aliens. We would be seeing both the archetype and the actual vistors from another world. But lovers must also resolve the anima and animus archetypes they project upon each other. The man seeks an ancient sea-nymph in himself, and the woman seeks the wise old man inside her; meanwhile, flesh-and-blood beings make a relationship with each other. [5]

There is a general and ancient tradition on Earth of numinous and fantastic events and entities in the firmament. Because the saucers were associated with intelligent beings in an overseer or savior role, Jung related them to the angelic and divine visitations that occurred under older heavens, especially during periods of widespread anxiety and millennial expectations. If seeing sentient-type objects in the sky is a general human activity, set off by internal psychic or external atmospheric phenomena, then peoples of different cultures would explain such sightings in ways reasonable to them. Even before explanation, they would see the things that required seeing, and this would be true whether physical UFOs existed or not. For instance, during periods of sightings elsewhere in the Southwest, Hopi Indians have observed bluestar kachinas in the night air above the mesas.

We expect the aliens now, enough so that we dream of them and our popular literature is filled with them in all guises. Thus, it is no accident that psychic energies are being transformed into UFO visions—from actual superconscious perceptions considered religious in other ages to fragmented subconscious and hysterical hallucinations of people in crazed states. Jung accepts the collective nature of the human unconscious, and he allows that things occurring in one mind can be transferred telepathically to others, or, more commonly, that forms originate simultaneously in all minds, leading to an intimation of flying saucers

in this case, an intimation which is then projected onto an unknown phenomenon or into a space where nothing exists but
darkness to which it can give form. In terms of the collective
unconscious, the contacts with Saturnians, Jovians, or Centau-
rians share an archetype with the descent of angels in Christian
tradition and with the delivery of tablets to the Mormons by
some sort of astral beings. Different archetypes lead to mass
hysteria about the devil or to sightings of goblins and elves. Or
perhaps these are the shadow forms of the inflated extraterrestrial gods.

After all, in general, the aliens are considered better than
ourselves. People plead with them to deliver us from the conditions we have created, by malice, blunder, or both. After Hiroshima, we began to solicit help from outside. Where else? And we
have been disappointed only by their shyness. The majority of
early reports indicated friendly, even helpful extraterrestrials,
usually anxious to guide the Earth from self-annihilation. For
instance, psychics have claimed (on numerous occasions) that
UFO intervention has prevented a third World War simply by
altering a minor detail in circumstances—a detail so obscure that
it would be overlooked by everyone else and yet so fundamental
that its alteration alone would circumvent an atomic miscalcula-
tion. (Uri Geller claimed a thought implantation by interstellars
into the mind of Anwar Sadat during the 1973 Arab-Israeli War:
the leader need not be a warmonger, and the suggestion need not
be peaceful; it need only be the right impulse at the right moment,
based on an outsider's clearer perception of our situation.)

In Gurdjieff's *All and Everything*, beings from other parts of
the universe visit the Earth and attempt to teach terrestrials how
to overcome the cosmic difficulties of their locale. This "account"
is over 1,200 pages in the English translation from a mixture of
Armenian and Russian, and it is not meant to be fictional in the
usual sense. If these exact aliens did not visit, then their esoteric
others did. Either way, there is a spiritual training that comes
from outer space, and its esoteric form combines arrival in a
spaceship with an indigenous Rosicrucian brotherhood, already
the two poles of the scientific-spiritual dichotomy.

Everything the aliens do is anonymous and secret, and (if they
do not exist) protects the myth of their beneficent presence.

They do not end hunger or brutality; they do not brazenly interfere by using their "superior" machinery. They do the bare minimum, or we feign the bare minimum in their name to allow some other part of ourselves to come into being by projection and externalization. Even when they come with prophecies of earthquakes and erupting volcanoes, or upheavals of government, they reassure us that we have entered a natural cosmic cycle—in, say, 1958 or 1969—and that we will be through it by 2025 or 2107. They tell us that they are Venusians or Saturnians and that their own planets have come through a similar cosmic evolution. They tell us they travel between galaxies by a space-time warp. And we try to understand what they mean by this, and whether it comes from us or them.

As we saw earlier, Erich von Daniken posits that UFOs are true outer-space craft perceived by ancient humanity as gods and mythic beings because of their own collective primitivity. [6] By this materialist and supertechnological interpretation of the universe, religion itself becomes a system arising only from the misinterpretation of the visitations of aliens. The extraterrestrial "gods" become the magicians and shamans of primitive tribes from whom we inherit imitations of alien psychic powers. And we await their return, this time ready to deal instead of worship.

> Ancient religious mythology [wrote Norman Davidson] placed higher intelligences among the stars. Modern scientific mythology places higher intelligences among the stars. The gods have become extraterrestrial civilizations. [7]

Von Daniken leaves us with a difficult problem: so powerfully has he posed his own blonde Charioteers of the Gods, so compellingly has he redefined the Egyptian and Mesoamerican civilizations, that we now find it difficult to look at the artifacts on the surface of Mars (for example) without assuming they are "accomplices" in von Daniken's cosmic plot. Even though these anomalous objects were discovered independently on NASA data tapes by scientists with little sympathy for von Daniken, many reject the "Face" and "city" out of hand because they seem mere projections of the "ancient astronaut" theory.

The astronomer Robert Temple has noted that the Dogon

people of Africa apparently inherited from their ancestors un-
cannily precise information about the star Sirius, notably that it
has a dark companion circling it every fifty years. Scientists were
unable to observe this companion until 1970, so there is a real
question about how the Dogon came by this information and
whether it is real information or a coincidence between a native
myth and a scientific observation. Temple himself pursues the
most obvious fantasy. The ancestors of the Dogon were visited
by beings from the star system of Sirius sometime around 4500
B.C., and they were taught these facts, which they integrated as
mythology, in keeping with their assumption that the visitors
were gods. Temple goes on to show that much of the esoteric
knowledge of the Egyptians, which forms the basis for parts of
the hermetic and magical traditions in the West, has connections
with the Sirius material. The ancestors of the Dogon were not
the only contactees. Other information, from a visitation in Su-
meria, was passed on through Near Eastern mystery cults and
continued into the Middle Ages.[8]

Robert Anton Wilson takes this possibility to its limits in his
book *Cosmic Trigger.*[9] The occult material of the Sirius connection lodges in the olden mystery cults and continues to the present as a fundamental aspect of the hermetic-Rosicrucian doctrine and the Golden Dawn, and by other paths through
alchemy, anthroposophy, and Sufism, so that Crowley, Reich,
and Gurdjieff are all modern disciples of the Sirians. The hermetic material is our most fundamental magical instruction. It
is concerned directly with higher orders of being, intelligence
elsewhere in the universe, ritual contact and influence, awakening humanity from its present troubled sleep, and invoking
spirits and controlling events superconsciously and telepathically.

The Sirians, then, are enlightened visitors. If, hypothetically,
their wisdom lies behind Sufism, the Golden Dawn, and alchemy, and also an interstellar capacity (as evidenced by their journey to Earth), then the scientific and magical must have joined
into a single force for them and is being transmitted as a unified
knowledge to us. The alternative is that primitive societies have
embedded the scientific Sirian message in their own native occult systems.

If our esoteric tradition originated in the Sirian star-system, then the Earth forfeits its intrinsic responsibility for generating its own mystical systems. The consequence is the same as the one which follows from von Daniken's chariots of the gods: once we assume the existence of wiser teachers from elsewhere in the remote past, we undermine our own achievements and their indigenous local meanings, and we become addicted to future contact. And if we allow that the Rosicrucian and alchemical message was brought here from another solar system, we must admit that the postindustrial science that will allow interstellar travel in the distant future is very much like the occult sciences we have abandoned. Telepathic communication, teleportation, and faster-than-light speeds take on new meaning in alliance with homoeopathy, alchemy, and astral travel.

Ultimately, Wilson finds the UFO visitations interesting but not essential. Once we admit the hermetic-technological synthesis, it is no longer necessary to assume that astronauts came here at the dawn of history. The advanced beings in the star system of Sirius could have other ways to send us their knowledge. They could project it in visions. It is not that these messages would surpass the speed of light; they would be irrelevant to it because they would contain information passing instantaneously between sentiences. Thought influencing matter, faster-than-light messages, synchronicity, and parallel universes have all been suggested as resolutions of the contradictions contained in quantum mechanics. If the extremely confusing conditions of quantum theory are to stand as posed, then something else must change. We must give up the pure boundary of the speed of light, or the simple dimensional framework of events in time and space, or the forward flow of time, or the separation of mind and matter. And if quantum theory is not to stand, we have problems at least as great as these. The nature of mind and matter, with or without interstellar travel, and of UFOs, with or without the Sirians, hangs in the balance here.[10]

Wilson also mentions the fairly remarkable experimental results claimed by electronics engineer L. George Lawrence in Oak Grove Park, California, in 1971. Lawrence's study was unconventional to begin with: he was using electronic equipment to study the behavior of plants as receptors of biological signals.

Tapping oak trees, cacti, and yuccas, he intended only to pick up signals transmitted across the desert. However, with his device pointed inadvertently at the sky, he received regular pulses that lasted anywhere from a few minutes to hours. Given the precise terms of the experiment as stated by Lawrence, the only conclusion, shocking as it was, was that signals were being sent from out in the galaxy in such a way that they would be received by the preconscious cellular fabric.[11] If these messages reach plants unconsciously, then what could be the effects on human beings, who have so many more cells of such greater complexity? Data from higher civilizations throughout the universe could be seeding our neural systems, and all of human wisdom could be a latent response to those signals. We would live, then, not in our own cities, but in replicas of cities on the other side of the universe. Likewise, we should not be surprised to find them—or ourselves—there.

Lawrence repeated his experiment with plants at the Pisgah Crater in the Mojave Desert. The crater itself lies in the center of lava beds without any plant life for thirty miles around. Not only did he pick up additional signals, but the signals appeared strongest in the direction of Ursa Major, leading him to wonder if they might not be spillover from the dense star center of the Galaxy.[12]

Lawrence called these signals "an apparent train of interstellar communication signals of unknown origin and destination."[13] They are not the standard radio and electrical signals that man has sought as evidence of intelligent life in the universe. They are *biological* communications. The inference is not that they are messages aimed at the Earth, but that the universe itself is filled with this kind of "radiation," like a vast unconscious mind-net. The consequences of receiving the signals are unknown. Their purpose is obviously unknown, and no doubt even the meaning and accuracy of the experiment is unknown. Lawrence followed a logical sequence. He made many unconventional assumptions, and his proposition can be attacked from numerous vantages. It is a very leaky boat to set out anywhere in.

But that need not concern us here, for we are working with the images and projections. Experiments with plants yield inexplicable signals. The equipment is aimed at the sky. There are regular pulses with a seeming center of origin. Suddenly we are in a galactic jungle. The wild grasses and dense forests of the Earth are blown not just by the wind and receive not just the photosynthetic sunlight; they are also touched unconsciously by interstellar signals, which reach us too. To cells which are blind and virtually senseless, the sky is a din of "noise" and "light." The stars are fields of flowers too. Perhaps the vegetation of this world broadcasts its own chlorophyl-language secrets into a vast cosmic Intelligence.

It is our famous, unvoiced hope that the peoples of the universe are joined, even though they may never know of one another, and even though they may never come to each other as astronauts; they are engaged in the same cosmic archetypes, local representations of which their lives and artifacts portray. And they are joined by the possibility of unconscious signals among all living things. In fact, plants and animals and cells may compose a vast unconscious field that receives the collective wisdom of the universe through an inner sky—higher centers of being engulfing all the lesser provinces of night. One occultist, Douglas Baker, even proposes, quite apart from Robert Temple's hypothesis, that if the Earth and Sun lie at the heart of a giant cosmic being, then the star system of Sirius is his third eye. It is entirely appropriate that wisdom should flow from the third eye to the heart, and perhaps back from the heart to the third eye. Compared to the night skies of astronomy and astrophysics, this loom is very rich, both harmonic and harmonious.

It is also very confusing. Once we open the framework of the universe to this degree, we are everywhere and nowhere. The night sky has vanished. It has turned into a nerve-filled skin, a synapse of the cosmos. The source of our own traditions, or their many sources, become blurred and distorted. Why need the information have come from Sirius? Could it not have come from the unknown vaults of space itself? Could it not have originated somehow within ourselves? If our unconscious mind is merged with the unconscious mind of a cosmic being traced in the sky, how do we tell anymore what is terrestrial and what is extraterrestrial? How do we distinguish between unconscious information and objective external events? How can we distinguish between our own intentions and directions and the general mesh of cosmic entities? The information about the dark companion of Sirius is really minor compared to these problems.

The interstellar brotherhood and the sentient sky are hints of another way of thinking and being. Long before their puzzles can be resolved, they reveal both the extent of our hope and the intricacy of our cosmic paranoia. There are some madmen among us who obviously think that Humpty-Dumpty can be put back together again, and that the universe that lies around us in pieces is a mirage. They would have astrophysics lead back finally to the third eye and the lineage of Hermes Trismegistos. Or they would have the gnostic and hermetic rituals lead eventually to a new galactic science, one that would carry us both into the heavens and the esoteric meaning of the human ceremony. Like astronomers before Copernicus, they would place the throne out among the fixed stars; but unlike the pre-Copernicans, they would do so in full understanding of the atomic nature and mortality of those stars.

Something is meant by all this. It may not be, as Timothy Leary has said, that the Sirian science is a blueprint for life-extension and space-migration, ultimately carrying us to the makers themselves, though he has commented that he fully expects to be alive when the Sun burns itself out in a cinder. It does portend that spacecraft and UFOs are not the crowning revelations in a theory of interstellar civilization. We are driven back into cellular and symbolic material, as we were by creation itself in the making of us, to reach the remotest stars. Or we find that we are already there, lacking only the courage to see ourselves for who we are. We are the aliens we fear. We are the body snatchers, the invaders. We need no visitors to teach us the cosmic truth. We need not travel to reach the ends of space and time.

In recent years, the nature of UFOs has changed dramatically, and, although we have not returned to Wells's Martian invaders or even pure body-snatchers, we are faced with perhaps more insidious versions of both. Two current events mark the transition: cattle mutilations and abductions by aliens. It is possible that both of these activities (certainly the latter) occurred with some frequency before the last two decades, but the recent episodes seem so widespread and ominous that they suggest a fundamental change in the alien presence. Either we are being visited by different aliens, by the same aliens with revised agendas, or we are suffering a new collective fragmentation of personality.

When flying saucers first appeared globally in the late forties, the general assumption was that they were experimental military craft originating on the Earth: Russian, American, or transnational. This was a major premise on which the Air Force opened Project Bluebook. For the optimistic fifties and sixties, ready to welcome the aliens, such a proposition was right-wing paranoia, but it has gained a new credibility coming from the prominent Jacques Vallee, the French computer scientist on whom the researcher in *Close Encounters* was based.

Vallee argues that a paramilitary organization could have come into being in the aftermath of World War II. He does not identify the group or their goals, but concludes that their activities are an attempt to brainwash mankind into believing in UFOs. This camouflage is either meant to prepare people for some event on a global scale (which this organization is planning) or to distract general attention from terrestrial to extraterrestrial phenomena in order to disguise the organization's operations by associating them with aliens. Its goal is some particular destiny for humanity. This alarms Vallee because he feels we know little or nothing about these people, and their activities behind the UFO cover seem manipulative and self-serving. They use, he says, a psychotronic technology, that is, an advanced technological science whose "machines" project mind-altering images that make people think they have seen certain things. With psychotronics, people may report sighting a UFO, being taken aboard, making contact with aliens, and traveling to other planets or star systems—when all these activities are actually thought patterns broadcast from an airborne craft or ground station.[14]

Visitors from outer space could have psychotronic technology also. If such a disguise were used by either aliens or unknown terrestrial groups, UFOs could be mind-waves on a global scale, creating in people the sense that something is happening at the same time that the forces behind the projection are doing something else. It is as though a demonic star-form were projecting a ray from the heavens and creating in its victims another fantasized sky from which come spacecraft carrying aliens; these aliens then take the victims for an imaginary ride. Like the old astral travelers, the kidnapped "go" to planets and stars and visit people there. The images they see are not their own unconscious ones; instead, they are science fiction stories that someone else has written for the occasion and to which chosen contactees are submitted. Following the Freudian laws of thought, the tales and their images will carry something of the person's own personality structure and unconscious needs—but the primary narrative will be manipulated. It will be an outer-space fantasy created either by fellow Earth-beings or by aliens, from unknown motives. Of course, some yogis even claim that the whole life we live is such a post-hypnotic suggestion.

Vallee called the psychotronic masters "messengers of deception." *They* are the UFO phenomenon (there are possibly no extraterrestrials). This same intelligence organization, he claimed, is responsible for the bizarre mutilation of livestock globally. Since the early 1970s, primarily dead cattle have been discovered surgically disfigured. The area most affected has been in Colorado and Wyoming. There have been reports, however, from throughout the United States and South America, with hundreds of additional cases in Western Europe. In each incident, a sheep, a cow, or sometimes another creature has had its sexual organs removed. The incisions have been made with an extremely sharp surgical instrument, apparently by intruders who arrived in some sort of flying vehicle, leaving no "footprints." In the most affected areas, local people have been disturbed by both the ghoulish phenomenon and its seeming senselessness. Unusual precautions have been taken, guards have been posted, but still the animals are attacked and the intruders escape unseen. Sometimes the cattle are lifted to a height above the ground and then smashed by being dropped. In one case, a cavity inside the sexual organs was packed with sand after mutilation. The people may realize that something extraordinary is happening, but they are like any primitive population subjected to the activities of an advanced technology. It little matters that they live in the most technological nation in the history of the Earth. They sense their inferiority and lack of control, which is exactly what the mutilators intend, Vallee tells us.[15]

There seems to be no way that any known group could carry

out these slaughters. They require not only elaborate airborne machinery ostensibly well out of the range of most occult and Satanic organizations, but also worldwide implementation, which would suggest collaboration on a scale heretofore un-imaginable. It is a scheme that any nation would have difficulty carrying out. Some unknown factor, perhaps psychotronic, al-lows persons or entities to steal in directly under guard, like the invisible spellbinding thieves of mythology, to carry out their deeds. In fact, cattle have been mutilated and deposited right at the heavily guarded gateway to NORAD, the Rocky Mountain missile-defense center. Both the skill of this foray and the choice of target suggest to Vallee a direct military dare or diversionary tactic. But this is because there seems to be no purpose to the cattle mutilations, and one instinctively seeks a purpose. It is too unsettling to think that somehow these events just happen; circumstantial evidence links them to the UFOs in some way. The one mystery engulfs the other. The psychotronic smoke-screen seems the only likely way that daredevils could carry out their brazen acts. But once we accept that possibility, we are almost tempted to suggest that the mutilations themselves could be psychotronic or paranormal physical events.

It is our failure to come up with any other explanation that has lent credence to the paramilitary psychotronic hypothesis. But why should we trust Vallee? Might he not be covering for extra-terrestrials by proposing a transnational diversionary tactic in exactly the same way that he claims the mysterious intelligence community is covering its own activities by saucers and livestock disfigurement? Would that not be more in keeping with his earlier work?

Either way, Vallee has rightly pointed out how the mutilations cast a pall over the whole UFO phenomenon. At a time when cults are proclaiming the goodness of our space brethren and some are likening them to the famous Brothers of the Rosy Cross who secretly visited Western Europe during the troubled seventeenth century, the new image of malevolent or prankish surgeons is a shock and a disappointment. Such beings are nei-ther benevolent nor rational. All that distinguishes them from the average canine scavenger is the advanced instruments they use and the scale and whimsy of their operations. Not only are such activities seemingly pointless, they are cruel. What else can we now expect from creatures who cross millions of miles or light-years to come to our planet and, without notifying us of their arrival, disfigure harmless and helpless domestic animals? It is not a reassuring scenario. It is almost easier to blame it on ourselves and leave outer space to more compassionate and intelligent beings. Vallee's choice of an Earth-based operation comes in part from an essential incredulity that this kind of thing makes any sense in extraterrestrial terms. But then, it doesn't make sense in any terms.

Not everyone accepts this pessimistic interpretation. On a number of rural Southwestern communes, members have regularly observed UFOs, and some have claimed communication, either spiritual or person-to-person, with alien beings. They remain uniformly convinced that these beings are well-meaning and wise, and that they are monitoring the Earth for our own good, presiding, like the communes themselves, over the transition of our society from primitive violence to global sharing. The aliens have ostensibly explained their bizarre activity. It is neither mindless nor pointlessly sadistic, but a scientific operation to detect radioactive pollutants in the areas where the samples are taken, pollutants that might lodge in the genitals. In fact, the trail of the cattle mutilations reported in Colorado appears to follow the watershed. Thus, the aliens would be checking runoff to see how afflicted the soils are. Other people, however, think that this same operation is being carried out by the CIA for the same purpose.

The radicals of our own culture find their counterparts in more advanced beings from other worlds, thus legitimizing and explaining their own existence on the edge of society and at the edge of history and giving themselves a cosmic image to work toward in their daily lives. Likewise, the apocalyptic rejection of nuclear energy becomes associated, through the insoluble mystery of mutilated animals, with the peaceful outer-space brotherhood. The mutilations prove that our nuclear activities are a profound violation, with long-term consequences of radiation in the environment. People so much more advanced than we are seem to think so. One violation calls into play another. The mutilations and the nuclear activity cancel each other out as two uncomfortable signals, but with one justifying the other, leaving someone more intelligent and powerful keeping watch.

But all of this is wild supposition, and though it is interesting and in some ways appealing, its simplicity is discouraging—as if the whole phenomenon resolved down to a Hardy Boys mystery. Even Vallee has rejected his own supposition in recent years, acknowledging that the UFO phenomenon is too ubiquitous and complex for such a heavy-handed scam. The sheer number of reports defies any terrestrial explanation, and the seemingly pointless and irreconcilable behavior of the "aliens" is in contradiction to the high technology needed to cross outer space. Creatures able to move so far so fast and to conceal their tracks so well clearly do not require animal dissections to get data on our contamination. They could probably draw this information—as well as our whole immunological history—from remote-distance blood-probes. And, as Richard Hoagland has pointed out, they likely have advanced enough genetic engineering to replicate biological materials too.[16]

In his more recent lectures, Vallee has suggested that a transdimensional origin for UFOs fits the facts better than an outerspace or indigenous terrestrial one. Aliens from another plane could manifest equally as meteorological apparitions or channelled messages, with the distinction being one of more ontological significance to us than to them. The science fiction writer Ian Watson draws on this new level of paradox in his book *Miracle Visitors*,[17] inventing aliens who work simultaneously through spaceships, psychotronic devices, parapsychological experiments, dreams, shamans, mediums, and the traditional occult. As the story develops, his characters are not able to tell which events actually happened and which were implanted by suggestion. Even their "validated" metallic vehicles are phantasms. Or how else can the main character deal with being driven to the Moon in a red Ford Thunderbird by a "tortoise."

Perhaps it is true that the harder we try to force our way through the paradoxes by ingenuity, the deeper into nonsense we will go. It is hardly an enlightened path to come by, but here surely we approach both Hinduism and Zen.

Abductions of Earthlings by extraterrestrials in spaceships have been reported periodically for the last forty years, and certain pre-UFO events can be construed as abductions if we take into account their cultural context. However, descriptions of these incidents have had such a phantasmagoric quality to them that they have generally been dismissed as dreams or other kinds of out-of-the-body experiences. Even the famous Betty and Barney Hill kidnapping has a peculiarly flaccid quality to it in their retelling, as if more a trance or fugue than a brutal invasion of person. However, accounts from the late 1980s, particularly Whitley Strieber's *Communion* and Budd Hopkins's *Intruders*, are anything but vague somnambulations. The victims give dramatic, often horrifying descriptions not only of abductions by aliens but ensuing medical exams with mutilation. The memory of these episodes is routinely suppressed by the intruders, to be recovered only under hypnosis.

It is hard to gauge whether these abductions themselves have increased, or whether the wool has suddenly been pulled from our eyes. Certainly if the encounters are anesthetized by the perpetrators, then any number of them could have occurred throughout history with the only traces being symbolic and fragmentary memories of something else. These new books, however, have raised public consciousness about the phenomenon, so that increasing numbers of people with haunting and incomplete memories have volunteered for regressive hypnosis and have uncovered traces of what certainly seem to be intimate encounters of more than the third kind. Perhaps the most shocking aspect of this is that the accounts (like the mutilations) are consistent worldwide. So, once again, we are dealing either with collective hallucination or actual experience.

The current recruitment of "abductee support groups" corroborates the desire of these people to be taken seriously, to be regarded as kidnap victims rather than story-tellers. For the most part these are not psychically inclined individuals, and, to a one, they insist that they didn't choose to be kidnapped, nor was the event a psychedelic tea-party. They out and out reject any fantasy explanation, and they warn the rest of us to take heed:

"This is a major failsafe event. When policemen, housewives, and other citizenry minding their own business are swept up into vehicles, submitted to invasive exams, and mind-zapped, everyone should open their windows and bang pots and pans before it is too late. Each of us could be seized and compromised at any time. We are all under attack."

Strieber could not have been more graphic as he described his clothes thrown about the floor, his legs drawn apart, and an "extremely ugly object, gray and scaly, with a sort of network of wires on the end" inserted into his rectum where "it seemed to swarm...as if it had a life of its own..... I had the impression that I was being raped...."[18]

In his descriptions and those of others, these creatures are small humanoids, either doll- or robot-like. They have wide expressionless faces and black, slanted almond-shaped eyes. Strieber recalls them moving like an army so that their hands on him in the examination felt "as if I were being passed along by rows of insects."[19] He also describes their odor as being of something alive but not human, sour with a hint of cardboard and cinnamon. They seemed to him fragile, dependent on their numbers and technology, as if they had captured a Bigfoot and were handling it delicately.

He notes their dispassionate mien but also what looks like occasional bemused jollity. He describes an utter terror at being controlled and examined by them but also a sense that no harm would come to him. He wavers between malevolent and benevolent interpretations and ultimately comes out in favor of the latter. He ponders a prognosis of induced hallucination but feels that the creatures themselves are exogenous (from wherever they arise) and thus must be confronted and judged as real beings:

> This is not a "mere" matter, to be explained away by one facile dodge or another. It is an immense human reality, vast in its impact and complexity....
>
> Something is here, be it a message from the stars or from the booming labyrinth of the mind...or from both. It must have left a signature somewhere, a thread in the snow, the scratch of a strange nail upon a wall.... In taking the thread we might find ourselves in possession of a very real key to the universe....
>
> And we will all go down the labyrinth, to meet whatever awaits us there.[20]

Budd Hopkins recruited his candidates for hypnotic regression mostly from people who had the experience of "missing time," that is, of losing the thread of their memory in one time or place and picking it up discontinuously in another, with no explanation of what happened in between. The accounts he took exposed a widespread and provocative form of alien intrusion, at least as disturbing as the animal mutilations. Numerous women (and a few men) described quasi-sexual encounters with the "same" aliens that kidnapped Strieber (at least, their "camouflage" was the same). The encounters were not sexual in the manner of Aphrodite's seduction of Anchises; instead, they recalled Strieber's exam: the men had sperm removed, the woman were mechanically impregnated. Seven or eight months later the women were abducted again and their babies were sucked out of them by machine and taken away. Actual bodily scars and excruciating discomfort upon recall testify to some real event. In a few cases, discernible burns and other spaceship landing marks appeared on the ground in the vicinity of the incident.

These kidnappings are sealed from memory by luminous and impenetrable images, usually animals, phantasmal beasts that suggest in every way they are more than they seem, that guard the gates to a great mystery. Strieber, for instance, describes a barn owl staring at him through the window, an owl that left no tracks in the snow. A woman recalls a beautiful deer, losing time, then blood on her blouse, a scar. A man describes seeing "a bunch of rabbits hopping around outside his car." Then nothing.[21]

When Hopkins leads Kathie Davis to the traumatic moment of the theft of her baby, she begins to wail:

"It's not right, it's not fair! IT'S NOT FAIR. IT'S MINE! (Sobbing) I *HATE* YOU *I HATE YOU*! IT'S NOT FAIR!"[22]

She describes the pain, a feeling of being squashed, of being opened like a flower.

When she had calmed down somewhat, I asked if they— those who had done this to her—ever told her why, ever offered a reason? She answered in a coldly angry voice: "No." I asked if she ever said anything to them, ever told them that it was cruel, that they had no right to take her baby. She spoke to me almost in a whisper, calmly furious: "I screamed it at them." Then, in a sad, ironic mix of incomprehension and profound personal loss, she added this: "And the fucker looked surprised."[23]

As we have already observed, it is impossible to assign meanings or contexts to these events. We are dependent on the veracity and objectivity of the authors and publishers of the books as well as basic validity of the content. In a business in which Carlos Castaneda is routinely accused of making up Don Juan Matus, we cannot any longer be too cautious. However, the consistency of many of these accounts with one another gives a check that we do not have with Castaneda. Strieber's earlier "science fiction" and "ecocatastrophe" writings might cast some suspicion on the motivation behind *Communion*, but as Strieber himself has pointed out, such encounters with aliens have happened all his life (and been blocked by post-hypnotic suggestions); thus, his other writings do not lead up to *Communion*; they and it issue from the same underlying event. He cites the verification by the "hypnotic regression" process, but not every psychiatrist would concur.

Accepting these episodes as "real" in some sense, we are left grasping for the nonexistent common thread, the integrating theme. How do cattle mutilations and baby stealing go together? How do we square seemingly benign nonmanipulative aliens with the compassionless, intrusive humanoids described by Hopkins? Are they the same creatures operating under different aliases? Are they totally different phenomena? What does the lovely and very typically human lady from the Pleiades (Semjasse) have to do with Strieber's insectlike familiars? And most crucial of all perhaps, why are they all humanoid?

The impregnations and the Face on Mars speak, in different ways, to this one enigma. As Richard Hoagland puts it succinctly:

> Either these features on Mars are natural and this investigation is a complete waste of time, or they are artificial and this is one of the most important discoveries of our entire existence on Earth. If they are artificial it is imperative that we figure them out, because they 'do not belong there.' Their presence may be trying very hard to tell us something extraordinary.[24]

So is Kathie Davis.

The Face does not belong at Cydonia because it is humanoid. Assuming life could not have evolved on Mars (and if it had that it wouldn't have looked like us), the Face must have been put there by people who had significant prehistoric contact with us or who are actually related to us, i.e., genetically involved with the human race. This brings us to that other "impossibility": that aliens could be interfertile and breeding with humans. Not only could aliens not be interfertile with us, they shouldn't even carry DNA.... unless some primeval event once brought our fledgling species into the most intimate of all contact with space-travelers.

Given our affinity to the other animals on this planet, it is ridiculous to suppose that we could be the pure offspring of aliens. But it is not *as* impossible that we are the result of an alien-conducted breeding experiment with primates, an experiment apparently still in progress. It doesn't explain why the aliens are primate-like to begin with, but then normal biological rules seem suspended anyway. Impregnation by extraterrestrials, hybrid babies, and a Face on Mars are all biology-busting. If they are real, they cry out for explanation—with terrestrial science hanging in the balance.

Why, for instance, would Betty Hills's aliens, who were careful enough to disguise and hypnotically "erase" all traces of their intrusion, blatantly reveal a starmap identifying their home system as the double-star Zeta Reticulii (33 light-years away)? Why would these super-technicians leave "erased" memories susceptible to amateur hypnosis anyway? It is almost as though they mean for us to discover them. Or is it that they mean for us to think they mean for us to think ... etc.? Is it their intention to delude us as to where they originate because, for some reason, we must not know? Or do they mean only for us to *suspect* them of the same? What is the game here, and is it alien-directed or in our minds?

Hoagland feels the cattle mutilations must finally be more symbolic than scientific. The aliens, he muses, might want us to connect the themes of blood, genitals, genes, and sacred cows, even as they want us to puzzle about humanoids on Mars:

> It is my opinion that the bewildering, contradictory, even irrational behavior of the "UFO phenomenon" over the past forty or so years has been a carefully calculated "recent" strategy whose true intent is nothing less than direct "mass psychological manipulation" of terrestrial populations. ..."they" apparently have been attempting through a superior technology to insinuate themselves in all levels of our human consciousness for years—
>
> As representatives of our "creator"—if not as "gods" themselves![25]

We could propose an alien attempt to strengthen their own frail stock by breeding or cloning our apelike, "primitive" genes. We could propose a renegade colony on Mars, later "mating" with terrestrials in order to migrate here through mutated offspring. These sorts of wonders require an incredible genetic engineering, but then to cross interstellar space requires an equally incredible physics. By this explanation no wonder Kathie Davis's abductor looked surprised. Does the scientist ever permit his lab animal to show "human" emotions, to claim personal rights?

But then who is Semjasse to Hamlet, et al.? She tells an entirely different story, one that has nothing to do with the almond-eyed intruders or baby-theft—a tale of intergalactic empires and lost tribes; she is generally upbeat and spiritual, not unlike Ramtha or Seth in her New Age advice. She poses stylishly for cameras and allows her very metallic spaceship to be photographed too. But still she keeps her visits to one remote rural area of Denmark and to one uneducated and possibly psychopathic contactee, Billy Meier.

Hoagland feels there is more likely a link between her and the Face, for her tale of interstellar exile and a colony on Mars 500,000 years ago matches the approximate dating for the complex at Cydonia (as well as the age of Pithecanthropus, the closest model for the Face). Semjasse at least provides a possible scenario for Pleiadian visits to the prehistoric Earth and subsequent genetic experiments with hominids. The Face would thus be a monument to the connection between the Earth and the Galaxy; direct investigation of it would be crucial to our further evolution (remember C. S. Lewis's "silent planet" and Arthur Clarke's monolith on the Moon and moons of Jupiter).

The other thing about the Face is that it is there: Semjasse and the willowy buglike creatures come and go in shadow, but we can visit Cydonia in the flesh and confirm a concrete alien presence. In fact, Hoagland toys with the notion that the precise purpose of the Face is to lead us to the UFO connection in a way that does not overwhelm us and lets us explore the universe by our own powers and come to our own conclusions. It is our body that lands on "their" world, not the other way around.

Our deepest fears may be evasions of beauty. Perhaps someday

we will understand why the extraterrestrials sit over us in judgement, and try to save us, and frighten us, and fail in their contact
with us, and steal from us, and give us strange gifts—why this
world is an isolated and dark place, why we are born here helpless
and afraid (no, Velikovsky is not explanation enough). Perhaps
we are the night, the sky, and the rest of it is fields of golden
flowers and astral levity, on to eternity.

25

The Pop Star Cult
of the Fifties
and Sixties

THE LEGACY of World War II was the atom bomb, and those born then and in the eras thereafter lived under the omen of the air-raid sirens. Mounted on lampposts in the cities and on fire stations and barns in the country, they were the Cyclopes of our time, and they screamed for our blood. We were born into postwar prosperity, and our elders demanded gratitude for a bounty neither they nor we understood. They pretended to be giving us a gift for which they slaved all their lives, but they laid false claim to an unknown history, and, in any case, their other oblation was a dearth of meaning, a pathological greed and mistrust. They continue to dismantle the Earth.

The sirens warned us of another holocaust for which the atom bomb was an emblem. For all the times they accidentally went off, we still survived into the sixties. By then it was clear that the threat was fundamental. We had forgotten that the Earth was a planet, so strong had artificial reality become. Collective pollution, overpopulation, and consumption of the world would lead to holocaust too. The threat was so much more serious because it did not rest on any one episode like Eisenhower's shelling of Quemoy or Kennedy's blockade of Cuba. No single confrontation resolved our destiny. It was everything we were. And the nuclear war we seemed to have evaded, against the odds, was happening to us anyway, as radiation leaked into the rivers and the air, and Joan Baez sang *"What have they done to the rain?"*

This was the dark Plutonian half of the era, when a star cult began, like the one that visited the Southeast Indian tribes during the Mississippian Era of the thirteenth century. We had no temple mounds or imported Aztec jewelry, but the candy stores of the nation were filled with colored trading cards of Flash Gordon and the Martian princesses and warlords. Baseball cards came too as totems, figureheads on bright yellow and blue backgrounds, the insignias of dark brown cubs and of orange cardinals on a sprig. They were totem beings, and they generated the full zodiac of baseball statistics. Many young occultists and radical astrologers were trained in the first level of meditation and evocation by these cards and walked their first astral pathways through those blue and orange skies.[1] This was not the legacy of the generation before us, which was prepared only to turn sports figures and pop musicians into industries, convert the star symbols into cash, and join zombie armies which now waged magical war for the planet on both sides of the Iron Curtain. Why else, years later, were the Beatles in Eastern Europe singing *"Back in the USSR"?* The star-cult was our only antidote to planetary invaders who pretended to be our benefactors and our protectors and who enlisted half of our generation in their cause.

The filmmaker Kenneth Anger describes returning to the United States in 1962 after eight years in Europe, and spending the first part of that summer at Coney Island on the beach under the boardwalk. There the kids sat playing their transistor radios; the early rock music was a magical transmission, recalling Jean Cocteau's *Orpheus* and the radio in Death's car on which the poet-hero also listened to the broadcasts of another world.[2] Cocteau's radio was a prophecy of a mutant generation. *"Fools rush in,"* sang Ricky Nelson, and the stars flickered over the sea at the tip of the New World city. Years later, dark berserk warriors were to arise from the shadows of this astral music. The costume angels were kicked out of the heavens, as Richard Alpert warned they would be, before he became Baba Ram Dass. We can enter the wedding party on such a high as a guest, but we *cannot stay there*. Near Pearl Harbor, John Lennon's killer-to-be handed Kenneth Anger three .38 slugs, marking the end of the ceremony. *"And though I know the danger there,"* sang Ricky Nelson, *"if there's a chance for me, then I don't care."*

It is impossible to forget the rocket launchings of the fifties and sixties against the rich tradition of science fiction that preceded them. Ten, nine, eight, seven, six. . . . For years afterward, lying awake at night, seeing those spaceships depart the planet. . . . Ignition, liftoff, *t* minus two seconds—and then fiery separation before the main stage darted past stray clouds through the blue sky into the night beyond. In that blackness lay everything the world was not. Before the Buddha came to America, it was our only hope.

In first grade, I had a fantasy saucer in which I went to the planets of the Solar System and those of other stars. By the time I was twelve, I had met with imaginary beings all over the universe and had helped found whole civilizations with my friends. At night, I would see my saucer picking up waves of speed as it transcended time and space, and with that thrust my mind would rush forward into images, and finally sleep.

There was a star-cult because we needed a star-cult, and a star-cult alone would do. We were born into a tremendous heat and a prophecy. We knew that we were going to be something different because the world had become absurd. The passion we felt went beyond anything we could feel the passion for, so we transformed each other into angels and messengers, and we listened to the interstellar debris.

The signals passed into the night and began their movement toward the stars. From radio stations in New Orleans and the American South, they penetrated the Caribbean and gave a voice to the reggae music of the Rastafarian revival. It didn't matter what the words said. The intention of the sound was clear. To the Rastafarians it said: kill the Pope; return to Africa; Haile Selassie, Emperor of Ethiopia, reigns, an immortal star-king. It was an astral message twisting slang pop English to its purposes, and it could as easily have been a Japanese song about a fisherman or a Zulu chant to a lion.

"Go, go, go Johnny go! Go, go Johnny go!" sang Chuck Berry, and a billion years from now, again, when alien creatures find this cut on the Voyager disk somewhere on the other side of the Galaxy, they may be less puzzled than the generation of elders

who suspected a danger hidden in the sound and who sought
both to choke and exploit it in its infancy. In the end, we returned it to unknown stellar entities.

"*I'll build a stairway to heaven,*" sang Neil Sedaka. "*I'll climb
to the highest star.*"

The night sky and the astral heavens were both hidden from
us, born as we were in the darkness of cities among those who
had torn down their own temples. We knew intuitively that *star*
and *night* were esoteric words that unlocked secret realms. We
knew, in fact, more than those who wrote the songs. When the
heavens cried out for their "stars above," and tens of thousands
of jukeboxes and radios wailed variants of the word *love,* didn't
we understand that our whole civilization was praying for the
return of the gods, the return of those powers within us that had
brought us into being?

Yes, it is *love which brings us here* and *love which gives us life.*

Yes, we stand, every man and every woman, within the stars.

Who else has survived the incredible galactic and atomic violence to be here for a day of song?

When the old prayers are lost, tribes reinvent offerings out
of the rubble and static. The gods are no less attentive.

Bobby Darin called his *"Dream Lover"* from a faraway world.
A zodiac figure, like Paul Anka's Venus, she kneeled on the
grassy meadow of an unknown science fiction planet beneath
eight sun-stars, filling and emptying her pitchers of sacred water,
in the Star Card of the tarot, a pelican behind her, awaiting the
brief Aquarian era of the sixties. She was Flash Gordon's interstellar daughter.

Del Shannon shrieked: *"I'm a-walkin' in the rain,"* and Frankie
Laine *"gambled for love in the moonlight."* *"The Great Pretender"*
was invoked by the Platters. Elvis went to *"Heartbreak Hotel,"* as
remote as the house of Cepheus. There he dreamed of *"a warmer
sun"* in a world long past his own brief life.

The melodies and the dances were otherworldly and exotic.
They came out of American-melting-pot/African/folk-Europe-
an/Oriental/Navajo/Iroquois culture; English ballads merged
with Bantu and Hausa chants, Lithuanian folk songs, *"Green-
sleeves,"* and *"Danny Boy"*—and the message was global and pan-
cultural. It was as wild as the land itself and the fiery night. We

approached a parting more fragrant than body and soul. *"But you must go, and I must stay."*

I can remember leaving a dance at summer camp with feelings of great loneliness—the music of *"Michael, row your boat ashore"* fading in the distance behind me as I walked through fields of high grass with my eyes on the star-filled heavens. I felt both enormous and tiny, and though I thought myself in exile, I also felt utterly liberated, and I sang aloud with Dion and the Belmonts: *"Each night I ask the stars up above: Why must I be a teenager in love?"* The stars and the song together carried an unknown power. It may have been adolescent, but the bigness felt was authentic. All our lives our inner self reaches out for the connection.

The baseball cards changed to tarot cards, and they fell like meteors across an older sky. *"Do you believe in magic?"* the Lovin' Spoonful asked at the cusp of changing times. The Beatles visited India, and they returned with a cosmic instrument. Jimi Hendrix arrived with his songs of the outer Solar System. He traveled faster than sound, and he set his guitar on fire to the gasps of his audience. Other visionaries flocked to the deserts to watch the ancient ceremonies of the Native Americans. The old horned priests went about their business as always. They did not seek new visions; it was all they could do to handle the spirits that were already there. So the new tribes gathered at Woodstock. It was no costume party. The stars were coming to claim their own, as they had with Sufis and Cherokees for millennia. If the magic was in the music, the music was in us.

When the astral prophecy of the sixties made it to Broadway with the nude dancers of *Hair*, the message to the stars could not have been clearer: *"You twinkle above us, we twinkle below."*

And in 1980, in a movie called *Fame*, thirty years after the beginning of the cult, the chorus sang: *"Someday we'll all be stars."* The magicians and astral priests promised likewise.

By the late sixties, the star music had disintegrated into acid rock, atomic residue, and things were to get crazier. We had brought something into being that was equal to our passion, and

it arrived in a glittering star-suit within the ceremony, by invocation. It told us: this is now outer space.

"How many years?" Bob Dylan had asked before he set out
on his aeonic journey to Osiris. An extraterrestrial being lurked
outside our world—lover, rescuer, star-dancer, demon, and devil
woman. We stared through a thousand veils; we tried every
imaginable code. We called, but it never answered. Every song
of lover's abandonment told us that: the aliens had come as close
as they were going to come, and we could cry our hearts out,
and we could die for them, but that law would not be changed.
The Stones knew: *"Nobody else's hand will ever do. Nobody else's
hand."*

The Big Bopper and Johnny Horton died in the early space
missions. David Bowie fell to Earth years later with Valentine
Michael Smith and the Spiders from Mars. *"There's a star man /
Waiting in the sky,"* he told us. Only our incapacity to meet him
keeps him away. But was that star man finally Bowie himself in
his synthetic spaceflesh and rock-and-roll-suicide costume? Was
it Spock the Vulcan? Juan Matus the sorceror? Baba Ram Dass
the Harvard-psychologist-turned-holy-man?

Suzanne held the mirror and her tea and oranges showed the
whole intergalactic trade that was now possible. But Leonard
Cohen left North America and moved to the Aegean to await
the final war, back in darkness. Charles Manson leapt from darkness and bloodied the street altar. How vulnerable we were still:
that would not change either. The deaths of Janis Joplin and Jimi
Hendrix told us we could not survive on a planet that corrosive,
that close to the Sun. The death of John Lennon taught us how
fragile a glimmer it always was. We had thought we stood within
a lit palace, but it was a momentary phantasm, a message from
a distant star magnified by the media to give the sense of a
nearby nova, put out by a single quick gust. Those who huddled
in the cold in the park in a star memorial now truly feared that
all could be lost.

Eldridge Cleaver came home to tell his people there was no
Africa, no Cuba, no socialist republic. Abbie Hoffman went into
hiding. Porn stores and stage orgies took over the downtown
theater strips. And heroin replaced the sacred Indian plants. We

had forgotten the Mafia and the Soviet bear. As naked angelic stars, we weren't very good.

And the Beatles, crashing with Hamlet's Mill into Celtic and Germanic star debris, promised: *"There will be an answer. Let it be."*

The American space program faded after the Moon landings, but Ophiel told us to walk down hallways of light and to speak to beings of flame. Posters revealed other worlds with triple stars for suns and spiral nebulae in their heavens, emerald oceans and purple and yellow vines and flowers—the outer galaxies or the insides of atoms and cells. But this was the decorative decay of the cult.

Then the Tibetan Lama Tarthang Tulku sent us into the blue sky, region by region, atom by atom. Space was not outer; it didn't require lavish or luminous imagery; it was the actual ground of our existence. "Space is projecting space into space," he wrote.[3]

We talked peace, but the world knew better. We had tried to become anti-macho in putting the deep sirens to rest—but this was the wrong planet. The Pentagon despaired of our standing up to the dark challenge of the eighties. It was time to rearm.

The vision now vanished from the central plaza. The star cult was over, but its children built hidden cities, some of them as small as a room. They bought the sacred hot springs, and lay under real stars in medicinal water. They sat in rows staring back and forth, trying to see God in one another. They replaced the rock stars with a mantra; they transformed the cult.

John Lennon set his faith against the rock and roll holocaust, for he was barely a survivor of it. But Dylan stayed a prophet, leaving his family, moving on to the next deadly cult. The stars had led us to another Earth, another plane of this world. Now, all that was left was to return to the roots of art, the roots of human life. Those who remained in the temples would become robots of the negative afterlife. Punk and cold, they proved that men were sorry gods.

Jimi Hendrix stood in the Watchtower, his guitar on fire. And Rob Brezsny sang, *"When I fantasize the bomb vaporizing me into its own primeval heat and radiation, I remember that you and I are made of the same stuff.... We all live and die together... we are all born out of Adam, the invisible hermaphrodite god of our species.... We become one potently concentrated demonic imagination, a single meditator casting an irreversible spell to bind the great satan bomb."*

And Willie Nelson sang, *"Don't cross him, don't boss him, he's wild in his sorrow."*

David Bowie: *"And I Want to Believe / In the madness that calls 'Now.'"*

But: *"I ain't got the power.../No I ain't got the power anymore."*

Who are we to march so boldly from the oath sealed in cell and egg?

What promise have we kept to the dead creatures whose life is now our life?

Why have we come so far through shadows only to betray?

The old songs remain in the night air. Smokey Robinson: *"You've really got a hold on me."* And Sam Cooke, shot dead in a motel: *"What a wonderful world this could be."* Elvis dead on the star cult altar. *"We shall overcome someday,"* but on what planet and when? If not on this planet, will there ever be a planet? Is this our last chance, or as Seth the spirit promised: only the beginning?

A gunman in the night, thinking he was John Lennon, shot himself, shot into the chaos of unfulfilled messages and failed potential. When we are empty, dark forces use us for their ends. *"Oh yes we will find out":* the Stones.

We stand in darkness in an unknown corner of the Galaxy. And await further messages in the night air.

26

The Light Within

ND ON A NIGHT in 1969, hundreds of commune-dwellers gathered in a mountain meadow, close to the New Mexico stars, and sat among the crickets in darkness. They were joined, in time and space, by comrades in the deserts of eastern Oregon, by others on a mountain in India, and by still others who climbed to the sacred hot springs of Lake County, California, the realm of Orion and earth water tinted by Sirius. Together they sang: "Thank God / For the light within us."

At first this might have been a sacral cliché. But they shared the moment with each other and no one else—except those on other worlds around other stars with whom they might have imagined they were sharing it to do honor to the whole of creation, and with the crickets and grasses in their own night. It was better than our electric insistence that we are here. For once, in this century in the West, we were serious and sincere before the cosmos. We didn't need an answer. Of course, we are not alone.

Each time they sang those words, the light within them was different, weighed slightly differently, felt in tenderness as the thing they were projecting out into space.

In the distant resonance, in their cells, the sounds of the cities called them back to a shattered civilization in which their lives began and would end, and the Everly Brothers sang: "I can make you mine, taste your lips of wine / Any time, night or day."

Whose lips? Whose wine? Which light? When?

It is foolhardy to say that the whole creation is inside us. The stars are there all right, and without their vast sparkling cataclysm, nothing would happen. But it's also clear—imaginary or not—that a spirit, a light, is inside us. From ceaseless angles of being, we look out to see it reflected back—from the lake at dusk, from the streaks of clouds on the horizon, from the distant meadows on the mountainside, and from each other's faces. It is reflected through us, our memories, and the billions of flowers in the fields.

We are the marriage of vision and light. We bring the inner and outer lights together, or we see the one light passing from our center into the heart of the cosmos.

And this light stands out regardless of the Soviet bear's claw which smacks millions of souls into line, and notwithstanding the deadening materialism of the Western world, and despite all the dictators of the Orient and the Tropics.

The light must finally penetrate even cold granite stone, billions of meters deep. Factory workers in Poland, Japanese monks, West Virginia miners, migrants in the desert—it is all they have. We are all made of ancient hives of infinitesimal shimmers of that light. We don't have to know why or how. We are dense enough that we can't get at its source, that it can't pass through us all the time; but when it does, in moments of grief or joy, the old songs play, and the singers of our beginning sing with us; we know then how we are alive.

There is much yet to be done. Every echo tells us that, and every whisper tells us that too. We must act for ourselves, and we must act for the speechless animals. They stand before the ceremony, and they will stand before it, motionless, forever. The manifold design has entrusted us with this single moiré—a warble of blue sky, a throbbing of organdy and loam, and a clarity so lucid and final nothing can be seen through it but itself. We are creatures entangled in a primitive oil. We are dancers to the muffled drum. Fuzziness and nausea mark the limits equally of mind and matter. We struggle to recover and retain the dwindling past, and, in the same gesture, we grasp toward the unshaped future. We are surrounded by lords, avatars, yogis, aliens, science fiction heroes, clones, and memories of memories—diamonds reflecting through us, and a faint aura of sandalwood and brine. But we are the heroes of this masque, just as we are the singers of this song. For having come so far through flesh and cells in darkness, for being the mysterious stranger and the one whom the mysterious stranger affrights, we stand on this enchanted evening bathed in a richness even the gods cannot imagine—and with no other clue in the darkness. Something in us wants the Christ and Boddhisattva functions to be fulfilled. Something in us wants the aliens to come, to merge with us. Something in us wants to get back every memory, every thing we have lost, every thing that was put together ever and once to make us. It *is* a sickness, but it is a wonder and a gift too. And though nothing yet in this century has worked out, we still expect to survive intact, and to deliver the torch to those who will revive us in some other place in some other way. That is the garden of childhood we come from and return to, beyond the stars, and beyond the figments and mirages of space and time.

Appendix:
Giving Them A
Name*

I HAVE NO PERSONAL EXPERIENCE with UFOs and aliens, but like the rest of you I am a visitor to a strange and haunting planet. No matter what else is loose in the cosmos, our inhabitation of this body, this life, is the first mystery—and one of undiagnosable profundity.

Why us? Why here?

What next?

In the last century or two, scientists have catalogued us as insignificant accidents among the infinities of space, taking what limited satisfaction remains from their goal of mastering the physical parameters of that universe.

But we and they are also protagonists in a shadow play, and it is not even certain they speak for themselves, let alone for us. At the deepest level we have another agenda that no one dares speak of, no one even knows. It is also unclear whether modern science represents the expression or repression of our most far-reaching intelligence and powers.

The parapsychologist Jule Eisenbud claims that there are no

---

*Lecture given at "Angels, Aliens, and Archetypes" Conference, sponsored by Omega Foundation, Palace of Fine Arts, San Francisco, November 1987; some material added to this version from UFO talk at Arthur Young's Institute for the Study of Consciousness, December 1987.

UFOs not associated with paranormal mental phenomena. With all theories of reality still patent pending, he notes, what isn't a combination of hypnosis, amnesia, and hypermnesis—from mediums flying miles through the air to crash onto seance tables to multiple personalities speaking ancient languages and deriving cube roots of twenty-seven figures, to say nothing of a menagerie of ghosts, ouija boards, and spirit possessions?[1]

Fifteen years ago, in an interview with me, Eisenbud suggested that much of our scientific and technological activity was "in some way that I cannot yet comprehend, a defense against ...other capacities in us that we don't wish to realize. To put it schematically, and simplistically," he said, "and almost absurdly, because we don't wish to realize that we can just kill with our minds, we go through this whole enormous play of killing with such, of overkilling with such overimplementation.... It's a caricature of saying: how can I do it with my mind; I need tanks; I need B-52 bombers; I need napalm, and so on.... What I'm trying to say is: there must be, I feel, a relationship between this truth, which we will not see, and this absurd burlesque of aggression that goes on all around us."[2]

The UFO literature is itself a book of riddles and conundrums. Beings of reputedly remote origin reach us through both mediums and spacecraft; at least "they" say the same things through these very different channels. The messages may suddenly interrupt ordinary radio transmissions, assemble themselves through table tapping, or get delivered in sealed envelopes by humanoids debarking from toruses. Their content generally suggests ordinary theosophy or science fiction: "We have passed our souls, bodies, and minds into computers and moved several of millions of light-years backwards toward your time and dimension"; "A cosmic morality such as the one we share forbids us to intervene"; "We will return to see you two more times"; "We believe in the Almighty Power of the Universe. You must understand that there are over 150 billion universes, and that there are many forms and orders of Gods in each and every one of them"; "We will harmonize this world with the rest of the universe"; "Rentre dans ton silence et souffle tes chandelles"; and so on.

Even the UFOs do not have to be metallic ships; they can

manifest as the Holy Virgin Mary, Khidr the Sufi angel, or a Hopi blue kachina. Jacques Vallee describes the initial sighting at Fatima:

> The first apparition of the woman took place on May 13, 1917. Three children were watching their sheep when a bright flash surprised them, and they walked toward the large hollow pasture called Cova da Iria ... to see what had happened. They found themselves caught in a glowing light that almost blinded them, and in the center of the light they perceived a little woman, who spoke to them, begging them to return every month to the same spot....
>
> On August 13 there were eighteen thousand people at the site of the apparitions.... A clap of thunder was heard, followed by a bright flash. A small whitish cloud was forming around the tree. It hovered for a few minutes, then rose and melted away. The clouds in the sky had turned crimson red, and then changed to pink, yellow, and blue. 'Colored light like a rainbow on the ground'; 'clouds around the sun reflecting different colors on the people'—such are some of the terms that witnesses used to describe it. The witnesses saw 'falling flowers,' the famous phenomenon of 'angel hair' so consistently reported after the passage of a UFO, and sometimes interpreted as an ionization effect. One man, Manual Pedro Marto, reported seeing clearly *a luminous globe spinning through the clouds....*[3]

At subsequent visitations through October 13, the crowd gradually swelled to seventy thousand; there were flashes of light, a sudden end to heavy rain, rainbow-colored disks that doused the throng in lights, sweet aromas, spontaneous healings, the manifestation of a "Lady" who introduced herself as the Angel of Peace, then the delivery of a communiqué to be read in 1960. Vallee adds:

> A man whose word I trust received an interesting report from one of the Pope's secretaries, who introduced the highest men in the Church into the presence of John XXIII for the opening of the secret part of the Fatima prophecy in 1960. Although the solemn event took place behind closed doors, the secretary had the opportunity to see the cardinals

as they left the Pope's office; they had a look of deep horror on their faces. He got up from behind his desk and tried to speak to one of them whom he knew intimately, but the prelate gently pushed him aside and walked on with the expression of someone who has seen a ghost.[4]

This probably means that the message was little different from those received by 1950s Air Force pilots whose radio channels were coopted, for instance, with descriptions of beings who live on the interior of Saturn and prophecies of the Earth entering the Fourth Dimension with an uprising of Atlantis in the Bermuda Triangle. (The deadlines for all of these have long since passed.)

An institution based on interpreting exogenous messages must suffer the literalism of both the carrier and the text. *The Book of Mormon, Oahspe,* and *The Book of Urantia* are all the products of such originless transmission. The notion of the immaculate Son of God has mostly time and tradition behind it to separate it from more garish visitations: Jesus can no longer be debunked by a panel of experts. But once the Church is lured into a contemporary interaction with mediums and UFOs, it too becomes part of the grand unresolved science-fiction conspiracy and rests on the same footing as any other paraphysical cult.

Because of our rock video/soap opera mentality we are seduced by a melodramatic, inflated interpretation of what is happening to us. Certainly the 'big event' in which we all exist is unfolding today as it always was, but it is not intrinisically more apocalyptic now, either in the positive or negative sense. To the degree that some critical moment is precipitating, it is not likely to be the one we are heralding anyway. Communications with disembodied entities, realms perceived during astral travel, etc., still await determination. They cannot be simultaneously experienced, described, decoded, and marketed. I think even the most committed believers must sense that they are the targets of the packaging of an image rather than the image itself.

All our lives we are the recipients of messages even if these messages (like dreams) turn out to be from the depths of our own beings. From one standpoint our own depth and the depth of the universe—at least the signified universe—must be the same. A primary cause of New-Age confusion is that we cannot *ever* tell the difference between ostensible voices of aliens who evolved far from here and voices of the Earth (be those our own unconscious selves, telepathic transmissions from the minds of fellow humans, or channellings from so-called other dimensions or the dead). In fact, as much as we know (and it is not really very much) about the shape of the three-dimensional universe, we know almost nothing about the topology of consciousness, so when someone like the famed astral traveller Robert Munroe reports on meetings with entities who have gotten sidetracked on the Earth, we cannot tell if these are terrestrially-created intelligences (perhaps from his own multiple-personality, story-telling potential, perhaps from shamanic entities), or if they are authentic visitors who arose indigenously in their geospheres and travelled here. As long as we entertain the notion of intrinsic identity separate of embodiment we also cannot tell the difference between entities who never had "bodies" (at least in our three-dimensional sense of them), entities who are permanently disincarnate, and entities who (like Munroe) are temporarily travelling out-of-flesh.

If a minor hypnotic trance causes someone to believe that the chair on which he is sitting does not exist, that the raisin in his mouth is a grapefruit, that he was once married to the Queen of England, what major occurrence is likewise unfolding before our noses? If the vast caul of light we are wrapped in is a chimera (within a mirage), what progression of aliases does it mask?

This conference is entitled "Angels, Aliens, and Archetypes," which is free territory for spirits, visions, and entities from all sources. The list is endless because it encompasses not only a possible kingdom of distinct phenomena but the names and explanations assigned to these phenomena in different cultures and at different periods of history.

Here I would like to focus on the particular theme of celestial UFOs, spaceship-like manifestations in the night sky—to draw our attention back to a simpler time when it was possible to wonder only about the exotic planets on which life evolved, the creatures dispatched from there to explore the universe. Their heydey was not so long ago, sometime in the mid to late fifties, sustained in many ways into the sixties and seventies, and pervasive enough in the early eighties to evoke the mood in the desert at the beginning of *Close Encounters of the Third Kind.*

In early science fiction, tens of thousands of distinct alien beings piloted material yet sublime vehicles through a geography of fireballs, cosmic dust, and sun-stars. Their myths were background to the beeps of our own first Sputnik and Explorer satellites—countdown followed by the slow rise of a rocket ship, a statement of our willingness to go bodily into the mystery that has covered our species since its entry to consciousness. We were rewarded with stunning images of the three-dimensional radiance of our planet, right to the actual dust and stones of the Moon. Through remote eyes we viewed a Martian day, sunrise to sunset, across a boulder-strewn landscape, then luminescent photographs of Saturn, Jupiter, and their moons, some mottled, some covered with ice, at least one fiery and volcanic, one submerged beneath clouds and perhaps harboring oceans.

This is the universe of radio messages from extraterrestrials to Air Force jets, UFO crashes in Texas, bodies of aliens in the White House vault—into which Spielberg's chandelier spacecraft descends as a chilling reminder of the "once upon a time" yet to be. It is also the universe of blue sky, summer days, windblown seeds, fields of purple and yellow flowers after the rain, birds rising in single dense waves, their cries filling the air with glyphs, layers of cumulus, waves rolling shells, gulls following fishing boats.

This is the only world we know from within, the genesis of our mystery and wonder. It is the world to which the old-fashioned UFOs came as magnificent intruders because it is the world of our own unfathomability. We received these aliens first in our intimations of them, so long evolving in their own biosystems and landscapes, so remote from the Earth that all of their history and biology would be different from ours. They might even include us someday in their interstellar laws and commerce so our dilemmas would fall to a wise and neutral court. Of course, they might also be insectoid, semi-conscious, conquistador, but our imagination of that through countless science-fiction tales merely added to the peril of the vision. Back in the fifties and sixties, when we went UFO-exploring, we were summoning a range of images and emotions from the edge of our existence, but we kept them within the ground of our daily lives.

My intuition is that this universe with its UFOs is now all but dead. We may be telling ourselves these days we're in better shape, on the brink of a whole new consciousness, a hierarchy of dimensions, cosmic convergences, a birthing beyond this physical shell, but so far (as usual), we're our own preachers; we're the ones doing the telling as well as the listening, and this risks the compensating shadow of spiritual inflation. We have seen some of our wisest gurus become so powerful they could only reclaim their souls by enacting petty decadences—molesting young disciples, driving fleets of sacred cars.

I believe we are evolving slowly; I do not think the universe creates souls to obliterate them, but I also do not expect we are going to be pulled pellmell out of our neuroses, romances, and unfinished cities into the dreamtime. And that is no cause for disappointment, for there is a great deal of mystery and subtlety to explore in these bizarre flesh crystals, each of them containing an unconscious cellular history of the Earth.

Isn't it strange that the early manned capsules and 1969 Moonwalk already seem innocent and nostalgic? U.S. space missions, when they begin again, will be on the level of government committees weighing economic and military priorities. Meanwhile, our intrepid visitors in unimaginable vehicles and bodies and costumes have turned into impalpable riddles such that they seem maybe not to have crossed the vast distances among stars nor even to be true aliens.

Not only have they become less benign since animal slaughter, kidnapping, and baby-stealing have been ascribed to them, but they have become less confidently identified with the stars and possible planets of the night sky and more with poltergeists and spontaneous psi phenomena.

For every incident in which a UFO leaves an analyzable relic, there seems to be a trickster event in which, for instance, an alien deposits a chemically conventional pancake in the hands of a startled contactee or delivers a nonsensical message, or in which a sample of extraterrestrial manufacturing disappears from the laboratory, or turns out to be a mundane alloy. Even more disruptive are the cases in which ostensible UFO encounters have been wiped from contactees' memories by post-hypnotic commands and other forms of tampering. In these circumstances we are hardput to claim that any experience of contact, even a simple sighting, is more than a projection or hallucination. We truly do not know enough about ourselves to guess at who "they" are, especially when "they" are unwilling or unable to present themselves through regular diplomatic channels. Clearly the simplicity of the old days of UFOs was our own simplicity, an innocence in our culture, not a simplicity of the phenomenon.

The distinction between spirit and matter has been challenged so extensively that it is now merely situational, and the goblins, ghosts, and disembodied entities of occult science have combined with outer-space UFOs in a muddle of phenomena. Some of those aliens who remain potentially extraterrestrial have been acting out, at best (and I mean "at best" here) B grade movies, telling us tales about Orion confederacies, about transgalactic wars, celestial migrations, and imperial star systems, or they have been performing elaborate masquerades. And what can we say in behalf of other beings who murder and cut up the sentient creatures of the fields, kidnap and experiment on human beings, and suck babies out of pregnant women? They certainly aren't travelling Buddhists.

A number of factors have contributed to the transformation of the traditional celestial UFO into the multidimensional, metaphysical one, and, like all changes in consciousness, it has occurred mostly on a subliminal level so that we cannot pinpoint the moment of change. In the relatively early days of UFOs, Carl Jung raised the possibility that unidentified lights and shapes we saw in the heavens were actually forms we projected there, alien beings reifying the shadow of our scientistic civilization. Before spaceflight, Jung pointed out, flying entities were gods or spirits. Unable to return to a spiritual universe and equally unable to bring peace and well-being to this technological one, we transpose our images and fears into archetypal machines across the tableau of night.

Jung's insights about UFOs were accepted quite widely for many years, even by those who continued to believe in actual spaceships carrying aliens. After all, just because we have projections and even collective hallucinations doesn't mean that there aren't also aliens. The validity of the metaphysical processes generating shamanic jaguars and condors is not affected by the existence of animal ones, and in fact there is an important synchronistic connection between the two that lies at the heart of a universe seamlessly producing creatures through flesh and archetype both.

In recent years Jung's theory has gained new credibility in a somewhat different guise. The issue now is not so much whether archetypal and real UFOs could coexist as whether there are UFOs that do not come from outer space and are also not pure transpositions of unconscious material, i.e., UFOs that represent materializations of psychic or paraphysical material independent of individual mentation. In such a condition objects and entities are simultaneously concrete and real, psychic and hallucinatory—and we can never tell the difference. This includes the shamanic forms described by Carlos Castaneda and others, possible visitors from other dimensions, from the future, from realms of disembodied mind (including the dead), and, more deviously, channels of psychotronic mind-manipulation and hypnosis with vision implants. The person experiencing an exogenous alien form cannot tell not only if that form is material or psychic but, if it is psychic, whether it is generated inside himself, outside, or both, and, if an implant, whether it is channelled, or cosmic static.

I don't think there is any way out of this dilemma short of the mythical full disclosure by "them" on the White House lawn. And that is not going to resolve the whole riddle of paradoxical experiences with entities; it is only going to silence the professional debunkers and carve out a certain small part of the territory as explicable in conventional terms, maybe.... Because the inventions of our psychic life will go on.

It strikes me, for instance, as odd—though not necessarily incriminating—that the piloters of UFOs have been taking on aspects of our own most disturbing behavior: they are treating sentient beings with precisely the kind of scientific contempt we now exhibit epidemically, carrying out clandestine operations complete with cover stories. They even seem to have picked up the superpowers' repetoire of brainwashing and dirty tricks. In an era of drugs and torture, they have an arsenal second to none. Are they mocking us? Are they reflections of us? And then, are they even all the same aliens?

I am not alone in advancing the idea that perhaps we are dealing with a variety of different phenomena even under the catchall category of space visitors. The crew from the Pleiades seems to have nothing to do with the genetic experimenters and baby-stealers described by Budd Hopkins among others. The former are unintrusive, informative, conventional to the point of *Book of Mormon*-cliché-ed in their cosmic history and politics (sort of like in the *Star Trek* series where everyone speaks English and is acquainted with conventional political systems, and some of the most advanced cultures are organized like interplanetary Aztecs and Egyptians); the frail, almond-eyed biotechnicians are intrusive and tell us nothing—except as one abductee so eloquently reported, "Yes, we have the right (to treat you this way)."⁵

How could there be two such different cosmic strategies and why are both types of aliens apparently humanoid?; why should we be interfertile with creatures arising in a different biology not even based on DNA (could genetic engineering on a cosmic scale be that good?), and why don't they ever talk to each other and get it straight what they want from us?

There are also many *other* styles of visitors who claim to be from a variety of star systems and such patently uninhabitable planets in this Solar System as Mercury and Uranus, and who also seem to take no cognizance of one another, *or* the Pleiadians, *or* the baby thieves. I should add: *apparently* they are different entities, and *apparently* they don't talk to each other. We might be experiencing the faint and remote ripple of a transdimensional phenomenon, translated into our ken through layers of resistance and symbolic distortions, much as dreams are, hence fragmentary and condensed in the same way. Such UFOs would be harbingers of the depth and subtlety of the creation. In a less optimistic version, though, the explanations we can presently imagine are not reassuring because the aliens come off as mechanically-obsessed, materialistic, not respectful or compassionate of sentient life, sort of like small-time crooks with flashy machines (we've also made up that story many times). We can always argue, as with the old gods, that their ways are not our ways—but I'd rather not give them that honor until we are talking about *bona fide* gods. If you think it's even remotely reassuring that we might be someone else's genetic experiment, you'd better dig deep into the darkest possible nightmares, because there is no salvation there inside or outside of history, and none in the dharma either.

So let us move away from both the original metallic UFOs and the new psychic and psychotronic ones. Let us consider that we have an original and unassailable integrity because it is on that ground alone that we meet the aliens and on that ground alone that the term "alien" has any meaning. We are led by sweet layers of flesh and psyche, and when we are no longer able to trust them, we become just one more note in a chaos of transgalactic noise—radio, metaphysical, bodily, extrabodily, and other.

When "*It* Came from Outer Space," we were *here*, in our cities and villages, with ordinary hopes and fears. The real Earth, with its immediate sun-star, great seas, and profound mysterious landscapes, is our protector and our solace; it is the source of our psychic and emotional strength. All things meaningful come from our hearts, and in that sense no UFO can be as wondrous as the birth in blood of a single child, or even the birth of a furry mole, the arising by cells of a dragonfly from its egg. The metaphysical UFOs, abductors, maintainers of bases in the Andes, and generators of bigfeet and Loch Ness monsters are prophetic, but they are also restrictive and authoritarian, if not in themselves, then in the hands of those who interpret them for us; we become reduced to their unsolved paradigm at the risk of the things that make us real, that define our world as home to which anything else comes from beyond, our lives as worth preserving in the strange and unknown cosmos. That is why the ancient, enormous Sphinx of a human face carved into a Martian mesa has a special significance even among more intimate and contemporary meetings with aliens. That one we can go out and see in our own spaceships just as we went to the pyramids of Egypt and the temples of Greece. We can touch it in our own terms.

The original ground on which we stand is this world, the familiarity of our body/minds, language, and civilization, however much in crisis that might seem and no matter that we judge ourselves to have made a mess of it. It is still what we are, by karmic law what we have chosen to be, a materialization of our profoundest desires. We shouldn't be looking any more for a literal biblical god, or his fundamentalist equivalent in a super alien biologist. There are probably billions of possible manifestations in the universe and we could transmute among them authentically for innumerable lifetimes, all manner of planets and dimensions and subatomic particles. That's not yet our destiny; even unenlightened, we live, experience wondrous things, breed, and die, and we should not stand ready to cede that to aliens, to submit it to their judgement, or to deem them automatically superior to it—not out of false pride but because we exist only as the legitimate outcome of the forces that we express. We cannot be anything else, and I would argue that this is true even if we *are* someone else's experiment—and I will get right to the point on that one: even if we are the genetic experiment of a scientifically advanced race, the experiment can only be a manipulation of existing lifeforms; it does not include the invention of our whole existence. Our genes can be synthesized, or rearranged; the biological frame of our life can be altered, but biology itself cannot be invented out of nothing by something that is itself an evolutionary product of the universe. Frank Herbert fashioned the genetic priesthood and Tleilaxu flesh tanks, wrote the whole *Dune* series to arrive at this single truth.

If the aliens are biological, to use the term in its broadest trans-DNA sense, then we are biological in the same way, and the experience to which biology refers remains intact. Put another way—genetic manipulation (which is just an intense form of natural selection) may determine what range of phenomena we deal with as organisms, but it cannot invent the original phenomenology, the impulse for something to become in a universe where nothing might as easily have been. That creationary force, operating through intelligent entities or through randomly distributed pools of local planetary starstuff, that archetypal, individuating force (if you prefer) is still going to incarnate creatures at the same level of enlightenment and existence. Our creators are not going to be any more enlightened than we are; they will just have advanced technologies. They know no more about how the universe came to be, why it is, and what anything in it is. Their missions and experiments should not trap us and our civilization in the meanings they give to them and the ostensible goals they set (any more than we can change the existential fact of a genetically-altered rabbit).

If the UFOs contain or *are* authentic evolved beings—and if they mean to compel and even midwife us into our destined maturities—we can still wait for their actual surprise. Nothing said here will prepare us for an experience of them. No one else's account can stand in place of our own ("No one else's hands will ever do," the Stones sang years ago, and also: "Stand up coming years, escalation fears; oh, yes, we will find out...."). There is no reason to leave this conference feeling as though we have to evolve faster in order to fulfill a prophecy or respond to the UFO warning. Because the gods have yet to make any rules for us, and I doubt that they are going to change strategies now and simply say, "Be good—or be high." We are far too perverse and unconscious to respond to such a message anyway. Most people don't want to evolve, and won't; they'll scratch and claw their way out of any power trip, however posed in the language of love and beneficence. If need be, they'll vandalize the ships of heaven and spray the gods themselves with graffiti. And they certainly don't want *us* to lead them. But when the real thing arrives, they'll be ready too, and they won't even know it's a UFO. Nor will we.

That is why I am reminding us of the old green and blue Flash Gordon "African Queen" Earth to which the aliens first came, Al Jolson singing "Old Man River," and a thousand other native songs in the air from Siberia to Somalia to Peru. When we are able to meet them there, to be us and let them be them, and they are neither our projections nor our inventors, then the story they tell us, rather than a horror story and the intimation of our own nightmare, is something truly mysterious and from the other end of matter.

Notes

Preface

1. Michel Foucault, *Les Mots et Les Choses* (Paris: Editions Galli-mard, 1966); excerpt entitled "The Writing of Things," translated by William Christian, in *Io*, No. 5 (*Doctrine of Signatures*), Ann Arbor, Mich., 1968, p. 20.
2. Ibid.
3. Ibid., pp. 20–21.

CHAPTER 1
The Night Sky

1. Richard Hinckley Allen, *Star Names: Their Lore and Meaning* [1899] New York: Dover Books, 1973), pp. 303–320.
2. Johann Heinrich Lambert, *The System of the World*, translated from the French by James Jacque (1800); excerpted in *Theories of the Universe: From Babylonian Myth to Modern Science*, edited by Milton K. Munitz (Glencoe, Ill.: The Free Press, 1957), p. 251.
3. Stephen Fulder, *The Root of Being: Ginseng and the Pharmacology of Harmony* (London: Hutchison, 1980).
4. Robert Kelly, "Re: The Occult", *Io*, No. 6 (*Ethnoastronomy Issue*), Ann Arbor, Mich., 1969, p. 107.
5. Ibid.
6. D. H. Lawrence, *The Rainbow* [1915] (New York: Random House, 1943), p. 42.

CHAPTER 2
Scientific and Occult Astronomy

1. Fred Hoyle, *The Nature of the Universe* (New York: Harper and Bros., 1950); excerpted in *Theories of the Universe: From Babylonian Myth to Modern Science,* edited by Milton K. Munitz (Glencoe, Ill.: The Free Press, 1957), p. 426.

2. Munitz, *Theories of the Universe,* p. 428.

3. Da Free John, *The Transmission of Doubt: Talks and Essays on the Transcendence of Scientific Materialism through Radical Understanding* Clear Lake, California: The Dawn Horse Press, 1984), pp. 360–362.

4. Ibid., p. 261.

5. *The Celestial Elder's Canon of the Spirit Lights (An Ancient Chinese Book of Interior Astrology),* translated by Nathan Sivin, *Io,* No. 4 (*Alchemy Issue,* enlarged edition), Plainfield, Vermont, 1973, p. 234.

6. Ibid.

7. Ibid.

8. Hugh A. Moran and David H. Kelley, *The Alphabet and the Ancient Calendar Signs* (Palo Alto, Calif.: Daily Press, 1969), p. xvii.

9. Ophiel, *The Art and Practice of Astral Projection* (St. Paul, Minn.: The Gnostic Institute, 1961).

10. Julia Lorusso and Joel Glick, *Healing Stoned: The Therapeutic Use of Gems and Minerals* (Alburquerque, N.M.: Brotherhood of Life, 1976).

11. Hermes Trismegistus, *The Divine Pymander and Other Writings,* translated by John D. Chambers (1882); republished by Samuel Weiser, Inc., New York, 1972.

12. Ibid., p. 5.

13. Ibid., p. 8.

14. Ibid., p. 25.

15. Hua-jui fui-jen, "Kung tz'u": quoted in Edward H. Schafer, *Pacing the Void* (Berkeley: University of California Press, 1977), p. 38.

16. P. D. Ouspensky, *In Search of the Miraculous: Fragments of an Unknown Teaching* (New York: Harcourt, Brace & World, 1949), p. 205 repunctuated).

17. Ibid., p. 211.

18. Ibid., p. 212.

19. Ibid., p. 85.

20. Rodney Collin, *The Theory of Celestial Influence* (London: Stuart and Watkins, 1954), pp. 72–73.

21. Ibid., p. 77.

22. Pierre Teilhard de Chardin, *The Phenomenon of Man*, translated from the French by Bernard Wall (New York: Harper and Row, 1959).

23. Ibid., p. 73.

24. Ibid.

25. Carl Sagan, "Interview," conducted by Richard Grossinger (January 23, 1972), *Io*, No. 14 (*Earth Geography Booklet*, No. 3: *Imago Mundi*), Cape Elizabeth, Maine, 1972, pp. 374–386.

26. Ibid., p. 384.

CHAPTER 3
Ancient Astronomy

1. Kjell Akerblom, *Astronomy and Navigation in Polynesia and Micronesia: A Survey*, Ethnographic Museum of Stockholm Monograph Series, No. 14 (Stockholm, 1968), p. 18.

2. Ibid., p. 24.

3. Ibid., pp. 24–25.

4. Ibid., pp. 104 and 114.

5. Eldon Best, *The Astronomical Knowledge of the Maori, Genuine and Empirical: Including Data Concerning Their Systems of Astrogeny, Astrolaty, and Natural Astrology, with Notes on Certain Other Natural Phenomena*, Dominion Museum Monographs, No. 3 (Wellington, New Zealand, 1922).

6. Ibid., p. 6.

7. Akerblom, *Astronomy and Navigation*, p. 13.

8. Edwin Krupp, ed., *In Search of Ancient Astronomy* (Garden City, N.Y.: Doubleday, 1977), p. 187.

9. Ibid., p. 91.

10. Ibid., pp. 149, 156, and 159.

11. Henry Wright, Department of Anthropology, University of Michigan, personal communication, 1969.

12. Gerald S. Hawkins, *Stonehenge Decoded* (New York: Dell, 1965).

13. Alexander Marshack, *The Roots of Civilization: The Cognitive Beginnings of Man's First Art, Symbol and Notation* (New York: McGraw-Hill, 1972).

14. Ibid., p. 202.

15. Ibid., p. 452.

16. Ibid., pp. 453–456.

17. Philip Wheelwright, ed., *The Presocratics* (Indianapolis: Odyssey Press, 1966), pp. 44–52.

18. Ibid., p. 57.

19. Ibid., p. 59.

20. Ibid., p. 58.

21. Ibid., pp. 69–89.

22. Ibid., pp. 27–28.

23. Ibid., pp. 182–199.

24. Werner Heisenberg, *Physics and Beyond,* translated from the German by Arnold J. Pomerans (New York: Harper and Row, 1971), p. 241.

25. Lucretius, *The Nature of the Universe,* translated from the Latin by R. E. Latham (Baltimore: Penguin Books, 1951); excerpted in *Theories of the Universe: From Babylonian Myth to Modern Science,* edited by Milton K. Munitz (Glencoe, Ill.: The Free Press, 1957), p. 55.

26. Ibid., pp. 44 and 53.

27. Ibid., p. 45.

28. Quoted here from Wheelwright, *The Presocratics,* p. 162.

29. Ibid., p. 160.

30. Plato, *Timaeus,* translated from the Greek by H. D. P. Lee (Baltimore: Penguin Books, 1965).

31. F. M. Cornford, ed. and trans., *Plato's Cosmology: The Timaeus of Plato* (New York: Humanities Press, 1937); excerpted in Munitz, *Theories of the Universe,* p. 79.

32. Plato, *Timaeus,* pp. 45 and 47.

33. Aristotle, *On the Heavens,* translated from the Greek by W. K. C. Guthrie (Cambridge, Mass.: Harvard University Press, 1939).

34. Elias Bickerman and Morton Smith, *The Ancient History of Western Civilization* (New York: Harper and Row, 1976), p. 143.

35. A remark made by Robert Kelly in private conversation, ca. 1966.

36. Arthur Koestler, *The Sleepwalkers: A History of Man's Changing Vision of the Universe* (New York: Grosset and Dunlap, 1959), pp. 49–50.

37. Rudolf Thiel, *And There Was Light: The Discovery of the Universe,* translated from the German by Richard and Clara Winston (New York: Knopf, 1957).

38. Michael Collins, *Carrying the Fire: An Astronaut's Journey* (New York: Farrar, Straus and Giroux, 1974), p. 472.

39. Thiel, *And There Was Light.*

40. Ibid., p. 50.

41. J. L. E. Dreyer, *A History of the Planetary Systems from Thales to Kepler* (Cambridge, England: Cambridge University Press, 1905);

excerpted in Munitz, *Theories of the Universe*, pp. 120–124.

42. Dante Alighieri, *Paradise*, translated from the Italian by Dorothy Sayers and Barbara Reynolds (Baltimore: Penguin Books, 1962).

CHAPTER 4

The History of
Western Astronomy:
The Sun in the Center

THE BULK OF THE BIOGRAPHICAL MATERIAL on Copernicus comes from Arthur Koestler, *The Sleepwalkers: A History of Man's Changing Vision of the Universe* (New York: Grosset and Dunlamp, 1959).

1. Nicolaus Copernicus; quoted in Koestler, *The Sleepwalkers*, p. 202.

2. Nicolaus Copernicus, *De Revolutionibus* (1543), translated from the Latin by John F. Dobson and Selig Brodetsky, in *Occasional Notes of the Royal Astronomical Society* (London, 1947); excerpted in *Theories of the Universe: From Babylonian Myth to Modern Science*, edited by Milton K. Munitz (Glencoe, Ill.: The Free Press, 1957), pp. 158 and 162.

3. Ibid., p. 169.

4. Cyrus Gordon, *Before Columbus: Links Between the Old World and Ancient America* (New York: Crown, 1971).

5. Carl O. Sauer, *Northern Mists* (Berkeley, Calif.: Turtle Island Foundation, 1968).

6. Ibid.

7. Ibid.

8. Ibid.

9. Frances A. Yates, *Theatre of the World* (Chicago: University of Chicago Press, 1969).

10. Ibid.

11. Diane di Prima, *Selected Poems 1956–1976* Plainfield, Vermont: North Atlantic Books, 1977), p. 294.

12. Giordano Bruno; quoted in Rudolf Thiel, *And There Was Light: The Discovery of the Universe*, translated from the German by Richard and Clara Winston (New York: Knopf, 1957), p. 112.

13. Ibid., p. 112.

14. Giordano Bruno; quoted in Yates, *Giordano Bruno*, p. 244.

15. Ibid., p. 256.

16. Robert Kelly, "The Alchemist"; reprinted in *Alchemy: pre-Egyptian Legacy, Millenial Promise* (*Io*, No. 26), edited by Richard Grossinger (Richmond, Calif.: North Atlantic Books, 1979), p. 130.

17. Giordano Bruno; quoted in Thiel, *And There Was Light*, p. 113.

CHAPTER 5

The History of Western Astronomy: The Planets

THE BULK OF THE BIOGRAPHICAL MATERIAL on Kepler and Galileo comes from Arthur Koestler, *The Sleepwalkers: A History of Man's Changing Vision of the Universe* (New York: Grosset and Dunlap, 1959).

1. Johannes Kepler, Letter to Michael Maestlin; quoted in Koestler, *The Sleepwalkers*, pp. 261–262.

2. Johannes Kepler, *Harmonice Mundi* (1619); quoted in Koestler, *The Sleepwalkers*, p. 262.

3. "Unerringly impelling this dead, impregnable, uninjurable wall, and this most buoyant thing within; there swims behind it all a mass of tremendous life, only to be adequately estimated as piled wood is—by the cord; and all obedient to one volition, as the smallest insect." (Herman Melville, *Moby Dick* (1851) [New York: New American Library, 1961], p. 327.)

4. Johannes Kepler, *Mysterium Cosmographicum;* quoted in Rudolf Thiel, *And There Was Light*, translated from the German by Richard and Clara Winston (New York: Knopf, 1957), p. 116.

5. Johannes Kepler, Letter to Herwart von Hohenburg; quoted in Koestler, *The Sleepwalkers*, p. 304.

6. Johannes Kepler, *Astronomia Nova* (1609); quoted in Koestler, *The Sleepwalkers*, p. 332.

7. Johannes Kepler, *Harmonice Mundi* (1619); quoted in Thiel, *And There Was Light*, p. 295.

8. Galileo Galilei, *Sidereus Nuncius* (1610); quoted in Koestler, *The Sleepwalkers*, p. 365.

9. Johannes Kepler; quoted in Koestler, *The Sleepwalkers*, p. 367.

10. "The whole of this visible world is only an imperceptible fleck in the ample bosom of nature. No idea of ours can approach it. . . . Let man

think of himself as one who has strayed into this out-of-the-way corner of nature, and, from this narrow prison in which he finds himself lodged—I mean the universe—let him learn to estimate at their just value the earth, kingdoms, cities, and himself. What is a man, in the midst of infinity?" (Blaise Pascal, *Pensé es sur la Religion* (1647); quoted in Arthur O. Lovejoy, *The Great Chain of Being* [Cambridge, Mass.: Harvard University Press, 1936], p. 127.)

11. John Milton, *Paradise Lost* (1667), Book II, lines 891–893; in *John Milton: Complete Poems and Major Prose,* edited by Merritt Y. Hughes (New York: Odyssey Press, 1957), p. 253.

12. Galileo Galilei, *Dialogue Concerning the Two Chief World Systems* (1632), translated from the Latin by Stillman Drake (Berkeley: University of California Press, 1953); quoted in Koestler, *The Sleepwalkers,* p. 474.

CHAPTER 6

The History of Western Astronomy: The Gravitational Field

1. Arthur Koestler, *The Sleepwalkers: A History of Man's Changing Vision of the Universe* (New York: Grosset and Dunlap, 1959).

2. Isaac Newton, "Four Letters to Richard Bentley" (1692); reprinted in *Theories of the Universe: From Babylonian Myth to Modern Science,* edited by Milton K. Munitz (Glencoe, Ill.: The Free Press, 1957), p. 212.

3. Ibid., p. 210.

4. Isaac Newton, *Philosophiae Naturalis Principia Mathematica* (1687), translated from the Latin by Andrew Motte (Berkeley: University of California Press, 1946); reprinted in Munitz, *Theories of the Universe,* p. 209.

5. Isaac Newton; quoted in A. Pannekoek, *A History of Astronomy* (London: Allen and Unwin, 1961), pp. 264–265.

6. Steven Weinberg, *The First Three Minutes: A Modern View of the Origin of the Universe* (New York: Basic Books, 1977), p. 149.

7. Bertrand Russell, source unavailable.

8. Isaac Newton; quoted in Pannekoek, *A History of Astronomy,* p. 273.

9. Ibid., p. 274.

10. Ibid.

11. William Blake, *Jerusalem* (1804–1820); excerpted in *The Portable Blake*, edited by Alfred Kazin (New York: Viking Press, 1946). p. 463.

12. William Blake, *The Four Zoas* (1797); excerpted in Kazin, *The Portable Blake*, p. 379.

13. Percy Bysshe Shelley, "Adonais: An Elegy on the Death of John Keats" (1821), in *Selected Poems*, edited by Edmund Blundin (London and Glasgow: Collins, 1954), pp. 441, 443, and 449.

14. Edgar Allen Poe, "Eureka" (1848), in *The Works of Edgar Allen Poe*, Volume 9 (New York: Funk and Wagnalls, 1904), p. 41.

15. Rudolf Thiel, *And There Was Light: The Discovery of the Universe*, translated from the German by Richard and Clara Winston (New York: Knopf, 1957).

16. Pierre Simon Laplace; quoted in Thiel, *And There Was Light.*

CHAPTER 7
The History of Western
Astronomy: The Stars

GENERAL INFORMATION IN THIS CHAPTER comes from Rudolf Thiel, *And There Was Light,* translated from the German by Richard and Clara Winston (New York: Knopf, 1957); A. Pannekoek, *A History of Astronomy* (London: Allen and Unwin, 1961); Richard Berendzen, Richard Hart, and Daniel Seeley, *Man Discovers the Galaxies* (New York: Science History Publications, 1976); William Graves Hoyt, *Planets X and Pluto* (Tucson: University of Arizona Press, 1980); and A. F. O'D. Alexander, *The Planet Uranus: A History of Observation, Theory, and Discovery* (New York: American Elsevier, 1965).

1. Christian Huygens; quoted in Thiel, *And There Was Light,* p. 177.

2. Walter H. Hesse, *Our Evolving Universe* Encino, Calif.: Dickenson, 1977), pp. 68–69.

3. Christian Huygens, *Cosmotheros* (English translation, 1698); excerpted in *Theories of the Universe: From Babylonian Myth to Modern Science,* edited by Milton K. Munitz (Glencoe, Ill.: The Free Press, 1957), p. 222.

4. Thomas Wright, *An Original Theory or New Hypothesis of the Universe* (1750); reprinted in Munitz, *Theories of the Universe,* p. 230.

5. Ibid., p. 225.

6. Immanuel Kant, *Universal Natural History and Theory of the Heavens* (1755), translated from the German by W. Hastie (Glasgow, 1900); excerpted in Munitz, *Theories of the Universe,* p. 232.

7. Ibid., p. 238.

8. Ibid., p. 243.

9. Ibid., p. 237.

10. William Herschel; quoted in Pannekoek, *A History of Astronomy,* p. 318.

11. Ibid., p. 317.

12. William Herschel; quoted in Berendzen et al., *Man Discovers the Galaxies,* p. 313.

13. William Herschel; quoted in Alexander, *The Planet Uranus,* p. 52.

14. Sir Joseph Banks; quoted in Hoyt, *Planets X and Pluto,* p. 21.

15. William Herschel; quoted in Alexander, *The Planet Uranus,* p. 59.

16. William Herschel; quoted in Thiel, *And There Was Light,* p. 237.

17. Ibid., p. 233.

18. George Adams, *Astronomical and Geographical Essays,* 5th edition, corrected and enlarged by William Jones (London: W. and S. Jones, 1803), pp. 7–9.

CHAPTER 8

The History of Western Astronomy: The Elements

GENERAL INFORMATION IN THIS CHAPTER comes from Rudolf Thiel, *And There Was Light,* translated from the German by Richard and Clara Winston (New York: Knopf, 1957); A. Pannekoek, *A History of Astronomy* (London: Allen and Unwin, 1961); Richard Berendzen, Richard Hart, and Daniel Seeley, *Man Discovers the Galaxies* (New York: Science History Publications, 1976); Bentley Glass, Owsei Temkin, and William L. Straus, Jr., eds., *Forerunners of Darwin* (1745-1859) Baltimore: Johns Hopkins University Press, 1959); and Otto Struve and Velta Zebergs, *Astronomy of the Twentieth Century* (New York: Macmillan, 1962).

1. Joseph Addison, *Spectator,* No. 519; quoted in *The Great Chain of Being,* by Arthur O. Lovejoy (Cambridge, Mass.: Harvard University Press, 1936), p. 239.

2. George Ellery Hale; quoted in Struve and Zebergs, *Astronomy of the Twentieth Century*, p. 121.

3. Ibid., p. 122.

4. D. H. Lawrence, *The Rainbow* [1915] (New York: Random House, 1943), pp. 416–417.

CHAPTER 9

The History of
Western Astronomy:
The Space-Time Continuum

GENERAL INFORMATION IN THIS CHAPTER comes from Rudolf Thiel, *And There was Light*, translated from the German by Richard and Clara Winston (New York: Knopf, 1957); Richard Berendzen, Richard Hart, and Daniel Seeley, *Man Discovers the Galaxies* (New York: Science History Publications, 1976); and Otto Struve and Velta Zebergs, *Astronomy of the Twentieth Century* (New York: Macmillan, 1962).

1. Arthur M. Young, *The Reflexive Universe: Evolution of Consciousness* (Mill Valley, California: Robert Briggs Associates, 1976, p. 6.

2. Rodney Collin, *The Theory of Celestial Influence* (London: Stuart and Watkins, 1954), p. 38.

3. Harlow Shapley; quoted in Berendzen et al., *Man Discovers the Galaxies*, p. 183.

4. Albert Einstein, *Relativity: The Special and General Theory*, translated from the German by R. W. Lawson (New York: Peter Smith 1920); excerpted in *Theories of the Universe: From Babylonian Myth to Modern Science*, edited by Milton K. Munitz (Glencoe, Ill.: The Free Press, 1957), p. 275.

5. Philippe Le Corbeiller, "The Curvature of Space," in *The New Astronomy*, compiled by the editors of *Scientific American* (New York: Simon and Schuster, 1954), pp. 49–65.

6. Herman Melville, *Moby Dick* [1851] (New York: New American Library, 1961), p. 360.

7. Ibid., p. 302.

8. Ibid., p. 221.

9. Sigmund Freud, *The Interpretation of Dreams*, translated from the German by James Strachey (New York: Avon Books, 1965), p. 313.

10. Ibid., p. 651.

11. Herman Melville, *Pierre or, The Ambiguities* [1852]; quoted in Paul Metcalf, *Genoa: A Telling of Wonders* (Highland, North Carolina: The Nantahala Foundation, 1965), p. 107.

CHAPTER 10

The History of Western Astronomy: The Atom

GENERAL INFORMATION IN THIS CHAPTER comes from Steven Weinberg, *The First Three Minutes: A Modern View of the Origin of the Universe* (New York: Basic Books, 1977); Werner Heisenberg, *Across the Frontiers*, translated from the German by Peter Heath (New York: Harper and Row, 1971); Banesh Hoffman, *The Strange Story of the Quantum* (New York: Dover Books, 1947); and Nigel Calder, *The Key to the Universe* (Baltimore: Penguin Books, 1978).

1. Niels Bohr, *Atomic Physics and the Description of Nature* (Cambridge, England: Cambridge University Press, 1934), p. 57.

2. Gell-Mann took this phrase from Joyce's *Finnegan's Wake* (1939).

3. Gary Snyder, "The Manichaeans," in *The Back Country* (New York: New Directions, 1960); reprinted in *Inside Outer Space: New Poems of the Space Age*, edited by Robert Vas Dias (Garden City, N.Y.: Doubleday, 1970), p. 291.

4. Edward Dorn, "This is the way I hear the Momentum," in *Io*, No. 6 (*Ethnoastronomy Issue*), edited by Richard Grossinger (Ann Arbor, Mich., 1969), p. 109.

5. Ibid., p. 110.

6. Emile Durkheim, *Suicide* (1897), translated by J. Spaulding and G. Simpson (New York: The Free Press, 1938).

7. P. D. Ouspensky, *In Search of the Miraculous: Fragments of an Unknown Teaching* (New York: Harcourt Brace and World, 1949).

8. Steven Weinberg, *The First Three Minutes*, p. 154.

9. Morris Edward Opler, "Myths and Tales of the Jicarilla Apache Indians," *Memoirs of the American Folklore Society*, Volume 31 (New York, 1938), pp. 133–134.

10. Weinberg, *The First Three Minutes*, pp. 154–155.

11. Samuel Beckett, *Murphy* (New York: Grove Press, 1957), p. 1.

12. Samuel Beckett, *Waiting for Godot* (New York: Grove Press, 1954), p. 51.

13. Ibid.

CHAPTER 11

The Creation

THE BASIC ASTRONOMICAL SOURCE for this chapter was Steven Weinberg, *The First Three Minutes: A Modern View of the Origin of the Universe* (New York: Basic Books, 1977); and the basic mythological source was *Primal Myths: Creating the World*, edited by Barbara C. Sproul (New York: Harper and Row, 1979).

1. Aleister Crowley (The Master Therion), *Magick in Theory and Practice* (New York: Castle Books, no date), p. xiv.

2. Hesiod, *Theogony*, translated from the Greek by Charles Olson in his poem "Maximus from Dogtown—I," *Maximus Poems IV, V, VI* (London and New York: Cape Goliard/Grossman, 1968), p. 2.

3. Edward H. Schafer, *Pacing the Void: T'ang Approaches to the Stars* (Berkeley: University of California Press, 1977), p. 28.

4. Ibid., p. 27.

5. Paracelsus, *The Hermetic and Alchemical Writings of Parcelsus the Great*, translated from the Latin by A. E. Waite (London: James Elliott, 1894), Volume I, p. 307.

6. Maria Leach, *The Beginning* (New York: Funk and Wagnalls, 1956); excerpted in *Primal Myths: Creating the World*, edited by Barbara C. Sproul (New York: Harper and Row, 1979), p. 44.

7. E. W. Nelson, *The Eskimo About Bering Strait*, 18th Annual Report of the Bureau of American Ethnology (Washington, D.C., 1899); excerpted in Sproul, *Primal Myths*, p. 221.

8. F. H. Cushing, *Outlines of Zuni Creation Myths*, Thirteenth Annual Report of the Bureau of American Ethnology (Washington, D.C., 1896); excerpted in Sproul, *Primal Myths*, pp. 284–286.

9. *The Popul Vuh*, translated from the Mayan into Spanish by Adrián Recinos, English translation from the Spanish by Deli Goetz and Sylvanus G. Morley (Norman, Oklahoma: University of Oklahoma Press, 1950); excerpted in Sproul, *Primal Myths*, p. 288.

10. T. G. H. Strehlow, *Aranda Traditions* (Melbourne: University of Melbourne Press, 1947); excerpted in Sproul, *Primal Myths*, p. 321.

11. Teuira Henry, *Ancient Tahiti*, Bernice P. Bishop Museum Bulletin, No. 48 (Honolulu: Bishop Museum Press, 1928); excerpted in Sproul, *Primal Myths*, p. 350.

12. *The Nihongi*, translated from the Japanese by W. G. Alston (London: Allen and Unwin, 1956); excerpted in Sproul, *Primal Myths*, p. 212.

13. Edward Dorn, *Some Business Recently Transacted in the White World* (West Newbury, Mass.: Frontier Press, 1971), p. 82.

CHAPTER 12

The History of Western Astronomy: Quasars, Pulsars, and Black Holes

GENERAL INFORMATION IN THIS CHAPTER comes from Richard Berendzen, Richard Hart, and Daniel Seeley, *Man Discovers the Galaxies* (New York: Science History Publications, 1976); Otto Struve and Velta Zebergs, *Astronomy of the Twentieth Century* (New York: Macmillan, 1962); *The New Astronomy*, compiled by the editors of *Scientific American* (New York: Simon and Schuster, 1954); Nigel Calder, *Violent Universe* (New York: Viking Press, 1969); and Walter Sullivan, *Black Holes: The Edge of Space, The End of Time* (Garden City, N.Y.: Doubleday, 1979).

1. Johannes Hevelius; quoted in Richard Hinckley Allen, *Star Names: Their Lore and Meaning* [1899] (New York: Dover Books, 1963), p. 473.

2. Robert Duncan, *The H. D. Book*, Part 2, Chapter 3, in *Io*, No. 6. (*Ethnoastronomy Issue*), edited by Richard Grossinger (Ann Arbor, Mich., 1969), p. 127.

3. Kip S. Thorne, "Gravitational Collapse," *Scientific American*, 217:5 (November 1967), p. 97.

4. William H. Press; quoted in Sullivan, *Black Holes*, p. 202.

5. James Bogan, "Rhapsody for McCoy Tyner," unpublished poem.

CHAPTER 13
Language, Mind, and Astrophysics

1. Jane Roberts, *Seth Speaks: The Eternal Validity of the Soul* (Englewood Cliffs, N.J.: Prentice-Hall, 1972), p. 12.

2. Charles Stein, transcript of a discussion with Richard Grossinger, in *Alchemy: pre-Egyptian Legacy, Millennial Promise* (*Io*, No. 26), edited by Richard Grossinger (Richmond, Calif., 1979), pp. 220–221.

3. Wilhelm Reich, *Ether, God and Devil—Cosmic Superimposition*, translated from the German by Therese Pol (New York: Farrar, Straus and Giroux, 1972).

4. D. H. Lawrence, *The Rainbow* [1915] (New York: Random House, 1943), p. 303.

5. John Wheeler; transcribed from verbal remarks at a conference in *The Nature of Time*, edited by Thomas Gold (Ithaca, N.Y.: Cornell University Press, 1967), p. 234.

6. R. Buckminster Fuller, "Visions 65 Summary Lecture," in *The American Scholar*, 35:2 (Spring 1966), 215.

7. Benjamin Lee Whorf, *Language, Thought, and Reality* (Cambridge, Mass.: M.I.T. Press, 1956), pp. 52–55.

8. Alexander Stephen, *Hopi Journal* (1892); excerpted in *Io*, No. 3 (Winter 1966–1967), edited by Richard Grossinger (Ann Arbor, Mich.), pp. 39–40.

9. Whorf, *Language, Thought, and Reality*, p. 55.

10. C. S. Lewis, *Out of the Silent Planet* (New York: Macmillan, 1965), pp. 43–44.

11. Whorf, *Language, Thought, and Reality*, pp. 55–56.

12. Ibid., pp. 58–60.

13. Claude Lévi-Strauss, *The Savage Mind*, translation from the French anonymous (Chicago: University of Chicago Press, 1966), p. 59.

14. Claude Lévi-Straus, *From Honey to Ashes*, translated from the French by John and Doreen Weightman (New York: Harper and Row, 1973), pp. 288–290.

CHAPTER 14

The Planets: The Solar System

IN CHAPTERS 14–18, my two main sources for general information are Alan E. Nourse, *Nine Planets: Astronomy for the Space Age* (New York: Harper and Row, 1960), and Wernher von Braun and Frederick I. Ordway, *New Worlds: Discoveries from Our Solar System* (Garden City, N.Y.: Doubleday, 1979). I would also like to thank Ken Wilson of the Morrison Planetarium in San Francisco for his close reading of these chapters.

1. William Graves Hoyt, *Planets X and Pluto* (Tucson: University of Arizona Press, 1980), pp. 161–162.
2. Ibid., p. 162.
3. Alex Haley, *Roots* (Garden City, N.Y.: Doubleday, 1976).
4. Johannes Kepler, *Somnium, Sive Astronomia Lunaris* (1630), translated from the Latin by Patricia Frueh Kirkwood, in *Kepler's Dream*, edited by John Lear (Berkeley: University of California Press, 1965).
5. Johannes Kepler, *Somnium, Sive Astronomia Lunaris* (1630), translated by Ludwig Gunther; quoted in Arthur Koestler, *The Sleep-walkers: A History of Man's Changing Vision of the Universe* (New York: Grosset and Dunlap, 1959), p. 417.
6. Lear, *Kepler's Dream*, pp. 155–157; also, for an earlier version of this passage, see Richard Grossinger, *The Continents* (Los Angeles: Black Sparrow Press, 1973), pp. 49–52.
7. Norman Davidson, "Astronomical Aphorisms," *News from the Goetheanum* (Sept./Oct. 1987), Dornach, Switzerland, p. 10.

CHAPTER 15

The Planets: Mercury and Venus

1. Rudolf Hauschka, *The Nature of Substance*, translated from the German by Mary T. Richards and Marjorie Spock (London: Stuart and Watkins, 1966).
2. Svante Arrhenius, *The Destiny of the Stars* (1918); quoted in Patrick Moore, *The Planet Venus* (New York: Macmillan, 1957), pp. 108–109.

3. C. S. Lewis, *Perelandra* (New York: Macmillan, 1965), pp. 37–38.

4. I. S. Shklovskii and Carl Sagan, *Intelligent Life in the Universe* (New York: Dell, 1966), pp. 467–468.

5. Immanuel Velikovsky, *Worlds in Collision* (New York: Dell 1965).

CHAPTER 16

The Planets: The Moon, the Earth, and Mars

1. Rudolf Hauschka, *The Nature of Substance*, translated from the German by Mary T. Richards and Marjorie Spock (London: Stuart and Watkins, 1966), pp. 193–195.

2. William Faulkner, *Absalom, Absalom!* (New York: Random House, 1936).

3. P. D. Ouspensky, *In Search of the Miraculous: Fragments of an Unknown Teaching* (New York: Harcourt, Brace & World, 1949), p. 89.

4. Rudolf Thiel, *And There Was Light*, translated from the German by Richard and Clara Winston (New York: Knopf, 1957), p. 64.

5. Lucretius, *The Nature of the Universe*, translated from the Latin by R. E. Latham (Baltimore: Penguin Books, 1951); quoted here from *Theories of the Universe: From Babylonian Myth to Modern Science*, edited by Milton K. Munitz (Glencoe, Ill.: The Free Press, 1957), p. 45.

6. See Daniel K. Statnekov, *Animated Earth* (Berkeley: North Atlantic Books, 1987), p. 91.

7. Percival Lowell; quoted in Otto Struve and Velta Zebergs, *Astronomy of the Twentieth Century* (New York: Macmillan, 1962), pp. 143–144.

8. Father Athanasius Kircher; quoted in Thiel, *And There Was Light*, pp. 60–61.

9. Richard C. Hoagland, "The 'Face' on Mars," in *Planetary Mysteries*, Revised Edition, edited by Richard Grossinger (Berkeley: North Atlantic Books, 1986), pp. 33–34.

10. Edgar Rice Burroughs, *A Princess of Mars* [1912] (New York: Ballantine Books, 1963), p. 60.

11. Richard C. Hoagland, *The Monuments of Mars: A City on the Edge of Forever* (Berkeley: North Atlantic Books, 1987), pp. 3–4.

12. Hadley Cantril, *The Invasion from Mars: A Study in the Psychology of Panic* (Princeton, N.J.: Princeton University Press, 1940), p. 141.

CHAPTER 17

The Planets: Jupiter and
Its Moons

1. Richard Grossinger, *Solar Journal: Oecological Sections* (Los Angeles: Black Sparrow Press, 1970), p.34.

2. Ibid., pp. 34–35.

3. Ibid., pp. 35–36.

4. I. S. Shklovskii and Carl Sagan, *Intelligent Life in the Universe* (New York: Dell, 1966), pp. 471–473. For a further discussion of the moral implications of the Dyson Sphere, see Gary Snyder, "Interview," conducted by Richard Grossinger and David Wilk (November 9, 1971), in *Io*, No. 25 (*Ecology and Consciousness*), edited by Richard Grossinger (Richmond, Calif., 1978), pp. 152–154.

5. Arthur C. Clarke, "A Meeting with Medusa," in *Jupiter*, edited by Carol Pohl and Frederik Pohl (New York: Ballantine Books, 1973), pp. 252 and 254.

6. Fred Haddock, "Interview" (1968), conducted by Richard Grossinger, in *Io*, No. 6 (*Ethnoastronomy Issue*), edited by Richard Grossinger (Ann Arbor, Mich., 1968), pp. 43–46.

7. Much of the new information on the Jovian moons comes from Rick Gore, "What Voyager Saw: Jupiter's Dazzling Realm," *National Geographic*, 157:1 (January 1980), 2–29.

8. Jonathan Eberhart, "Io: Charting the Fire," *Science News*, 117:16 (April 19, 1980), 251–252.

9. Haddock, "Interview."

10. Arthur C. Clarke, *2001: A Space Odyssey* (New York: New American Library, 1968).

11. Rudolf Hauschka, *The Nature of Substance*, translated from the German by Mary T. Richards and Marjorie Spock (London: Stuart and Watkins, 1966), pp. 167–169.

CHAPTER 18

The Planets: Saturn, Uranus,
Neptune, Pluto, and Their Moons

1. Galileo Galilei; quoted in Wernher von Braun and Frederick I. Ordway, *New Worlds: Discoveries from Our Solar System* (Garden City, N.Y.: Doubleday, 1979), p. 246.

2. Christian Huygens; quoted in von Braun and Ordway, *New Worlds*, p. 246.

3. James Maxwell; quoted in von Braun and Ordway, *New Worlds*, p. 247.

4. Quoted in the *San Francisco Chronicle* (Nov. 13, 1980), p. 1.

5. Ibid.

6. J. Kelly Beatty, "Voyager at Saturn, Act II," in *Sky and Telescope*, 62:5 (November 1981), p. 436.

7. Charles Poncé, *Working the Soul: Reflections on Jungian Psychology* (Berkeley: North Atlantic Books, 1988), pp. 48–49.

8. Rudolf Hauschka, *The Nature of Substance*, translated from the German by Mary T. Richards and Majorie Spock (London: Stuart and Watkins, 1966), pp. 170–174.

9. Barbara Hand Clow, *Chiron: Rainbow Bridge Between the Inner and Outer Planets* (St. Paul, Minnesota: Llewellyn Publications, 1987), p. xix.

10. Andrew Chaikin, "Voyager Among the Ice Worlds," in *Sky and Telescope*, 71:4 (April, 1986), pp. 339–340.

11. Piers Anthony, *Macroscope* (New York: Avon Books, 1969), pp. 182–183.

12. Gerrit Lansing, "The Neptunian Character," in *Io*, No. 16 (*Earth Geography Booklet*, No. 4: *Anima Mundi*), edited by Richard Grossinger (Plainfield, Vermont, 1973), pp. 6–7.

13. Percival Lowell; quoted in William Graves Hoyt, *Planets X and Pluto* (Tucson: University of Arizona Press, 1980), p. 141.

14. Vesto Slipher; quoted in Hoyt, *Planets X and Pluto*, p. 179.

15. Clyde Tombaugh; quoted in Hoyt, *Planets X and Pluto*, p. 188.

16. Dale Cruikshank, Carl Pilcher, and David Morrison; quoted in Hoyt, *Planets X and Pluto*, p. 245.

17. Fritz Brunhübner, "Pluto" (1934); reprinted in *Io*, No. 14 (*Earth Geography Booklet*, No. 3: *Imago Mundi*), edited by Richard Grossinger (Plainfield, Vermont, 1972), pp. 281–290.

18. Oskar Seyffert, *A Dictionary of Classical Antiques* (New York: Meridian Books, 1956), p. 263.

19. William Lonsdale, unpublished talk, Goddard College, Plainfield, Vermont, 1977.

20. Brunhübner, "Pluto."

21. Ibid.

22. James Hillman, *The Dream and the Underworld* (New York: Harper and Row, 1979), pp. 27–28.

CHAPTER 19

Science Fiction:
The Origin of Celestial Worlds

1. Claude Lévi-Strauss, *The Raw and the Cooked*, translated from the French by John and Doreen Weightman (New York: Harper and Row, 1969), p. 168.

2. Ellen Russell Emerson, *Indian Myths or Legends, Traditions, and Symbols of the Aborigines of America, Compared with Those of Other Countries Including Hindostan, Egypt, Persia, Assyria, and China* [1884] (Minneapolis: Ross and Haines, 1965), p. 337.

3. Robert Graves, *The Greek Myths* (Baltimore: Penguin Books, 1955), Volume 1, p. 49.

4. Hesiod, *The Homeric Hymns and Homerica*, translated from the Greek by H. G. Evelyn-White (Cambridge, Mass.: Harvard University Press, 1914), pp. 417–419.

5. Robert K. G. Temple, *The Sirius Mystery* (New York: St. Martin's Press, 1976), p. 207.

6. Ibid., pp. 211–212.

7. *The Gilgamesh Epic*, translated from the Sumerian by Alexander Heidel; quoted in Temple, *The Sirius Mystery*, p. 92.

8. Eric von Daniken; quoted in Temple, *The Sirius Mystery*, back cover.

9. Graves, *The Greek Myths*, Volume 1, pp. 120–121.

10. *The Egyptian Book of the Dead*, translated by E. A. Wallis Budge (New Hyde Park, N.Y.: University Books, 1960), pp. 268–278.

11. *The Tibetan Book of the Dead*, translated and edited by W. Y. Evans-Wentz (Oxford, England: Oxford University Press, 1960), pp. 145 and 162.

12. Geoffrey Ashe, *Land to the West: A Search for Irish and Other Pre-Viking Discoverers of America* (New York: Viking Press, 1962), pp. 73–143.

13. For the original version of this passage, see Richard Grossinger, *The Continents* (Los Angeles: Black Sparrow Press, 1973), pp. 102–104.

14. William Shakespeare, *The Tempest* (ca. 1609), Act I, Scene ii, line 331, in *The Complete Works of William Shakespeare*, edited by William Aldiss Wright (Garden City, N.Y.: Doubleday, 1936), p. 1304.

15. Ibid., Act V, Scene i, lines 181–182, p. 1322.

16. See Carlos Castaneda, *The Teachings of Don Juan: A Yaqui Way of Knowledge* (Berkeley: University of California Press, 1969); *A*

Separate Reality (New York: Simon and Schuster, 1971); and *Journey to Ixtlan* (New York: Simon and Schuster, 1972).

17. Brian W. Aldiss, *Billion Year Spree* (Garden City, N.Y.: Doubleday, 1973).

18. Ibid., p. 16.

19. Ibid., pp. 20–30.

20. Poul Anderson, *The High Crusade* (Garden City, N.Y.: Doubleday, 1960).

CHAPTER 20

Science Fiction: Self and Cosmos

1. Carlos Castaneda, *A Separate Reality* (New York: Simon and Schuster, 1971), indirect quote.

2. Charles Dickens, *Great Expectations* [1861] (New York: Holt, Rinehart, Winston, 1963), p. 84.

3. Ursula K. LeGuin, *City of Illusions* (New York: Ace Books, 1967), pp. 204–205.

4. Olaf Stapledon, *Star Maker* [1937] (New York: Dover Books, 1968), p. 262.

5. Ibid., pp. 424–425.

6. Ibid., p. 424.

7. Roger Zelazny, *Lord of Light* (New York: Avon Books, 1967).

8. Paramahansa Yogananda, *Autobiography of a Yogi* (Los Angeles: Self Realization Fellowship, 1946), p. 316.

9. Lama Yongden, *Mipam: A Tibetan Novel* [1938] (San Francisco: Mudra, 1971), pp. 324–325.

10. Philip José Farmer, *The Maker of Universes* (New York: Ace Books, 1965).

11. Ibid., pp. 8–9.

12. Frank Herbert, *Children of Dune* (New York: Berkley, 1976), p. 271.

13. Ibid., pp. 345–346.

14. Piers Anthony, *Macroscope* (New York: Avon Books, 1969).

15. Ibid., p. 324.

16. Ibid., p. 309.

17. Ibid., pp. 437–480.

18. Frank Herbert, *Dune Messiah* (New York: Berkley, 1969), p. 144.

19. Ibid., pp. 123–124.
20. Ibid., p. 129.
21. Ibid., p. 206.
22. Ibid., p. 237.

CHAPTER 21

Science Fiction: Jesus of Nazareth

1. Arthur C. Clarke, *Childhood's End* (New York: Ballantine Books, 1953).
2. Clarke, *Childhood's End*, p. 170.
3. C.S. Lewis, *Out of the Silent Planet* (New York: Macmillan, 1965).
4. C.S. Lewis, *Perelandra* (New York: Macmillan, 1965).
5. C.S. Lewis, *That Hideous Strength* (New York: Macmillan, 1965).
6. Lewis, *Out of the Silent Planet*, p. 32.
7. Lewis, *Perelandra*, pp. 81–82.
8. Robert Silverberg, *The Book of Skulls* (New York: Berkley, 1972), pp. 25–27.
9. Lewis, *Perelandra*, pp. 218–219.

CHAPTER 22

Astrology

1. Rudolf Steiner, *The Spiritual Guidance of Man and of Mankind* (Dornach, Germany: Rudolf Steiner Press, 1911); quoted and translated from the German in John Meeks, "Johannes Kepler and the Philosophical Defence of Astrology," *Io*, No. 27 (*Star Rhythms: Readings in a Living Astrology*), edited by William Lonsdale (Richmond, Calif.: North Atlantic Books, 1979), p. 73.
2. Marc Edmund Jones, *Horary Astrology* (Berkeley, Calif.: Shambhala, 1971), p. 25.
3. Carl G. Jung, *The Interpretation of Nature and Psyche*, translated from the German by R. F. C. Hull, in *Psyche and Symbol* (Garden City, N.Y.: Doubleday, 1958).

4. Norman Davidson, "Astronomical Aphorisms," *News from the Goetheanum* (Sept./Oct. 1987), Dornach, Switzerland, p. 10.

5. C.S. Lewis, *Perelandra* (New York: Macmillan, 1965), pp. 147–148.

6. Dane Rudhyar, *The Astrology of Personality* (Garden City, N.Y.: Doubleday, 1963).

7. Michael Gauquelin, *The Cosmic Clocks: From Astrology to a Modern Science* (Chicago: Henry Regnery, 1967), p. 131.

8. Ibid.

9. Edward H. Schafer, *Pacing the Void: T'ang Approaches to the Stars* (Berkeley: University of California Press, 1977).

10. Charles Poncé, *Working the Soul: Reflections on Jungian Psychology* (Berkeley: North Atlantic Books, 1988), pp. 54 and 47.

11. Ibid., p. 45.

12. William Sampson, *The Zodiac: A Life Epitome* [1928] (New York: ASI Publishers, 1975), p. 13.

13. Ibid.; this image is developed on pp. 245–249.

14. Ibid., pp. 360–361.

CHAPTER 23
Star Myth

1. Giorgio de Santillana and Hertha von Dechend, *Hamlet's Mill: An Essay on Myth and the Frame of Time* (Boston: Gambit, 1969), p. 48.

2. Ibid.

3. Ibid.

4. Ibid., p. 343.

5. Robert K.G. Temple, *The Sirius Mystery* (New York: St. Martin's Press, 1976), pp. 58–59.

6. De Santillana and von Dechend, *Hamlet's Mill*, p. 5.

7. Ibid., pp. 5–6.

8. Edward Kelly, "The Theatre of Terrestrial Astronomy" (ca. 1590); reprinted in *Alchemy: pre-Egyptian Legacy, Millennial Promise* (*Io*, No. 26), edited by Richard Grossinger (Richmond, Calif.: North Atlantic Books, 1979), pp. 56–68.

9. Norman Davidson, "Astronomical Aphorisms," *News from the Goetheanum* (Sept./Oct. 1987), Dornach, Switzerland, p. 10.

10. Dante Alighieri, *The Divine Comedy*, Cantica 1: *Hell* (1314), translated from the Italian by Dorothy Sayers (Baltimore: Penguin

Books, 1949), p. 71 (Canto 1, lines 2 and 3).

11. Giorgio de Santillana and Hertha von Dechend, *Hamlet's Mill: An Essay on Myth and the Frame of Time* (Boston: Gambit, 1969), pp. 204 and 337.

12. Ibid., pp. 275–277 and 313–315

13. Frances A. Yates, *Giordano Bruno and the Hermetic Tradition* (Chicago: University of Chicago Press, 1964), pp. 367–370.

14. Carl L. Becker, *The Heavenly City of the Eighteenth-Century Philosopher* (New Haven: Yale University Press, 1932), p. 129.

15. Ibid., p. 45.

16. Isaac Bashevis Singer, *The Family Moskat*, translated from the Yiddish by A. H. Gross (New York: Knopf, 1950), p. 594.

17. Charles Olson, *The Maximus Poems. Volume Three* (New York: Grossman, 1975), p. 39.

18. Isaac Bashevis Singer, *Shosha*, translated from the Yidddish by Joseph Singer (New York: Fawcett, 1978), pp. 129–130.

19. De Santillana and von Dechend, *Hamlet's Mill*, p. 5.

20. Ibid., pp. 5–6.

21. De Santillana and von Dechend, *Hamlet's Mill*, p. 6.

22. Ibid., pp. 41–42, 63, 156, 166, 173, 220, 249, 251–252, and 291–292.

23. Denis Diderot, *Oeuvres*, Volume 18 (1765); quoted in Becker, *The Heavenly City*, p. 147.

24. George Bernard Shaw, *Back to Methuselah* (New York: Brentano's, 1921), p. xlvi.

CHAPTER 24

Flying Saucers and Extraterrestial Life

1. Mel Noel, "UFO Lecture" (1966), *Io*, No. 4 (*Alchemy Issue*), edited by Richard Grossinger (Ann Arbor, Mich., 1967), p. 111.

2. Ibid., p. 114.

3. Lt. Col. Wendelle C. Stevens, ed., *UFO . . . Contact from the Pleiades*, Volume 1 (Phoenix, Arizona: Genesis III Productions, 1979), no page numbers.

4. Ibid.

5. Carl G. Jung, *Flying Saucers: A Modern Myth of Things Seen in the Sky*, translated from the German by R. F. C. Hull, in *Civilization in*

Transition (New York: Pantheon Books, 1964), pp. 307–433.

6. Erich von Daniken, *Chariots of the Gods?* (New York: Bantam Books, 1970).

7. Norman Davidson, "Astronomical Aphorisms," *News from the Goetheanum* (Sept./Oct. 1987), Dornach, Switzerland, p. 10.

8. Robert K. G. Temple, *The Sirius Mystery* (New York: St. Martin's Press, 1976).

9. Robert Anton Wilson, *Cosmic Trigger* (Berkeley, Calif.: And/Or Press, 1977).

10. Ibid.

11. Peter Tompkins and Christopher Bird, *The Secret Life of Plants* (New York: Harper and Row, 1973), pp. 46–48.

12. Ibid., p. 49.

13. Ibid., p. 50.

14. Jacques Vallee, *Messengers of Deception: UFO Contacts and Cults* (Berkeley, Calif.: And/Or Press, 1979).

15. Ibid.

16. Richard C. Hoagland, "Reassessing Sacred Cows: A White Paper on Possible Connections between Martian 'Monuments' and UFOs," unpublished paper, 1988.

17. Ian Watson, *Miracle Visitors* (New York: Ace Books, 1978).

18. Whitley Strieber, *Communion* (New York: Beech Tree Books, William Morrow, 1987), p. 30.

19. Ibid.

20. Ibid., p. 295.

21. Ibid., p. 31.

22. Budd Hopkins, *Intruders: The Incredible Visitations at Copley Woods* (New York: Random House, 1987), p. 122.

23. Ibid.

24. Richard C. Hoagland, *The Monuments of Mars: A City on the Edge of Forever* (Berkeley: North Atlantic Books, 1987), back cover.

25. Richard C. Hoagland, "Reassessing Sacred Cows," op. cit.

CHAPTER 25

The Pop Star Cult
of the Fifties and Sixties

1. See Rob Brezsny, "Qabalistic Sex*Magic for Shortstops and Second Basemen," in *Baseball I Gave You All the Best Years of My Life*,

edited by Kevin Kerrane and Richard Grossinger (Richmond, Calif.: North Atlantic Books, 1978), pp. 381–390.

2. Kenneth Anger, "Interview," conducted by *Spider Magazine* (1965); reprinted in *Io*, No. 12 (*Earth Geography Booklet*, No. 1: *Economics, Technology, and Celestial Influence*), edited by Richard Grossinger (Cape Elizabeth, Maine, 1972), pp. 24–15.

3. Tarthang Tulku, *Time, Space, and Knowledge* (Emeryville, Calif.: Dharma Publishing, 1977), p. 10.

APPENDIX

Giving Them A Name

1. Jule Eisenbud, "Interview (January 8, 1972)," in *Ecology and Consciousness*, edited by Richard Grossinger (Richmond, California: North Atlantic Books, 1978).

2. Ibid., 168–169.

3. Jacques Vallee, *The Invisible College* (New York: E. P. Dutton, 1975), pp. 143, 145.

4. Ibid., 153.

Bibliography

Adams, George. *Astronomical and Geographical Essays.* 5th edition. Corrected and enlarged by William Jones. London: W. and S. Jones, 1803.

Agrippa, Henry Cornelius. "Astronomical Geomancy" (1655). Reprinted in *Io,* No. 5 (*Doctrine of Signatures*), edited by Richard Grossinger. Ann Arbor, Mich., 1969.

Akerblom, Kjell. *Astronomy and Navigation in Polynesia and Micronesia: A Survey.* Ethnographic Museum of Stockholm Monograph Series, No. 14. Stockholm, 1968.

Aldiss, Brian W. *Billion Year Spree.* Garden City, N.Y.: Doubleday, 1973.

Alexander, A. F. O'D. *The Planet Uranus: A History of Observation, Theory, and Discovery.* New York: American Elsevier, 1965.

Allen, Richard Hinckley. *Star Names: Their Lore and Meaning* (1899). New York: Dover Books, 1963.

Anderson, Poul. *The High Crusade.* Garden City, N.Y.: Doubleday, 1960.

Anger, Kenneth. "Interview," conducted by *Spider Magazine* (1965). Reprinted in *Io,* No. 12 (*Earth Geography Booklet,* No. 1: *Economics, Technology, and Celestial Influence*), edited by Richard Grossinger. Cape Elizabeth, Maine, 1972.

Anthony, Piers. *Macroscope.* New York: Avon Books, 1969.

Aristotle. *On the Heavens.* Translated from the Greek by W. K. C. Guthrie. Cambridge, Mass.: Harvard University Press, 1939.

Ashe, Geoffrey. *Land to the West: A Search for Irish and Other Pre-Viking Discoverers of America.* New York: Viking Press, 1962.

Becker, Carl L. *The Heavenly City of the Eighteenth-Century Philosopher.* New Haven: Yale University Press, 1932.

Beckett, Samuel. *Murphy.* New York: Grove Press, 1957.
————. *Waiting for Godot.* New York: Grove Press, 1954.

Berendzen, Richard, Richard Hart, and Daniel Seeley. *Man Discovers the Galaxies.* New York: Science History Publications, 1976.

Best, Eldon. *The Astronomical Knowledge of the Maori, Genuine and Empirical: Including Data Concerning Their Systems of Astrogeny, Astrolatry, and Natural Astrology, with Notes on Certain Other Natural Phenomena.* Dominion Museum Monographs, No. 3. Wellington, New Zealand, 1922.

Bickerman, Elias, and Morton Smith. *The Ancient History of Western Civilization.* New York: Harper and Row, 1976.

Blake, William. *The Four Zoas* (1797) and *Jerusalem* (1804–1820). In *The Portable Blake,* edited by Alfred Kazin. New York: Viking Press, 1946.

Bogan, James. "Rhapsody for McCoy Tyner." Unpublished poem.

Bohr, Niels. *Atomic Physics and the Description of Nature.* Cambridge, England: Cambridge University Press, 1934.

Brezsny, Rob. "Qabalistic Sex*Magic for Shortstops and Second Basemen," In *Baseball I Gave You All the Best Years of My Life,* edited by Kevin Kerrane and Richard Grossinger. Richmond, Calif.: North Atlantic Books, 1978.

Brunhübner, Fritz. "Pluto" (1934). Reprinted in *Io,* No. 14 (*Earth Geography Booklet,* No. 3: *Imago Mundi*), edited by Richard Grossinger. Plainfield, Vermont, 1972.

Buckstaff, Ralph N. "Stars and Constellations of a Pawnee Sky Map" (1927). Reprinted in *Io,* No. 6 (*Ethnoastronomy Issue*), edited by Richard Grossinger. Ann Arbor, Mich., 1969.

Burroughs, Edgar Rice. *A Princess of Mars* (1912). New York: Ballantine Books, 1963.

Calder, Nigel. *The Key to the Universe.* Baltimore: Penguin Books, 1978.

———. *Violent Universe.* New York: Viking Press, 1969.

Cantril, Hadley. *The Invasion from Mars: A Study in the Psychology of Panic.* Princeton, N.J.: Princeton University Press, 1940.

Castaneda, Carlos. *Journey to Ixtlan.* New York: Simon and Schuster, 1972.

———. *A Separate Reality.* New York: Simon and Schuster, 1971.

———. *The Teachings of Don Juan: A Yaqui Way of Knowledge.* Berkeley: University of California Press, 1969.

The Celestial Elder's Canon of the Spirit Lights (An Ancient Chinese Book of Interior Astrology). Translated by Nathan Sivin. In *Io,* No. 4 (*Alchemy Issue,* enlarged edition), edited by Richard Grossinger. Plainfield, Vermont, 1973.

Clarke, Arthur C. *Childhood's End.* New York: Ballantine Books, 1953.

———. "A Meeting with Medusa." In *Jupiter,* edited by Carol Pohl and Frederik Pohl. New York: Ballantine Books, 1973.

———. *2001: A Space Odyssey.* New York: New American Library, 1968.

Collin, Rodney. *The Theory of Celestial Influence.* London: Stuart and Watkins, 1954.

Collins, Michael. *Carrying the Fire: An Astronaut's Journey.* New York: Farrar, Straus and Giroux, 1974.

Copernicus, Nicolaus. *De Revolutionibus* (1543). Translated from the Latin by John F. Dobson and Selig Brodetsky. In *Occasional Notes of the Royal Astronomical Society.* London, 1947.

Cornford, F. M., ed. and trans. *Plato's Cosmology: The Timaeus of Plato.* New York: Humanities Press, 1937.

Crowley, Aleister. *Magick in Theory and Practice.* New York: Castle Books, no date.

Cusanus, Nicolas. *Of Learned Ignorance* (1440). Translated from the Latin by Fr. Germain Heron. New Haven: Yale University Press, 1954.

Cushing, F. H. *Outlines of Zuni Creation Myths.* Thirteenth Annual Report of the Bureau of American Ethnology. Washington, D.C., 1896.

Dante Alighieri. *Hell.* Translated from the Italian by Dorothy Sayers. Baltimore: Penguin Books, 1949.

———. *Paradise.* Translated from the Italian by Dorothy Sayers and Barbara Reynolds. Baltimore: Penguin Books, 1962.

Davidson, Martin. *The Stars and the Mind.* London: Watts, 1947.

de Santillana, Giorgio, and Hertha von Dechend. *Hamlet's Mill: An Essay on Myth and the Frame of Time.* Boston: Gambit, 1969.

Dickens, Charles. *Great Expectations* (1861). New York: Dodd, Mead, 1947.

Dorn, Edward. *Some Business Recently Transacted in the White World.* West Newbury, Mass.: Frontier Press, 1971.

———. "This is the way I hear the Momentum." In *Io,* No. 6 (*Ethnoastronomy Issue*), edited by Richard Grossinger. Ann Arbor, Mich., 1969.

Dreyer, J. L. E. *A History of the Planetary Systems from Thales to Kepler.* Cambridge, England: Cambridge University Press, 1905.

Duncan, Robert. *The H.D. Book* (Part 2, Chapter 3). In *Io,* No. 6 (*Ethnoastronomy Issue*), edited by Richard Grossinger. Ann Arbor, Mich., 1969.

Durkheim, Émile. *Suicide* (1897). Translated by J. Spaulding and G. Simpson. New York: The Free Press, 1938.

Eberhart, Jonathan. "Io: Charting the Fire." *Science News,* 117:16 (April 19, 1980), 251–254.

Eddington, A. S. *The Expanding Universe.* Cambridge, England: Cambridge University Press, 1933.

The Egyptian Book of the Dead. Translated by E. A. Wallis Budge. New Hyde Park, N.Y.: University Books, 1960.

Einstein, Albert. *Relativity: The Special and General Theory.* Translated from the German by R. W. Lawson. New York: Peter Smith, 1920.

Emerson, Ellen Russell. *Indian Myths or Legends, Traditions, and Symbols of the Aborigines of America, Compared with Those of Other Countries Including Hindostan, Egypt, Persia, Assyria, and China* (1884). Minneapolis, Minn.: Ross and Haines, 1965.

Enslin, Theodore. "Note." In *Io,* No. 6 (*Ethnoastronomy Issue*), edited by Richard Grossinger. Ann Arbor, Mich., 1969.

Farmer, Philip José. *The Maker of Universes.* New York: Ace Books, 1965.

Faulkner, William. *Absalom, Absalom!* New York: Random House, 1936.

Finney, Jack. *The Invasion of the Body Snatchers.* New York: Dell, 1954.

Fletcher, Alice C. "Pawnee Star Lore" (1904) and "Star Cult Among the Pawnee" (1902). Reprinted in *Io,* No. 6 (*Ethnoastronomy Issue*), edited by Richard Grossinger. Ann Arbor, Mich., 1969.

Freud, Sigmund. *The Interpretation of Dreams* (1900). Translated from the German by James Strachey. New York: Avon Books, 1965.

Fulder, Stephen. *The Root of Being: Ginseng and the Pharmacology of Harmony.* London: Hutchison, 1980.

Fuller, R. Buckminster. "Vision 65 Summary Lecture." *The American Scholar,* 35:2 (Spring 1966), 206–218.

Galileo Galilei. *Dialogue Concerning the Two Chief World Systems— Ptolemaic and Copernican* (1632). Translated from the Latin by Stillman Drake. Berkeley: University of California Press, 1953.

Gauquelin, Michel. *The Cosmic Clocks: From Astrology to a Modern Science.* Chicago: Henry Regnery, 1967.

Glass, Bentley, Owsei Temkin, and William L. Straus, Jr., eds. *Forerunners of Darwin (1745–1859).* Baltimore: Johns Hopkins University Press, 1959.

Gold, Thomas, ed. *The Nature of Time.* Ithaca, N.Y.: Cornell University Press, 1967.

Gordon, Cyrus. *Before Columbus: Links Between the Old World and Ancient America.* New York: Crown, 1971.

Gore, Rick. "What Voyager Saw: Jupiter's Dazzling Realm." *National Geographic,* 157:1 (January 1980), 2–29.

Graves, Robert. *The Greek Myths.* Volume 1. Baltimore: Penguin Books, 1955.

Grossinger, Richard. *The Continents.* Los Angeles: Black Sparrow Press, 1973.

———. *The Long Body of the Dream.* Plainfield, Vermont: North Atlantic Books, 1974.

———. *Planet Medicine: From Stone-Age Shamanism to Post-Industrial Healing.* Garden City, N.Y.: Doubleday, 1980.

———. *The Planet with Blue Skies,* unpublished manuscript.

———. *The Provinces.* Plainfield, Vermont: North Atlantic Books, 1975.

———. *The Slag of Creation.* Plainfield, Vermont: North Atlantic Books, 1975.

———. *Solar Journal: Oecological Sections.* Los Angeles: Black Sparrow Press, 1970.

———. *The Unfinished Business of Doctor Hermes.* Plainfield, Vermont: North Atlantic Books, 1976.

———. *The Windy Passage from Nostalgia.* Plainfield, Vermont: North Atlantic Books, 1974.

———, ed. *Alchemy Issue (Io,* No. 4, enlarged edition). Plainfield, Vermont, 1973.

———, ed. *Alchemy: pre-Egyptian Legacy, Millennial Promise (Io,* No. 26). Richmond, Calif.: North Atlantic Books, 1979.

———, ed. *Doctrine of Signatures (Io,* No. 5). Ann Arbor, Mich., 1968.

———, ed. *Earth Geography Booklet,* No. 1 *(Io,* No. 12: *Economics, Technology, and Celestial Influence).* Cape Elizabeth, Maine, 1972.

———, ed. *Earth Geography Booklet,* No. 3 *(Io,* No. 14: *Imago Mundi).* Plainfield, Vermont, 1972.

———, ed. *Earth Geography Booklet,* No. 4 *(Io,* No. 16: *Anima Mundi).* Plainfield, Vermont, 1973.

———, ed. *Ecology and Consciousness (Io,* No. 25). Richmond, Calif.: North Atlantic Books, 1978.

———, ed. *Ethnoastronomy Issue (Io,* No. 6). Ann Arbor, Mich., 1969.

———, ed. *An Olson-Melville Sourcebook.* Volume 1 *(Io,* No. 22: *The New Found Land, or North America).* Plainfield, Vermont, 1976.

Haddock, Fred T. "Interview" (1968), conducted by Richard Grossinger. In *Io,* No. 6 *(Ethnoastronomy Issue),* edited by Richard Grossinger. Ann Arbor, Mich., 1969.

Haley, Alex. *Roots.* Garden City, N.Y.: Doubleday, 1976.

Hauschka, Rudolf. *The Nature of Substance.* Translated from the German by Mary T. Richards and Marjorie Spock. London: Stuart and Watkins, 1966.

Hawkins, Gerald S. *Stonehenge Decoded.* New York: Dell, 1965.

Heisenberg, Werner. *Across the Frontiers.* Translated from the German by Peter Heath. New York: Harper and Row, 1971.

———. *Physics and Beyond.* Translated from the German by Arnold J. Pomerans. New York: Harper and Row, 1971.

Henry, Teuira. *Ancient Tahiti.* Bernice P. Bishop Museum Bulletin, No, 48. Honolulu: Bishop Museum Press, 1928.

Herbert, Frank. *Children of Dune.* New York: Berkley, 1976.

———. *Dune.* New York: Berkley, 1965.

———. *Dune Messiah.* New York: Berkley, 1969.

Hermes Trismegistus. *The Divine Pymander and Other Writings.* Translated by John D. Chambers (1882). New York: Samuel Weiser, 1972.

Hesiod. *The Homeric Hymns and Homerica.* Translated from the Greek by H. G. Evelyn-White. Cambridge, Mass.: Harvard University Press, 1914.

———. *Theogony.* Translated from the Greek by Charles Olson. In *Maximus Poems IV, V, VI,* by Charles Olson. London and New York: Cape Goliard/Grossman, 1968.

Hesse, Walter H. *Our Evolving Universe.* Encino, Calif.: Dickenson, 1977.

Hillman, James. *The Dream and the Underworld.* New York: Harper and Row, 1979.

Hoffman, Banesh. *The Strange Story of the Quantum.* New York: Dover Books, 1947.

Hoyle, Fred. *The Nature of the Universe.* New York: Harper and Bros., 1950.

Hoyt, William Graves. *Planets X and Pluto.* Tucson: University of Arizona Press, 1980.

Hubble, Edwin. *The Realm of the Nebulae.* New Haven: Yale University Press, 1936.

Johnson, Francis R. *Astronomical Thought in Renaissance England.* Baltimore: Johns Hopkins University Press, 1937.

Jones, Marc Edmund. *Horary Astrology.* Berkeley, Calif.: Shambhala, 1971.

Jung, Carl G. *Flying Saucers: A Modern Myth of Things Seen in the Skies.* Translated from the German by R. F. C. Hull. In *Civilization in Transition.* New York: Pantheon Books, 1964.

———. *The Interpretation of Nature and Psyche.* Translated from the German by R. F. C. Hull. In *Psyche and Symbol.* Garden City, N.Y.: Doubleday, 1958.

Kant, Immanuel. *Universal Natural History and Theory of the Heavens* (1755). Translated from the German by W. Hastie (1900). Glasgow, 1900.

Kelly, Edward. "The Theatre of Terrestrial Astronomy" (ca. 1590). Reprinted in *Io*, No. 26 (*Alchemy: pre-Egyptian Legacy, Millennial Promise*), edited by Richard Grossinger. Richmond, Calif.: North Atlantic Books, 1979.

Kelly, Robert. "The Alchemist" (1961). Reprinted in *Io*, No. 26 (*Alchemy: pre-Egyptian Legacy, Millennial Promise*), edited by Richard Grossinger. Richmond, Calif.: North Atlantic Books, 1979.

————. "Re: The Occult" (1963). Reprinted in *Io*, No. 6 (*Ethnoastronomy Issue*), edited by Richard Grossinger. Ann Arbor, Mich., 1969.

Kepler, Johannes. *Somnium, Sive Astronomia Lunaris* (1630). Translated from the Latin by Patricia Frueh Kirkwood. In *Kepler's Dream*, edited by John Lear. Berkeley: University of California Press, 1965.

Kerrane, Kevin, and Richard Grossinger, eds. *Baseball I Gave You All the Best Years of My Life* (*Io*, No. 24). Richmond, Calif.: North Atlantic Books, 1978.

Koestler, Arthur. *The Sleepwalkers: A History of Man's Changing Vision of the Universe*. New York: Grosset and Dunlap, 1959.

Krupp, Edwin, ed. *In Search of Ancient Astronomy*. Garden City, N.Y.: Doubleday, 1977.

Lansing, Gerrit. "The Neptunian Character" (1963). Reprinted in *Io*, No. 16 (*Earth Geography Booklet, No. 4: Anima Mundi*), edited by Richard Grossinger. Plainfield, Vermont, 1973.

Lawrence, D. H. *The Rainbow* (1915). New York: Random House, 1943.

Leach, Maria. *The Beginning*. New York: Funk and Wagnalls, 1956.

Le Corbeiller, Phillipe. "The Curvature of Space." In *The New Astronomy*, compiled by the editors of *Scientific American*. New York: Simon and Schuster, 1954.

Lévi-Strauss, Claude. *From Honey to Ashes*. Translated from the French by John and Doreen Weightman. New York: Harper and Row, 1973.

————. *The Raw and the Cooked*. Translated from the French by John and Doreen Weightman. New York: Harper and Row, 1969.

————. *The Savage Mind*. Translation from the French anonymous. Chicago: University of Chicago Press, 1966.

Lewis, C. S. *Out of the Silent Planet*. New York: Macmillan, 1965.

————. *Perelandra*. New York: Macmillan, 1965.

————. *That Hideous Strength*. New York: Macmillan, 1965.

Lonsdale, William. *The Signs of the Zodiac in the Late Twentieth Century*. Richmond, Calif.: North Atlantic Books, 1981.

————, ed. *Star Rhythms* (*Io*, No. 27). Richmond, Calif.: North Atlantic Books, 1979.

Lorusso, Julia, and Joel Glick. *Healing Stoned: The Therapeutic Use of Gems and Minerals*. Albuquerque, New Mexico: Brotherhood of Life, 1976.

Lovejoy, Arthur O. *The Great Chain of Being*. Cambridge, Mass.: Harvard University Press, 1936.

Lucretius. *The Nature of the Universe*. Translated from the Latin by R. E. Latham. Baltimore: Penguin Books, 1951.

Marshack, Alexander. *The Roots of Civilization: The Cognitive Beginnings of Man's First Art, Symbol and Notation*. New York: McGraw-Hill, 1972.

Meeks, John. "Johannes Kepler and the Philosophical Defence of Astrology." In *Io*, No. 27 (*Star Rhythms*), edited by William Lonsdale. Richmond, Calif.: North Atlantic Books, 1979.

Melville, Herman. *Moby Dick* (1851). New York: New American Library, 1961.

————. *Pierre or, The Ambiguities* (1852). New York: New American Library, 1964.

Metcalf, Paul. *Genoa: A Telling of Wonders*. Highland, North Carolina: The Nantahala Foundation, 1965.

Milton, John. *Paradise Lost* (1667). In *John Milton: Complete Poems and Major Prose*, edited by Merritt Y. Hughes. New York: Odyssey Press, 1957.

Moore, Patrick. *The Planet Venus*. New York: Macmillan, 1957.

Moran, Hugh A., and David H. Kelley. *The Alphabet and the Ancient Calendar Signs*. Palo Alto, Calif.: Daily Press, 1969.

Munitz, Milton K, ed. *Theories of the Universe: From Babylonian Myth to Modern Science*. Glencoe, Ill.: The Free Press, 1957.

Nelson, E. W. *The Eskimo About Bering Strait*. 18th Annual Report of the Bureau of American Ethnology. Washington, D.C., 1899.

The New Astronomy. Compiled by the editors of *Scientific American*. New York: Simon and Schuster, 1954.

Newton, Isaac. *Philosophiae Naturalis Principia Mathematica* (1687). Translated from the Latin by Andrew Motte. Berkeley: University of California Press, 1946.

The Nihongi. Translated from the Japanese by W. G. Alston. London: Allen and Unwin, 1956.

Noel, Mel. "UFO Lecture" (1966). In *Io*, No. 4 (*Alchemy Issue*, enlarged edition), edited by Richard Grossinger. Plainfield, Vermont, 1973.

Nourse, Alan E. *Nine Planets: Astronomy for the Space Age.* New York: Harper and Row, 1960.

Olmstead, A. T. *History of the Persian Empire.* Chicago: University of Chicago Press, 1948.

Olson, Charles. *Maximus Poems IV, V, VI.* London and New York: Cape Goliard/Grossman, 1968.

————. *The Maximus Poems, Volume 3.* New York: Grossman, 1975.

Ophiel. *The Art and Practice of Astral Projection.* St. Paul, Minn.: The Gnostic Institute, 1961.

Opler, Morris Edward. "Myths and Tales of the Jicarilla Apache Indians." *Memoirs of the American Folklore Institute,* Volume 31. New York, 1938.

Ouspensky, P. D. *In Search of the Miraculous: Fragments of an Unknown Teaching.* New York: Harcourt, Brace and World, 1949.

Pannekoek, A. *A History of Astronomy.* London: Allen and Unwin, 1961.

Paracelsus. *The Hermetic and Alchemical Writings of Paracelsus the Great.* Translated from the Latin by A. E. Waite. London: James Elliott, 1894.

Plato. *Timaeus.* Translated from the Greek by H. D. P. Lee. Baltimore: Penguin Books, 1965.

Poe, Edgar Allen. "Eureka." In *The Works of Edgar Allen Poe,* Volume 9. New York: Funk and Wagnalls, 1904.

The Popul Vuh. Translated from the Mayan into Spanish by Adrián Recinos. English translation from the Spanish by Deli Goetz and Sylvanus G. Morley. Norman, Oklahoma: University of Oklahoma Press, 1950.

Ptolemy. *The Almagest.* Translated from the Greek by R. C. Taliaferro. Chicago: Encyclopedia Britannica, 1952.

Reich, Wilhelm. *Ether, God and Devil—Cosmic Superimposition.* Translated from the German by Therese Pol. New York: Farrar, Straus and Giroux, 1972.

Roberts, Jane. *Seth Speaks: The Eternal Validity of the Soul.* Englewood Cliffs, N.J.: Prentice-Hall, 1972.

Rudhyar, Dane. *The Astrology of Personality.* Garden City, N.Y.: Doubleday, 1963.

Sagan, Carl. "Interview," conducted by Richard Grossinger (January 23, 1972). In *Io,* No. 14 (*Earth Geography Booklet,* No. 3: *Imago Mundi*), edited by Richard Grossinger. Plainfield, Vermont, 1972.

Sampson, William. *The Zodiac: A Life Epitome* (1928). New York: ASI Publishers, 1975.

Sauer, Carl O. *The Early Spanish Main.* Berkeley: University of California Press, 1966.

————. *Northern Mists.* Berkeley, Calif.; Turtle Island Foundation, 1968.

Schafer, Edward H. *Pacing the Void: T'ang Approaches to the Stars.* Berkeley: University of California Press, 1977.

Seyffert, Oskar. *A Dictionary of Classical Antiques.* New York: Meridian Books, 1956.

Shakespeare, William. *The Tempest* (ca. 1609). In *The Complete Works of William Shakespeare,* edited by William Aldiss Wright. Garden City, N.Y.: Doubleday, 1936.

Shaw, George Bernard. *Back to Methuselah.* New York: Brentano's, 1921.

Shelley, Percy Bysse. "Adonais: An Elegy on the Death of John Keats" (1821). In *Selected Poems,* edited by Edmund Blunden. London and Glasgow: Collins, 1954.

Shklovskii, I. S., and Carl Sagan. *Intelligent Life in the Universe.* New York: Dell, 1966.

Silverberg, Robert. *The Book of Skulls.* New York: Berkley, 1972.

Singer, Dorothea Waley. *Giordano Bruno: His Life and Thought with an Annotated Translation of His Work, On the Infinite Universe and Worlds.* New York: Abelard-Schuman, 1950.

Singer, Isaac Bashevis. *The Family Moskat.* Translated from the Yiddish by A. H. Gross. New York: Knopf, 1950.

————. *Shosha.* Translated from the Yiddish by Joseph Singer. New York: Fawcett, 1978.

Snyder, Gary. *The Back Country.* New York: New Directions, 1960.

————. "Interview," conducted by Richard Grossinger and David Wilk (November 9, 1971). In *Io,* No. 25 (*Ecology and Consciousness*), edited by Richard Grossinger. Richmond, Calif.: North Atlantic Books, 1978.

Sproul, Barbara C. *Primal Myths: Creating the World.* New York: Harper and Row, 1979.

Stapledon, Olaf. *Star Maker* (1937). New York: Dover Books, 1968.

Stephen, Alexander. *Hopi Journal* (1892). Excerpted in *Io,* No. 3 (Winter 1966–1967), edited by Richard Grossinger. Ann Arbor, Mich.

Stevens, Lt. Col. Wendelle C., ed. *UFO . . . Contact from the Pleiades.* Phoenix, Arizona: Genesis III Productions, 1979.

Strehlow, T. G. H. *Aranda Traditions.* Melbourne: University of Melbourne Press, 1947.

Struve, Otto, and Velta Zebergs. *Astronomy of the Twentieth Century.* New York: Macmillan, 1962.

Sullivan, Walter. *Black Holes: The Edge of Space, The End of Time.* Garden City, N.Y.: Doubleday, 1979.

Tarthang Tulku. *Time, Space, and Knowledge.* Emeryville, Calif.: Dharma Pulishing, 1977.

Teilhard de Chardin, Pierre. *The Phenomenon of Man.* Translated from the French by Bernard Wall. New York: Harper and Row, 1959.

Temple, Robert K. G. *The Sirius Mystery.* New York: St. Martin's Press, 1976.

Thiel, Rudolf. *And There Was Light: The Discovery of the Universe.* Translated from the German by Richard and Clara Winston. New York: Knopf, 1957.

Thorne, Kip S. "Gravitational Collapse." *Scientific American,* 217:5 (November 1967), 88–98.

The Tibetan Book of the Dead. Translated and edited by W. Y. Evans-Wentz. Oxford, Engand: Oxford Univerity Press,1960.

Tompkins, Peter, and Christopher Bird. *The Secret Life of Plants.* New York: Harper and Row, 1973.

Vallee, Jacques. *Messengers of Deception: UFO Contacts and Cults.* Berkeley, Calif.: And/Or Press, 1979.

Vas Dias, Robert, ed. *Inside Outer Space: New Poems of the Space Age.* Garden City, N.Y.: Doubleday, 1970.

Velikovsky, Immanuel. *Worlds in Collision.* New York: Dell, 1965.

von Braun, Wernher, and Frederick I. Ordway. *New Worlds: Discoveries from Our Solar System.* Garden City, N.Y.: Doubleday, 1979.

von Daniken, Erich. *Chariots of the Gods?* New York: Bantam Books, 1970.

Waite, A. E. *The Holy Kabbalah.* New Hyde Park, N.Y.: University Books, 1960.

Weinberg, Steven. *The First Three Minutes: A Modern View of the Origin of the Universe.* New York: Basic Books, 1977.

Wheelwright, Philip, ed. *The Presocratics.* Indianapolis: Odyssey Press, 1966.

Whitehead, Alfred North. *Process and Reality.* Toronto: Macmillan, 1929.

Whorf, Benjamin Lee. *Language, Thought, and Reality.* Cambridge, Mass.: M.I.T. Press, 1956.

Wilson, Robert Anton. *Cosmic Trigger.* Berkeley, Calif.: And/Or Press, 1977.

Yates, Frances A. *Giordano Bruno and the Hermetic Tradition.* Chicago: University of Chicago Press, 1964.

————. *Theatre of the World.* Chicago: University of Chicago Press, 1969.

Yogananda, Paramahansa. *Autobiography of a Yogi.* Los Angeles: Self-Realization Fellowship, 1946.

Yongden, Lama. *Mipam: A Tibetan Novel* (1938). San Francisco: Mudra, 1971.

Zelazny, Roger. *Lord of Light.* New York: Avon Books, 1967.

Additional Bibliography for 1988 Edition

Beatty, J. Kelly. "A Place Called Venus." *Sky and Telescope*, 71:4 April, 1986, 333–337.

Beatty, J. Kelly. "Voyager at Saturn, Act II." *Sky and Telescope*, 62: 5 November 1981.

Chaikin, Andrew. "Voyager Among the Ice Worlds," in *Sky and Telescope*, 71: 4 April, 1986, 338–343.

Clow, Barbara Hand. *Chiron: Rainbow Bridge Between the Inner and Outer Planets*. St. Paul, Minnesota: Llewellyn Publications, 1987.

Da Free John, *The Transmission of Doubt: Talks and Essays on the Transcendence of Scientific Materialism through Radical Understanding*. Clear Lake, California: The Dawn Horse Press, 1984.

Davidson, Norman. "Astronomical Aphorisms." *News from the Goetheanum* Sept./Oct. 1987, Dornach, Switzerland, p. 10.

di Prima, Diane. *Selected Poems 1956–1976*. Plainfield, Vermont: North Atlantic Books, 1977.

Grossinger, Richard. *Embryogenesis: From Cosmos to Creature—The Origins of Human Biology*. Berkeley: North Atlantic Books, 1986.

———. *Planetary Mysteries*, Revised Edition. Berkeley: North Atlantic Books, 1986.

Hoagland, Richard C. "The 'Face' on Mars." *Planetary Mysteries*, edited by Richard Grossinger. Berkeley: North Atlantic Books, 1986.

———. *The Monuments of Mars: A City on the Edge of Forever*. Berkeley: North Atlantic Books, 1987.

———. "Reassessing Sacred Cows: A White Paper on Possible Connections between Martian 'Monuments' and UFOs," unpublished paper, 1988.

Hopkins, Budd. *Intruders: The Incredible Visitations at Copley Woods*. New York: Random House, 1987, p. 122.

LeGuin, Ursula K. *City of Illusions*. New York: Ace Books, 1967.

Poncé, Charles. *Working the Soul: Reflections on Jungian Psychology*. Berkeley: North Atlantic Books, 1988.

Statnekov, Daniel K. *Animated Earth*. Berkeley: North Atlantic Books, 1987.

Strieber, Whitley. *Communion*. New York: Beech Tree Books, William Morrow, 1987.

Watson, Ian. *Miracle Visitors*. New York: Ace Books, 1978.

Young, Arthur M. *The Reflexive Universe: Evolution of Consciousness*. Mill Valley, California: Robert Briggs Associates, 1976.

Index

Aborigines, Australian, 7–8, 281; myths of, 130, 149, 281
Abstract expressionism, 164
Adams, John, 96–99, 318
Addison, Joseph, 101
Aesop, 272
Aetius, 41
Airy, George, 98
Akkad, 8
Alchemy, 316; mentioned, 197, 204, 205, 241, 258, 343, 350, 378, 379
Alcor, 20
Aldebaran, 344
Aldiss, Brian, 282
Aldrovandi, xviii-xix
Alexander the Great, 45, 345–46
Alexandria, 45–46, 313; library, 45
Alien abductions, 382–84, 387 388, 392, 412
All and Everything, 376
Almagest, 48, 51
Alnilam, 7, 8
Alpert, Richard, 396
Alpha Centauri, 182
Alphabets, 22
Amalthea, 235, 249
Amazing Stories, 272
America, 348
Ananke, 236
Anaxagoras, 43
Anaximander, 40–41, 45
"Ancient astronaut" theory, 377
Anderson, Poul, 284–85, 288
Andromeda Galaxy, 106, 113; mentioned, 92
Angel of Peace, 406
Anger, Kenneth, 396
Animate versus morphological, 117–19, 146–47
Anka, Paul, 398
Antares, 4
Anthony, Piers, 263, 298–300
Antimatter, 124

Anti-Terra, 192
Apollonius of Perga, 48
"Appearances of the Planets" (Labashi), 38
Apuleius, 272
Aquarius, 263, 331–32
Aquarian Age, 317–18
Aquinas, St. Thomas, 45
Arab culture, 50
Aranda myth, 149
Archaeology, development of, 94–95
Archetypal geometry, 48, 67–69, 81, 347
Archetypes, 337, 366, 374–76, 413
Archimedes, 47; mentioned, 50
Architecture, sacred, 35–37
Aries, 327–28
Arctic snowcap, life in the, 109
Arcturus, 33
Argo, 154
Ariel, 97, 261–62
Aristarchus of Samos, 47, 54; mentioned, 55
Aristophanes, 272
Aristotle, 40, 45, 48; mentioned, 52, 59
Armstrong, Neil, 150
Arrhenius, Svante, 197–98
Art expressing our sense of cosmos, 163–64
Asteroids, 94; -belt, 183, 224–25
Astounding Science Fiction, 272
Astral projection, 23, 180
Astral sky, 22–23, 25, 29, 60, 112, 170, 180, 216, 273, 378, 396, 398
Astro-biology, 316, 379–81
Astrology, xxiv, 20–23, 30, 88, 204, 207, 224, 241, 244, 258–59, 262, 264, 299–300, 268–69, 306, 309–10, 313–33; as millennial science, 315–17; and radio astronomy, 155, 311–12; relationship to astronomy of, 190–91
Astromancy, 62, 87
Astronomers, as priests, 353
Astronomia Nova, 68–69
Astronomy: ancient, 32–52; history of Western, 53–165; internal, xiii, 19, 20, 21, 28, 61, 208, 308, 309, 310, 319,

321, 327, 338, 342, 381, 382; moral
dimension of, 353–61; occult, 190–
91; postmodern, 152; Ptolemaic, 48;
relationship to astrology of, 190–91,
315–16, 318; secularization of, 352–
55; subjectivity of, 190–91, 335–36
Astrophysics, xii, xxiv, 87, 316, 317;
relationship of, to language and
mind, 168. *See also* Atom, the; Black
holes; Pulsars; Quasars; Space-time
continuum; *individual planets by
name*, 181–270 *passim*
Astro-Theology, 8
Astrum, the, 23, 24
Atom, the, 111, 122–39, 140–45
Atom bomb, the, 395
Atlantis, 224, 280, 344, 409
Atomic theory, 42–44, 101–02
Atomic weights, 102
Atomists, 45
Australia, 33; mythology of, 7–8, 130,
149, 281
Australopithecus, 187
Aztec calendar, 22

Baba Ram Dass, 396, 400
Babylonians, 275, 314; astronomy, 39,
326
Bach, Johann Sebastian, 153
Background of civilizations, 336, 347
Bacon, Francis, 71
Baez, Joan, 396
Baker, Douglas, 381
Ballot, Christoph Hendrik Didericus
Buys, 113
Banks, Sir Joseph, 93
Bantu myth, 147–48
Baryons, 125
Baseball cards, 396
Basques, fishing in New World, 59
Beatles, the, 396, 399, 401
Becker, Carl, 348
Beckett, Samuel, 138
Bell, Jocelyn, 153
Bellatrix, 7
Bentley, Richard, 83
Bermuda Triangle, the, 409
Berry, Chuck, 397

Best, Eldon, 34
Betelgeuse, 7
Big Bang theory (as initial creationary
event), xxi, 15–19, 82, 128–36, 140–
46, 157, 163, 187, 327, 328, 352
Big Bopper, the, 400
Big Dipper, 20
Bigfoot, 371
Big Horn Medicine Wheel, 36
Billion Year Spree, 282
Biological signals, 379–81
Biology, extraterrestrial, 364
Black holes, 157, 161–63, 267–68
Blake, William, 84, 317
Bode, Johann, 96, 97, 98, 99
Bogan, James, 164
Bohr, Niels, 124
Bolyai, Janos, 118
Bonaparte, Napoleon, 86, 345, 346
Book of the Craft of Dying, The, 11
Book of Mormon, The, 409, 415
Book of Skulls, The, 307
Book of Urantia, The, 409
Bowie, David, 400, 402
Bradbury, Ray, 218
Brahe, Tycho, 48. *See also* Tycho Brahe
Brazil, 2, 58, 273
Brendan, 278, 284
Brezsny, Rob, 401–402
Brothers Grimm, the, 278
Brothers of the Rosy Cross, the, 385
Bruno, Giordano, 60–64; mentioned,
84, 106, 188, 307
Buddhism, 138, 167, 209, 258, 291,
311–12, 403
Burmese constellations, 22
Burroughs, Edgar Rice, 218, 222, 223,
224
Bushongo mythology, 147–48

Calder, Nigel, 155
Calendars, 36–39, 314–15
Calendric number systems, 23
Callisto, 235, 238
Caloris Basin, 196
Cambodian lunar animals, 22
Campanella, Tommaso, 346, 347
Cancer, 328–29, 330–31

Capella, 113
Capricorn, 330–31
Caracol, 35
Carme, 236
Caroline Islands, 34
Cassini, Giovanni, 88, 253
Cassini's Division, 248
Castaneda, Carlos, 208, 281–82, 287, 391, 412
Castle of Otranto, The, 282
Cathay, 279, 284
Cattle mutilations, 382, 384–87, 391, 392, 410
Celestial influence, theory of, 314–15, 322–23, 325–26
Celestial Worlds Discovered, The, 89
Centrifugal force, 72
Cepheids, 113
Ceres, 96, 224
Chaldeans, astronomy of, 38–39, 314
Challenger, space shuttle, 244
Charm, 128–29
Charon, 266
Chemistry, universality of, 365–66
Childhood's End, 292, 303–05
Chinese cosmology, 8, 22, 48–49, 146, 314; classical music, 153. *See also* Taoism
Chiron, 259
Christian Topography, 51
Christianity, 23, 310–12, 342, 344, 367
Christy, James, 266
Church, the, and scientists, 75–76, 409
CIA, the, 386
Cidenas, 39
Città del Sole, 346, 360
City of Illusions, 288
City of the Sun, the, 346–47
Clarke, Arthur C., 228, 232, 238–40, 292, 303–05, 393
Cleaver, Eldridge, 400
Close Encounters of the Third Kind, 292–93, 373, 383, 411
Cocteau, Jean, 396
Cohen, Leonard, 400
Collective unconscious, the, 375–76
Collin, Rodney, 27–28, 112
Collins, Michael, 47, 214, 350

Color force, 127–28
Colorado, 384
Columbia, space shuttle, 215
Columbus, Christopher, 51, 58, 60; mentioned, 97
Comets, 182–83, 202–03
Communication, interstellar, 365–66, 378–80, 382–83, 397–98, 407, 411
Communion, 388, 391
Communist Manifesto, 264
Consciousness, human, 166–80. *See also* Extraterrestrial life
Constellation astrology, 324–25
Constellations, described, 1, 3, 7–8
Cook, James, 280
Cooke, Sam, 402
Copernicus, Nicolaus, xviii, 53, 54–60, 188; mentioned, 81, 106, 192, 273, 318
Cosmic superimposition, 171–72
Cosmology, 156–57, 159–63, 164, 167–68, 172, 271, 272–82, 285, 334–61; Chinese, 8, 22, 48–49, 146, 314; Egyptian, 8, 19–20, 61, 197, 277, 314, 357;; mediaeval, 51–52; mythocosmology, 337–39, 341–46, 357–58. *See also* Astrology; Astronomy; Creation myths; Stellar mythology
Cosmic Trigger, 378–79
Cosmotheoros, 89
Crab Nebula, the, 154
Creation, xii-xvii, 16–19; Big Bang theory of, xxi, 15–19, 82, 107, 128–29, 129–46, 163, 327–28, 352; and consciousness, 166–67; Kant on, 90–91; myths, 129, 137–38, 146–47; without a Creator, 86, 107
Creek Indians, burial mounds of, 36
Crowley, Aleister, 378
Cruikshank, Dale, 266
Cubism, 164
Curvature of space, 114–15, 161
Cusa, Nicholas of, 54; mentioned, 58, 188
Cygnus, 33
Cytherean cloud cover, 197

Da Free John, 18

da Vinci, Leonardo, 362
Dalton, John, 101
Dante Alighieri, 52, 344–45; mentioned, 272
Darin, Bobby, 398
Darwin, Charles, 104–08, 118
Darwinism, 104–07, 359
Davidson, Norman, 190, 321, 343, 377
Davis, Kathie, 390, 393
Dead, World of the, 276–78, 410
Death, discussion of, 9–13; and Moon, 208–09
Dechend, Hertha von, 337–38, 341–42, 357
Dee, John, 59; mentioned, 280
Deimos, 218
Delta Cephei, 113
Democritus, 42, 44, 45; mentioned, 50
De Revolutionibus orbium coelestium, 56, 57
Derham, William, 8
Descartes, René, 77, 79
Destiny of the Stars, The, 197
Dickens, Charles, 288, 289
Diderot, Denis, 359
Digges, Thomas, 56
Dion and the Belmonts, 399
Dione, 252, 253
di Prima, Diane, 61
Divine Pymander, The, 24
DNA, 19, 158, 209, 364, 374, 415
Dogon, the, 275, 377–78
Donne, John, 57, 355
Doppler, Christian, 112
Doppler effect, 112–13
Dorn, Edward, 132
Dostoevsky, Fyodor M., 288
Dream Lover, 398
Dreams, 354; of stars and planets, 157–60, 165, 240–41, 269–70, 397
Dr. Strangelove, 163
Druidic tradition, 59
Duncan, Robert, 158–59
Dune trilogy, 296–98, 417
Dune Messiah, 300–02
Durkheim, Emile, 134
Dylan, Bob, 400, 401
Dyson, Freeman, 231

Earth, the, 143–44, 213–17; mentioned passim
East St. Louis mounds, 36
Eclipses, 40
Ecology, considerations of, 202, 212, 231–32, 340, 350, 386
Economy, inflation of world, 356
Eddington, Arthur, 113
Egyptian Book of the Dead, 8
Egyptian cosmology, 8, 19–20, 61, 277, 314; and hermetic enlightenment, 348; Temple on, 378; tradition in Europe, 59; mentioned, 197, 357
Einstein, Albert: on atomic particles, 161–62; on relativity, 114–17; on space, 115; mentioned, 11, 70, 74, 122, 123, 125, 135, 334
Eisenbud, Jule, 406–407
Elara, 235
Electric charge of universe, 131
Electricity, 347
Electromagnetism, 20, 110–11, 114, 116–17, 122
Electrons, 123–25, 134
Elements, study of, 40, 100–109, 142, 186
Embryo, 146–47, 335; as love which bring us life, 398
Embryogenesis, xxiv
Enceladus, 252–53, 262
Energy, 143; atomic, 143; relationship to inertia, 116–17; solar, 195, 211 350–51
Enlightenment, European, 348–49
Enslin, Theodore, 101
Epistemology (human existence itself as cosmology), xiv-xv, xvii, xxv, 2–3, 6–7, 9–14, 30, 83, 92–93, 109, 121, 129, 132–33, 145–46, 151, 163–64, 167–74, 321, 333, 335, 339, 351–52, 394, 399, 403–404, 409–11, 416–18
Eratosthenes, 47
Eridamus, River, 343–44, 345
Erik the Red, 278
Erikson, Erik, 66
Eros, 40, 52, 146; planetoid, 96
Eskimo myths, 148

Esoteric astrology, 325
Ethnoastronomy (also Archaeoastronomy), xiv-xv, 3, 21–22, 32–38, 174, 176, 178–80, 313, 315–16, 361, 375, 378–79, 396
Ethnography, 281
Ethology, 119
Euclid, 47; mentioned, 118
Eudoxus, 44
"Eureka," 86
Europa, 235, 237, 238
Everly Brothers, the, 403
Evolution, human, 304
Expanding universe, 16
Experimentation, 47, 68–72, 78–79, 81–82, 85–86, 87–89, 91, 93–94, 96–99, 110–117, 156, 221–22, 264–65
Exploitation of other worlds, 212, 243, 304–306
Extraterrestrial life, 62, 74, 89, 92, 93, 107, 151, 158, 164, 175, 198, 216, 221–22, 229–33, 238, 239, 244–45, 256–57, 271–72, 275–78, 292–93, 319, 325, 356, 364–69, 372–74, 377–81, 405–09, 412–13
Extraterrestrial visitors, 275–76, 284, 292–93, 309–11, 362–394, 400, 406–418

Face on Mars, xxiii, 223, 244, 262, 277, 377, 391–92, 393, 416
Fairy tales, 278
Fame, 399
Faraday, Michael, 110, 117, 122; mentioned, 118
Faraday-Maxwell field, 110, 114
Farmer, Philip José, 294–96
Fatima, 408–09
Faulkner, William H., 207; mentioned, 288
First Three Minutes, The, 82, 136
Flammarion, 8
Flamsteed, John, 87
Flash Gordon, 222–23, 396, 398
Flying saucers (UFOs), 368–94
Forces, vital, xvi-xvii
Forerunner to Cosmographical Treatises, A, 67–68

Foucault, Michel, xviii-xix
Fourth dimension, the, 26–28, 114, 116, 215, 371, 410, 415
Frankenstein, 282–83
Fraunhofer, Joseph von, 102
Freud, Sigmund, 107, 117, 119–20, 270; mentioned, 122, 196, 384
From Honey to Ashes, 178–79
Fuller, R. Buckminster, 173
Fundy, Bay of, 5

Galaxies, formation of, 141
Galileo Galilei, 53, 54, 72–76, 188–89; on light, 88–89, 99; and Newton, 77–78; on Saturn's rings, 248; mentioned, 87, 95, 182, 238, 273, 280, 338
Galle, Johann, 97, 98
Ganymede, 235, 237–38, 253
Gauss, Karl Friedrich, 96, 114
Gawain, 336
Geller, Uri, 376
Gell-Mann, Murray, 126, 127
Gemini, 328
Genesis, 272
Geometry, 66, 166. *See also* Mathematics
Georgium Sidus, 93. *See also* Uranus
Germanic myths, 278
Gilgamesh, 275–76, 336
Ginseng, 8
Gnostic tradition, 58, 309, 313
God, 54, 57; astronomy's loss of faith in, 86, 91, 95, 346; Enlightenment's view of, 348–49; Kepler on, 65–66; Newton on, 80
Goethe, Johann Wolfgang von, 317
Gold, Thomas, 154–55
Golden Dawn, the, 378
Gordon, Cyrus, 58
Gravitation, 77–86, 104, 133; and astrology, 322
Gravity, 107, 112, 122, 126, 132, 141, 215, 346; and black holes, 161; effect of moon on Earth, 206, 321–22; Einstein on, 114; Galileo on, 74; Kepler on, 72, 79; Newton on, 74, 77–86
Great Chain of Being, the, 107, 117

Great Expectations, 288, 289
Great Nebula of Orion, 103
Great Pretender, The, 398
Great Serpent Mound, 36
Greek: astronomers, 39–51; cosmology, 197, 313, 343; myths, 129, 146, 235, 252, 258, 268–69, 274–75, 276–77, 357; philosophers, 40–48
Greening of America, a, 349, 360
Greenland, 7
Gulliver's Travels, 272
Gurdjieff, G. I., 26–27, 135, 153, 208, 212, 376, 378; mentioned, 258

Hadrons, 125
Hair, 399
Hale, George Ellery, 104–05
Haley, Alex, 187–88
Hall, Aseph, 222
Halley, Edmund, 87, 99
Halley's comet, 85
Hallucinogens, 264, 400
Hamlet's Mill, 286, 337–38, 341–42, 401
Harmonic Convergence, the, 262
Harmonice Mundi, 72
Hawaii, 33
Hawking, Stephen, 163, 170–71
Haydn, Franz Josef, 153
Healing, xix–xxii, 316
Healing by stars (also by star concepts, ideas, cosmologies), xx–xxii, 64, 341, 343, 346–47, 350–51, 380–81, 402, 409
Heartbreak Hotel, 398
Heinlein, Robert, 218
Heisenberg, Werner, 42, 102, 123, 173; mentioned, 135, 144
Heliocentricity, 53–64
Helium, 131, 134, 245
Helmholtz, Hermann von, 105, 115
Hendrix, Jimi, 399, 400, 401
Heracleides, 46–47; mentioned, 55
Heraclitus, 41, 46
Herbert, Frank, 296–98, 300–02, 417
Hercules, 91
Hermes, 24, 58, 59; planetoid, 96
Hermes-Thoth, 196

Hermeticism, 58, 60, 346, 347–48, 354, 377–79; texts of, 24–26. See also Qabala, the
Herschel, Caroline, 92, 94, 100
Herschel, Frederick William, 88, 91–94, 95, 100, 252, 261; mentioned, 98, 182, 318
Herschel, Sir John, 94, 97
Hesiod, 39, 59, 146, 258
Hevelius, 154
Hewitt, Anthony, 266
Hierarchy of cosmoses, 26–27, 29, 127, 325
High Crusade, The, 284–85
Hill, Betty and Barney, kidnapping, 388, 392
Hillman, James, 269
Himalia, 235
Hinduism, 8, 22, 138, 291–92, 311–12, 342, 352, 357, 387
Hipparchus, 47
Hitler, Adolf, 268, 291, 355–56
Hoagland, Richard, 222, 223, 387, 391, 392, 393
Hoffman, Abbie, 400
Hohokam people, 3
Homer, 60, 344, 362
Hooke, Robert, 95
Hopi: grammar, 174–77; Indians, 292, 375
Hopi Journal, 174
Hopkins, Budd, 388, 389–90, 391, 413
Horton, Johnny, 400
Hoyle, Fred, 17
Hoyt, William Graves, 99
Hubble, Edwin, 90, 113, 130
Huggins, William, 103, 113
Humanoid aliens, 107, 223, 229, 244–45, 364, 391–93, 415
Hunting Dogs, the, 106
Huygens, Christian, 87–88, 89; on Saturn's rings, 247
Hydrogen, 102–04, 125, 131, 133–34, 140–41, 144, 184, 245
Hyperion, 252, 254
Hypnosis, 389, 407, 410, 412

Iapetus, 252, 254–55

Icarus, 96

Ice Age cosmology, 51

I Ching, 350

Idealism, archetypal, 44

Imaginary planets, 98, 183–84, 192, 194, 264–67, 271–72

Immortality, quest for, 306–08

Immrama, 278

Impregnation, alien, 390, 391–82, 393, 413

Impressionism, 164

Incarnation, xiii, 1, 5, 7, 10–12, 135, 215, 406, 416

India, 8

Indians, American, 2, 59, 280–81; mounds of, 35–36

Individuality, human, 283–85, 292, 294–98, 300–02, 314, 319–20, 327–30, 333

Industrialism, 106

Inertia, 72; and energy, 116–117

Infinity (including moral implications of), xi, 4–5, 43, 63, 67, 73–74, 87, 92–93, 99–100, 112, 121, 216, 286, 290–91, 326, 333, 341, 355

Intelligence, human, 166–80. *See also* Consciousness

Interpretation of Dreams, The, 119

Introduction to the Study of the Starry Sky, 96

Intruders, 388

Invasion of the Body Snatchers, 374

Io, xxii–xxiii, 153, 234–35, 236–37, 238, 253

Ionia, astronomers of, 40, 45

Ionian philosophy, 102, 106, 352

Iran, 324, 358

Irish, the: mythology of, 278–79; exploration of the New World, 58, 59; mentioned, 8

Iron, 142

Islam, 358, 367

It Came from Outer Space, 373, 416

Jain cosmology, 22

Janus, 252, 254

Jeans, Sir James, 135, 166

Jefferson, Thomas, 348

Jerusalem, 84

Jesus Christ, 309–12, 344, 406, 409

Jicarilla Apache myth, 137

Jones, Marc Edmund, 320

Joplin, Janis, 400

Jovians, 229–32

Joyce, James, 126

Jung, Carl Gustav, 320, 374–76, 411–12; psychology, 45

Juno, 96

Jupiter,, 153, 226–41, 246, 273; astral, 241; life on, 229–233; moons of, 73, 234–38, 254; rings of, 248; mentioned, 96, 202

Kalevala, 336

Kali Yuga, 342

Kant, Immanuel, 3, 86, 90–91, 317

Kelley, David, 22

Kelly, Edward, 343

Kelly, Robert, 13, 14, 46, 63

Kelvin, William (Lord), 105

Kepler, Johannes, 53, 65–72, 73, 75, 81, 188; and Newton, 77–79; *Somnium* of, 189–90; mentioned, 31, 90, 95, 97, 153, 166, 266, 318, 334, 346, 349

Khomeini, the Ayatollah, 358

Kidinnu, 39

Kierkegaard, Søren, 11

Kircher, Athanasius, 221

Kirchhoff, Gustav Robert, 103

Koestler, Arthur, 66, 69, 70; mentioned, 72

Kohoutek (comet), 23

Koppernigk, Nicolas, *see* Copernicus

Kosmas Indicopleustes, 51

Kronos, 258, 259

Kuiper, Gerard, 261, 263

Labashi, 38

Laboratory, 120

Laine, Frankie, 398

Lalande, Joseph J. F. (De la Lande), 97

Lambda, 91

Language, 10, 174–77

Lansing, Gerrit, 264

Laplace, Pierre Simon, 86, 91, 93, 96; mentioned, 107, 135
Lassel, William, 97, 261, 263
Laughter, cosmic, 167, 372
Lawrence, D. H., 14, 108–09, 172
Lawrence, L. George,, 379–80
Leary, Timothy, 382
Leavitt, Henrietta Swan, 113
Leda, 235
Leeuwenhoek, Anton van, 101
LeGuin, Ursula K., 288
Leibnitz, Gottfried Wilhelm von, 54, 110
Lennon, John, 396, 400, 401, 402
Leo, 329
Leonardo da Vinci, 362
Leptons, 125
Leverrier, Urbain, 96–99, 195, 318
Lévi-Strauss, Claude, 177–79
Lewis, C. S., 175, 198, 305–07, 308–09, 321; mentioned, 296, 393
Libra, 329
Life: evolution of, 104–08, 209; on Jupiter, 229–33; on Titan, 255–57
Light, 27–28, 47, 88–89, 99, 110, 115, 117, 122–23, 134, 140–41, 152–53, 242, 267; Collin on, 27–28
Linguistic patterns, 174–75, 180
Lobachevski, Nikolai, 118
Lonsdale, William, 268, 327–34
Lord of Light, 291–92
Louis XIV, 87
Lovin' Spoonful, the, 399
Lowell, Percival, 217–18, 219, 220, 264–65, 266, 318
Lucian of Samosata, 272
Lucretius, 42–43, 214
Luna, 205
Lunar alphabet, 23
Lunar effects, 208
Lunar rhythms, 206, 322
Lysithia, 235

Macroscope, 263, 298–300
Magi, 360
Maker of Universes, The, 294–96
Malevolent aliens, xxiii, 374, 383–92, 411–15
Manson, Charles, 400

Maoris, 34, 38
Mariner missions, 186, 194, 195–96, 200, 218–19, 222. See also Spacecraft missions
Marius, Simon, 88
Mars, 217–26, 244–45; Kepler on, 70; Lowell on, 217; moons of, 222; occult, 224; Schiaparelli on, 193; mentioned, 96
Mars and Its Canals, 217
Mars as the Abode of Life, 217
Martians, 193, 217–18, 222, 224
Marshack, Alexander, 37
Marxism, 144, 347
Mass, and relativity, 113, 116–17
Mathematical messages, 365
Mathematical relationships (both scientific and occult), 39, 44–49, 67, 71–72, 81–82, 116, 133–34, 141, 154, 238, 250, 260–61, 313, 321, 334, 337
Mathematical Principles of Natural Philosophy, 81
Mathematical relationships, 102
Mathematics: astronomical, 81, 82, 346; and linguistics,174; and natural forms, 102, 134; prehistoric, 38–39; universality of, 365. See also Geometry
Maxwell, James Clerk, 110, 117, 122, 201; on Saturn's rings, 247–48; mentioned, 118
Mayan: astronomy, 35; calendar, 22; myth, 149
Mécanique Céleste, 86
Mediaeval astronomy, 50–52
Medicine, xix-xxii, 316
Meier, Billy, 393
Melville, Herman, xviii, 117–19, 121; mentioned, 67–68
Mendeleev, Dmitri, 102
Mercury, 98, 105, 192–97; occult, 23, 54, 196–97
Mesons, 124, 125
Mesopotamia, 38
Messages, interstellar, 402
Messenger from the Stars, 73
Meteorites, 185–86
Meteoroids, 185
Meteors, 94

Mexico, 281
Microcosm/Macrocosm, as a pair (including Atom/Star, Earth/Sky, River/Galaxy, Embryo/Cosmos, Archaeology/Astronomy), 67, 94, 101, 109, 117–19, 122, 130, 145–50, 180, 187–88, 210–11, 215, 224, 320, 322–26, 343, 345, 348, 401
Micronesia, 33
Microscope, 100–01
Microwaves, 115, 132, 134–35
Milky Way, the, 6, 89–91, 95, 113, 129, 184, 298–99, 343; origin of, 90
Millennial sciences, the, 315–17
Milton, John, 74; mentioned, 272
Mimas, 250, 252, 253
Mind, 166–80. *See also* Consciousness
Mintaka, 7, 8
Mipam, 293–94
Miracle Worker, 387
Miranda, 244, 261, 262
Miró, Joan, 164
Misner, Charles, 163
Missouri Breaks, The, 11
Moby Dick, 117–19
Monte Alban, 35
Moon, the, 205–13; attraction of, 27; and death, 208–09; first landing on, 150, 338, 410; and gravity, 205–06, 321–22; historical speculations about, 188–90, 205; occult, 207; origin of, 187, 209–10; phases of, 36–39; von Braun and Ordway on, 184–85
Moral issues, 341–60
Moran, Hugh, 22
Morrison, David, 266
Mortality, xii, 2, 5–6, 8–13, 180, 307
Mounds, Indian, 35–36
Mount Palomar mirror, 152
Mozart, Wolfgang Amadeus, 153
Mundus Subterraneus, 221
Munroe, Robert, 410
Muons, 125
Murphy, 138
Music, 153; popular, 395–402
Mysterium Cosmographicum, 67–68, 69

Mystery cults, Near Eastern, 378
Mythology, 280. *See also* Cosmology; Creation myths; Star Myth

Naming astronomical bodies, 88, 93, 109, 154, 237, 266
Napoleon Bonaparte, 86, 345, 346
NASA, 30, 377
Natural Selection, Law of, 104–108, 134, 417
Navigation, celestial, 33–35
Nebula: as ambiguous category, 103; first dark, 92; primordial, 140–41
Nelson, Ricky, 396, 397
Nelson, Willie, 402
Neoteny, 304
Neptune, 242, 263–64, 267; discovery of, 95–99, 182; moons of, 97, 263; occult, 264
Nereid, 263
Neutrinos, 125–26, 134
Neutrons, 123, 125, 126; creation of, 133; -stars, 154–55
New Age, xvii, xxiv, 216, 326, 393, 409–10
New Age inflation, xvii, xxv, 162, 166, 282, 318, 331, 386, 399–400, 409–410, 412
New Astronomy Based on Causation, A, 71
New Mexico, 137
Newton, Sir Isaac, 53, 74, 77–86, 88, 104, 112; mentioned, 31, 72, 90, 95, 97, 107, 110, 114, 116, 117, 118, 120, 125, 134, 153, 176, 184, 249, 346, 347, 349
New World, discovery of, 58–59
New Zealand, 33
Night sky, as universal field, xii–xiii, 3, 6, 13, 21, 24–25, 78, 80, 84, 101, 110–12, 115, 117–19, 121–22, 128–30, 133–34, 141, 143–47, 150, 161, 323, 344, 354
Nihilism of astrophysics and professional science, xvi, xxi, 16, 75–76, 82, 84–86, 108, 120, 135–39, 150, 162–63, 168–69, 180, 290–91, 317,

340, 349, 351, 353–59, 395
Nile, inundation of the, 22
Nixon, Richard M., 24
Noel, Mel, 368
NORAD, 385
Norse: invasions, 58–59; myth, 278–79
Nuclear forces, 125, 133
Nuclear war, prospect of, 349, 395–96
Number systems, 35. *See also* Mathematics
Numerology, 43–44

Oahspe, 409
Oberon, 93, 261
Occult, the, xv, 19, 180, 361. *See also under names of individual planets*
Occult and medicinal energy from stars (*See also* Healing by stars), 60–63, 171–72, 197, 205, 207, 259, 306, 322–23, 349, 360–61
Odysseus, 278, 344–45
Ohio, 36
Olbers, H. Wilhelm, 96, 132
Olbers' paradox, 99, 113–14
Olson, Charles, 350
On the Size and Distances of the Sun and Moon, 47
Oort, Jan, 183
Oort cloud, 183
Ophiel, 401
Ordway, Frederick I., 184
Orgones, 63–64, 171–72, 370
Origin of Species, The, 105
Origin of time and space; flow of time, 15–18, 91, 94, 114, 116–17, 129, 131–32, 318, 320, 326, 332
Orion, 7–9, 73
Orpheus, 396
Osage Indian cosmology, 178
Osiris, 277
Out of the Silent Planet, 175, 305
Oxygen, 144, 213

Paedomorphism, 304
Pallas, 96
Panspermia theory, 198, 374
Papacy, 16

Paracelsus, Philippus Aureolus, 147
Paradiso, the, 52
Paranormal mental phenomena, 407, 412–14
Pascal, Blaise, 73
Pasiphae, 236
Pauli, Wolfgang, 126, 320
Perceptual patterns, 175, 198
Perelandra, 198–99, 305–07, 308–309, 321
Perfit Description of the Caelestiall Orbes, 56
Periodic table, 104; development of the, 102
Persian astronomers, 39, 358
Philolaus, 56
Philosophers, Greek, 39–46
Phobos, 218
Phoebe, 252, 254, 255
Phoenician navigators, 58
Photons, 125, 134, 227
Physics: quantum, 45; universality of, 365–66. *See also* Quantum theory
Piazzi, Giuseppe, 96
Pickering, William H., 183–84, 266
Pilcher, Carl, 266
Pilgrim's Progress, 283
Pioneer missions, 201, 243, 248–49, 252. *See also* Spacecraft missions
Pisces, 327, 332–33
Plains Indians, 345
Planck, Max, 111, 117, 122; mentioned, 135
Planck's Constant, 123
Planetariums, 13
Planetesimals, 185
Planet Medicine: From Stone-Age Shamanism to Post-Industrial Healing, xix-xx, xxi
Planetoids, 152
Planets, 65–76, 181–270; hypothetical, 183–84; as worlds, 39, 74, 188, 226–27, 273
Planet X (Pluto), 264–66
Plato, 42, 43–45; mentioned, 48, 52, 59, 272, 338, 346, 361
Platters, the, 398
Pleiades, 103

Pleiadians, 369, 373, 391, 393, 415
Plutarch, 188, 284, 345; mentioned, 337
Pluto, 99, 182, 242, 266–70; moon of, 266; occult, 268–69, 396
Poe, Edgar Allan, 86
Polaris, 105
Polo, Marco, 279–80
Polynesia, 33–34, 362
Poncé, Charles, 258, 326–27
Pop star cult, the, 395–402
Pope John XXIII, 408–09
Praesepe cloud, 73
Preons, 127
Presley, Elvis, 398, 402
Press, William H., 162
Prime numbers as interstellar messages, 365
Professional astronomy (*See also* Nihilism of astrophysics), xxi, xxiv, 29–30, 50, 121, 136–37, 139, 167–68, 351–53, 368, 406
Project Bluebook, 383
Protons, 123–25; creation of, 133
Psychic wholeness, 339–40
Psychotronic technology, 383–85, 389–90, 412, 414
Ptolemaic system, 51, 52, 53, 55, 57, 80; mentioned, 164
Ptolemy, 45, 48, 62, 164, 313
Pulsars, 153–55
Pythagoras, 41–42, 54, 153; mentioned, 65, 97, 102
Pytheas, 284

Q, letter of alphabet, 158
Qabala, the, 25, 26, 137–38, 316
Quantum, the, 124
Quantum: theory, 111, 117, 124, 144, 380; physics, 45
Quarks, 122, 126–28, 144; creation of, 133
Quasars, xix, 73, 153, 155–57, 160–61, 163

Radiation: released by stars, 105; from atoms, 111
Radio: astrologers, 155; noise, 16

Radio emissions, 111, 134, 152–53, 154; from Jupiter, 234; from Saturn, 251
Radioactivity in ancient rocks, 143
Rainbow, The, 172
Rastafarians, 397
Reagan, Ronald, xxiv, 244
Red shift, 112–13, 131, 161
Refutation of Heresies, 40–41
Reggae, 397
Reich, Charles, 349
Reich, Wilhelm, 63–64, 171–72, 370, 378
Reincarnation, 291, 293–94, 311
Relativity theory, 114–18
Rhea, 252, 253
Rheita Antonia Maria de, 95
Riemann, Bernhard, 114
Rigel, 7
Roberts, Jane, 167
Robinson, Smokey, 402
Rolling Stones, the, 400, 402, 418
Roman beliefs, 8
Romanticization, of primitive and alien cosmology, 177, 180, 376, 381, 386, 417–18
Rosen, Nathan, 161–62
Rosicrucians, 84, 106, 303, 347–48, 376, 378, 379
Rudhyar, Dane, 321
Rudolph, Emperor, 190
Russell, Bertrand, 82
Russell, Henry Norris, 99
Rutherford, Ernest, 122

Sacred geometry, refutation of, 49
Sacred number, 49
Sadat, Anwar, 376
Saga Tale, The, 279
Sagan, Carl, 29–30
Sagas, Norse, 60, 278
Sagittarius, 330
St. Augustine, 41, 45
St. Hippolytus, 40–41
Samoans, 34
Sampson, Walter, 327
Santillana, Giorgio de, 337–38, 341–42
Saturn, 54, 245–59; moons of, 73, 88,

252–57, 357; occult, 23, 241, 244, 257–59; rings of, 247–52

Sauer, Carl, 58

Saving the appearances, 48, 66, 164

Schiaparelli, Giovanni, 193, 217, 220

Schwarzschild, Karl, 161–62

Science, itself a mythology, xiv, xxiv, 18, 27, 121, 161, 164–66, 168, 178, 180, 191, 315–17, 335–36

Science and occult, dialectic of, xiv, xxi, xxiv–xxv, 19, 29–31, 72, 74, 79–85, 104, 107–108, 121, 155, 168–70, 189–90, 212, 272, 281, 305–306, 308–309, 312, 316–18, 322–24, 338–40, 347, 349, 357, 360–61, 369, 370–72, 377, 382, 409

Science fiction, 271–312, 409; creatures, 271, 280–81, 283–85, 287–88, 290–91, 294–97, 301, 303–06, 308, 314, 363, 387; essential quality of, 288–302; as stellar mythology, 285–86; transformation, 163, 180, 239, 281–82, 287, 294–96, 299, 302, 303–06, 352, 360

Scorpio, 329–30

Sea journeys, 278–80, 344–45; by night sky, 33–35, 344–45

Secularization of stellar law, 49, 84, 189–91, 231, 273, 282, 286, 337, 340–49, 351–52, 354–56, 358–59, 367, 377

Self-development (versus technological improvement of race), 162–63, 169, 180 231, 281–82, 287–88, 291–99, 301–11, 315–17, 321, 331, 366–67, 377, 379, 382, 400, 412

Semjasse, 369, 373, 393

Sexuality of stars, 171–72

Seyfert galaxies, 156

Shakespeare, William, 280, 286

Shannon, Del, 398

Shapley, Harlow, 113–14

Shaw, George Bernard, 359

Shelley, Mary Wollstonecraft, 278, 282–83

Shelley, Percy Bysshe, 85; mentioned, 282

Sherente, the, 273–74

Shih K'uang, 20

Shiism, 358

Sierra Club Books, xxiii-xxiv

Silverberg, Robert, 307

Singer, Isaac Bashevis, 355–56

Singleness of world, 214, 233, 350

Sinope, 236

Sirians, the, 378–79

Sirius, 116; occult, 378–79, 381–82; mentioned, 4, 21

Sirius Mystery, The, 339–40

Sleepwalkers, The, 66

Slipher, Vesto, 113, 265

Smith, Bradford, 250

Smith, John, 59

Smith, Valentine Michael, 400

Snyder, Gary, 129

Soderblom, Laurence, 250

Sol, 19, 205

Solar aspect of life, 28–29, 186–87, 322, 351

Solar energy, 195, 211, 350–51

Solar system, 112, 181–91, 350–51; origin of, 86, 185–87

Solstice, summer, 22

Somnium, 189–90

Sophocles, 58

Sorrow, cosmic, xxv, 5, 187–88, 209, 293–94, 301–02, 329–30, 340, 402

Spacecraft missions, xxiii, 103, 199–201, 215–16, 218–19, 221, 224, 228, 235, 236, 237, 243–44, 248–49, 252, 260–61, 362–63

Space Odyssey, 228

Space probes, 243–44, 411

Space program, xxi, 210–12, 215, 260, 397, 401, 410; value of, 244, 349, 352

Spaceships, 215, 369, 410–12

Space-time continuum, the, 110–21

Spectroscopy, 102–03, 113

Speed of light, 215–16

Spiders from Mars, the, 400

Spielberg, Steven, 411

Spirit: and consciousness, 167, 401, 403–05; -forms, 281

Spirits, 363, 371, 408, 410, 413

Spiritual astronomy (including limitations of), xvi-xviii, 67, 180, 291,

326–27, 360–61, 400
Stalin, Joseph, 144
Stapledon, Olaf, 290–91
Star dreams, 157–60, 165, 240–41, 269–70, 397
Star loss, 338–40, 342, 355, 358
Star Maker, 290–91
Star mounds, 35–36
Star of Bethlehem, 23, 409
Star-paths, 33–34
Star pebbles, 37, 38
"Starring of the Earth," the, 356
Stars, the, 87–99; brightness of, 91–92; death of, 105–06; density of field, xii, 9, 73, 90–92, 94–96, 113–14, 165; heat of, 105–06; as meaning, xi, xv, xix, xx, xxiv–xxvi, 2, 3, 7, 8, 21, 32, 121, 130, 158–59, 166, 169, 172, 180, 243–44, 258–59, 268–69, 283, 287–89, 292, 307–08, 312, 315, 319, 334–50, 352, 354, 356–61, 366, 374–76, 387; multiple, 91; reflecting natural, moral, and ecological law, xiii, 3 74, 143–44, 163, 214, 334, 346–47, 349–52, 358, 360
Star Trek, 136, 162, 283, 292, 415
Star Wars, 374
Star-wisdom, 360–61. *See also* Occult, the
Statnekov, Daniel, 216–17
Steady State theory, 16–19, 136
Stein, Charles, 171
Steiner, Rudolph, 319
Stellar architecture, 35–36
Stellar chemistry, 103
Stellar hermeneutics, xiv, xvii, xviii, xix, 7, 11, 12, 22–24, 30, 37, 153, 159, 162, 164, 171–77, 179–80, 319–20, 334–35, 342, 346, 349, 409
Stellar mythology, 178–79, 190, 203, 259, 272–74, 285, 287–90, 296, 298, 307–08, 313–14, 319, 325, 336–37, 339, 341, 343–46, 353, 357, 367, 373
Stephen, Alexander, 174
Stone Age, 314
Stonehenge, 36–38, 313
Strangeness, 127–29
Strieber, Whitley, 388–91

Strings, 122
Sufism, 378
Sumerians, 39, 314; Temple on, 378
Sun, the, 7, 19, 143–44; as center of Solar System, 53–64; Collin on, 28; mortality of, 105–106, 125, 142; gravitational field of, 80, 181–82; movement of, 144; nuclear force of, 125; Teilhard on 28–29; Kepler on, 68
Supernovae (supernovas), 106, 155
Swedenborg, Emanuel, 319
Swift, Jonathan, 272
Synchronicity, 315, 320–21, 379, 411–12, 414

Tahiti, mythology of, 149
T'ai chi ch'uan, 215
Taoism, 20, 26, 48, 326; mentioned, 166, 350
Tarot, 398–99
Tartarus, 277
Taurus, 96, 327, 328
Teilhard de Chardin, Pierre, 28–29
Telescope, 73, 75, 94, 100, 152–53, 182, 193, 243, 248
Tempest, The, 280
Temple, Robert, 275, 339, 377–78, 381
Teotihuacan, 35
Tethys, 252, 253
Thales, 40
That Hideous Strength, 305, 306
Theory of consciousness, 107, 119–20, 354
Theosophy, 407
Thiel, Rudolf, 209
Thompson, Hunter, 372
Thorne, Kip, 162, 163
Tibetan Book of the Dead, The, 11, 277
Tibetan myth, 277–78
Tides, 206
Tikopia, 34
Timaeus, 42
Time, 32; Einstein on, 115–17; sacred sense of, 314–15
Titan, 252, 254, 255, 372
Titania, 93, 261
Titius, Johann, 96

Tombaugh, Clyde, 265–66
Trismegistus, Hermes, 58, 382
Triton, 97, 263
Tulku, Lama Tarthang, 401
2001, 238–40
Tycho Brahe, 48, 53, 69–70, 72. *See also* Brahe
Tyner, McCoy, 164

UFOs, 368–94, 406–18. *See also* Flying saucers
Umbriel, 97, 261, 262
Uncertainty theory, 111
Unconscious mind, 120, 162, 269, 335, 354, 375, 381, 384, 410, 418
United States, 348
Universal Natural History and Theory of the Heavens, 90
Uranium, 142
Uranus, 96, 97, 242, 259–64; discovery of, 93; effect of Neptune on orbit of, 97–99; moons of, 93, 97, 261–62; occult, 244, 262–63, 264; rings of, 248, 260–61
Ursa Major, 380
Uru-anna, 8

Vallee, Jacques, 383–87, 408–09
Van Allen belt, 249
Varela, Andia y, 33–34
Vega, 112
Velikovsky, Immanuel, 202–03, 394
Venera missions, 200
Venus, 197–204, 273; occult, 190, 204; mentioned, 96, 192
Verae Historiae, 272
Verne, Jules, 283
Vesta, 96
Viking missions, 221, 224. *See also* Spacecraft missions
Vikings, 58–59
Virgo, 329
Visions, 408
Vital forces, xvi-xvii
von Braun, Werner, 184
von Daniken, Erich, 275, 377, 379; mentioned, 229
Voyager missions, xxiii, 228, 235–37,

243–44, 245–57, 260–61. *See also* Spacecraft missions
Vulpecula, 154
Vulcan, 98, 192

Waiting for Godot, 138, 139
Walker, Sears, 97
Walpole, Horace, 282
War of the Worlds, 224, 374
Water, 144, 213; on Mars, 220; on Pluto, 267; on Saturn's moons, 255
Watson, Ian, 387
Waves (electrical), 110–11, 124, 129
Weinberg, Stephen, 82, 136–38
Wells, H. G., 283, 374, 382
Wheeler, John, 163, 173
Whistling jugs, 215–17
White dwarf, 267
Whitehead, Alfred North, 336
Whole Earth consciousness, 350, 360
Whorf, Benjamin Lee, 174–76
Wilson, Robert Anton, 378–79
Winnebago Indians, 129, 274
Woodstock, 399
World Ages, 342
World of the Dead, the, 276–78, 410
World War II, 395
Wright, Thomas, 89–91
Writing systems, origin of, 22
Wyoming, 384

X-rays, 154

Yeti, the, 371
Yogananda, Paramahansa, 293
Yongden, Lama, 293–94
Yucatán, 35

Zapotec, 35
Zedong, Mao, 144
Zelazny, Roger, 291–92
Zen, 121, 360, 387
Zeta Reticulii, 392
Zodiac, 22, 23, 44, 265, 313, 314, 318, 323–33; and UFOs, 370. *See also* Astrology
Zuni myths, 148; mentioned, 350

Photograph of author by George Leonard

ABOUT THE AUTHOR

Richard Grossinger is a native of New York City and a graduate
of Amherst College and the University of Michigan from
which he received a doctorate in Anthropology. He has taught
at the University of Southern Maine and Goddard College
in Vermont and is the co-founder and Publisher
of North Atlantic Books in Berkeley, California.
Other recent titles by him include *Planet Medicine: From
Stone-Age Shamanism to Post-Industrial Healing* and
Embryogenesis: The Origins of Human Biology.
He has also edited a number of anthologies, including
*The Alchemical Tradition in the Late Twentieth Century, The
Temple of Baseball, Nuclear Strategy and
the Code of the Warrior,* and *Planetary Mysteries.*
Currently he is writing a narrative about childhood
entitled *New Moon.*

ACF 4037